Putting Development First

Putting Development First

The Importance of Policy Space in the WTO and IFIs

**edited by
Kevin P. Gallagher**

ZED BOOKS
London & New York

Putting Development First was first published in 2005
by Zed Books Ltd, 7 Cynthia Street, London N1 9JF, UK,
and Room 400, 175 Fifth Avenue, New York, NY 10010, USA

www.zedbooks.co.uk

Designed and typeset in Monotype Bembo by Illuminati, Grosmont
www.illuminatibooks.co.uk
Cover designed by Andrew Corbett
Printed and bound in Malta by Gutenberg Press Ltd

Distributed in the USA exclusively by Palgrave Macmillan,
a division of St Martin's Press, LLC, 175 Fifth Avenue, New York, NY 10010

A catalogue record for this book is available from the British Library
Library of Congress Cataloging-in-Publication Data available

ISBN 1 84277 634 7 (Hb)
ISBN 1 84277 635 5 (Pb)

Contents

List of Tables and Figures

Acknowledgements

This book would not have been possible without the help of others. I thank all of the authors in this book for their excellent chapters and their willingness to participate in the project. Ha-Joon Chang and Nagesh Kumar deserve special thanks not only for their pioneering work in this field, but also for their help in securing the involvement of Zed Books. Robert Molteno at Zed has been enthusiastic about this project from the moment Ha-Joon and Nagesh "introduced" me to him via email. It has been a pleasure to work with Zed from the beginning.

Special thanks go to Melissa Birch, a Ph.D. student at the Fletcher School of Law and Diplomacy, who presided over the editing and formatting of the manuscript with precision and cheer. I thank Ha-Joon Chang and Peter Evans for very helpful comments on the first chapter.

Some of the chapters in the volume first appeared in working paper form or at various conferences. Ha-Joon Chang's chapter is a summary of his book published by Anthem Press. Ajit Singh's chapter was first presented at a conference as part of the International Centre for Trade and Sustainable Development (ICTSD) and the UNCTAD–UNDP Global Programme for Globalization, Liberalization and Sustainable Human Development. An earlier version of the Cho and Dubash chapter was issued as Working Paper 16 (December 2003) of the South Centre, as part of its Trade-Related Agenda, Development and Equity (TRADE) series. An earlier version of Amit Bhaduri's chapter was presented at a conference on globalization and sustainable development held at El Colegio de Mexico, 20–21 February 2003. Dr Bhaduri wishes to thank Alejandro Nadal for both comments and permission for publication in English. Robert Wade's chapter was originally published in the *Review of International Political Economy*, 10:4, November

2003. Sanjaya Lall's chapter originates in a paper that was commissioned by the G24 and that is also being published in *The IMF and the World Bank at Sixty*, edited by Ariel Buira (Anthem Press, 2005). Carlos Correa's chapter is an elaboration on an earlier piece that appeared in the *Journal of World Intellectual Property*. We thank all of these venues for their early and continued support of these writings.

Extra thanks go to the Rockefeller Foundation and Boston University's College of Arts and Sciences for financial support toward this effort. In addition, Boston University's Department of International Relations and Tufts University's Global Development and Environment Institute provided and continue to provide wonderful homes for this work.

The most profound gratitude goes to my wife, Kelly Sims Gallagher. This book is for her.

Globalization and the Nation-State:
Reasserting Policy Autonomy for Development

Kevin P. Gallagher

In the face of increasing poverty, inequality, and environmental degradation across the developing world, the global community has reasserted the need for development through the Millennium Development Goals and the global commitment to sustainable development signed at the World Summit for Sustainable Development. At the same time, most of the world's nations have also embarked on a new round of global trade negotiations – the Doha Round under the World Trade Organization (WTO). Citing the fact that developing countries gained very little from the Uruguay Round, developing countries agreed to enter a new round of trade negotiations only on condition that development be the centerpiece. There are growing concerns that this promise will go unfulfilled. Key among those concerns is the notion that additional commitments will not give the developing world the "policy space" to use the very instruments and tools that many industrialized nations took advantage of to reach their current levels of development.

This volume brings together prominent development economists – from North and South – who in their earlier work have shown how effective state intervention in national economies was a key ingredient for the development success stories that we have witnessed since World War II. Most of the authors here referred to such nations as "developmental states." For this volume, the authors are asked the following questions:

- To what extent do new and proposed global trade rules under the WTO and other measures required by the International Financial Institutions (IFIs) restrict the ability of developing nations to establish effective development policy?

- To the extent that policy space is being limited, what policies should developing nations put in place to preserve and expand upon the existing spaces now available?

There is a consensus among the authors of this volume that existing and proposed rules for the global economy are restricting policy spaces for development in the nations that need development most. After analyzing the relationship between trade rules and policy space, the authors offer various avenues for reform. The chapters in this volume can be thought of as having three parts. First, drawing on economic theory and development success stories in East Asia, the chapters by Stiglitz, Lall, and Wade argue that state management to make markets more development friendly is more important now than it ever was. Yet these authors show that the spaces to use development policies have shrunk considerably. Articles by Chang, Kumar, and Cho and Dubash show that many of the development policies that are now scorned by industrialized nations are the very policies that were so essential to industrial development in the industrialized world. They also demonstrate that experiments with variations of those policies proved successful in many developing country contexts. Third, the cluster of articles by Bhaduri, Amsden, Singh, and Evans offers a range of alternative perspectives and policies that can help nations preserve and expand current policy space.

A Commitment to Development

Although the twentieth century ushered in an unprecedented level of technological change and advancement, poverty and inequality remain key characteristics of the global economy in the twenty-first century. The World Bank defines poverty as earning less than $2 per day (1999 purchasing power parity) and extreme poverty as earning less than $1. Using this definition, about half of the world's population are poor, almost 3 billion people. Close to half of the poor — 1.4 billion people — live in extreme poverty.

The world's poor are not always located where one would think. The economist William Cline has shown that "three-fourths of the world's poor live in countries that are considered too developed to qualify for any of the special regimes oriented toward benefiting countries in these groupings" (Cline 2004: 10). Cline shows that only one-quarter of the world's poor live in the least developed countries (LDCs), the heavily indebted poor countries, or sub-Saharan Africa. Since many countries fall in all three categories, the proportion may be even smaller due to double counting. Half of the poor live in China and India (Cline 2004).

With this as the backdrop, the United Nations General Assembly forged the Millennium Development Goals (MDGs) in 2000. Under the MDGs, governments have committed to the following by 2015: eradicating hunger and extreme poverty, reducing child mortality, achieving universal primary education, promoting gender equality, combating diseases such as HIV/AIDS and malaria, and ensuring environmental sustainability. The MDGs recognize that trade policies can play a role in achieving these goals, but only if done properly and with recognition of special and differentiated treatment for developing countries:

> We believe that the central challenge we face today is to ensure that globalization becomes a positive force for all the world's people. For while globalization offers great opportunities, at present its benefits are very unevenly shared, while its costs are unevenly distributed. We recognize that developing countries and countries with economies in transition face special difficulties in responding to this central challenge. Thus, only through broad and sustained efforts to create a shared future, based upon our common humanity in all its diversity, can globalization be made fully inclusive and equitable. These efforts must include policies and measures, at the global level, which correspond to the needs of developing countries and economies in transition and are formulated and implemented with their effective participation. (UNDP 2000a)

Parallel to these efforts at the UN, the WTO has been working to liberalize trade further. The Uruguay Round of world trade negotiations was completed in 1994 and culminated in the establishment of the WTO in 1995. It is estimated that the annual gains from the Uruguay Round were approximately $200 billion annually. However, it has also been estimated that 70 per cent of those gains have gone to the developed countries and most of the rest have gone to a small handful of developing countries. Indeed, it is estimated that in the first six years following the Uruguay Round the forty-eight LDCs were worse off by $600 million per year (Stiglitz and Clayton 2004). When the developed world proposed another round of global trade talks in 2001 in Doha, Qatar, the developing countries accepted on the condition that development form a core part of the negotiations.

Trade, Growth, and Development

Although the WTO has a stated "commitment to the objective of sustainable development," the primary goal of the organization is to increase trade and investment. Many developed country free trade proponents argue that increasing trade and investment through WTO and more regional arrangements will automatically lead to growth and development. Though grounded in economic theory, such claims rest on numerous assumptions that often do not hold, especially in the poorest of nations. It will come as no surprise, then, that the empirical evidence of a positive relationship between trade and growth is quite limited. Such empirical evidence is not reflected in the vast majority of predictions relating to the benefits of global trade liberalization.

The economist David Ricardo (1817) showed that because countries face different costs to produce the same product, if each country produces and then exports the goods for which it has comparatively lower costs, then all parties benefit. The effects of comparative advantage (as Ricardo's notion became called) on factors of production were developed in the "Heckscher–Ohlin" model. This model assumes that in all countries there is perfect competition, technology is constant and readily available, there is the same mix of goods and services, and that factors of production (such as capital and labor) can move freely between industries. Within this rubric, the Stolper–Samuelson theorem adds that international trade can increase the price of products (and therefore the welfare) in which a country has a comparative advantage. Foreign direct investment (FDI) can contribute to development by increasing employment and by human capital and technological "spillovers," where the foreign presence crowds in new technology and investment. In a perfect world, then, free trade and increasing exports could indeed be unequivocally beneficial to all parties.

The assumptions in these theories – such as full employment, perfect competition, and no technological change, among others – are one reason why there is limited evidence that trade openness and unbridled foreign investment lead to economic growth. In a comprehensive review of the literature, Rodriguez and Rodrik (1999) have shown that there is no systematic relationship between a nation's average level of tariff and non-tariff barriers and its economic growth rate. An assessment of the literature on FDI and development came to similar conclusions: FDI alone was not correlated with local spillovers in developing countries (Gallagher and Zarsky 2004). Whereas developing country per capita income growth was 3 per cent on an annual basis between 1960 and 1980 – a period of considerable levels of state management of developing economies – the more integrated period from 1980 to 2000 yielded average annual growth rates of 1.5 per cent in the developing world. The latter rate is less than 1 per cent per annum if India and China (two interventionist countries) are taken out (Chang 2003b).

Perhaps no region of the world has experimented with economic integration more than Latin America. Since the late 1980s, many Latin American nations have introduced a package of deep reforms, including: reducing tariffs and other protectionist measures; reducing barriers to foreign investment; restoring "fiscal discipline" by reducing government spending; and promoting the export sector of the economy.

Different countries in the hemisphere adopted these policies at differ-ent times and to different degrees, but as a region Latin America and the Caribbean for the last twenty years has followed such policies. In recent years, this orientation has been promoted through a growing range of trade agreements that seek more rapid global economic integration and a deeper liberalization process. After twenty years of reforms, the region has not expe-rienced the promised economic growth. According to a sweeping assessment of the impacts of the reforms conducted by the Economic Commission for Latin America and the Caribbean (ECLAC), the region's economies grew at an annual rate of less than 2 per cent between 1980 and 2000, compared to a rate of 5.5 per cent between 1960 and 1980. Growth was faster during the 1990s than in the 1980s, but it still did not compare to the period prior to the reforms. The ECLAC report concludes that the reforms contributed to an increase in inequality in the region (Stallings and Peres 2000).

An exception is Chile, where growth rates almost doubled over the past twenty years compared to the 1960 to 1980 period. In this volume Stiglitz shows how the Chilean case has to some degree been due to the heterodox approach taken toward integration in Chile. Stiglitz illustrates how Chile did not fully open itself to portfolio investments but instead levied a tax on the inflow of short-term capital. This measure played a key role in protecting Chile from the currency crises that plagued Latin America in the 1990s. Chile also undertook a highly selective and managed privatization process. Indeed, 20 per cent of all Chilean exports come from one government-owned enterprise. Alongside these measures, Chile put a great deal of expenditure into education and health, without needing to finance such activities through deficit spending.

Of course no country has developed successfully by turning away from global trade. What the vast array of studies show, however, is that the positive relationship between trade and investment and growth is contingent upon numerous other institutional factors. Earlier econometric studies found a positive relationship between liberalization and growth (Sachs and Warner 1995; Frankel and Roemer 1999). These studies have since been called into question. Although different countries have approached openness in vastly different ways, the definition of "openness" in many studies has included nations where the state has played a key role in economic development. For instance, in contrast to Latin American countries that were lax in terms of restrictions on FDI, South Korea strongly encouraged exports and borrowed funds from abroad but was very restrictive in terms of FDI. Nevertheless,

South Korea and many Latin American nations are treated the same in many models – as open economies (Rodriguez and Rodrik 1999).

More recent work has shown that trade liberalization alone is not a sufficient condition for economic growth. Institutional innovation coupled with macroeconomic and political stability is key to the growth process (Wacziarg and Welch 2003). Indeed, there is now fairly widespread agreement among growth economists that institutional quality is the strongest driver of economic growth, more so than trade or geographical contexts (Rodrik et al. 2004). Whereas traditional trade theory emphasizes obtaining welfare gains through specialization, institutional approaches emphasize obtaining welfare gains from increasing productivity by means not necessarily based on specialization. Two key elements of institutionalist success have been the focus on improving individual capacity to be productive and on improving the ability of people and firms to work together. To those successes we now turn.

In contrast with the empirical evidence, virtually every quantitative estimate of the benefits of trade liberalization predict that unbridled integration in the Latin American mode will bring growth and development to the countries that need it most. Such estimates are derived from and are built into computable general equilibrium models (CGE models) (Anderson 2004).

Drawing on prevailing economic theory and numerous simplifying assumptions, CGE models attempt to present a quantitative picture at one point in time of the full interaction of markets and industries throughout the economy. One of the more controversial assumptions necessary for CGE models to work properly is the assumption that there is no technological change in the economy. The assumption that is perhaps most unrealistic is the assumption that there is perfect competition in the economy. In other words, there are no barriers to entry among buyers and sellers (Munk 1990; Stanford 1993; see also Tims 1990). In essence, there is no room for oligopolistic multinational corporations in these models. These models also have to hold all other aspects of economic activity constant, such as inflation, exchange rate fluctuations, full employment, and so forth. In most developing countries unemployment, inflation, and exchange rate fluctuations are rampant. Moreover, these models will only examine the effects of tariff reductions, not investment and factor mobility factors related to further liberalization. Although the economic impacts of such provisions are forming a growing part of world trade, it is difficult to model them in a CGE framework.

In the end, the results of these exercises also ignore the distributional consequences of trade liberalization. On the one hand, CGE models will provide estimates about which sectors will gain or experience losses from a particular measure. Moreover, if the net benefits (where the winners win more than the losers lose) are positive then there is the potential for real development benefits – the increase in net welfare can be used to benefit the poor. However, it is well known that in developing countries a redistribution of the net benefits often does not occur, a factor that explains much of the resistance to globalization (Kanbur 2001, 2002). In fact, distributional policies and others that form the very institutions that are key to economic growth, if introduced into a CGE model, would cause distortions and provide estimates of negative effects.

In summary, the empirical evidence shows us that the relationship between trade and economic growth is very limited in the absence of the proper institutional mechanisms to make increases in imports and exports a force for growth. Yet the dominant modeling techniques are uniformly "built" to show that any increase in trade will be beneficial for growth and that most institutional interventions will distort such growth. This is cause for great concern, as CGE-based estimates drive public and official discussions of the benefits of integration.

The Developmental State

In the post-World War II era, developing countries found themselves far behind the technological frontier and in a global economy rife with market failures. Important among those market failures was imperfect competition. Many of the markets for manufacturing and high technology products that are a key to value-added growth were virtually impossible to enter. In the face of these market failures, a small number of states successfully orchestrated a set of institutions and policies that eventually led to strong growth. Such nations have been termed "developmental states" (Wade 1990; Evans 1995). While many of the measures used by developmental states for development policy are justified in neoclassical economics, they are scorned by current and proposed trade rules.

As Stiglitz, Lall, Singh, Wade, and others in this volume show, states such as Taiwan, South Korea, Thailand, Singapore and to some extent Brazil and Mexico (among others) focused on the reliance on major public outlays for infrastructure, planning, tariffs, import licensing, quotas, exchange rate controls, wage controls, and direct government investment in key sectors. The engine of growth was the development of a strong manufacturing sector. Government subsidies and international protection, in addition to loans from national development banks, were given to industry in exchange for concrete results. Lending and support were conditional on local content requirements, price controls, technological innovation, capacity, and exports. Through this process, nations created "national leaders" in the form of key state-owned and state-patronized enterprises in the petroleum, steel, and other industries. These sectors were linked to chemical, machinery, transport, and textiles industries that also received government patronage (Amsden 2001).

Many of these measures have been shown to be economically efficient in a second-best world. Rodrik (1987) has shown that performance requirements on FDI are often necessary to maximize welfare benefits in the context of imperfect competition. Dasgupta and Stiglitz (1985) have shown that industrial policies are important for dynamic learning effects and correcting for market failures. Other economists have argued for such policies on justifications beyond efficiency. Amsden (2001) and Krugman (1990) have shown that some protections may "get the prices wrong" but can be beneficial for countries looking to enter new markets. In this volume, Stiglitz, Lall, and Singh stress that the theoretical justification for such interventions is even stronger in today's global economy.

The chapters by Chang, Cho and Dubash, and Kumar in this volume show that the very policies that have now fallen out of favor in global trade circles are mirror images of policies once (and still) employed by developed countries. Chang shows how in the United States "we can say that US in- dustries were literally the most protected in the world until 1945." Cho and Dubash, and Kumar, show how many protectionist policies to create infant industries and attract investment are still present in the United States in the form of subsidies for alternative energy sources and to lure foreign car firms to enter the United States. Indeed, Dani Rodrik has noted that

> Almost all successful cases of development in the last fifty years have been based on creative and often heterodox policy innovations.... At the time, GATT rules were sparse and permissive, so nations combined their trade policy with unorthodox policies: high levels of tariff and non-tariff barriers, public ownership of large seg- ments of banking and industry, export subsidies, domestic content requirements, import–export linkages, patent and copyright infringements, directed credit, and restrictions on capital flows.... In all of these countries, trade liberalization was a gradual process, drawn out over a period of decades rather than years. (Rodrik 2004)

Intervening policies alone, however, will not ensure success. The notion of 'reciprocity' has been shown to be a key to success. Amsden has shown how a select group of developing nations industrialized through pure learning (rather than through proprietary innovation) by creating control mechanisms whereby subsidies and other forms of support were allocated to certain industries in return for monitorable performance standards that were redistributive and results oriented (Amsden 2001). In a comprehensive volume on the develop- ment of national high technology industries in Brazil, India, and South Korea, Peter Evans showed that getting the right balance between state and market was often very tricky. To Evans, success required "embedded autonomy," where states and private sectors acted together but with enough distance so as not to erode innovation and development. Evans witnessed that, in addition to the establishment of basic "custodial" rules and institutions in an economy, success was also determined by states playing roles as producers of certain types of goods; acting as "midwives" to assist in the development of new entrepreneurial groups; and performing "husbandry" activities in the form of "greenhouses" that allowed firms to experiment with innovation while protected from international competition (Evans 1995). In this volume, Lall sets out a number of institutional roles that are essential for state-facilitated development in the newly globalized economy:

- selectivity (picking a few activities at a time) rather than promoting all industrial activities indiscriminately and in an open-ended way;
- picking activities and functions that offer significant technological benefits and linkages;
- forcing early entry into world markets and using exports to discipline bureaucrats and enterprises;
- giving the lead role in productive activity to private enterprises but using public enterprises as needed to fill gaps and enter exceptionally risky areas;
- investing massively in skill creation, infrastructure and support institutions, all carefully coordinated with interventions in product markets;
- using selectivity in FDI to help build local capabilities (by restricting FDI or imposing conditions on it) or to tap into dynamic, high technology value chains;
- centralizing strategic decision-making in competent authorities that could take an economy-wide view and enforce policies in different ministries;
- improving the quality of bureaucracy and governance, collecting huge amounts of relevant information and learning lessons from technological leaders;
- ensuring policy flexibility and learning, so that mistakes could be corrected en route, and involving the private sector in strategy formulation and implementation.

Rodrik emphasizes that

> The secret of economic growth lies in institutional innovations that are country-specific, and that come out of local knowledge and experimentation. These innovations are typically targeted on domestic investors and are tailored to domestic realities. Accordingly, a development-friendly trading regime evaluates the demands of institutional reform not from the perspective of integration ("What do countries

need to do to integrate?") but from that of development ("What do countries need to do to achieve broad-based, equitable economic growth?"). (Rodrik 2004)

If variations of these policies worked so well for developmental states toward the end of the last century, are they viable for other developing countries in the future?

The Shrinking of Policy Space

The authors in this volume unanimously argue that the trading regime is restricting the ability of developing countries to put in place the proper policies to raise standards of living in their countries. Most of the authors in the volume focus on WTO trade policies and corresponding IMF policies. The increasing bilateral and regional trade negotiating agenda shrinks policy space to an even greater degree.

In the WTO, four key agreements have been singled out in this volume as not being friendly toward development:

- *Trade-Related Investment Measures (TRIMs) Agreement* TRIMs affect trade in goods and restrict the use of instruments traditionally used to steer local benefits from FDI. Such tools include: local content requirements, technology transfer, local employment requirements, and so forth (see Kumar, Cho and Dubash, and Wade in this volume).
- *Trade-Related Aspects of Intellectual Property Rights (TRIPS) Agreement* TRIPS' copyright and patent restrictions make it very difficult for nations to develop strategies for R&D, reverse engineering, and generic drug development (see Wade, Correa, and Lall in this volume).
- *General Agreement on Trade in Services (GATS)* This restricts the ability to set market-correcting policies to ensure competition regarding FDI (mode 3) for each subsector that a nation lists to other WTO members (called a positive list approach, discussed most in Wade).
- *Subsidies and Countervailing Measures (SCM) Agreement* Whereas it was once permissible (non-actionable) for states to put targeted subsidies toward R&D, regional inequality, and environmental protection, such measures are now actionable (see Amsden in this volume).

In the Doha Round, developed countries have proposed deepening these restrictions on investment, intellectual property, and services. Moreover, developed countries have proposed to add competition policy and other issues to the negotiations. In response to developing country objections, investment and competition have now fallen off the negotiating agenda, but they have not gone away. The WTO has created committees for each of these issues, where ongoing debate over their merits will take place. If history is any guide, they will eventually show up on the agenda, regardless of their developmental merits. Das (2003) has shown that many of the controversial issues in the trading system that were the subject of opposition by developing countries ended up as committees by compromise. Then, in bilateral and regional deals where developing countries have less bargaining power, many countries end up agreeing to such measures. Thus, the eventual constituency is developed on a multilateral scale.

Because of the general sluggishness of the Doha negotiations, countries such as the United States have engaged in numerous bilateral and regional deals. In these agreements, asymmetric bargaining power is an understatement (Ann-Elliot 2003). Moreover, they run deeper than their counterparts in the WTO and are an indication of the developed world's wish list for future WTO agreements:

- The *North American Free Trade Agreement (NAFTA)* investment provisions are seen as "TRIMs plus" measures that run far deeper than TRIMs. Under NAFTA's investment agreements, all forms of local content, performance requirement, and technology transfer are restricted. Perhaps most alarming is the fact that private foreign investors can now directly sue governments (as opposed to state-to-state disputes under the WTO) if a regulation is seen as "tantamount to expropriation." Several social and environmental policies have been called into question in investor–state disputes under NAFTA and a host of bilateral deals. The United States has insisted on investor–state provisions in the Free Trade Area of the Americas (FTAA) negotiations and virtually every bilateral and regional treaty it has negotiated since NAFTA.
- The *United States–Chile Free Trade Agreement* restricts Chile's ability to install import controls on foreign portfolio investments, even though such controls were seen as a key reason that Chile avoided the contagion of the crises in the 1990s and when the IMF has begun to soften its stance on the relationship between portfolio investment and economic development (Ffrench-Davis 2002; IMF 2003). Interestingly, Singapore did not give in to similar pressure in the United States–Singapore Agreement.
- The *United States–Morocco Free Trade Agreement*'s intellectual property provisions are seen as "TRIPS plus" and make it increasingly difficult for Morocco to produce and import generic drugs.
- The *Central American Free Trade Agreement*'s services provisions adopt a "negative list" approach (as does NAFTA) where nations have to list every sector that they wish to be exempt from trade rules. The saying goes,

"if you don't list it you lose it." This is in contrast to the WTO where nations only list sectors that they will subject to rules.

Aside from trade agreements, numerous authors in this volume, especially Stiglitz and Evans, stress how the fiscal and monetary polices advocated by the IMF also restrict policy space in developing countries. Tight fiscal policies have prohibited nations from spending their way out of recessions – which were often caused in part by opening up capital markets too quickly. Other economists have argued that measures mandated by the IMF and foreign investors as needed to keep inflation in check generate high interest rates and an overvalued exchange rate that inevitably lead to current account deficits, which can eventually cycle back into instability and low growth (Nadal 2003).

Pull Together and Carve Out or Pull Out Altogether?

The São Paulo Consensus forged in the summer of 2004 at the eleventh meeting of the United Nations Conference on Trade and Development (UNCTAD) explicitly recognizes the restriction of policy space under various international arrangements and calls on nations to "take into account the need for appropriate balance between national policy space and international disciplines." The question is, how can the developing world do it and why should they? After all, whether it was under a WTO round or in specific agreements with the IMF, many countries have willingly signed on to the deep integration-based economic strategies.

It is true that developing countries have willingly signed on to many of the commitments that authors in this book argue are shrinking policy space. However, the concerted efforts that developing countries are conducting to make sure that no further shrinking occurs and that some space can be restored is evidence of the fact that many countries feel that mistakes were made during the last trade round. It is important to remember that concessions on intellectual property, investment, and services by the developing countries were seen as concessions in exchange for market access and institutional reforms in the industrialized world. As mentioned earlier, it has been documented that the industrialized nations have largely failed to follow through on their side of the deal. Blocking the negotiations on investment and competition policy in the Doha Round and the emergence of the G22 in general can be seen as attempts to correct for past mistakes.

Indeed, in his chapter in this volume, Peter Evans sees these current events as possible opportunities at both the international and the national levels. However, such an opportunity will arise only if states in the global South can overcome collective action problems. Contingent on this precursor, globally, Evans sees the WTO's 'one nation, one vote' consensus decision-making process as a mechanism for change that has just begun to be taken advantage of. It is true that developed countries generate close to 80 per cent of the world's GDP and have thus been able to frame negotiations successfully as bargains for entry into Northern markets. However, developing countries vastly outnumber the developed countries and have begun to use such voting power to their advantage. Evans points to the development of the G22's role in halting the Cancún talks because developed countries failed to table development-friendly proposals, and to Brazil's successful cases against developed country subsidies, as positive examples of what might come with a more concerted and coordinated effort on the part of the developing world. On the domestic front, Evans also sees existing WTO laws as opportunities for reform-oriented developing country governments to shed themselves of rent-seeking firms that are dependent on state funds for survival. Developing countries can say "my hands are tied" in order to let go of lobbies that have a hold on the state and build new alliances with more productive areas of their economies.

The chapter by Singh offers further proposals that could come from the developing world. He shows how the concept of special and differentiated treatment (S&DT) was radically changed with the establishment of the WTO. S&DT under GATT allowed nations to follow a different path toward development that did not necessarily require that each nation follow the rules. The WTO was established as a single undertaking that requires nations to endorse and comply with every single agreement under the WTO. Moreover, S&DT has been reconceptualized to be special treatment to make sure nations comply with the single undertaking, rather than special treatment to steer clear of certain provisions until a certain level of development is reached. Singh sees the endorsement of S&DT at Doha as a chance to change course and offers a new conception of the S&DT paradigm that gives developing countries the ability to join certain parts of the WTO system as they develop, but without the obligation to join all parts at once, in the absence of the proper institutions.

Amsden argues that the "bark of the WTO appears to be worse than its bite, and 'neodevelopmental States' in 'the rest' have taken advantage of this, where necessary." While acknowledging that policy space is shrinking under the WTO, especially in the form of industrial subsidies, Amsden points out how developing nations can creatively adhere to the letter but not necessarily the spirit of WTO law in order to achieve development. She outlines how nations such as Thailand and Taiwan have craftily set up effective control mechanisms to steer the private sector toward growth and innovation while avoiding the bite of the WTO.

The fact that the developing world was able to halt the Cancún ministerial because the proposed packages were not good for development, and subsequently to force the developed countries into offering real targets and timetables for agricultural support reductions, shows that the developing world means business. The new world trade politics will be very interesting to observe. On the one hand, new power in the South as a collective entity may end up stalling multilateral talks that could harm development. On the other hand, if talks don't yield positive outcomes for the developed countries, they have shown that they will sign bilateral and regional deals where Southern coalition-building is not as strong.

This volume will be far from the last word on this subject. However, it is the aim of this book to provide to policymakers and negotiators an immediate guide to current and proposed commitments under the WTO and in other regimes and the extent to which they are reducing policy space for development. Second, this book is a fresh and very contemporary look at the academic literature that examines the role of the nation-state in a globalizing world. The myriad commitments and agreements that have recently taken place or that are currently under way will have long-lasting effects on the world economy. Together, the chapters in this volume provide a solid theoretical and empirical analysis of the possible effects that current and proposed arrangements could have on development prospects in the nations that need development most. The volume also outlines a number of alternative policies and theoretical approaches that can help make a globalizing world economy work for development.

2

Development Policies in a World of Globalization

Joseph E. Stiglitz

Throughout Latin America today the question is being debated, has globalization failed us, or has reform failed? What is clear is that there is disappointment in the policies that have been pushed for the past two decades, the policies focusing on liberalization, privatization, and stabilization which collectively have come to be called the Washington Consensus policies. The data for the 1990s, the first true test of these policies, when the countries were freed from the shackles of overhanging debt, help explain the sense of disillusionment. Growth during that decade was just over half of what it was in the pre-reform and pre-crisis decades of the 1950s, 1960s, and 1970s. Even in those countries which have seen significant growth, a disproportionate share of the gains have gone to the better off, the upper 30 per cent, or even the upper 10 per cent, with many of the poor actually becoming worse off. Little if any progress has been made in reducing inequality, already the highest of any region of the world, and the percentages, let alone numbers, in poverty actually increased. Unemployment, already high, has increased by three percentage points. And the performance in the last half-decade has been, if anything, even more dismal; with income per capita stagnating or declining, it is beginning to be known as the lost half-decade (see ECLAC 2002).

I have argued that there was a clear connection between these failures and the policies that were pursued. The outcomes should not have come as a surprise. They reflect both what was on the agenda and what was left off the agenda. The seeming success of the first two-thirds of the decade was but a mirage, partly a surge in growth caused by an unsustainable inflow of foreign capital; partly, as so often happens after a period of stagnation, a "catch-up" from the lost decade. The growth was not sustained. A convincing argument can be made that it was not sustainable.

A closer look at the one often repeated success case, Chile, shows that in the years of its phenomenal performance, with growth of 7 per cent, it did not simply succumb to following the dictates of the Washington Consensus willy-nilly. Like the success cases of East Asia, it was selective, adding and subtracting to the standard recipes in ways that allowed it to shape globalization for its purposes. For instance, it did not fully liberalize its capital markets, retaining what amounted to a tax on the inflow of short-term capital, a tax which prevented surges into the country, which in turned dampened the surges out of the country in the aftermath of the East Asia crisis. It privatized, but selectively, even with IMF pressures, including accounting frameworks that tilt the deck unfairly and strongly against government enterprises; today, something like 20 per cent of exports still come from one government-owned enterprise, CODELCO. The social democratic governments emphasized education and health expenditures, especially for the poor. In this world, one often has to run to stand still: though there was little progress in reducing inequality, at least it did not increase as it did elsewhere. Perhaps most importantly, there was put in place a virtuous circle: the growth allowed the government to provide these vital social expenditures without deficit financing, so that today Chile's debt-to-GDP ratio stands at around 15 per cent,[1] making that country less subject to the whims of the international markets, which have had such devastating effects on other Latin American countries.[2]

Globalization: Opportunities and Challenges

Increasingly, the basic tenets of the Washington Consensus have come to be challenged.

- Stabilization policies do not ensure economic growth. Countries that have followed the recipes of the IMF, from Bolivia to Mongolia, are saying: we have felt the pain, we have done everything you have told us to do; when do we start to reap the benefits? Meanwhile countries that have taken an independent course, like China, or that have been selective, like Chile, have fared far better.
- Stabilization policies – defined as fiscal stringency and "sound" monetary policy – do not even ensure stability, as sudden changes in investor sentiment can, with open capital markets, lead to massive outflows, leaving in their wake economic havoc, even in countries with moderately strong institutions, but especially in those countries in which financial sector regulation is weak and safety nets are absent. The repeated financial crises of the past six years have provided ample evidence.

- Capital market liberalization – sequenced wrongly, effected prematurely – does not lead to faster economic growth, but does expose countries to high levels of risk: it is risk without reward.
- The benefits of trade liberalization are more questionable than the free-trade mantra would suggest, particularly when the free-trade agenda is the kind of asymmetric one that has characterized the world in recent years, with developed countries insisting that the developing countries take down their trade barriers to the goods that they produce, while developed countries maintain their barriers to the goods of the South. The United States, under the Bush administration, had led the way in this hypocrisy, with agriculture subsidies reaching new heights and with its newly imposed tariffs on steel. If the United States, the richest country in the world, a country where, even in a recession, fewer than 6 per cent of its workers face unemployment, and where those who do lose their jobs are protected by a safety net, says that it must resort to "safeguards" to protectionist measures, what must be true in the developing countries, where there are no safety nets, where unemployment is already high, where those who are thrown out of a job as a result of liberalization and their families may face truly bleak prospects? To make matters worse, in the face of austerity policies, the promised new jobs are not created: how could they be with interest rates as high as they often are, with IMF policies that worry more about inflation and what it would do to the value of investor bonds than they do about those thrown out of work? As a result, instead of workers moving from low-productivity jobs to high-productivity jobs, the "promise" of liberalization, workers move from low-productivity jobs to unemployment, or poorly paid jobs in the informal sector, which does not enhance growth but does increase poverty. As the United States and other developed countries resort increasingly to non-tariff protectionist measures, while they continue to espouse the rhetoric of free trade and globalization, a natural question is beginning to be repeatedly asked: why are there two standards for what is a "fair" or "unfair" trade practice? Internally, the United States has clearly defined standards for "dumping," for predatory behavior, under the anti-trust laws. Why shouldn't they be applied more generally?
- The last round of trade negotiations, the Uruguay Round, amply demonstrated the inequalities in the global regime. The intellectual property regime was dictated by commercial interests in the United States and elsewhere, paying little attention to the concerns of either the developing countries or of the research community throughout the world. It was unbalanced. Some of the problems, such as those arising from access to drugs, have already come to the fore. Others will only emerge more

gradually. Similarly, in the areas of services: while the extension of trade agreements to services is often lauded as one of the great achievements, it is noteworthy that it was financial services, of concern to the United States, that was on the agenda, not construction or maritime services, which would have been of greater interest to the developing countries.

- Privatization – done wrongly, and it is very hard to do well – may lead to higher prices of utilities, not lower, thereby undermining further a country's competitiveness, and, through the high levels of corruption which often accompany it, can further corrupt political processes and increase inequality, as Russia so amply demonstrated. But the difficulties that Britain experienced in both rail and electricity show that even countries with highly sophisticated institutions may find it difficult to "get it right," and the problems of electricity deregulation in the United States demonstrate not only that without adequate government regulation massive manipulation by private firms can disrupt the economy and destroy public finances, but that it is extremely difficult to get the regulatory framework "right."

- Ignoring the social and political dimensions – as the IMF and the Washington Consensus have done – is not only bad social policy, it is also bad economic policy. It will take years for Indonesia to recover from the riots to which IMF policies contributed in that country, just as one can argue that much of Latin America has suffered from urban violence and guerrilla activity that, in part, are a result of the mistaken policies that were pushed on those countries. In those countries with huge inequalities in land ownership, where sharecropping is a common form of tenancy, the 50 per cent of the crop that is turned over to the landlord acts as a heavy tax on the peasants, with enervating effects on growth.

More on the Globalization of Ideas and Global Hypocrisy

One powerful aspect of globalization is that those in developing countries can see the disparity between what is said and done in the North, and especially in the United States, and the policies that are recommended for, or imposed upon, them. I have already mentioned the hypocrisy in trade. I have touched briefly upon the problems of privatization and regulation in the North, which are leading to a rethinking of those issues there, including initiatives for renationalization. The widespread discussions of accounting, both in the public sector and in the private, have drawn attention not only to these problems but also to the inadequacies of the accounting frameworks imposed on developing countries by the IMF and the differences between those and the ones conventionally used in Europe and elsewhere.

In the United States, in the recession of 2001, both Democrats and Republicans agreed on the need for a fiscal stimulus to restore the economy; yet throughout the developing world, the IMF forces contractionary fiscal policies on countries facing downturns – just the opposite of the mission for which they were created. While the IMF has pushed privatization of social security, the initiative even for partial privatization in the United States has (except in Wall Street) received a lukewarm reception. The efficiency of America's public system, the fact that it has virtually eliminated poverty among the elderly, combined with studies which show that, in the case of Britain, transactions costs under privatization have reduced benefits by as much as 40 per cent, and the recognition of the risks for old-age security posed by stock-market volatility, have dampened enthusiasm.[3] (Of course, what from a societal point of view are called transaction costs look to others like a good source of income, and, not surprisingly, those who would gain from these costs remain ardent advocates.)

Learning from Others' Mistakes

Globalization has had another advantage: those all over the world have the opportunity not only to learn from the mistakes of others, but to look at the analytic studies which attempt to interpret those experiences. That the transition from Communism to a market economy in those countries which followed the Washington Consensus policies was a disappointment, to say the least, is clear (Stiglitz 2000c, 2001). They can follow the lively debate over the failure. They can read too the raging debate about the consequences of inflation. While there is a consensus that high levels of inflation have significantly adverse effects on growth, empirical and theoretical research (including that by George Akerlof, who won the Nobel prize in economics with me) suggests that not only may the benefits of pushing inflation lower and lower be limited, but there may actually be adverse effects from pushing it too low (see Akerlof et al. 1996). This was not the problem facing Latin America a quarter-century ago. But one has to be careful about the straitjackets into which the past puts one: today, Europe is facing a major problem. As it faces a major slowdown, it is unable to respond effectively, because of a monetary authority whose sole objective is inflation (unlike that of the United States, which also is concerned with unemployment and growth) and because of a stability pact which constrains the size of deficit financing. France, Germany,

Italy, and Portugal all recognize the potentially disastrous consequences, and are looking for ways of reinterpreting these commitments.

Challenges Posed by Globalization

Focusing more narrowly on the economy, globalization has three distinct advantages: the demand for a country's products is no longer constrained to its own markets; a country's investment is no longer constrained to what it can save itself; and a country's producers can have access (at a price) to the most advanced technology. But corresponding to these opportunities are some important challenges: the developed countries have learned how to use a variety of non-tariff barriers to keep out the goods of the developing world; while foreign direct investment (FDI) does bring with it not only access to capital but access to markets and technology, this is not so for short-term financial capital, which exposes a country to enormous instability. China, which has been the most successful in getting foreign direct investment, has shown that the assertion by advocates of capital market liberalization that one cannot get FDI without at the same time opening up oneself to short-term capital flows is simply wrong. Countries have been misled, too, into thinking that foreign purchases of existing capital goods (e.g. associated with privatizations) is foreign direct investment. In some cases it may be, but the contrast between greenfield investments, where a foreign firm creates new jobs, and these other forms of foreign investment should be clear. In many cases, the foreigners may make the purchase simply for purposes of asset stripping, not wealth creation; and in the long run the country will be poorer, not richer. Globalization poses other challenges: while there is not a free movement of labor, highly trained labor is more mobile, forcing a dilemma on developing countries – either they pay internationally competitive wages, which they can ill afford and which leads to massive inequality, or they lose these skilled workers. In some countries in Eastern Europe, the outflow of skilled labor has been massive, leaving behind those who are too old to move and those without skills, contributing to the downward spiral in those countries. Similarly, the asymmetries in mobility between labor and capital have forced reductions in the taxes imposed on capital, leaving more of the burden on labor, adding still another force to those leading to increasing inequality around the world. In this chapter, I have time to address only two of the challenges posed by globalization: those associated with borrowing from abroad and, in particular, with sovereign bankruptcy; and those associated with industrial policies.

Sovereign Bankruptcy

The access to capital when things are going well has proved irresistible to too many countries. There is a compelling economic argument for borrowing when the rate of return on these investments exceeds the cost of capital. And there is a corresponding compelling political argument: the gains from borrowing will be felt now, while the problems of repayment will occur under someone else's watch, as the case of Argentina forcefully showed.

The problem is that banks and lenders more broadly are, to use an American expression, fair-weather friends. While they are willing to lend when you don't need the money, they want their money back just when you need it most. That is one of the reasons why, throughout the continent, Latin American countries have pursued countercyclical policies (Easterly et al. 2001 and the references cited there). It is not that the economists have not taken their basic course in macroeconomics, where they should have learned about countercyclical policies. Rather, this lending acts almost as an automatic destabilizer. (As an economy goes into a downturn, banks become weaker; as confidence in the country's banks weakens, people look for safer havens abroad; as they pull their money out of the country, and as defaults increase, strict enforcement of, let alone tightening of, capital adequacy standards and reserve requirements leads to a contraction of lending, further contributing to the economic downturn.) Even countries with moderate debt-to-GDP ratios may not be able to service that debt, if the international capital markets suddenly decide that the risk premium they demand for emerging market debt in general, or that country in particular, must be increased dramatically. It is easy to show that there may be multiple equilibria. If the interest rate were reasonable, the country would have no problem servicing the debt, the default probability would be low, and, accordingly, the interest rate should remain moderate. But if the interest rate soars, the country will have a problem servicing the debt, the default probability will be high, and, accordingly, the high interest rate is perfectly rational (see Stiglitz and Greenwald 2003).

These problems are exacerbated by the design of debt contracts, which violates basic principles of efficient markets. The rich countries are more able to bear the risks associated with interest and exchange rate volatility, and the debt contracts should be designed accordingly, or would be in efficient capital markets. But this is not so in practice. With poor countries left to bear this risk, when matters get bad (or are simply *perceived* to be bad) a vicious cycle begins: fear of default leads to capital flight, leading to lower exchange rates and interest rates, which increases the debt burden to the point where it is not serviceable.

These problems are exacerbated by the fact that the world has no good way of handling sovereign defaults. There is no Chapter 11, no Chapter 9, speedy and equitable ways of resolving defaults which pay attention to the interests not only of creditors but also of other stakeholders, such as pensioners and those dependent on the government for vital services like health and education. To be sure, we have made some progress in the past hundred years.

A hundred years ago, in 1902, Dr. Luis Maria Drago, then foreign minister of Argentina, announced the Drago Doctrine, in response to the bombing of parts of Venezuela by European powers, with the express consent of the United States, which had followed upon Venezuela's default on its international debt. He stated:

> what the Argentine Republic supports is the principle, already accepted, that there can be neither European territorial expansion in America nor oppression of the peoples of this continent because of an unfortunate financial situation that could bring one of them to defer the payment of its obligations; that the public debt cannot bring about a military intervention or give merit to the material occupation of the soil of the American nations by a European power.

He went on to say, what is as true today as it was a hundred years ago,

> The creditor knows that it is contracting with a sovereign entity and it is an inherent condition of every sovereignty that no executive proceedings can be initiated or carried out against it, since the manner of collection would compromise its very existence, making the independence and the action of the respective government disappear. The acknowledgment of the debt, the settlement of its amount, can and must be made by the Nation without diminishing its essential rights as a sovereign entity, but the compulsive and immediate collection at any given time, by means of force, would not bring anything other than the ruin of the weaker nations and the absorption of their governments with all their inherent faculties, by the strong ones of the Earth.

A hundred years ago, Argentina rose to the defense of its fellow Latin American state. As Drago stated,

> we are not moved by any selfish sentiments, nor are we seeking profit for ourselves, as we express our wish that the public debt of the states would not serve as a reason for military aggression; it is because of that sentiment of continental fraternity and by the strength that always emanates from the moral support of a whole nation … a nation that has faith in its destiny and in that of this whole continent.

This was not the first time, nor the first place, the world military and financial powers – the G7 of those days – had used military means in an attempt to enforce debt: in the middle of the century they had occupied Mexico. Their occupation of Egypt was to last for decades. Nor was it to be the last.

Views of default have, in some ways, changed considerably in the course of a century. At the personal level, we no longer have debtor prisons. All the major countries of the world have passed bankruptcy laws that provide for the restructuring and discharge of debt. In the United States, the bankruptcy law also provides for the bankruptcy of local governments and other public authorities (Chapter 9). So too have views changed about how to respond to the inability or unwillingness of a sovereign state to repay its debt. The Drago Doctrine is now universally accepted. But at the international level, there are no bankruptcy proceedings. And there is a concern that economic pressure brought by the large and powerful nations of the world, sometimes through the international economic institutions, can be every bit as oppressive as that of the military measures of the nineteenth century, and possibly even more destructive of life and political freedom. To many within the developing world, the picture of Suharto signing the so-called Letter of Intent appeared no less a signing over of that country's economic sovereignty as those that followed upon military intervention. (Indeed, in the international arena the distinction between private and public debts is sometimes obscured, as pressure is exerted for the nationalization of private liabilities. Such nationalizations occurred both in the Latin American crisis of the early 1980s and in the more recent East Asia crisis.)

Many believe that the travails Argentina has been forced to go through are, in part at least, deliberate: debtors are being put on notice that there will be serious consequences to default. Policies could (and I would argue should) have been designed to reactivate the economy. It was moral outrage that stopped the military interventions, moral outrage that closed the debtors' prisons. Perhaps it will be our moral sensibilities that will bring on a new era in dealing with international debts. The good news is that there are glimmerings of a recognition that something is amiss in the current arrangements. In the East Asian crisis (as after the last Latin American crisis), critics of the IMF bail-outs argued that there needed to be greater reliance on standstills and bankruptcies, and that there needed to be improvements in bankruptcy procedures, a super-Chapter 11 as I called it. But the long debate about bankruptcy reform in the United States should have made clear that there is not a single "best" bankruptcy code. The fact that every government among the advanced industrial countries has taken a statutory approach (rather than relying on market mechanisms, modified by, for instance, mandatory collective action clauses) should have made it clear that the position of the US Treasury (which seemed to claim that *all* that was required was collective action clauses) makes little sense, reinforcing the results of theoretical and empirical research on bankruptcy and bargaining. Thus, it *is* good news that the IMF, after the failure of six bail-outs in as many years, finally recognized that an alternative approach was needed, and that some sovereign debt restructuring mechanism was desirable. They are right too that one cannot rely on market-based approaches (a fact which they failed to recognize in East Asia), that some version of a statutory approach was desirable. It should have been obvious that in any bankruptcy procedure which is viewed as fair, a major creditor (such as the IMF) cannot simultaneously play the role of the bankruptcy judge, nor even have a central role in the process, other than as one of the claimants. To many, the IMF's attempt to give itself such a central role says much about its political insensitivities. But these reforms, if they occur, will be a long time in the making. In retrospect, it is clear that the discussions about reforming the global financial architecture were more about calming frayed nerves than about anything else: one suspects that the hope on the part of the US Treasury was that the impetus for reform would pass before issues related to the offshore banking centers or hedge funds, or even deeper issues like bankruptcy and capital market liberalization, would be effectively addressed

Thus, countries in the developing world today need to face three harsh realities. First, capital markets are highly volatile; countries can be punished not only for mistakes that they have made, but for events for which they have no responsibility; countries may be punished not just for mistakes that they have made, but for mistakes that the capital market might think that they might make. Subjecting oneself to the so-called discipline of international capital markets does not ensure growth or efficiency; it does risk countries being forced to give up important elements of their sovereignty. This is especially true because short-term capital focuses, quite naturally, on the short term. Second, when there is a crisis the costs are enormous, and even when a crisis is averted the costs of dependence on foreign capital are great, as they, for instance, force contractionary policies exactly when expansionary policies are necessary. These costs more than offset the benefits that accrued earlier, when the borrowing was undertaken. Third, well-functioning capital markets would have rich countries bear the risks of exchange rate devaluations and interest rate increases; a well-functioning global financial architecture would have arrangements which limited the costs of bankruptcy, whether of sovereigns or firms engaged in cross-border borrowing. But we have neither well-functioning international capital markets nor a well-functioning global financial architecture (at least in this – and other – crucial respects). Yes, the costs of not borrowing are high – in terms of education or health projects not undertaken, roads not built – but the costs of borrowing are even higher. Countries facing these realities must trim expenditures and increase taxes.

Industrial Policies

Globalization has confronted countries with the challenge of how to compete in the global market place. Today, we recognize that what separates developed from less developed countries is not just a disparity in capital and other resources, but also a gap in knowledge.

Countries are asking what can they do to promote technology, to enhance their competitiveness to increase their exports and their ability to compete with foreign imports. Of late, industrial policies have obtained a bad reputation. As my predecessor at the Council of Economic Advisers put it, it makes no difference whether the economy produces potato chips or computer chips, the economy should produce whatever maximizes GDP, and the market is the best place to make those decisions.

Economic theory and industrial policy

The argument against industrial policies is based on a naive reading of economic theory and a misreading of economic history. Standard economic theory trumpets the efficiency of competitive markets, but Adam Smith's invisible hand theorem, asserting market efficiency, was based on extremely stringent conditions. It assumed, for instance, that information was perfect, that there were no information asymmetries, and that markets were complete – capital markets were perfect and one could obtain insurance against all risks. These assumptions clearly do not apply even to the best-functioning market economies. Of course, economists realized that information was imperfect and markets were incomplete, but the hope was that if information was not too bad, or information was not too imperfect, then the economy would be well described by the perfect information models. My research, and that of others, showed that this hope was not well founded: even small amounts of information imperfections could have marked effects. Work with Bruce Greenwald (Stiglitz and Greenwald 1986) showed that perhaps the reason why the invisible hand was invisible was that it was simply not there, or that if it was there, it was palsied. Thus there was a role for government: government could, in principle, enhance the efficiency of markets.

These arguments are even more compelling when it comes to innovation. Knowledge can be thought of as a particular form of *information*, and, as such, the results of the economics of information apply to the realm of the economics of innovation. The standard theories *assumed* a fixed technology, but of course at the center of growth and development is the change in technology, the development and adoption of new modes of production and new products. The standard theories about the efficiency of markets thus have *nothing* to say about this arena. On the contrary, there are strong reasons to believe that in general markets *do not* by themselves produce efficient outcomes. Knowledge has the attributes of a public good (that is, there are high costs to exclusion and low or zero costs to additional individuals enjoying the benefits of the good), and innovation generates enormous externalities. Moreover, there are large uncertainties associated with innovation, so that the consequences of the absence of insurance markets are likely to be particularly severe. Long ago, Schumpeter emphasized the importance of capital market imperfections, since investments in research are typically not collateralizable. Thus, modern economic theory has created a strong presumption for a role for government.

Economic history and industrial policy

This brings me, then, to the question of economic history. The two cases of successful development that I have studied most closely, that of the United States and East Asia, provide compelling evidence for the importance of industrial policies. The telecommunications industry was, in a sense, created by the government. The first telegraph line was built in 1842 by the federal government between Baltimore and Washington, and the modern Internet, which has done so much to create the New Economy, was itself created by the US government. The major *industry* of the nineteenth century was, of course, agriculture, and the US government, through its research and extensions services, transformed this industry, leading to the productivity increases that were the necessary precursor to the modern world. A central ingredient in the successful policies of the East Asian countries was a deliberate attempt to close the "knowledge gap." These countries realized that what separated them from the more developed countries was not just a gap in capital, but a gap in knowledge, and they worked hard, and successfully, to bring modern technology to their societies. Today, in many areas, they stand at the forefront.

Making industrial policy better: new instruments and approaches

Critics of industrial policy cite the failures and the abuses, and there have been failures and abuses. Sometimes, political pressures have brought huge subsidies to favored industries.

Government, it is claimed, does not have a credible record at "directing" the economy. Japan's pressuring Honda not to produce cars − saying there were already enough car manufacturers − is repeatedly cited as an attempt (fortunately for Japan unsuccessful) at misguided government intervention.

But the successes noted earlier suggest that societal benefits far outweigh the costs.

Indeed, with optimal risk taking, there should be failures: if there were none, clearly the government would have been pursuing too conservative a strategy. Research at the Council of Economic Advisers while I was Chair showed convincingly that in fact government support for research had an enormously high return, far higher than that for typical private investments (Council of Economic Advisers, Executive Office of the President 1995).

Principles

Still, we have learned from the mistakes, and I believe we are in a position to make an even more effective industrial policy. *Modern* industrial policy focuses on attempting to identify areas in which interventions to correct market failures are likely to be most successful. For instance, it looks for areas in which *coordination* failures may loom large, or where there are large spillovers, or significant problems of appropriability. The research on the Internet illustrates all of these problems. It would have been difficult for a private firm to appropriate the full benefits of the Internet; the value of the Internet has risen with the usage, but if a potential Internet developer were to have waited for the Internet application companies to demand the creation of the Internet, it would never have been developed. The Internet has produced enormous spillovers to all firms, and not just to those directly engaged in marketing over the Internet.

The economics of information has also helped us understand why capital markets are often imperfect, and why therefore government may need to play an important role in this arena. In the United States, in one recent year, 25 per cent of all finance was provided either by the government, with government guarantees, or through government-sponsored enterprises. The government helped create the national mortgage market, which has lowered the cost of capital for homeowners. Government loans to small businesses (through the Small Business Administration) have, in recent years, had a remarkable record. Every large business begins, of course, as a small business. Among the large ones that today play a major role in the US economy that began with an SBA is Federal Express.

In some sense, the government cannot avoid addressing issues of industrial policy. The government plays a central role in the economy. In addition to the large role just described in finance, it is pivotal in research and education as well. Infrastructure is another area where government is dominant. Decisions it makes in these areas – which areas of research to support, how to design the curriculum, where to build roads and airports – help shape the economy and its competitiveness. It is better that these decisions be made with a view to where the economy is going. Similarly, tax policies help shape the economy. Special tax treatment of real estate and energy is a form of industrial policy – it directs resources into these areas. But is this where the government should be directing resources? Again, thinking about these issues from a more global perspective can enhance the economy's performance.

Modern industrial policy is not involved in micro-management of the economy. Critics of industrial policy say that government is not in the best position to "pick winners." And it should not do so. But this misses the point, in two respects. The government intervenes in the market not because it does not have faith in the markets' ability to pick winners (though the misallocation of resources in the American technology bubble might raise questions), but rather because it recognizes that there are market failures of the kind noted earlier. The inventors of the laser, the Internet, the transistor appropriated but a small fraction of the societal benefits associated with their innovation. Thus, today, industrial policy is based on broad-gauged interventions, attempting in particular to address these market failures.

It begins by focusing on education and research. Countries like Costa Rica have recognized that if they are to be successful in the modern era, everyone must have mastery of computer skills and education. It identifies other areas where government naturally plays a large role, such as infrastructure, and asks how they should be shaped in ways that enhance the development of the economy.

By the same token, modern industrial policy is often "broad gauged" and, so far as possible, attempts to employ market-like mechanisms in implementation. Thus, it may make more sense for the government to encourage "energy efficient technologies," allowing competition among alternative approaches, than *ex ante* selecting a particular technology to push. In this competition, it may require those seeking support to contribute substantial sums of their own, so that their own money is at risk as well as that of the government. Similarly, in loans (such as those for small and medium-sized enterprises) the government may use commercial banks to help screen applicants, but require the originating banks to risk some of their own capital. In science and technology projects, peer review should be employed. (Some of America's experiences with these improvements carry with them a warning: as rents get eliminated, so too does political support for these programs wane!)

Labor markets and education

A key part of this broad-gauged industrial policy will be working to enhance the economy's flexibility: for example, through active labor market policies, lifelong education, and education aimed at learning to learn. There will need to be changes in the curriculum, and closer links between universities and industry. In the nineteenth century, public education was directed at developing the trained and disciplined labor force needed for industrialization. In the twenty-first century, education needs to be directed at developing entrepreneurship and the ability to cope with a fast-changing world.

Some countries will face a challenge in keeping skilled and well-educated populations at home. This is especially true of the economies in transition, which have seen an enormous outflow. Unless this outflow is stemmed, it is hard to see how a new modern economy can be reconstructed on the ashes of the old Communist one.

Negative industrial policies

Modern industrial policy may entail "negative" policies as much as positive, recognizing that speculative real estate may contribute less to employment and growth than other sectors, and may expose the economy to greater instability. Thus, it may make sense to restrict the extent of bank lending for speculative real estate. While such restrictions are not normally viewed as part of industrial policy, in a very real sense they are.

Small businesses and venture capital

While there are some instances of small economies developing large businesses (Nokia), it is more likely that small businesses will continue to predominate, and industrial policies will need to be particularly attentive to their needs, through the establishment of industrial and research parks and incubators. There may need, too, to be specialized financial institutions, venture capital firms that go beyond traditional approaches for providing credit to small and medium-size enterprises.

Vision

While broad-gauged industrial policies reduce the necessity of the government "picking winners," there is no way that government can avoid forming a "vision" of where the economy is going. Indeed, some might argue that forming that vision – in consultation with those in the private sector – was one of the important roles performed by the governments of East Asia. They were not engaged in the detailed planning associated with government *control*, but they were performing a perhaps more important *catalytic* role. Within Latin America, both the public and the private sectors will need to ask, what will be the comparative advantages in the future; how can they, how should they, alter those comparative advantages through investments? I cannot even begin to provide an answer to this central question, but I want to touch upon some aspects that relate to the questions of globalization.

Modern economies are increasingly service sector and knowledge economies. The transformation from agriculture to industry was a major reorientation, and it is clear that the transformation from manufacturing to the New Economy will be no less dramatic. There are no easy answers to the questions of what are a country's *dynamic* comparative advantages. But this much should be clear: in the New Economy, these are likely to be markedly different from what they were in the past. This will require rethinking government strategies in every one of the areas in which it is involved.

China, with its enormous pool of low-wage labor, increasingly well educated, will pose a challenge to manufacturing everywhere in the world, especially if that country continues policies which result in low exchange rates (partly through ever increasing reserves, which, given the instabilities associated with modern globalization, may make enormous sense, especially for a country that has experienced the risks of instability). Even the United States can, of course, find niches in which it can compete: computer-driven apparel manufacture provides a made-to-order product that, at the upper end, can compete with clothes produced in China. The globalization of technology has changed the nature of competition in fundamental ways. As much as America would like to claim that it is other countries' unfair subsidies which have put its steel industry at a competitive disadvantage, the fact is that South Korea, only a quarter-century ago a less developed country, can produce with *higher technical efficiency* (even in a state-run firm) than the old American steel behemoths.

There are niches that a country like Brazil can find, and some of these will be high-technology niches, like airplanes to serve a regional market. While new technologies in some areas have considerably reduced the advantages of proximity to the market, there are some areas in which these advantages remain. These will have to be identified, and the opportunities exploited.

There have been advances in trading services, and since these typically are highly labor intensive, countries like Brazil may find opportunities in this arena. At the same time, many services will remain highly non-traded, and improvements in the efficiency of this part of the economy can bring real increases in standards of living.

We should not forget that in many developing countries many of the poorest people remain in the rural sector, and are likely to remain there for several decades. If poverty is to be reduced, something must be done about this sector. Even if it does not directly contribute much to exports, it is the right thing to do. The experiences in the successful countries have demonstrated the importance of social stability, and one cannot maintain social stability if large fractions of the population remain left behind. Education for the children in these areas cannot just be a way out, but also must be a way up. It must be designed so that those who remain see their productivity rise, both by attuning them to better production technologies and sensitizing them to the products that are most valued by the market. But this will not be enough, if they are not at the same time equipped with resources – capital and land – to put their knowledge to work. In short, industrial policies cannot ignore agriculture, and the rural sector more broadly. (Indeed, China's and Taiwan's early success was built on a rural-based development strategy.)

Concluding Remarks

There are no easy formulas for success in the modern world. Ireland and Portugal show clearly, however, that countries that were on the periphery of Europe, and whose income levels were toward the bottom, can go a long way in catching up. Finance, education, and industrial policies all were central to their success. Markets – entrepreneurship – will be vital, but government has the responsibility, and the opportunity, for shaping the economic environment. There are some who sound the simplistic mantra of lower taxes and deregulation, suggesting that if only taxes were lowered and regulations eliminated, growth would come. There is no evidence in support of that approach. Yes, overbearing taxes and regulations can stifle an economy, and to some *any* tax or regulation is by definition overbearing. But a more balanced approach recognizes the vital role that government can, and must, play, and that includes *both* regulation and the provision of public services, like education. The problems that brought about the East Asian crisis were too little regulation, not too much, and the problems facing the US economy too come from underregulation, not overregulation. Industrial policies, when well constructed and well thought out, can be an important part of a more comprehensive strategy for economic management, one which can produce economic growth and stability with social justice. We may need to invent new names – like productivity-enhancing investment and technology strategies – and we need to be aware of the pitfalls, but such policies are essential for long-term growth.

A short while ago, there was discussion in Latin America about the second-generation reforms: the first-generation reforms, focusing on liberalization, privatization, and stabilization, were well on their way; it was *assumed* that they would be successful. It was time to build further reforms on the basis of those past successes. Today, the inadequacies of the Washington Consensus reforms are apparent, though some say it is too soon to pass judgment; that things would have been even worse but for the reforms. It is clear that some have benefited from the reforms, and it is also clear that some of the reformers have a stake in the reforms being judged to be a success. The reforms were supported too by free-market, market-fundamentalist ideologues, and they will continue to proclaim the success, whatever the evidence with which they are confronted.

Many of the old policies had to be changed. Governments cannot continue to mount large deficits without facing consequences. High levels of inflation are deleterious. Many of the state-run enterprises were inefficient. Rampant protectionism had enormous costs. We cannot go back to the past. But neither should we fail to recognize the failures of the present. Reform has to be reformed. In my Prebisch lecture, I spelled out several elements of such a reformed reform strategy. Here I have focused more narrowly on the consequences of globalization.

Globalization has enhanced the opportunities for success, but it has also posed new risks to developing countries. The rules of the game have been designed for the most part by the advanced industrial countries, or, more accurately, by special interests in those countries, for their own interests, and often do not serve well the interests of the developing world, and especially the poor. Countries like Brazil need to take an aggressive position in advocating a more balanced regime, not only for their own good, but for the benefit of the entire world.

Yet this will take a long time. In the meanwhile, countries have to learn to live within the rules of the game, as unfair as they may be. Even within these rules, I believe that countries like Brazil can help shape globalization, to make it work, not just for the rich within the country, but for everyone. But if they are to do this, they must choose their own course, free of the simplistic mantras that have played such a central role in guiding economic policy in Latin America over the past decade. It will not be easy, but there is no alternative.

Notes

The author is indebted to the Ford Foundation, the Mott Foundation, the MacArthur Foundation, and Columbia University for financial support, and to Sergio Goody for research assistance.

1. See Stiglitz 2002 for sources of the data cited in the previous discussion.

2. Most of that debt can be traced back to the cost of recapitalizing the banking system after the financial crisis in the Pinochet period. For excellent accounts on the Chilean failed liberalization and crisis see Diaz-Alejando 1985; Edwards and Edwards 1991; and de la Cuadra and Valdés 1992.

3. Murthi et al. (1999) calculate that in Britain, these transactions costs will result in benefits being 40 per cent lower than they would otherwise have been (for the privatized part of their social security system).

3

Rethinking Industrial Strategy: The Role of the State in the Face of Globalization

Sanjaya Lall

As liberalization and globalization gather pace, concern with industrial competitiveness is growing everywhere. Diverging competitiveness in the developing world is one of the basic causes of the growing disparities in income: the potential that globalization offers for growth is being tapped by a small number of countries, while liberalization is driving the wedge between them and others deeper. But there is little consensus on what should be done: should lagging countries persist with liberalization and hope that free-market forces will stimulate growth and bring about greater convergence? Or is there a need to re-examine national and international policies? What is the correct role of government in stimulating industrialization and using it as an engine for growth?

There are two approaches to the issue: neoliberal and structuralist. The *neoliberal* approach is that the best strategy in all situations is to liberalize – and not much else. Integration into the international economy, with re-source allocation driven by free markets, will let countries realize their natural comparative advantage. This will in turn optimize dynamic advantage and yield the highest sustainable rate of growth – any government intervention can only reduce welfare. The only legitimate role for the state is to provide a stable macro-economy with clear rules of the game, a fully open economy, and essential public goods like human capital and infrastructure. This approach is backed by industrialized countries and the Bretton Woods institutions and is enshrined in WTO rules.

The neoliberal approach has strong theoretical premises: markets are "efficient," institutions needed to make markets work exist, and serious deviations from optimality cannot be remedied by governments. These premisses are a mixture of theoretical, empirical, and political assumptions. The theory relies on a restricted view of technology. The empirical base is a particular interpretation of the experience of the successful "Tigers" of East Asia. The political element – that governments are necessarily less efficient than markets – has less to do with economics than with ideology.

The *structuralist* view puts less faith in free markets as the driver of competitiveness and more in the ability of governments to mount interventions effectively. It questions that free markets account for the industrial success of the East Asian Tigers (or, indeed, of the presently rich countries). Accepting the mistakes of past strategies, it argues that greater reliance on markets needs a more proactive role for the government. Markets are powerful, but they are not perfect; the institutions needed to make them work are often weak. Government interventions are needed to improve on market outcomes.

Structuralists accept that some industrialization policies have not worked well in the past. For the neoliberals this is a reason for denying any role for proactive policy: if there are market failures, the costs are always less than those of government failures. Structuralists, on the other hand, see a vital role for policy; past policy failure is not a reason for passive reliance on deficient markets but for improving policymaking capabilities. They note that many regions have implemented neoliberal policies recently without enjoying the industrial or export success that characterized more interventionist economies. To them, this suggests that persisting with passive liberalization will exacerbate divergence, not reverse it.

The growing unease with neoliberalism led the Zedillo Commission, in its "Report of the High-Level Panel on Financing for Development," to phrase the issue in diplomatic terms. Noting that "Sadly, increasing polarization between the haves and have-nots has become a feature of our world" it said the following on infant industry protection (a policy tool banned under the new rules): "However misguided the old model of blanket protection intended to nurture import substitute industries, it would be a mistake to go to the other extreme and deny developing countries the opportunity of actively nurturing the development of an industrial sector" (Zedillo Commission 2001, Executive Summary: 9–10).[1]

The controversy over industrial policy is not new; it goes back decades or even centuries (Reinert 1995; Chang 2002). Despite frequent assertions that the efficacy of free markets is established beyond doubt, this is not the case. We show why this is true and suggest that the case for policy is becoming stronger with technical change and globalization.

The New Dimensions of Industrial Competitiveness

Structural features

Competitiveness has always mattered for industrial growth, but its nature has changed. Rapid technical change, shrinking economic distance, new forms of industrial organization, tighter links between national value chains, and widespread liberalization have radically altered the environment that enterprises face. Competition now arises with great intensity from across the world, using a bewildering array of new technologies. To survive it, all producers must use new technologies at or near "best practice." The production system spans many countries, tapping differences in costs, skills and resources to optimize efficiency (Radosevic 1999).

Technical change is shifting industrial and trade structures towards more complex, technology-based activities. Table 3.1 shows the growth of manufacturing value added (MVA) for three technological sets of activities: resource based (RB), low technology (LT) and medium and high technology (MHT).[2] For exports the data allow us to show high technology products separately. Over the past two decades exports have grown faster than production, and complex activities have grown faster than other branches of manufacturing. Developing countries have done better in all branches than industrialized economies.

Table 3.1   Growth of manufacturing value added and manufactured exports by technology (% per annum, 1980–2000)

Activity	World	Industrialized countries	Developing countries
Manufacturing value added			
Total MVA	2.6	2.3	5.4
RB MVA	2.3	1.8	4.5
LT MVA	1.7	1.4	3.5
MHT MVA	3.1	2.6	6.8
Manufactured exports			
Total manufactured exports	7.6	6.6	12.0
RB manufactured exports	5.6	5.2	6.7
LT manufactured exports	7.4	8.4	11.4
MHT manufactured exports	8.4	7.3	16.5
of which hi-tech exports	11.5	9.9	20.2

Source: Calculated from UNIDO and Comtrade data.

Organizational structures and the location of production are changing in response to technical change. Industrial firms are becoming less vertically integrated and more specialized by technology, scouring the world for more economical locations. Shrinking economic space allows them to locate functions in far-flung corners of the globe. Some facilities are under the control of transnationals from the industrialized countries, but others are independent, interwoven with the leaders in intricate contractual and non-contractual relations. This "fragmentation" is rewriting the geography of industrial activity.[3]

New technologies change the institutional and policy structures needed for competitiveness. Countries require new skills to manage technical change and, therefore, the institutional ability to upgrade skills (Narula 2003). They need technical support agencies in standards, metrology, quality, testing, R&D, productivity, and SME extension. They need advanced infrastructure in information and communication technologies (ICTs), and they need to cushion the impact of new technologies on declining activities and disadvantaged groups.

Globalization also transfers productive factors across economies more rapidly. However, capital, technology, information and skills do not spread evenly. They go only to places where competitive production is possible, where there are inputs and institutions to complement the mobile factors. It requires, in brief, new industrial capabilities (Best 2001). Cheap unskilled labor or raw natural resources are no longer sufficient to sustain industrial growth: strong local capabilities determine competitive success. However, industrial capabilities develop slowly, in a cumulative and path-dependent manner subject to agglomeration economies. Economies that enter a virtuous circle of growth, competitiveness and new capabilities can continue to do better than those that are stuck in a "low-level equilibrium" and cannot muster the resources to break out. Industrial performance can continue diverging over time, with no built-in forces toward convergence.

Rules of the game

Liberalization in the developing world has been partly voluntary, partly driven by external pressures, and partly enforced by the rules of international economic relations. Some changes were initiated by developing countries disillusioned with earlier strategies, some by developed countries, the Bretton Woods agencies, and bilateral or regional agreements, and some by international agreements. One effect has been to constrict the scope for industrial policies. The most affected are protection of infant industries,[4] performance requirements for foreign investors, export targeting and incentives and other subsidies affecting trade,[5] slack IPRs (intellectual property rights) protection to promote copying and reverse engineering and local content rules.[6]

The rules cannot be analyzed here, but some points may be noted. First, rules on trade allow for exceptions, particularly for the least developed countries (though many exceptions are coming to an end). Second, rules now carry the threat of sanctions: trading partners can impose compensatory tariffs or other measures. Third, most important is the underlying *trend towards greater liberalization*. The scope and coverage of the rules are steadily increasing, and pressures are coming in many forms. The trade regime in developing countries is likely to become very similar to that in the OECD.

Policies on FDI and technology imports have undergone rapid liberalization to a greater extent than those on trade and domestic credit. Most liberalization has occurred over the past decade or so, with the pace accelerating in the 1990s. There are practically no policy controls left on technology transfer, in contrast to the 1970s, when there were extensive interventions by governments on licensing.

Some of the main issues in the multilateral agreements are as follows:[7]

- *Services* The General Agreement on Trade in Services (GATS) covers the supply to markets by foreign firms present in those markets under WTO. The GATS allows a "positive list" of permitted investments, allowing host countries freedom to exclude activities not on the list.

- *Performance requirements on TNCs* This is treated under the Agreement on Trade-Related Investment Measures (TRIMs). TRIMs affect trade in goods and are important in that they prohibit tools traditionally widely used to extract greater benefits from FDI: local content requirements, trade balancing, technology transfer, local employment and R&D, and so on.

- *Intellectual property rights* The protection of IPRs has moved in effect from the World Intellectual Property Organization to the WTO under the TRIPS (Trade-Related Aspects of Intellectual Property Rights) Agreement. The most important aspect of this shift is that trade sanctions can be applied to countries deemed deficient in protecting IPRs.[8] The implications for developing countries are worrying (Lall 2003). While stronger IPRs may benefit innovators in the developed countries, they can inhibit technological development in developing ones. They raise the cost of formal technology transfers by allowing technology sellers to impose stricter restrictions and by preventing copying and "reverse engineering," the source of much technological learning in newly industrializing countries.

Trends in industrial competitiveness in the developing world

This section uses two indicators: world market shares in *manufacturing value added* (MVA) and in *manufactured exports*. Developing regions are as follows: EA (East Asia) includes China and all countries in the Southeast Asian region except Japan, while EA2 excludes China. LAC (Latin America and the Caribbean) includes Mexico, while LAC2 excludes it. South Asia includes the five main countries in that region. MENA (Middle East and North Africa) includes Turkey but not Israel (an industrialized country). SSA (sub-Saharan Africa) includes South Africa, while SSA2 does not.

MVA

The developing world performed well in 1980–2000. Its share of global MVA rose by 10 percentage points (from 14 to 24 per cent) and its annual rate of growth (5.4 per cent) was over twice the 2.3 per cent recorded by the industrialized world. Does this mean that globalization and liberalization were conducive to development? Unfortunately not: success in the developing world was very concentrated (Figure 3.1). East Asia dominated, raising its world share from around 4 per cent to nearly 14 per cent – exactly the ten-point rise for the developing world as a whole (Figure 3.2). EA, while strongly export-oriented, was not "liberal" in the Washington Consensus sense.[9] LAC, the region that liberalized the most, the earliest and the fastest, was the worst performer.

LAC and East Asia illustrate the central issues nicely. The regions had different approaches to industrialization, first in developing industry,[10] and later

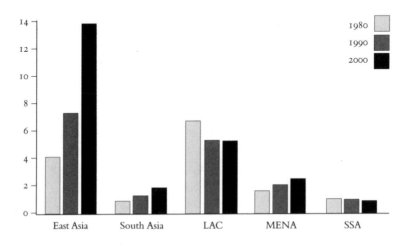

Figure 3.1 Developing regions' share of global MVA (%)

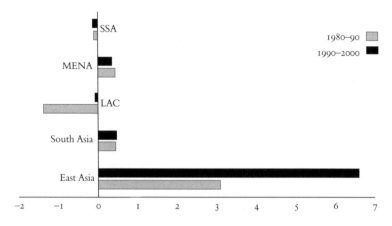

Figure 3.2   Changes in share of global MVA (%)

in liberalizing[11] – EA has had much more strategic industrial policy than LAC. The resulting differences in outcomes are interesting, as Figures 3.3 and 3.4 show. They separate out China in EA and Mexico in LAC, both regional outliers. Both did well in FDI-based manufactured exports, but their differences are of interest. The link between export and MVA growth is stronger in China than in Mexico: China is less exposed to import competition and has used industrial policy to induce greater local content in export activity. Figure 3.3 shows MVA market shares *within the developing world* for EA without China, China, LAC without Mexico, and Mexico.

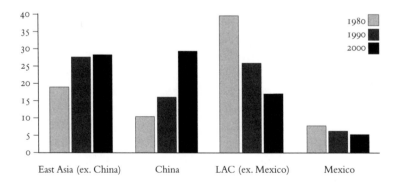

Figure 3.3   East Asia and LAC, shares of developing world MVA (%)

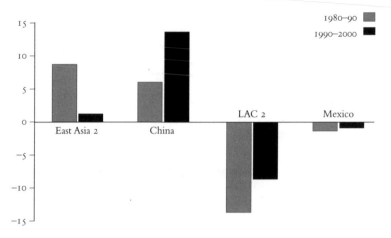

Figure 3.4 East Asia and LAC, change in shares of developing world MVA (%)

Figure 3.4 shows changes in market shares in the periods 1980–90 and 1990–2000. In 1980, LAC accounted for 47 per cent of developing world MVA and East Asia for 29 per cent; two decades later, the shares were 22 per cent and 58 per cent, respectively. The main surge in MVA in EA2 was in the 1980s, with a slowing in the 1990s because of financial crisis and global recession. In China the trends are reversed, with the more rapid growth in the 1990s, making its share of developing world MVA higher than the rest of East Asia. LAC2, excluding Mexico, loses MVA shares more rapidly than Mexico, with the 1980s (the "lost decade" after the debt crisis) being much worse than the 1990s.

LAC started the 1990s with considerable slack engendered by the "lost decade," which better macro-policy and liberalization should have allowed it to exploit for rapid production and export growth. However, the region continued to perform poorly: LAC2 had MVA growth of only 1.9 per cent p.a., much lower than developing countries as a whole (6.4 per cent) or East Asia (9.5 per cent). It underperformed relative to South Asia and MENA, both highly interventionist regions. Mexico's more robust growth of 4.4 per cent was largely a consequence of trade privileges over other developing regions under NAFTA – hardly a neoliberal recipe. In any case, it did not match EA2 (6.7 per cent) or China (13.1 per cent), and this despite the fact that the 1990s were a bad period for EA2, reeling from the effects of the 1997 financial crisis.

Export performance

Figure 3.5 shows world market shares for manufactured exports for 1981–2000 and the value of such exports in 2000, separating China from EA2 and Mexico from LAC2. East Asia as a whole accounted for 18.4 per cent of world manufactured exports in 2000, up from 6.8 per cent in 1981. Within it, EA2 raised its share from 5.8 per cent to 12.0 per cent, and China from 1.0 per cent to 6.5 per cent. China has a much higher share of regional MVA than exports – its industry, perhaps not surprisingly in view of the size of the economy and its late entry to export markets, is less export-oriented than its neighbors'. LAC lost world market share in 1981–1990 (from 3.2 per cent to 2.4 per cent), then raised it over the next decade to 5.1 per cent. The initial fall was due entirely to LAC2 (from 2.7 per cent to 1.9 per cent), with Mexico holding steady at a 0.5 per cent share. Other regions were relatively stagnant, though each did better in the 1990s than in the 1980s. Thus:

• MVA performance is broadly correlated with manufactured export performance, though the fit is not perfect. EA2 and Mexico fare better in exports than in MVA in the 1990s, while the opposite is true of South Asia and MENA.
• Neither MVA nor export growth is strongly related to liberalization in the Washington Consensus sense.

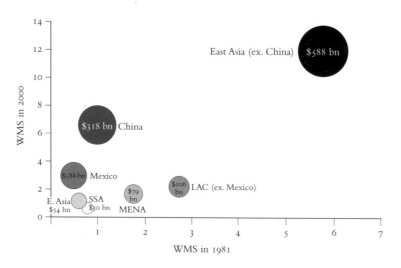

Figure 3.5 World market shares for manufactured products in 1981 and 2000 (%), with values of manufactured exports in 2000 ($ billion)

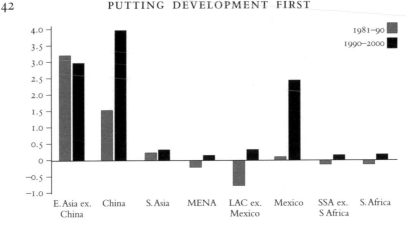

Figure 3.6   Changes in world market shares for manufactures (%)

• Industrial success remains concentrated. Liberalization is not leading to convergence, contradicting the neoliberal premiss that liberalization per se would promote industrial growth and competitiveness.

Why the World Differs from the Neoliberal Ideal

The neoclassical approach

Neoliberal economists accept a role for the state to provide basic public goods, law and order and sound macro-management. Selectivity (the support of particular activities, firms or technologies, or "picking winners") is taboo and became the arena for the industrial policy debate in the 1990s. The early neoliberal interpretation of East Asian success – that it was due to non-interventionist policies – was subjected to intense criticism. It was noted that most successful countries had been very interventionist in trade, FDI, technology and domestic resource allocation.[12] The neoliberals responded with a *"moderate neoclassical"* stance that devoted enormous effort to explaining why selectivity, while it existed, was redundant and unnecessary (World Bank 1993).[13] They admitted *some* market failures and *some* role for the state, but only as long as interventions were functional – there was no role for policy in influencing allocation at the activity, firm or technological level. This "market friendly" approach segmented market failures not according to whether market failures existed but according to the level at which policies affected investment decisions.

Neoclassical theory provides no reason for such a distinction; it arises instead from a *political economy premiss* that it is impossible for governments to mount effective selective interventions. The World Bank (1993) admitted that some selectivity may have worked in East Asia, but the circumstances were unique; other governments did not and *could not* have the capabilities needed. The moderate position, later called the "Washington Consensus," coincided with the World Bank's operations (in health, education, and infrastructure), policy advice (greater liberalization) and structural adjustment programs (stabilization, liberalization, and privatization).

The moderate position retained the simplifying assumptions of the strong position on technology. Both assumed that markets affecting technology were "efficient." In the theoretical sense, efficiency has stringent requirements: product markets give the correct signals for investment and factor markets respond to these signals. At the firm level there are no scale economies or externalities. Firms have perfect information and foresight and full knowledge of all available technologies. They choose the right technology if faced with free-market prices. Having selected the right technology they use it instantaneously at "best practice." There are no significant learning processes, no risks, no externalities and no deficiencies in the skills, finance, information, and infrastructure available to them.

In this model, any policy intervention in prices facing enterprises is by definition distorting.[14] The critical assumption concerns *learning and capability building* and changing it yields very different conclusions for policy (below). But showing that there may be market failures in technology markets does not establish the case for selectivity. It is also necessary to show that such failures are important in practice and not theoretical curiosities, and that governments can effectively remedy them in real life. Both *can* be shown, and the transition from an admittedly simplified neoclassical model to a universal, timeless neoliberal policy diktat is not justified in theory, history, or practice.[15] To do this we turn to the structuralist approach to technology in developing countries.

The technological capability approach

How enterprises in developing countries actually use technology is analyzed by a large recent literature on technological capabilities.[16] The literature is mainly empirical but has its theoretical roots in the evolutionary approach of Nelson and Winter (1982) and the modern information theory of Stiglitz.[17] It argues that industrial success in developing countries depends essentially on how enterprises manage the process of mastering, adapting and improving upon existing technologies. The process is difficult and prone to widespread and diffuse market failures, with important implications for policy (See Box 3.1).

Technology has "tacit" elements that need the user to invest in new skills, routines, and technical and organizational information. Such investment faces market and institutional failures whose remedies require intervention. Many interventions *have* to be selective because technologies differ inherently in their tacit features and externalities. Industrial success in the developing world – and indeed in the presently developed world in its early phases of industrialization – is thus traceable to how effectively governments overcome these market and institutional failures.

Box 3.1 Ten features of technological learning in developing countries

1. Technological learning is a real and significant process. It is vital to industrial development and is primarily conscious and purposive rather than automatic and passive. Firms using a given technology for similar periods need not be equally proficient: each will be at the point given by the intensity of its capability building efforts.

2. Firms do not have full information on technical alternatives. They function with an imperfect, variable and rather hazy knowledge of technologies they are using. There is no uniform, predictable learning curve for a given technology. Each faces risk, uncertainty, and cost. Differences in learning are larger between countries at differing levels of development.

3. Firms may not know how to build up the necessary capabilities – learning itself often has to be learned. In a developing country, knowledge of traditional technologies may not be a good base on which to build a mastery of modern technologies. For a latecomer to a technology, the fact that others have already undergone the learning process is both a benefit and a cost. It is a benefit in that they can borrow from the others' experience (to the extent this is accessible). It is a cost in that they are relatively inefficient during the process (and so have to bear a loss if they compete on open markets). The cost and risk depend on how new the technology is relative to the entrant's base of knowledge, how developed factor markets are, and how fast the technology is changing.

4. Firms cope with these uncertain conditions not by maximizing a well-defined function but by developing organizational and managerial routines (Nelson and Winter 1982). These are adapted as firms collect new information, learn from experience, and imitate other firms. Learning is path-dependent and cumulative.

5. The learning process is highly technology specific, since technologies differ in their learning requirements. Some technologies are more

embodied in equipment while others have greater tacit elements. Process technologies (like chemicals) are more embodied than engineering technologies (machinery or automobiles), and demand different (often less) effort. Capabilities built up in one activity are not easily transferable to another. Different technologies involve different breadths of skills and knowledge, some needing a narrow range of specialization and others a wide range.

6. Different technologies have different degrees of dependence on outside sources of knowledge or information, such as other firms, consultants, capital goods suppliers, or technology institutions.

7. Capability building occurs at all levels – shop floor, process or product engineering, quality management, maintenance, procurement, inventory control, outbound logistics, and relations with other firms and institutions. Innovation in the conventional sense of formal R&D is at one end of the spectrum of technological activity; it does not exhaust it. However, R&D does become important as more complex technologies are used; R&D is needed just for efficient absorption.

8. Technological development can take place to different depths. The attainment of a minimum level of operational capability (know-how) is essential to all activity. This may not lead to the development of deeper capabilities, an understanding of the principles of the technology (know-why): this requires a discrete strategy to invest in deepening. The deeper the levels of technological capabilities aimed at, the higher the cost, risk, and duration involved. It is possible for an enterprise to become efficient at the know-how level and stay there, but this is not optimal for its long-term capability development. It will remain dependent on other firms for all major improvements to its technologies, and constrained in what it can obtain and use. The development of know-why allows firms to select the technologies they need better, lower the costs of buying those technologies, realize more value by adding their own knowledge, and develop autonomous innovative capabilities.

9. Technological learning is rife with externalities and interlinkages. It is driven by direct interactions with suppliers of inputs or capital goods, competitors, customers, consultants, and technology suppliers. Other interactions are with firms in unrelated industries, technology institutes, extension services, universities, industry associations, and training institutions. Where information and skill flows are particularly dense in a set of related activities, clusters of industries emerge, with collective learning for the group as a whole.

10. Technological interactions occur within a country and abroad. Imported technology provides the most important input into technological

learning in developing countries. Since technologies change constantly, moreover, access to foreign sources of innovation is vital to continued technological progress. Technology import is not, however, a substitute for indigenous capability development – the efficacy with which imported technologies are used depends on local efforts. Similarly, not all modes of technology import are equally conducive to indigenous learning. Much depends on how the technology is packaged with complementary factors, whether or not it is available from other sources, how fast it is changing, how developed local capabilities are, and the policies adopted to stimulate transfer and deepening.

Source: Lall 2001a.

Capability development can face market failures in building *initial capacity* and in *subsequent deepening*. Both need support – functional and selective. Support entails a mixture of policies apart from infant industry protection.[18] In building initial capacity in new industrial activities, for instance, free markets may not give correct signals for investment in new technologies when there are high, unpredictable learning costs and widespread externalities. This is, in modern garb, the classic case for infant industry protection: classical economists clearly recognized that in the presence of such costs, an industrial latecomer faced an inherent disadvantage compared to those that had undergone the learning process.[19] To this can be added the extra costs and disadvantages faced by firms in developing countries. These include unpredictability, lack of information, weak capital markets, absence of suppliers, poor support institutions and so on. Exposure to full import competition is likely to prevent entry into activities with relatively difficult technologies. Yet these are the technologies that are likely to carry the burden of industrial development and future competitiveness.

Why do interventions have to be *selective*? Offering uniform protection to all activities makes little sense when learning processes and externalities differ by technology, as they inevitably do. In some activities the need for protection is low because the learning period is brief, information is easy to get and externalities are limited. In complex activities or those with widespread externalities, newcomers may never enter unless measures are undertaken to promote the activity. The only complex activities where investments may take place without promotion are those based on local natural resources, if the resource advantage is sufficient to offset the learning costs. However, the processing of many resources now calls for strong capabilities; both Africa and Latin America have large resource bases but advanced processing has only taken root in the latter, based on decades of capability building under import-substitution.

Infant industry protection is only one part of industrial policy, and by itself can be harmful and ineffective. First, protection cannot succeed if not offset by competitive pressures on firms to invest in capability building: cushioning the costs of capability building can remove the incentive for undertaking it. One reason why industrial policy failed in most countries is precisely that this dilemma was not overcome. But it is possible to do so by strengthening domestic competition, by setting performance targets and, most effectively, by forcing firms into export markets. Many such measures also have to be *selective*, since the costs of entering export markets differ by product. Thus, differentiated export targets, credits, and subsidies were often used in East Asia.

The second reason why industrial policy involves more than protection is the need for *coordination with factor markets*. Firms need new inputs for learning: new skills, technical and market information, risk finance, or infrastructure. Unless factor markets respond to these needs, protection cannot allow firms to reach competitive levels. Factor market interventions also have to be *selective as well as functional*, for three reasons. First, several factor needs are specific to particular activities; if they lack the coordination to meet these needs, interventions are needed to remedy the deficiencies. For instance, the skill needs of electronics may not be fully foreseen by education markets,[20] or the financial needs of emerging new technologies may not be addressed by capital markets. Second, government resources for supporting factor markets are limited, and allocating them among competing uses entails selectivity at a high level (say, between education and other uses). Third, where the government is already targeting particular sectors in product markets, factor markets have to be geared to those activities if the strategy is to succeed.

The *deepening* of capabilities suffers similar problems. The more complex the functions to be undertaken, the higher the costs involved and the greater the coordination required. Getting into production may be easy compared to design, development, and innovation. Neoclassical theory accepts that free markets fail to ensure optimal private innovative activity because of imperfect appropriability of information. However, developing countries face an additional problem. It is generally easier to import foreign technologies fully packaged than to develop an understanding of the basic principles involved – the basis of local design and development. "Internalized" technology transfer takes the form of wholly foreign-owned direct investment. This is an effective and rapid way to access new technology, but it may result in little capability acquisition in the host country apart from production skills.[21] The move from production to innovative activity involves a strategic decision that foreign investors tend to be unwilling to take in developing countries. While some relocation of innovative activity *is* taking place (UNCTAD 2002a), it is largely in advanced countries and a few newly industrializing economies.

Historically most countries that have built strong local innovative capabilities have done so in local firms, often by restricting FDI selectively. Some have done it by stimulating foreign investors to invest in R&D, but this also involved selective intervention. Thus, complete openness to internalized technology imports may not be a good thing if it truncates the process of technological deepening, and internalized transfers may need to be subjected to interventions to extract greater technological benefits.

Table 3.2   Industrial policy objectives of NIEs

	Deepening industrial structure	Raising local content	FDI strategy	Raising technological effort	Promotion of large local enterprises
Hong Kong	None	None	Passive Open Door	None except technology support for SMEs	None
Singapore	Very strong push into specialized high skill/ tech industry, without protection	None, but subcontracting promotion now started for SMEs	Aggressive targeting and screening of TNCs, direction into high value-added activities	None for local firms, but TNCs targeted to increase R&D	None, but some public sector enterprises enter targeted areas
Taiwan	Strong push into capital, skill and technology intensive industry	Strong pressures for raising local content and subcontracting	Screening FDI, entry discouraged where local firms strong. Local technology diffusion pushed	Strong technology support for local R&D and upgrading by SMEs. Government-orchestrated high-tech development	Sporadic: to enter heavy industry, mainly by public sector
Korea	Strong push into capital, skill and technology intensive industry, especially heavy intermediates and capital goods	Stringent local content rules, creating support industries, protection of local suppliers, subcontracting promotion	FDI kept out unless necessary for technology access or exports, joint ventures and licensing encouraged	Ambitious local R&D in advanced industry, heavy investment in technology infrastructure. Targeting of strategic technologies	Sustained drive to create giant private conglomerates to internalize markets, lead heavy industry, create export brands

Note: SMEs = small and medium enterprises, FDI = foreign direct investment, TNCs = transnational corporations, R&D = research and development.

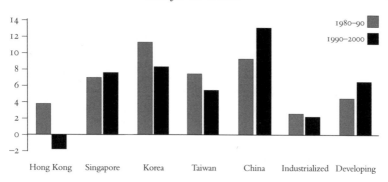

Figure 3.7 Growth rates of MVA (% per annum)

Industrialization Strategies in the Mature East Asian Tigers

There was no generic "East Asian model." Each country had a different model within the common context of export orientation, sound macro-management, and a good base of skills. Each model reflected different objectives and used different interventions. As a result, each had a different pattern of industrial and export growth, reliance on FDI, technological capability, and enterprise structure. However, for none was "getting prices right" sufficient for industrial success. The different objectives are shown in Table 3.2.

Figure 3.7 shows recent MVA growth for Hong Kong, Singapore, Taiwan, and Korea, as well as China and industrialized and developing countries for 1980 to 2000. Figure 3.8 shows manufactured export growth from 1981 to 2000, with very similar patterns except that Singapore marginally outperforms Korea in the 1990s.

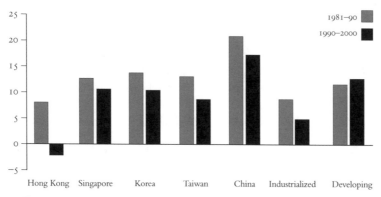

Figure 3.8 Growth rates of manufactured exports (% per annum)

Hong Kong was nearest to the neoliberal ideal, combining free trade with an open door policy to FDI. However, its success does not provide many lessons in the virtues of free markets to other countries. Hong Kong had unique initial conditions and its industrial performance, after the initial spurt, was weak. Its initial conditions included a long entrepôt tradition, global trading links, established infrastructure of trade and finance, the presence of large British companies (the "Hongs") with immense spillovers in skills and information, and an influx of entrepreneurs, engineers and technicians (with developed capabilities) from the mainland. This allowed it to launch into light export-based manufacturing: other entrepôt economies in the developing world have provided similar environments but not enjoyed similar success. Moreover, the colonial government did intervene to help industry, allocating land to manufacturers and setting up strong support institutions like the Hong Kong Productivity Council, an export promotion agency, a textile design centre, and a technical university.

The absence of industrial policy constrained industrial development as capabilities were "used up." Hong Kong *started with and stayed with* light activities where learning costs were low. There was progress in terms of product quality and diversification, but little technological deepening, in contrast to Singapore, a smaller entrepôt economy with strong industrial policy. Hong Kong deindustrialized as costs rose; manufacturing is now less than 5 per cent of GDP compared to over 25 per cent at the peak. Its manufacturers shifted to other countries, mainly China, and its own exports went into decline in the 1990s. The economy grew more slowly than the other Tigers, and its main competitive advantage – financial and other services to the mainland – is under threat as China builds its own capabilities.

Singapore used interventionist policies to promote and deepen industry in a free-trade setting, showing how industrial policy takes many forms apart from import protection. With half the population of Hong Kong, even higher wages, and a thriving service sector, Singapore did not suffer a similar industrial "hollowing out." Its industrial structure deepened steadily over time, allowing it to sustain rapid industrial growth. It relied heavily on TNCs but, unlike Hong Kong, the government targeted activities for promotion and aggressively sought and used FDI as the tool to achieve its objectives (Wong 2003).

Singapore started with a base of capabilities in entrepôt trading, ship servicing, and petroleum refining. After a decade or so of light industrial activity, the government acted firmly to upgrade the industrial structure. It guided TNCs to higher-value-added activities, narrowly specialized and integrated into their global operations. It intervened extensively to create the specific skills needed (Ashton et al. 1999), and set up public enterprises to undertake strategic activities where foreign investment was infeasible or undesirable.

Box 3.2 Singapore's use of FDI

The Singapore philosophy on foreign investment is that multinationals are to be "tapped" for the competitive assets they bring to the country. The government's goal is to maximize learning, technological acquisition, rapid movement up the industrial ladder, and the skills and incomes of its working population. To this end it is willing to contribute capital, tax concessions, infrastructure, education and skills training, and a stable and friendly business environment. While the country is well integrated into international production networks in certain sectors, its fortunes are not tied to those of particular multinational companies, which (like local companies) the government refuses to help if they are unable to compete in the rapidly changing local environment and the world market. Thus over time many multinational factories in Singapore have closed their doors – particularly in low-value, labor-intensive product lines and processes like simple electronic components and consumer goods – and shut down completely or relocated to neighboring countries, with the Singapore government's blessing.

The decisions of MNCs about what new technologies to bring into Singapore are strongly influenced by the incentives and direction offered by the government. The Singapore government is the only one in the region that, like many governments in Western countries, gives grants to firms for complying with specified requirements. These often have to do with entering particular (advanced) technologies. The government supports these incentives, acting in consultation with MNCs (or anticipating through proactive planning) by providing the necessary skilled manpower.

In many instances, it is the *speed and flexibility* of government response that gives Singapore the competitive edge compared with other competing host countries. In particular, the boom in investment in offshore production by MNCs in the electronics industry in the 1970s and the early 1980s created a major opportunity. The government responded by ensuring that all supporting industries, transport and communication infrastructure, as well as the relevant skill development programs, were in place to attract these industries to Singapore.

This concentration of resources helps Singapore to achieve significant *agglomeration economies* and hence first-mover advantages, and has allowed it to set up many advanced electronics-related industries. An example is the disk-drive industry, where all the major US disk-drive makers have located their assembly plants in Singapore. These industries demanded not only electronics components and PCB assembly support, but also various precision-engineering-related supporting industries such as tool and die, plastic injection molding, electroplating, and others. These supporting industries have been actively promoted by the government as part of a "clustering" approach to ensure the competitiveness of the downstream industries.

As labor and land costs have risen, the Singapore government has encouraged MNCs to reconfigure their operations on a regional basis, relocating the lower-end operations in other countries and making Singapore their regional headquarters to undertake the higher-end manufacturing and other functions. This has often led MNCs to set up regional marketing, distribution, service, and R&D centers to service the ASEAN and Asia–Pacific region. To promote such reconfiguration, various incentives have been offered under the regional headquarters scheme, the international procurement office scheme, the international logistics center scheme, and the approved trader scheme. There are now some 4,000 foreign firms located in Singapore, about half of them being regional headquarters. Some 80 of these regional headquarters have an average expenditure in Singapore of around US$18 million per year

The management of industrial policy and FDI targeting has been centralized in the Economic Development Board (EDB), part of the Ministry of Trade and Industry (MTI) that gave overall strategic direction. EDB was endowed with the authority to coordinate all activities relating to industrial competitiveness and FDI and was given the resources to hire qualified and well-paid professional staff (essential to managing discretionary policy efficiently and honestly). Over time the agency has become the global benchmark for FDI promotion and approval procedures. Its ability to coordinate the needs of foreign investors with measures to raise local skills and capabilities has also been critical – and a feature that many other FDI agencies lack. The government conducts periodic strategic and competitiveness studies to chart the industrial evolution and upgrading of the economy: the latest was published in 1998 (Ministry of Trade and Industry). Unlike many other countries, MNC leaders are actively involved in the strategy formulation process and are given a strong stake in the development of the economy.

Since its 1991 Strategic Economic Plan, the government has focused its strategy around *industrial clusters*. The term "cluster" was not used to denote geographical agglomerations (though in view of the tiny size of the economy all industry is in fact very tightly concentrated) but interlinked activities in a value chain. In the manufacturing sector cluster program (called "Manufacturing 2000"), the government analyses the strengths and weaknesses of leading industrial clusters and undertakes FDI promotion and local capability/institution building to promote their future competitiveness.

One explicit objective of the program is to avoid the kind of industrial "hollowing out" experienced by Hong Kong (and many other industrial countries).

This strategy has allowed it, for instance, to become the leading center for hard-disk drive production in the world, with considerable local linkages with advanced suppliers and R&D institutions. In 1994, the government set up an S$1 billion Cluster Development Fund (expanded to S$2 billion later) to support specific clusters like a new wafer fabrication park. It also launched a Co-Investment Program to provide official equity financing for joint ventures and for strategic ventures, not just in Singapore but also overseas (as long as this serves its competitive interests). The EDB can take equity stakes to support cluster development by addressing critical gaps and improving local enterprises.

As Box 3.2 shows, Singapore's heavy reliance on FDI reduced the initial need for local technological effort. Over time, however, the government induced TNCs to establish R&D and foster innovation in local enterprises (Wong 2003). This strategy worked well, and Singapore now has the third highest ratio in the developing world of enterprise financed R&D to GDP, after Korea and Taiwan (UNIDO 2002).

The two larger Tigers, *Korea* and *Taiwan*, adopted the most interventionist strategies, spanning product markets (trade and domestic competition) and factor markets (skills, finance, FDI, technology transfer, infrastructure, and support institutions). Their export drive was led by local firms, backed by a host of policies, including FDI restrictions that allowed them to develop impressive technological capabilities. The domestic market was not exposed to free trade; quantitative and tariff measures were used to give infant industries "space" to develop capabilities. The deleterious effects of protection were offset by strong export incentives.

Korea went much further than Taiwan in building heavy industry. To compress its entry into complex, large-scale and technology-intensive activities, its interventions were far more detailed and pervasive. Korea relied primarily on capital goods imports, technology licensing, and OEM agreements to acquire technology. It used reverse engineering, adaptation, and product development to build upon these arm's length technology imports and develop its own capabilities (Amsden 1989; Westphal 1990). Its R&D expenditures are now the highest in the developing world and are ahead of all but a handful of leading OECD countries. Korea accounts for some 53 per cent of the developing world's total enterprise-financed R&D (UNIDO 2002).

Box 3.3   Managing Korean industrial strategy

Korean industrial targeting and promotion were pragmatic and flexible, and developed in concert with private industry. Moreover, only a relatively small number of activities were supported at a given time, and the effects of protection were offset by strong export orientation (below). These features strongly differentiate its interventions from those in typical import-substituting countries, where infant industry protection was sweeping and open-ended, non-selective, inflexible, and designed without consultation with industry. One of the leading authorities on Korean industrial policy, Larry Westphal describes it thus:

> Since the economy's take-off in the early 1960s, the hallmark of the government's approach to developing the business sector has been its pragmatic flexibility in responding in an appropriate manner to changing circumstances. Several instances demonstrate this well: the means used at the outset to abolish the pervasive rent-seeking mentality that had been engendered by a decade of dependence on US foreign assistance; and the way that rampant pessimism about its growth prospects was overcome through sensible planning between government and business, the success of which soon created conditions that stimulated radical changes in the mode of economic planning.
>
> Another central feature has been the government's ability to adapt policy approaches borrowed from other countries. Here notable examples include the placement of the budget authority in the planning ministry and the entire apparatus of export promotion. But the most important characteristic of the government's approach has undoubtedly been its generally non-restrictive stance. More important, where many other governments have constrained business activities not in line with their development priorities, the government has practiced "benign neglect" rather than repression. As a result, entrepreneurial initiatives have identified significant business areas that were later incorporated into the government's priorities. (Westphal 1997)

Export promotion was a compelling system to force firms into export activity. Korea's export targeting system is well known. Targeting was practiced at the industry, product, and firm levels, with the targets set by the firms and industry associations in concert with the government. There were monthly meetings between top government officials (chaired by the president himself) and leading exporters.[22] These targets were also enforced by several punitive measures: access to subsidized credit and import licenses; income tax audits; and a number of other measures of suasion, publicity, and prizes. On a long-term basis, moreover, bureaucrats were held responsible for meeting export targets in their respective industries, and had to keep in close touch with enterprises and markets. These measures were supported by regular studies of each major export industry, with information on competitors, technological trends, market conditions, and so on.

One of the pillars of Korean strategy, and one that marks it off from the other Tigers (but mirrors Japan), was the deliberate creation of large private conglomerates, the chaebol. The chaebol were handpicked from successful exporters and were given various subsidies and privileges, including the restriction of TNC entry, in return for furthering a strategy of setting up capital- and technology-intensive activities geared to export markets. The rationale for fostering size was obvious: in view of deficient markets for capital, skills, technology, and even infrastructure, large and diversified firms could internalize many of their functions. They could undertake the cost and risk of absorbing very complex technologies (without a heavy reliance on FDI), further develop it with their own R&D, set up world-scale facilities, and create their own brand names and distribution networks.

This was a costly and high-risk strategy. The risks were contained by the strict discipline imposed by the government: export performance, vigorous domestic competition and deliberate interventions to rationalize the industrial structure. The government also undertook various measures to encourage the diffusion of technology, putting pressures on the chaebol to establish supplier networks. Apart from the direct interventions to support local enterprises, the government provided selective and functional support by building a massive technology infrastructure and creating general and technical skills. Korea today has the highest rate of university enrollment in the world and produces more engineers each year than the whole of India.

Even more striking than its creation of high-level skills was its promotion of industrial R&D. Enterprise-financed R&D in Korea as a percentage of GDP is the second highest in the world, after Sweden, and exceeds such technological giants as the United States, Japan, and Germany. Such R&D has grown dramatically in the past two and a half decades as a result of the promotion of the chaebol, export orientation, incentives, skill availability, and government collaboration. *All of this was an integral part of its selective industrial policy.*

Taiwan's industrial policy encompassed import protection, directed credit, selectivity in FDI, support for indigenous skill and technology development, and strong export promotion (Wade 1990). While this resembles Korean strategy in many ways, there were important differences. Taiwan did not promote giant private conglomerates; nor did it attempt a similar drive into heavy industry. Taiwanese industry remained largely composed of SMEs, and, given the disadvantages for technological activity inherent in small size, it supported industry through a mix of R&D collaboration, innovation inducements, and extension assistance. Taiwan has what is probably the developing world's most advanced system of technology support for SMEs, and one of the best anywhere. But it also built a large public sector in manufacturing to set up facilities where private firms were unwilling or unable to do so.

In the early years of industrialization, the Taiwanese government attracted FDI into activities in which domestic industry was weak and used a variety of means to ensure that TNCs transferred their technology to local suppliers. Like Korea, Taiwan directed FDI into areas where local firms lacked world-class capabilities. The government played a very active role in helping SMEs to locate, purchase, diffuse, and adapt new foreign technologies. Where necessary, the government itself entered into joint ventures, for instance to get into technologically very difficult areas such as semiconductors and aerospace (Mathews and Cho 1999).

Box 3.4 Taiwanese industrial targeting

In Taiwan early trade policies had "[e]xtensive quantitative restrictions and high tariff rates [that] shielded domestic consumer goods from foreign competition. To take advantage of abundant labor, the government subsidized light industries, particularly textiles." As import substitution started to run out of steam, by 1960

> [a] multiple exchange rate system was replaced with a unitary rate, and appreciation was avoided. Tariffs and import controls were gradually reduced, especially for inputs to export. In addition, the Bank of Taiwan offered low-interest loans to exporters. The government also hired the Stanford Research Institute to identify promising industries for export promotion and development. On the basis of Taiwan's comparative advantage in low-cost labor and existing technical capabilities, the institute chose plastics, synthetic fibers and electronic components. Other industries subsequently promoted included apparel, consumer electronics, home appliances, watches and clocks. (World Bank 1993: 131–2)

In the 1970s, the Taiwanese government again drew upon foreign advice, now from consultants Arthur D. Little, to upgrade the industrial structure and enter into secondary import substitution. These interventions included the setting up of "capital-intensive, heavy and petrochemical industries to increase production of raw materials and intermediates for the use of export industries." In the 1980s, as its light exports lost competitiveness, Taiwan's government "again moved to restructure the economy."

> After extensive consultation with domestic and foreign advisors, the government decided to focus on high-technology industries: information, bio-technology, electro-optics, machinery and precision instruments, and environmental technology industries.

The shift to a high-technology economy necessitated the close co-ordination of industrial, financial, science and technology, and human resource policies. (World Bank 1993: 133)

Individual tariff rates still varied widely, with widespread quantitative restrictions in use: the use of these protective instruments was made conditional on prices moving toward international levels in two to five years. The average legal tariff rate in 1984 was as high as 31 per cent, higher if additional charges are added; this is higher than the 34 per cent prevalent in the developing world (Wade 1990).

Mathews (2002) describes one of the most successful and distinctive recent tools of industrial policy used in Taiwan, *R&D consortia*.

Unlike the case of many of the collaborative arrangements between established firms in the US, Europe or Japan, where mutual risk reduction is frequently the driving influence, in the case of Taiwan it is technological learning, up-grading and catch-up industry creation that is the object of the collaborative exercises. Taiwan's R&D consortia were formed hesitantly in the 1980s, but flourished in the 1990s as institutional forms were found which encourage firms to cooperate in raising their technological levels to the point where they can compete successfully in advanced technology industries. Many of these alliances or consortia are in the information technology sectors, covering personal computers, work stations, multiprocessors and multimedia, as well as a range of consumer products and telecommunications and data switching systems and products. But they have also emerged in other sectors such as automotive engines, motor cycles, electric vehicles, and now in the services and financial sector as well. Several such alliances could be counted in Taiwan in the late-1990s, bringing together firms, and public sector re-search institutes, with the added organizational input of trade associations, and catalytic financial assistance from government. The alliances form an essential component of Taiwan's national system of innovation.

Taiwan's high technology industrial success rests on a capacity to leverage resources and pursue a strategy of rapid catch-up. Its firms tap into advanced markets through various forms of contract manufacturing, and are able to leverage new levels of technological capability from these arrangements. This is an advanced form of "technological learning", in which the most signifi-cant players have not been giant firms (as in Japan or Korea), but small and medium-sized enterprises whose entrepreneurial flexibility and adaptability have been the key to their success. Underpinning this success are the efforts of public sector research and development institutes, such as Taiwan's Industrial Technology Research Institute (ITRI). Since its founding in 1973 ITRI and its laboratories have acted as a prime vehicle for the leveraging of advanced technologies from abroad, and for their rapid diffusion or dissemination to Taiwan's firms.... This cooperation between public and private sectors, to overcome the scale disadvantages of Taiwan's small firms, is a characteristic feature of the country's technological upgrading strategies, and the creation of new high technology sectors such as semiconductors.

It is Taiwan's distinctive R&D consortia that demonstrate most clearly the power of this public–private cooperation, in one successful industry intervention after another. Taiwan's current dominance of mobile (laptop) PCs for example, rests at least in part on a public–private sector led consortium that rushed a product to world markets in 1991. Taiwan's strong performance in communications products such as data switches, which are used in PC networks, similarly rests on a consortium which worked with Taiwan's public sector industry research organization, ITRI, to produce a switch to match the Ethernet standard, in 1992/93. When IBM introduced a new PC based on its PowerPC microprocessor, in June 1995, Taiwan firms exhibited a range of computing products based on the same processor just one day later. Again this achievement rested on a carefully nurtured R&D consortium involving both IBM and Motorola, joint developers of the PowerPC microprocessor, as external parties. Taiwan is emerging as a player in the automotive industry, particularly in the expanding China market, driven by its development of a 1.2 litre 4-valve engine. Again, this is the product of a public–private collaborative research endeavour involving three companies, which have now jointly created the Taiwan Engine Company to produce the product. Thus, the R&D consortium is an inter-firm organizational form that Taiwan has adapted to its own purposes as a vehicle for catch-up industry creation and technological upgrading. The micro-dynamics of the operation of these alliances or consortia, is therefore a matter of some substantial interest.

Sources: Lall 1996; Mathews 2002; World Bank 1993.

The contrast between the success of industrial policy in the Tigers and its failures elsewhere suggests that there is no justification for the general neoliberal case against selective interventions. It shows that the outcome depends not on *whether* but on *how* governments intervene. On "how to intervene," the differences between import-substituting strategies and those used in the Tigers lay in:

- selectivity (picking a few activities at a time) rather than promoting all industrial activities indiscriminately and in an open-ended way;
- picking activities and functions that offered significant technological benefits and linkages;
- forcing early entry into world markets and using exports to discipline bureaucrats and enterprises;
- giving the lead role in productive activity to private enterprises but using public enterprises in order to fill gaps and enter exceptionally risky areas;

- investing massively in skill creation, infrastructure, and support institutions, all carefully coordinated with interventions in product markets;
- using selectivity in FDI to help build local capabilities (by restricting FDI or imposing conditions on it) or to tap into dynamic, high-technology value chains;
- centralizing strategic decision-making in competent authorities that could take an economy-wide view and enforce policies in different ministries;
- improving the quality of bureaucracy and governance, collecting huge amounts of relevant information and learning lessons from technological leaders;
- ensuring policy flexibility and learning, so that mistakes could be corrected en route, and involving private sector in strategy formulation and implementation (Lall and Teubal 1998).

The list could be longer but it suffices to show that *there are many ways to design and implement industrial policy*. The analysis offers important lessons on what to do now. There are also *many levels* of selectivity, and adopting "industrial policy" does not mean that the country has to copy the comprehensive and detailed interventions used in Korea or Singapore. In fact, the new setting may provide a case for lower degrees of selectivity in some areas. At the same time, the rigors imposed by globalization and technical change may well strengthen the case for more intervention in others.

Industrial Policy for the New Era

What difference do technical change and globalization make for the policies that developing countries need to promote industrialization?

Technical change

The rapid spread of information technology, the shrinking of economic distance, and the skill and institutional needs of new technologies have made the competitive environment more demanding. Minimum entry levels in terms of skill, competence, infrastructure, and "connectivity" are higher. All these raise the need for support for learning by local enterprises. Low wages for unskilled labor matter, but they matter less. Only natural resources give an independent competitive advantage, but only for extraction; subsequent processing needs competitive capabilities.

The policy needs of capability building have not changed much. They are *direct* – the infant industry case to provide "space" for enterprises to master new technologies without incurring enormous and unpredictable losses – and *indirect*, to ensure that skill, capital, technology, and infrastructure markets meet their needs. There is also a need to *coordinate learning* across enterprises and activities, when these are linked in the production chain and imports cannot substitute effectively for local inputs. At the same time, technical change makes it necessary to *provide more access to international technology markets*; it also makes it more *difficult to anticipate which activities are likely to succeed*. The information needs of industrial policy rise in tandem with technological change and complexity. The greater complexity of technology does not make selectivity unfeasible. Detailed targeting of technologies, products, or enterprises may be more difficult because of the pace of change, but targeting at higher levels is feasible and more necessary. Technological progress may actually make industrial policy easier in some respects: information on technological trends and markets is more readily available, more is known about the policies in successful countries and benchmarking is easier.

The *neoliberal alternative*, leaving capability development to free market forces, is hardly more promising. It can result in slow and truncated technological development, with gaps between countries rising. Some upgrading does take place, but is slower and more limited than with promotion. Given the speed at which technologies are changing, and given path-dependence and cumulativeness in capability building, the neoliberal approach can lead to latecomers being mired in low growth traps, unable to bridge the technological gap.

With weak local capabilities, industrialization has to be more dependent on FDI. But FDI cannot drive industrial growth without local capabilities, for several reasons:

- FDI concentrates in technology- and marketing-intensive activities and does not cover large areas of manufacturing with mundane skill, branding, and technological requirements (the heartland of industrial growth in latecomers). If local enterprises are not capable, the industrial sector cannot sustain lopsided growth in the long term.
- Attracting manufacturing FDI into complex activities needs strong local capabilities, without which TNCs cannot launch efficient operations.
- Retaining an industrial base with a strong foreign presence needs rapidly rising capabilities as wages rise and skill demands change.
- FDI is attracted increasingly to efficient agglomerations or clusters of industrial activity, again calling for strong local capabilities.
- The cumulative nature of capabilities means that once FDI takes root in particular locations, it becomes difficult for newcomers to break in, particularly in the more complex activities and functions. First mover advantages mean that late latecomers, countries seeking to industrialize

now on the basis of FDI, face increasing entry costs relative to those faced by earlier latecomers in Southeast Asia. Without strong local capabilities they will find it difficult to overcome these costs.

It is also difficult to see how host countries that have FDI can tap its potential fully without such strategies as local content rules, incentives for deepening technologies and functions, inducements to export, and so on. Performance requirements have been deployed inefficiently in many countries, but, as with protection, they have also been used very effectively.

Globalization

The spread of integrated production systems makes it more difficult and risky to take the autonomous route of Korea or Taiwan. It is much easier for countries to attract segments of TNC activity and build upon these rather than to develop local capabilities. In any case, local firms today would find it extremely hard to enter export markets emulating the OEM contractors from Korea and Taiwan. All the later entrants into globalized systems, from Malaysia to Mexico and Costa Rica, have taken the FDI route. As FDI regimes are more liberal, TNCs are also less willing to part with valuable technologies to independent firms.

Thus *globalization does not do away with the need for all selective industrial policies*; it only reduces the scope and raises the potential cost of some. FDI is complementary to local enterprises and capabilities after a certain level of development. Strong local capabilities raise the possibility of attracting high-value systems and of capturing skill and technology spillovers from them; these capabilities need selective policies. Moreover, attracting export-oriented FDI increasingly requires selective promotion and targeting; the most effective targeting is undertaken by advanced economies (Loewendahl 2001).

There is a more fundamental issue: how far *can* globalized production systems spread across the developing world? Fragmentation is feasible only when production processes can be separated in technological and geographical terms and where differences in labor cost affect the location of each process. In low-technology activities it is strong in clothing, footwear, sports goods, and toys; in high technology it is strong in electronics; in medium technology industry, it is strong in automobiles (but the weight of the product and its high capability requirements mean that it only goes to a few proximate, relatively industrialized locations). This leaves a broad range of industries in which FDI and exports are not driven by global production systems.

Where such systems exist, they are likely to continue relocating to lower wage countries in only some activities. Low-technology industries are the best candidates because of low entry requirements, but here the abolition of the Agreement on Textiles and Clothing (formerly MFA) next year raises the risk that garment production will shift back to East Asia. It is indicative that other labor-intensive systems that do not have trade quotas driving location – footwear, toys, and the like – have not looked for production bases in these regions.

In high-technology systems like electronics the picture is different. Entry levels are higher than in the late 1960s when the industry first moved to Southeast Asia. Production techniques have advanced and manufacturing systems have "settled down" in their new locations, with established facilities, logistics, infrastructure, and support institutions. If these systems grow, they are likely to cluster around established sites rather than spread to new, less developed ones. Entry by newcomers *is* possible, of course – China is the obvious case – but most poor countries lack the industrial capability, size, location, and other advantages of China. And most cannot use selective industrial policy to attract high-tech FDI and induce it to source local inputs in the way that China does (and is likely to continue to do after WTO rules come into play). The prospects of complex global production systems spreading to most of Africa, LAC, South Asia, or MENA are fairly dim.

New systems may emerge to catalyze the growth of FDI-driven production in new sites but they may not transform competitiveness in poorer economies. Those in resource-based activities are likely to be demanding in skills, technology, and infrastructure. Industrialization in the developing world thus continues to face many of the same constraints that it did before integrated systems. The need to foster the development of local capabilities remains the "bottom line" and globalization offers an alternative route only in some activities, to some countries, and even to these only for some time.

The desirable, the practical and the permissible

WTO rules do not prohibit all selective interventions, only those that affect trade. However, other forces for liberalization are less formal and rule-based (structural adjustment programs, bilateral trade, and investment agreements and pressures by rich countries) and they are as powerful. Together they constitute a formidable web of constraints on governments mounting industrial policy. Some constraints may be useful and may prevent the more egregious forms of intervention that have led to inefficiency, rent-seeking, and technological sloth. They are also beneficial to countries with strong capabilities developed behind protective barriers: India, Brazil or China should accelerate liberalization if they can combine this with a strategy to restructure activities and enter promising new activities.

At this time, it is possible to promote selectively skill formation, technology support, innovation financing, FDI promotion and targeting, infrastructure development, and other general subsidies that do not affect trade. These tools – and some not in line with the spirit of the rules (US tariff protection on steel) – are used vigorously by industrialized countries. Most semi-industrial countries also use them, but the less developed countries generally do not (on weaknesses in technology support in Africa, see Lall and Pietrobelli 2002). The critical issues facing the development community in industrialization are the following: Is the degree of policy freedom left to developing countries sufficient to promote healthy industrial development? If East Asia offers lessons for industrial policy, will the new environment allow them to be implemented? Without strong policy intervention, will persistence with liberalization suffice to drive industrialization?

The answer is "probably not." The permissible tools are probably not enough to foster the rapid development of technological capabilities. They may force poor countries with weak industrial bases to become overdependent on FDI to drive industrial development. This cannot meet a major part of industrialization needs. Even countries able to plug into global production systems can only do so as providers of low-level labor services; subsequent deepening may be held back by constrictions on capability development. For developing countries with a capability base, the rules can deter diversification into new technologies and activities. In general, the rules threaten to *freeze comparative advantage* in areas where capabilities exist at the time of liberalization, yielding a relatively short period of competitive growth before the stock is "used up." Subsequent upgrading of competitiveness is likely to be slower than if governments had the tools to intervene selectively.

While local capabilities matter more than ever in an era of globalization, this does *not* mean that all developing countries can replicate the selective policies of Singapore, Korea, or Taiwan. What it means is drawing appropriate lessons from their experience and adapting them to local circumstances.

- The first stage of a desirable international policy regime would be to provide policy makers with an objective and detailed analysis of what successful countries did to build industrial capabilities.
- The second would be to create greater "policy space" for industrial policy.
- The third stage would be to help develop the capability to mount industrial policy. An integral part of industrial policy must be the building of the administrative competence, information, and insulation that governments need.

• The fourth stage would be to help devise strategies appropriate to each country. Creating more policy space and strengthening government capabilities should not mean returning to the "bad old days" of import substitution. It should be used for careful and flexible policymaking, with clear targets and checks aimed at specific forms of technology development.

If this seems a forlorn hope, consider the alternative of continued whole-sale liberalization, which would support the strong and penalize the weak. Globalization by itself will not be able to catalyze industrial development. There is enough evidence that well-designed industrial policy can transform economic prospects. The development community should accept this, provide the "space" for policy and help countries to use it, not deny its usefulness and practicability.

Notes

This chapter originates in a paper that was commissioned by the G24, which is also being published in Ariel Buira, ed., *The IMF and the World Bank at Sixty* (Anthem Press, London, 2005). I am grateful to Larry Westphal for discussions and detailed comments on an earlier draft, to Robert Wade for sending me pre-publication copies of papers on the issues addressed here, and to Manuel Albaladejo for help in collecting the data.

1. For an interchange based on this recommendation, see Wood 2003. Rodrik 2001b raises similar issues.

2. For a description of the categories and the rationale behind the classification, see Lall 2001a.

3. The international fragmentation of value chains has, for economic reasons, gone furthest in activities with discrete and separable production processes and high-value products. Electronics is the best example, placing production in several countries, each site specializing in a process or function according to its labor costs, skills, logistics, and so on (Sturgeon 2002). The segmentation of software, business process services, and other IT-based activities like call centers is another manifestation of this phenomenon outside manufacturing. Fragmentation goes beyond the spread of transnational companies (TNCs). It encompasses the closer integration of national value chains under several governance systems, with direct ownership by TNCs being at one end and loose buying relationships at the other (Gereffi et al. 2001; Gereffi et al. forthcoming).

4. No new protection can be offered to products for which members have 'bound' their tariffs, though if actual tariffs are lower than bound tariffs they can be raised. Export processing zones may come under the purview of the subsidies ban in the future (LDCs are exempt so far).

5. General subsidies that do not create a cost advantage for identifiable activities may not be actionable. Only subsidies given to particular activities or locations that

create such an advantage are subject to potential sanctions.

6. Local content rules are actionable if there are specific subsidies or incentives linked to achieving the prescribed levels. All countries, regardless of income levels, are now subject to this restriction.

7. For a comprehensive analysis see UNCTAD 2003b.

8. The WTO Agreement on Subsidies and Countervailing Duties may also affect traditional means of supporting technological activity by subsidies. Although the Agreement excludes 'fundamental research' from its actionable provisions (i.e. governments may still subsidize research), the text leaves scope for interpreting what the limits of this are. In any case, R&D now comes under WTO scrutiny, and subsidies for research deemed non-fundamental could be limited in the future.

9. Most East Asian economies used infant industry protection, export subsidies and targets, credit allocation, local content rules, and so on to build their industrial capabilities, disciplining the process by strong export orientation (Amsden 1989; Stiglitz 1996; Wade 1990; Westphal 2002; World Bank 1993). There were strategic differences. Singapore, the Republic of Korea, and Taiwan province of China invested massively in human capital (particularly technical skills), fostered local R&D, and built strong support institutions (Lall 1996, 2001a). They tapped FDI in different ways, Singapore by plugging into global production systems and the other two by drawing on its technologies via arm's length means like licensing, copying, and original equipment manufacturing. The second-tier Tigers like Malaysia, Thailand, Indonesia, and the Philippines relied more heavily on FDI in export-processing enclaves and less on indigenous capabilities; their export success was driven by global value chains, particularly in electronics. China combined different strategies, some similar to its neighbors and others, like public enterprise restructuring, uniquely its own (Lall and Albaladejo 2003). The region as a whole liberalized cautiously and has retained a significant role for the state. As Stiglitz says in the *Human Development Report 2003*,

China and other East Asian economies have not followed the Washington Consensus. They were slow to remove tariff barriers, and China still has not fully liberalized its capital account. Though the countries of East Asia "globalized", they used industrial and trade policies to promote exports and global technology transfers, against the advice of the international economic institutions. (UNDP 2003: 80)

10. In the first phase, LAC, in common with other developing regions, relied heavily on protected import substitution, sheltering enterprises from international competition but failing to offset this with incentives or pressures to export. It did little to attract export-oriented FDI (in EPZs) and so missed the surge in global production systems in electronics. It did not deepen local technological activity (by encouraging R&D) or develop the new skills needed for emerging technologies. In concert with widespread macroeconomic (and in some cases political) turbulence, this meant that LAC failed to develop a broad base of industrial capabilities that would drive competitiveness as it liberalized. As a high-wage region, LAC needed competitive advantages in complex activities to offset wage disadvantage vis-à-vis Asia. Despite its tradition of entrepreneurship and base of skills, it failed to foster the necessary capabilities. There were exceptions, such as the automotive industry in the larger economies and resource-based activities more generally, but many such activities are not growing rapidly in world trade. LAC failed to raise export market shares rapidly, the exception being Mexico, due more to NAFTA than to strategy.

11. In the second (liberalization) phase, policy reform in LAC was rapid and sweeping, with no strategy to foster competitive capabilities and target promising activities. Again, there were exceptions, including the auto industry (restructured with the help of complementation programs, banned under new WTO rules), agro-based exports in Chile or national 'champions' like Embraer in Brazil, but the lack of industrial strategy meant that the region failed to catalyze export dynamism. Its main growth was in resource-based sectors where it largely exploited static advantages Some other developing regions that also used import substitution strategies liberalized more slowly and carefully – India is a good example – and did better in terms of MVA growth (but almost as poorly in terms of export competitiveness).

12. The objections to the strong neoliberal position came from such authors as Amsden (1989), Lall (1992b), Pack and Westphal (1986), Wade (1990) and Westphal (1982 and 1990).

13. The strong neoliberal stance was that *no* markets failed and that there was no role for the government apart from providing basic public goods and a stable setting for market-driven activity. For a critique of the World Bank (1993) publication see Lall 1996; and for a recent restatement of the moderate neoclassical position, see Noland and Pack 2003.

14. Neoclassical economists admit the possibility of market failure arising from such textbook cases as monopoly, public goods, and some externalities, although they tend to treat failures as special cases rather than the rule. The market failures that may call for selective interventions are capital market deficiencies, scale economies, and externalities arising from the imperfect appropriability of investments in knowledge, technology, and skills. However, the admission that these theoretical possibilities exist does not translate into recommendations that government actually mount selective policies to overcome them (as in World Bank 1993). Moreover, the neglect of firm-level learning processes (below) means that the list of market failures remains incomplete – the most critical ones for developing countries are ignored. For a longer discussion, see Lall and Teubal 1998.

15. Wade, in the introduction to the new edition of his pathbreaking book on industrial policy in Taiwan, *Governing the Market*, says:

> The remarkable thing about the core Washington Consensus package is the gulf between the confidence with which it is promulgated and the strength of supporting evidence, historical or contemporary. There is virtually no good evidence that the creation of efficient, rent-free markets coupled with efficient, corruption-free public sectors is even close to being a necessary or sufficient condition for a dynamic capitalist economy. Almost all now-developed countries went through stages of industrial assistance policy before the capabilities of their firms reached the point where a policy of (more or less) free trade was declared to be in the national interest. Britain was protectionist when it was trying to catch up with Holland. Germany was protectionist when trying to catch up with Britain. The United States was protectionist when trying to catch up with Britain and Germany, right up to the end of World War II. Japan was protectionist for most of the twentieth century up to the 1970s, Korea and Taiwan to the 1990s. Hong Kong and Singapore are the great exceptions on the trade front, in that they did have free trade and they did catch up – but they are city-states and not to be treated as economic countries. In Europe some countries abutting fast-growing

centres of accumulation were also exceptions, thanks to the "ink blot" effect. But by and large, countries that have caught up with the club of wealthy industrial countries have tended to follow the prescription of Friedrich List, the German catch-up theorist writing in the 1840s: "In order to allow freedom of trade to operate naturally, the less advanced nation [read: Germany] must first be raised by artificial measures to that stage of cultivation to which the English nation has been artificially elevated." (Wade 2003)

For a longer historical perspective see Reinert 1995.

16. See Lall 1992b, 1996, 2001; Westphal 2002; UNIDO 2002.

17. In his analysis of East Asian success Stiglitz argues that

whenever information was imperfect or markets were incomplete, government could devise interventions that filled in for these interventions and that could make everyone better off. *Because information was never perfect and markets never complete, these results completely undermined the standard theoretical basis for relying on the market mechanism.* Similarly the standard models ignored changes in technology; for a variety of reasons markets may under-invest in research and development.... Because developing economies have underdeveloped (missing) markets and imperfect information and because the development process is associated with acquiring new technology (new information), these reservations about the adequacy of market mechanisms may be particularly relevant to developing countries. (Stiglitz 1996: 156, emphasis added)

18. See the contributions by Wade and Lall in Wood 2003.

19. On the case for infant industry protection John Stuart Mill, the most powerful advocate of free trade in classical economic thought, says:

The only case in which, on mere principles of political economy, protecting duties can be defensible, is when they are imposed temporarily (especially in a young and rising nation) in the hopes of naturalising a foreign industry, in itself perfectly suitable to the circumstances of the country. The superiority of one country over another in a branch of production often arises only from having begun it sooner. There may be no inherent advantage on one part, or disadvantage in another, but only a *present superiority of acquired skill and experience*.... But it cannot be expected that individuals should, at their own risk, or rather to their certain loss, introduce a new manufacture, and bear the burden of carrying on until the producers have been educated to the level of those with whom the processes are traditional. *A protective duty, continued for a reasonable time, might sometimes be the least inconvenient mode in which the nation can tax itself for the support of such an experiment.* But it is essential that the protection should be confined to cases in which there is good ground for assurance that the industry which it fosters will after a time be able to dispense with it; nor should the domestic producers ever be allowed to expect that it will be continued to them beyond the time necessary for a fair trial of what they are capable of accomplishing. (Mill 1940: 922, emphasis added)

The nineteenth century saw intense debates, particularly in the United States, on the need for infant industry protection, and most early industrializing countries used the tool extensively.

20. On the selectivity of education and training policies in East Asia and their

intimate relationship to industrial policy more narrowly defined, see Ashton et al. 1999. Also see Narula 2003.

21. TNCs also have to undergo costly capability development in new locations but the costs are generally lower for them. They know how to go about building capabilities, have "deeper pockets," more information, and better training resources. If a developing host country engages only in simple assembly operations, TNCs may be able to achieve competitive production without protection because the learning period is short and relatively predictable. However, deepening and diversification into more advanced activities or functions may need government support to improve the quality of local factors and suppliers and to induce TNCs to transfer these activities and functions. This may not involve protection if the local workforce is sufficiently skilled – the Singapore story. However, Singapore had to use a battery of selective interventions to attract and target TNCs and provide them with the factor inputs, infrastructure, and incentives needed to force the pace of upgrading. FDI may reduce the need for interventions for capability building but cannot remove it altogether. Once countries move beyond simple processing, they have to provide the factors that allow TNCs to undertake complex functions efficiently.

22. According to Rhee et al. (1984),

> The export targets and monthly meetings provide some of the most important in-formation needed to administer the Korean export drive. Perhaps the most important is the up-to-date information on export performance by firm, product, and market and on reasons for discrepancy between target and performance. The government also gets much solid information on what is going on in the world. (The firms, meanwhile, get much solid information about the priorities and undertakings by government.) But the government has not only acquired this information. The ministries, in concert with the firms, have sought first to identify the problems and opportunities and to determine appropriate actions. These actions have been characterized by pragmatism … speed … flexibility…. This willingness to imple-ment new policies without careful, deliberate planning was generally a virtue for export policy-making – primarily because the test of those policies was success in the international market place. Firms thus saw the flexibility and frequent adjust-ments in the incentive system not as characteristics that would create uncertainty about the automaticity and stability of that system. They saw them as part of the government's long-term commitment to keep exports profitable – a commitment made possible by the continuity of the government. Without such commitment, firms would have faced much more uncertainty in their export production, and exports would have suffered as a result. (Rhee et al. 1984: 35–6)

4

Toward the Optimum
Degree of Openness

Amit Bhaduri

Some Implications of Globalization
for Developing Countries

Country-specific "optimum" openness

For most developing countries, globalization essentially means opening up their economies more or less unilaterally to the global market. The critical issue is not whether this opening up should take place at all, but how the country should try to achieve the "optimum degree of openness" from its point of view, given its level of development. In other words, the considerations involved in defining the strategy of attaining the optimum degree of openness are not independent of time and space, but specific to a particular country, its size, polity and society, as well as its stage of economic development. This has at least one important implication. Any sweeping generalization regarding how to deal with the forces of globalization is likely to be misleading. In particular, there is no great virtue in dogmatically following either a totally outward-looking or a totally inward-looking set of policies. It is the country-specific optimum mix between the two that needs to be strived for. And, in this respect, it is different in its economic philosophy from the disappearing "Washington Consensus" for which the Bretton Woods institutions were well known.

Asymmetries of globalization: four aspects

The reasons for this difference across country-specific perspectives may be stated briefly. They originate in some important asymmetries that characterize the current phase of globalization. First, and perhaps most obvious, is the asymmetry between the freedom of movement of capital, especially financial capital, and the severe restrictions on the movement of labor, especially unskilled labor from the developing world. Unless one evokes the mythical world of "factor-price equalization" through commodity trade, trade liberalization alone is unlikely to alleviate the problem of income inequality among and within nations.[1] A passing mention may be made here to the recent "convergence debate." It has recently been claimed (Fischer 2003) that, although there is little statistical evidence that countries across the world are tending to converge in terms of per capita income, the two largest countries in terms of population, China and India, are showing a tendency toward convergence, because their growth performance since the 1980s has been higher than the average. So, one might have the comfortable thought that more people, if not more nations, are tending toward convergence in terms of per capita income. This argument is fallacious, because the income distribution pattern *inside* a country like China or India has to be reasonably stable and not too adversely affected by the process of globalization. And yet, almost certainly in China (and there is a raging debate on this subject in India), domestic liberalization policies ushered in to take advantage of the global market have worsened the distribution of income inside the country, perhaps with a higher percentage of people now below the poverty line. If we know anything at all about the link between globalization, liberalization, and poverty, it is that the poorest segments – especially in rural areas – are often unreachable though the global or local market process and the price mechanism, simply because a lack of even the minimal purchasing power condemns them to marginalization and near exclusion from the market. Without direct action and intervention, widening relative and, at times, absolute poverty becomes a very likely outcome of the market process.

Second, there is an important asymmetry between trade in goods and services and that in the knowledge embodied in their production. In the emerging regime of trade-related intellectual property rights (TRIPS), developing countries will find it increasingly difficult to learn and adopt the production technology involved in the new goods and services they import. At the same time, they will be under increasing pressure in a more liberalized trade regime to import more goods and services rather than produce them at home. Yet trade is very often about trade in knowledge and in technology embodied in the newly traded goods; indeed, the learning process involved in international trade may well be the most important dynamic gain occurring from trade (Pasinetti 1981). Thus the asymmetry of the emerging trade regime is to promote freer trade in goods and services while largely denying the developing countries the dynamic gains from trade through faster diffusion of learning of processes and products.[2]

Third, an almost paradoxical asymmetry exists at the heart of the current process of globalization regarding the role of the state in monitoring and regulating economic activities. The market-oriented economic philosophy championed by institutions like the IMF and the World Bank seeks to restrict the reach of the state as far as possible in terms of monetary and fiscal policies. Its fiscal effectiveness is drastically curtailed by the received wisdom of monetarism, elaborating on the virtues of a balanced budget, and IMF-style conditionalities relating to the fiscal deficit of the government under all circumstances. Its monetary policies are blunted by moving toward capping the extent of public debt and toward an independent central banking system.[3] This leaves open possibilities of serious conflict between monetary and fiscal policy objectives, rendering the economic policies of the state less effective. Yet the same state that on the one hand is considered too irresponsible and inefficient to pursue the right kind of fiscal and monetary policy is entrusted on the other hand with carrying out far more complex tasks like privatization, setting up and regulating the stock exchange or making the market more flexible. The asymmetry lies in an almost schizophrenic view of the state, which cannot be trusted with its traditional fiscal and monetary role but can be assigned the more difficult role of wielding instruments like privatization to extend the scope of the market at the cost of the state. The root of this asymmetry is to be found in denying the state its developmental role but using it to promote "marketization" and globalization.[4]

A similar and perhaps even deeper asymmetry is to be found in the postulated relation between democracy and greater reliance on the global market. Although the two are treated as almost overlapping concepts in the economic philosophy of neoliberalism, the relationship between the "freedom" of the market economy and the "freedom" of political democracy is often troublesome, especially in a developing country. It is well known that the democratic principle of "one adult, one vote" coexists rather uneasily with the free-market philosophy that the rich have more "votes" with their greater purchasing than the poor in the marketplace. This asymmetry becomes all the more pronounced with greater inequality in the distribution of income and with a larger proportion of the voiceless poor nearly excluded from the market system. In these circumstances of widespread poverty and income inequality, which are typical in many developing countries, the democratic form of government becomes difficult to sustain in the context of too much freedom for the market. However, the forces unleashed by the process of globalization drive most developing countries toward a situation of integrating rapidly with the global market at almost any cost.

It must also be added that the relationship between economic development and democracy has been far more complex historically than received wisdom in line with "political correctness" suggests. It has often been the case historically that the per capita income of a country had to reach a relatively high level, relative to the present per capita income in many developing countries, before steps toward political democracy could be taken (Chang 2002). Nor is it true in the light of existing evidence that greater integration with the world economy through globalization has resulted in higher growth performance in the developing countries in general to raise their per capita income faster. Growth in GDP per capita fell from an average annual rate of 4.1 per cent in the "pre-globalization" 1950–73 period to 0.6 per cent in the period 1973–98 in the "other Asia" (excluding Korea, Taiwan, Singapore, Hong-Kong, Thailand and Malaysia, and eight other somewhat less successful Asian countries, including China and India). It fell during the same period from 2.5 per cent to 1 per cent in Latin America, from 2.1 per cent to 0 per cent in Africa, and from 3.5 per cent to −1.1 per cent in Eastern Europe and the former Soviet Union (Maddison 2001).[5] In short, historically democracy has often been the consequence, rather than the cause, of economic development of a country. Moreover, recent evidence suggests that economic development and per capita growth in GDP are often hampered and not helped by unrestricted opening to the global market.

A two-pronged development strategy: international and national

The fact of the matter is that, to date, globalization has turned out to be a flawed game whose asymmetrical rules are fixed to the advantage of the richer, more powerful nations. The list of asymmetries mentioned earlier could be made longer, but they are sufficient to point to the need for greater flexibility in setting rules, taking into account the different stages of development of different countries. Thus, some considerations for international equality in setting the rules of globalization have to be built into the system, if it is to become a voluntary, participatory process compatible with national sovereignty. An analogy might explain the point better: just as in an economically advanced country like the United States, "affirmative action" has been accepted in principle, or in a developing country like India "reservation" is often constitutionally guaranteed for disadvantaged groups, it is essential to devise similar principles to democratize the process of globalization. It hardly needs to be emphasized that neither the price mechanism nor "the richer-have-more-votes-than-the-poor" principle of the market system is meant to achieve this.[6] It requires concerted international action on the part of developing countries.

Let one recent example from World Trade Organization negotiations suffice to illustrate the point. A group of developing countries has been pressing for a firm WTO commitment to create a fair global market for agricultural trade without subsidies to farmers in developed countries.[7] This is not only required for a freer trade regime, but it affects largely the poorest 1 billion people in the world, most of whom are connected directly or indirectly with rural agricultural activities in the least developed countries. Indeed, there is hardly any other trade-related example where so great a degree of compatibility exists between freer trade and greater global equality, and, unless it is viewed in this light, such negotiations are likely to be reduced to a "tit-for-tat" strategy by countries, where "concessions" in terms of reduced agricultural subsidies in richer countries are to be reciprocated immediately by developing countries accepting disadvantageous global rules on foreign direct investment, capital inflows, and so on.

The essence of the broader argument is clear: just as national political democracies are not merely about majority rule but also about respect and protection of minority rights, at times through affirmative action or reservation, similarly globalization cannot aspire to democratic participation by nations on the economic plane without some considerations of equality being built into the system of global rules. This is the central international issue that needs to be addressed in the present process of globalization.

However, international issues almost invariably have an important national dimension in both developed and developing countries, especially in democracies. For instance, lower agricultural subsidies would particularly hurt the cotton and the sugar lobbies in the United States. The problem of reconciling domestic concerns for development with international aspects is even more difficult for a developing economy. Thus the demand for international solidarity with other developing countries may adversely affect domestic economic prospects. This is an issue that each individual developing country has to face candidly, taking into account the specific features of its economy, polity, and society, to bargain collectively. Country-specific requirements without too much generalization are essential here.

External and internal sector in country-specific strategies

Nevertheless, at least one generalization seems a valid starting point in forming country-specific strategies. Globalization, almost by definition, means an increase in the relative importance of the external vis-à-vis the internal sector of the economy. While the internal sector roughly coincides with the domestic production of goods and services and, in a broader definition, the institutions that sustain it, the external sector includes not only trade in goods and services, but, even more importantly in some cases, trade in financial assets and foreign exchange and the resulting capital flows, as well as the institutions that sustain them. An increased importance of the external sector for almost any country, developed or developing, has an important economic consequence that is seldom realized. It shifts attention from demand- to supply-side issues. Or, put differently, from the management of demand, the focus of policy shifts to the reduction of production costs. This shift surfaces in many different forms that may be outlined briefly.

Labor market strategy under globalization

The emphasis on increasing labor productivity is viewed primarily not as a source of greater availability of output per capita, but merely as a tool for enhancing national and international competitiveness (Krugman 1996). This also means that attention is diverted from generating employment to productivity increases at any cost. The recent waves of corporate "downsizing" (i.e. gaining productivity at the cost of lower employment) are the most obvious case in point. While it may help an individual firm gain a larger national or international market share by reducing unit costs, its overall effect may well be a shrinking of the size of the market in terms of aggregate demand. From the double-entry format of national income accounting, it is easy to see this. Employment growth would tend to be negative if productivity growth on the supply side exceeds the weighted average of consumption, investment, and export surplus growth on the demand side.[8] In such cases, downsizing for productivity increases would turn out to be a recipe for growing unemployment microeconomically at the level of the firm, as well as macroeconomically for the economy as a whole. Nevertheless, the pressure to increase labor productivity competitively through downsizing becomes an almost inevitable feature of globalization, with its emphasis on capturing a larger share of the external market by using the tool of increasing labor productivity relative to that of rivals.

Similarly, what is often described as greater labor market flexibility – primarily through restraining wages – is another way of cutting labor costs, but it may have the unintended effect of creating greater unemployment through its impact on demand. In a way, globalization through increases in the relative importance of the external market revives the pre-Keynesian argument for wage cuts as a means to greater employment in a different context. It emphasizes competitive cost reduction through downsizing and labor market flexibility without considering its implications in terms of aggregate demand, just as the wage cut argument ignored the impact on demand. However, there is an obvious fallacy in this strategy: not all countries can achieve export surplus simultaneously through competitive cost reduction! In addition, developing countries are often set in a hopeless fight over shares of the international market in a "beggar-my-neighbor" policy, the likely outcome of which is a downward spiraling of the employment situation.

Demand management from the wrong perspective under globalization

Competitive labor productivity growth, like competitive devaluation, hardly solves the problem of trade or current account deficits for most developing countries. Therefore it becomes necessary for the losers to resort to other solutions for managing their external sector. Since a move toward a more liberalized trade regime rules out increased import control through tariffs. or quotas, import restraints have to be sought indirectly through depressing aggregate demand. Thus many of the policies recommended by the Bretton Woods institutions in their stabilization and structural adjustment policies share this common characteristic. They are not even neutral to demand management, but often have the vicious effect of reducing demand in already depressed economic conditions. A close link between the government budget deficit and the current account deficit is postulated without sufficient reason to make expansionary fiscal policies unacceptable. Independence of the central bank and insistence that the government borrow from the capital market at the market interest rate restrains accommodative or expansionary monetary policies. By discouraging borrowing at home to finance investment, a high interest rate forces firms that have access to the international money market to borrow abroad, and vulnerability to growing external debt increases as domestic firms become more exposed internationally. This too becomes a vicious spiral in many developing countries, as the recent experiences suggest, especially in several Central and Latin American countries. The growing debt service cost and the threat of a "run" on the large foreign debt force them to impose even more restrictive monetary and fiscal policies (leading to further shrinking of growth and employment) in a desperate attempt to generate a surplus on the current account. It is a battle that most developing countries cannot win if they play according to the rules of the game fixed by the WTO and the "Washington Consensus."

Capital flows and the external sector

The logic of this mistaken perspective is to be found not in sound economic reasoning, but in the uninhibited market-oriented economic philosophy propagated by the Bretton Woods institutions. Its primary characteristic is to view all types of government intervention as essentially undesirable, except those government "interventions" that weaken the economic role of the government.[9] Its obvious manifestation is the unwillingness to allow developing countries to impose capital controls, in spite of the recent and relatively successful experiences of countries like Malaysia during the 1997–98

East Asian crisis or Chile in moderating speculative foreign portfolio invest-ment. The market-oriented philosophy requires covering current account deficits through international capital flows whenever possible, rather than through capital controls and devaluation. However, capital controls typically imply offering competitively higher interest rates, as well as restrictive fiscal policies. As a result, the domestic market and aggregate demand tend to shrink, discouraging genuine foreign direct investment that could be at-tracted for upgrading and expanding production at home. On the other hand, since successive devaluation or steady depreciation of the domestic currency would weaken international confidence in the domestic currency, upsetting capital inflows, even higher interest rates and indirect compres-sion of imports through the restraint of domestic demand are called for to service external debt. This typically amounts to increasing dependence on portfolio investment and short-term capital inflows, which – at best – buy some time to postpone the final showdown of a financial crisis. A process of globalization whose defining characteristic has been an unrestrained and phenomenal expansion in private trade in foreign exchange, increasing from a daily average of US$776 to US$1,173 billion between 1992 and 2001 (BIS 2001), can hardly be expected to act against its own dominant tendencies, leading to more controlled inflows or outflows of capital in developing countries. Consequently, globalization cannot be expected to reduce either the severity or the frequency of financial crises in the developing countries, unless developing countries themselves devise sensible coping strategies.

An Alternative Path to Optimum Openness for Development and Sectoral Policies

The conventional view that "There is no alternative" (TINA) to globalization needs to be countered with an opposite interpretation of TINA: "This is no alternative." Indeed, the ability to imagine this viable alternative is the central job of contemporary economic theory. Apart from international negotiations on trade, finance, property rights, environment, and migration – where, like in the marketplace, the rich countries necessarily have a stronger voice than the poor – the responsibility of individual developing countries is to devise specific strategies suited to their conditions and to strive for an optimum degree of openness. In this context, they would do well to be guided by *three fundamental principles* in the light of which country-specific policies may be formulated, especially with respect to various sectors.

First, there should be greater emphasis on the internal rather than the external market by national governments, contrary to the present trends in globalization. This is, of course, more viable for larger countries than for smaller countries. Consequently, the latter in particular might engage more seriously in building regional blocs to extend their internal market.

The primary implications of concentrating more on the internal market are twofold. In the first place, it places far greater emphasis on management and expansion of domestic demand with an active role for the government. In this respect, a relatively novel innovation in developing countries would be for the government to have an inventory of investment projects. These would be placed in order of priority, as agreed in conjunction with the opposition political parties transparently and ahead of time, with rough estimates of cost involved. The timing of the projects may be flexible for managing demand, to be implemented as and when the need arises. In the second place, greater emphasis on domestic demand with equity entails greater emphasis on the welfare role of the state. This is different from the usual view that the disruptions caused by unrestrained globalization need to be moderated by creating "safety-nets." The priorities should be the other way around: governments need to spend more on the social sector of welfare, health, unemployment, and old age insurance without being constrained drastically by an artificial fiscal discipline. It is not a change in the level of spending but rather a change in the composition of spending that increases the social component of income. Most developing countries fail miserably in this respect (e.g. an inability to rein in their defense expenditure or the expansion of salaries and wages in the public sector at the cost of spending on the social sector).

The second principle is to view productivity growth not primarily as a tool for international competitiveness, but as a source of greater availability of goods and services at home. This means that the corporate philosophy of productivity increases to reduce unit cost is to be abandoned in favor of an alternative view that requires productivity growth to rise hand in hand with total output, implying that productivity and employment growth should be complementary, not competitive, strategies.

In particular, public investments either in the social sector or in infrastructure, energy, and communications are essential for creating such complementarities. Many developing countries have the capabilities in terms of their existing industrial structures and excess capacities to undertake such investments without waiting for foreign investment. The false doctrine that "sound" public finance would not permit this – a doctrine propagated by the monetarist view of the economy as mere housekeeping – needs to be abandoned in favor of the Keynesian view that investment creates most of its own savings through expansion of income in situations of unemployment and excess capacity. In the present context, it means that the increase in domestic employment and productivity would create additional supply largely to meet the additional demand created by those investments and would also raise government revenue through greater tax collection in an expanding economy. To the extent that unaccommodating monetary policies or restrictions on budget deficits inspired by IMF-style conditionalities are impediments to this process of economic expansion, national governments must have the courage to challenge them.

The third principle follows from the first two. Developing countries should concentrate on sectors where production, on the one hand, is easier to attain in a more self-reliant way and, on the other hand, where it has powerful demand propagation effect in the rest of the economy. This must vary from country to country. For a large and still predominantly agricultural economy like India, growth in agricultural productivity and more employment through increased cropping intensity (resulting from greater irrigation and water management and allied services) would illustrate how to pursue such a strategy. While the government currently maintains a "price support system" as a supply incentive to the surplus farmers, it runs into a pathetic paradox in a poor country. Food grain collected by the government piles up and rots in warehouses, while the poorest segment of the population, which lacks the minimum purchasing power, starves, partly because the government does not have an adequate rural distribution system. Yet if this food grain could be better utilized to finance rural infrastructure, partly in kind, both agriculture and the non-agricultural sectors (industry and services) would do better. Agriculture would benefit from a guaranteed market to sell its products, while industry and services could expand through the larger market created by the higher purchasing power of agriculture (see Bhaduri 2003; Bhaduri and Skarstein 2003). At the same time, this would avoid a major source of inflationary pressure on the economy through rising food grain prices. This type of sectoral policy, favoring agriculture in the Indian case, could illustrate how a policy guided by the above principles of focusing on the internal market could hasten the pace of development without undue attention being paid either to "comparative advantage" forced upon a country by globalization, or to the monetarist doctrine of "sound public finance." To break out of these old habits of thought is the first step towards attaining the "optimum degree of openness" in a globalizing world.

Notes

1. Within this framework, the Samuelson–Stolper theorem is applied to explain lower real wage differentials between unskilled labor in developed and developing counties, while the differential widens between skilled and unskilled labor. Like all results in this framework, it assumes, along with many other highly questionable assumptions, full employment, and thus ignores the problem of unemployment due to lack of demand in the internal market, on which this chapter will have more to say later.

2. We abstain here from discussing the relative merits of "product" versus "process" patent. Instead, note Article 27(3) of the TRIPS Agreement on the patentability of biotechnology provides an illustration of the tension in this area. On the one hand, it seems to allow all biotechnology to be patented, while, on the other, it tries to protect traditional knowledge of plants and animals through exclusion. One result of this is expensive international litigation in which richer countries have a decided advantage.

3. This applies to developing as well as developed countries. The so-called "Stability Pact" of the common currency members of the European Union, which sets an upper limit on both government budget deficit and public debt as a proportion of GDP, illustrates this with full force.

4. The overwhelming importance of private trading in foreign exchange as the characteristic feature of globalization compels governments to tailor their policies in a "market-friendly" way, even if the government wants to act otherwise. This is perhaps the main force driving "globalization" through "marketization."

5. An important difference between the two periods 1950–73 and 1973–98 is the liberalization of capital markets in the latter period. See also the previous note for its economic significance.

6. Broadly speaking, "affirmative action" as practiced in the United States gives preference to a disadvantaged group when other things (e.g. qualifications) are more or less the same. "Reservation," on the other hand, as in India, is stronger in its intent insofar as it reserves a certain percentage of places exclusively for the disadvantaged groups.

7. The inability to come to a consensus at the WTO meeting in Cancún (September 2003) is the most recent example.

8. Weighted by their respective shares in GDP.

9. As discussed earlier in connection with "privatization" or deregulation.

5

What Strategies Are Viable for Developing Countries Today? The World Trade Organization and the Shrinking of "Development Space"

Robert Hunter Wade

Developing countries as a group are being increasingly tightly constrained in their national development strategies by proliferating regulations formulated and enforced by international organizations. These regulations are not about limiting companies' options, as "regulation" normally connotes. Rather, they are about limiting the options of developing country governments to constrain the options of companies operating or hoping to operate within their borders. In effect, the new regulations are designed to expand the options of developed country firms to enter and exit markets more easily, with fewer restrictions and obligations, and to lock in their appropriation of technological rents.

Developed country governments, led by the United States and the United Kingdom,[1] are driving this proliferation of international market-opening and technology-rent-protecting regulations, using multilateral economic organizations, international treaties and bilateral agreements. They have come together to legitimize a level of intrusion into the economies and polities of developing countries hitherto frowned upon by the international community, framing the intrusion in the shape of international agreements. Ironically, in view of the common belief that globalization is weakening the power of states to regulate, they are requiring developing country governments to regulate – themselves and their national firms – more, not less. At the same time the United States and the European Union have not followed through on their general commitments to improve market access for developing countries.[2] Both have kept large parts of their economies off the negotiating table.[3]

The net result is that the "development space" for diversification and upgrading policies in developing countries is being shrunk behind the rhetorical commitment to universal liberalization and privatization. The rules being written into multilateral and bilateral agreements actively prevent developing countries from pursuing the kinds of industrial and technology policies adopted by the newly developed countries of East Asia and by the older developed countries when they were developing, policies aimed at accelerating the "internal" articulation of the economy (about which more below). At the same time, developed country tariff escalation in sectors of interest to developing country exporters limits their export growth and their rise up the value chain.[4] All this constitutes a shrinkage not only of development space but also of "self-determination" space. It ties the hands of developing country governments "forever" to *the North's interpretation* of a market-opening agenda ("you open your markets and remove restrictions on incoming investment, in return for [promises of] improved access to our markets").

Here I shall show how the main international agreements from the Uruguay Round – TRIPS, TRIMs and GATS – systematically tip the playing field against developing countries. The agreements do not do for developing countries what their sponsors, the G7 states (Group of Seven major economies), say they will do, and they do help to lock in the economic, political, and military dominance of these and other states in the core of the world economy. Why does this matter? Partly for moral reasons. I describe a system in which bargains are struck between strong players and weak players. They each need – or see advantage in having – the cooperation of the others, so they reach agreements. But to the extent that bargaining is steered by morality, the balance of advantage in the agreements depends on which of two moralities prevails. One is the a-bit-better-than-the-jungle morality of "tit-for-tat," or reciprocity, which sanctions that the agreements reflect relative bargaining strengths; thus the strong do best. The second is the all-men-are-brothers morality, which says that the strong have a duty to restrain themselves to help the weaker. This is the morality behind the decision of early-twentieth-century British judges to grant trade unions legal privileges in order to force a degree of restraint on the part of employers. In what follows I bring out the extent to which the recent round of WTO agreements on intellectual property, investment, and trade in services expresses the a-bit-better-than-the-jungle morality, and show the implications of applying the all-men-are-brothers morality.

Yet the basis for not accepting the present agreements is not only moral. The case for "development space" also rests on the costs to the world, including the citizens of the prosperous democracies, of making the creation of dynamic capitalisms in the non-core zone of the world economy even more difficult than it has been to date. The fear of the social instability caused by the unrestrained power of employers over employees drove the decision of those early-twentieth-century British judges to choose the second morality over the first. Developed world policymakers would do well to keep this precedent in mind. Globalization erodes the insulation of the North from the responses to poverty, inequality, and subordination in the South – including migration, imploding states, civil wars, religious fundamentalism, and destruction of symbols of the structure of domination.

Shrinking the Development Space 1:
The TRIPS Agreement

The Agreement on Trade-Related Aspects of Intellectual Property Rights (TRIPS) was forged in the course of the Uruguay Round (1986–94), and entered into operation in 1994.[5] It covers protection of trademarks, copyrights, industrial designs, data secrets, and patents (on drugs, electronic and mechanical devices, etc.). The big two are copyrights and patents. The agreement seems innocent enough. Under patents, all it does is to oblige WTO members to introduce minimum standards for intellectual property protection, and it provides a dispute resolution and enforcement mechanism. The minimum standards include: limits on states' abilities to *deny* patents to certain types of products; a period of twenty years for all patents (many countries granted patents for shorter periods); and limits on states' flexibility in the use of technologies or products patented in their territory, including states' ability to insist on compulsory licensing.[6] The agreement handicaps developing countries through both economic and political mechanisms.

TRIPS economic handicaps

The economic handicaps operate through the market for knowledge. The North is a net producer of patentable knowledge, the South a net consumer. Even in the case of Mexico, an advanced developing country and member of the OECD, domestic residents made only 389 patent applications in 1996, compared to over 30,000 from foreign residents (World Bank 2002a: 136). TRIPS raises the price of patentable knowledge to consumers, and so raises the flow of rents from South to North. According to World Bank estimates, US companies would pocket an additional net $19 billion a year in royalties from full application of TRIPS. They own many patents in many countries required to tighten intellectual property protection, while TRIPS does not require tightening of US patent law.

TRIPS defenders say that the higher returns to knowledge generation in the North will yield even more innovation, which will diffuse to the South.

There is no credible evidence that this is the case (Helpman 1993). In the case of copyright, tougher protections raise the cost of scientific publications. Research libraries around the world paid out 66 per cent more for scientific monographs in 2001 than they did in 1986 and got 9 per cent fewer monographs for their money, and paid out 210 per cent more for 5 per cent fewer periodicals. These price escalations widen the North–South gap in access to scientific knowledge.

Yet it is not just a matter of the rising cost of knowledge in relation to the not-rising ability to pay of the South. It is also that as most natural science research is being privatized, less and less research is being done on issues from which the researchers and right holders are unlikely to receive a significant economic pay-off. This includes many problem areas of primary interest to populations in developing countries.

TRIPS political handicaps

The political handicaps operate through two main mechanisms. First, developing countries' rights and developed countries' obligations are unenforceable, while developing countries' obligations and developed countries' rights are enforceable. On paper, the rights and obligations of members look to be balanced between patent-holding (developed) and patent-using (developing) countries. In practice the agreement is skewed in favor of the developed countries, because of the difference in enforceability.

For example, the developing countries have a wide array of obligations about what they allow to be patented and how they treat and enforce patents. If they do not meet their obligations they may be taken to the dispute settlement mechanism (DSM) of the WTO. The developed countries supposedly have obligations too, directed at ensuring that their governments and firms do provide technology to developing countries. But the agreement gives no recourse: nothing happens if they do not meet their obligations. No developing country has taken a developed country to the dispute settlement mechanism for not transferring technology. Why not? Because the costs of mounting a case are high for a developing country, the United States and the European Union may threaten reprisals, and the obligations of developed countries with regard to technology transfer and everything else are vague.[7]

The second political mechanism is the use of the TRIPS' standards by the United States and European Union as merely the starting point for negotiating even tougher "TRIPS-plus" standards of patent protection in bilateral trade and investment treaties (although the agreement's minimum standards are themselves typically much tougher in favor of patent holders than developing countries had in place before the agreement).[8] This will

give the developing countries even less protection under TRIPS than they
have already.

Developing country representatives have argued for years that TRIPS must
be revisited. The response from the United States and European Union has
been, "We are happy to renegotiate, but there can be no change between [a
favorite phrase] *the balance of rights and obligations struck in the Uruguay Round*."
This is a good wheeze – because the developed countries effectively placed
themselves under no obligations in the TRIPS agreement.

Indeed, the United States has been active in trying to reopen the TRIPS
negotiations – so as to secure even stronger protections for intellectual
property. But in the face of developing country resistance it has recently
abandoned this strategy and is relying more on tighter enforcement of the
existing rules: making more use of the threat to take a country through the
WTO dispute resolution process; more use of TRIPS review procedures to
press countries to enforce intellectual property rules; more use of informal
bilateral pressure, including threats to withdraw aid and to support rival states
in geopolitical disputes, complaints to ministries or prime ministers about
unconstructive or "aggressive" ambassadors in Geneva, and sweet deals for
those who cooperate;[9] more intensive monitoring of countries under the
United States' Super 301 trade sanctions process; and more use of bilateral and
regional trade negotiations to require countries to implement even stronger
national intellectual property legislation than called for by TRIPS.

Tightening the noose: Doha and Brazil

Were the negotiations over TRIPS at the Doha Ministerial meeting of the
WTO in 2001 not intended to improve the position of developing countries?
The Doha Declaration on "TRIPS and Public Health" is widely understood
to have modified TRIPS sufficiently to improve developing countries' access
to certain drugs. To this extent it could expand – if developed countries
deliver on their promise – developing countries' TRIPS-consistent options in
a *humanitarian* direction. But it does not expand their options in industrial
transformation.

Even after the Doha modifications TRIPS leaves in place a much more
restrictive environment for technology transfer than the older industrialized
countries enjoyed during the early stages of industrialization and the new
industrialized countries of East Asia enjoyed during theirs. Recall that Japan,
Taiwan, and South Korea were each known as "the counterfeit capital" of
the world in their time (Wade 2003a). And the nineteenth-century United
States, then a rapidly industrializing country, was known – to Charles Dickens,
among many other aggrieved foreign authors – as a bold pirate of intellectual

property.[10] In all these cases foreign firms had little legal redress against patent- or copyright-infringers in those countries of the kind that they did have against infringers at home. But today, reverse-engineering, imitation, and many strategies of innovation to develop technology are either outlawed or made significantly more difficult by the high level of patent and copyright protection mandated by TRIPS. Thus, TRIPS raises significant development obstacles for many countries that the earlier developers did not face. These issues were not on the table at Doha.

The nub of the issue is caught in a recent pharmaceuticals dispute between the United States and Brazil (which resembles the 1980s' dispute between the United States and Brazil over computers). Brazil has taken the lead among developing countries in developing domestic capacity to produce HIV/AIDS drugs at low cost. It has thereby helped to avoid a catastrophe on the scale afflicting many African and Asian countries.

Brazil's efforts have generated controversy regarding the country's intellectual property law. The government has relied on two particular articles of its 1997 industrial property law to advance the fulfillment of its national health objectives. Article 71 authorizes compulsory licenses in the case of national health emergencies – it allows the government to authorize local producers to produce generic drugs needed to fight a national health emergency or to import from a generic producer elsewhere, despite patent protection. This article is generally understood to be consistent with TRIPS. While Brazil has not actually used this law to issue a compulsory license, it has frequently used the threat of a compulsory license to facilitate fairer negotiations with pharmaceuticals companies regarding the terms of licensing to Brazilian companies and the prices of drugs in Brazil.

The Brazilian law also contains an article (Article 68) that authorizes licenses when manufactured goods are not produced locally. If a foreign company has obtained a patent for a product or process in Brazil but does not establish local production within three years, the law authorizes the Brazilian government to license local producers to produce the good (the term of art here is "local working"). This is the "industrial policy" article, with application far beyond pharmaceuticals. By spurring foreign firms to establish local production it contributes to a more developmental foreign investment regime. But it is arguably in violation of TRIPS, and has been strongly opposed by the United States.

The United States brought a WTO panel dispute against Brazil in 2000. In June 2001 the two countries signed a communiqué announcing the withdrawal of the US challenge, but they also affirmed that the fundamental conflict over Article 68 remains unresolved. The United States threatens that if the Brazilians use Article 68 to issue a compulsory license for nonpharmaceutical products (as part of a wider industrial policy) the WTO case will be restarted.

The signal sent to other developing countries is that emulating Brazil's program for distributing AIDS medicines is acceptable, but emulating Brazil's efforts to use intellectual property rights policy as a tool of industrial strategy is not acceptable. This demonstrates the point made earlier, that expanded opportunities for TRIPS-consistent developing country action secured at Doha are for humanitarian relief, not industrial transformation.

Shrinking the Development Space 2: The TRIMs Agreement

The Agreement on Trade-Related Investment Measures (TRIMs), another product of the Uruguay Round, limits the development space of developing countries even more than TRIPS, because it covers a broader swathe of their economic activity.[11] The central point about TRIMs is that it moves trade rules from the principle of "avoid discrimination" between countries (the "most favored nation" principle of the old General Agreement on Tariffs and Trade), to "avoid trade and investment distortions." It interprets most "performance requirements" on foreign firms as distortions, and bans or aspires to ban them.[12]

The TRIMs agreement bans performance requirements related to local content, trade balancing, export requirements, and it also bans requirements on public agencies to procure goods from local suppliers. A country that tries to impose such requirements can be taken to the Dispute Settlement Mechanism, and will surely lose the case. In theory the complainant (normally the United States or the European Union) has to provide *evidence* that the specific requirement is distorting, but in practice the United States and the European Union do not; they simply assert that such requirements are distorting *by definition*, and – being dominant actors – their assertions generally prevail.

Moreover the United States and the European Union want to modify the current TRIMs agreement so as to ban *all* performance requirements, including for joint venturing, technology transfer, and research and development. At the Doha Ministerial meeting of the WTO in 2001 the United States and the European Union pressed this agenda, but India and Brazil prevented the ban being approved. However, the language in the relevant part of the current TRIMs is not legally clear, and many developing countries fear that if they do use such non-banned performance requirements the United States or the European Union will still threaten to take them to the DSM – whose rulings, they have seen, are almost always in favor of the most restrictive interpretation of allowable performance requirements; and the threat to take them to the DSM may well be reinforced by other threats, such as to cut foreign aid, as noted earlier. What is more, states currently negotiating to join the WTO (the "accession countries") are finding that the rules they are being asked to sign on to are even more restrictive than those for existing members. There is not a standard set of rules.

TRIMs defenders point to the exemption clauses, which allow categories of developing countries "special and differential treatment." The catch is that the exemptions are defined only in terms of the *time period* for complying. The time period has to do with administrative and legal handicaps in getting up to speed on TRIMs enforcement. It has nothing to do with the time needed to nurture infant industries, nothing to do with competitiveness. In this fundamental respect the TRIMs agreement narrows the scope of "special and differential treatment" allowable for developing countries, compared to the scope pre-TRIMs (Pangestu 2002).

Shrinking the Development Space 3: The GATS agreement

The General Agreement on Trade in Services (GATS) also came out of the Uruguay Round, and has been in a new round of intensified negotiations at the WTO since 2000. GATS represents the extension of WTO rules from trade in products to trade in services – including everything from banking, to education, to rubbish collection, tourism, health delivery, water supply and sanitation. "Trade" includes companies setting up in a foreign country to provide services there, so GATS is also an investment agreement. Foreign investment in services accounts for roughly half of world foreign direct investment, and developing countries have been assured that complying with GATS commitments will boost FDI inflows.

The central thrust of the GATS, as with TRIMs (but not TRIPS), is market liberalization. The articles of the agreement are a list of ways in which governments should not interfere in the market, should not place barriers in the way of service trade between countries; and should not regulate the behavior of multinational corporations operating in their country (World Development Movement 2002).[13] Because the responsibility for affordable provision of public services is fundamental to a government's responsibility to its citizens – to the whole idea of social compact between government and taxpayers – the GATS agreement is intruding even further into domestic political economy than the other two. It makes it next to impossible for developing country governments to protect their own service industries from competition from well-established foreign firms, in the way that virtually all the successful developers have done in the past.

For example, GATS requires "most favored nation" treatment, such that a government must treat firms from all WTO members equally.[14] GATS also requires "national treatment," such that all foreign service providers must be treated at least as well as domestic firms. They cannot be required to use local suppliers, managers or staff, unless local firms are under the same requirement. And GATS requires "market access," which prevents a government from putting a limit on the number of service suppliers or outlets and on where they operate. All this is done in the name of fairness.

However, GATS has a larger exemption provision than the other two agreements. Governments can specify limitations on *some* of the commitments they make in a particular service sector, and hence wall-off particular government laws or regulations from GATS. Governments list which sectors and which requirements they wish to exclude (though not all requirements can be excluded – the most-favored-nation principle, for example, cannot be excluded in any sector). The presumption is that anything not on their list is subject to the full commitments. In actuality, however, this exemption procedure is less than meets the eye. The exemptions have to be signaled at the beginning, because it is almost impossible for governments to get them introduced later. Yet it is also almost impossible to predict what limitations should be put on commitments in advance.

As for the promised benefits to developing countries, an UNCTAD study concludes, "There is no empirical evidence to link any significant increase in FDI flows to developing countries with the conclusion of GATS" (UNCTAD 2000a: 172). The World Bank reports similar findings. FDI location decisions are much less sensitive to the protections of GATS than they are to factors like physical infrastructure and nests of local support services.

What the New Agreements Mean for Development

The new agreements must be seen in the context of the norms underlying the pre-Uruguay Round regime. At that time the "development" norm carried some weight in trade negotiations, even if mainly when it could be deployed as a tool of Cold War and post-colonial objectives. The general push toward trade liberalization was conditioned by recognition that developing countries, and particularly least developed countries, needed "special and differential" (S&D) treatment by definition of their being developing countries. The answer to the question, "what do countries need to do (need to be permitted by international rules to do) to achieve equitable development" was not assumed to boil down to "liberalize" and "integrate." Many poor countries were allowed to maintain protection.

As noted earlier, the past decade has ushered in an era of new market access dynamics much more favorable to the developed countries. Now, in the "globalization plus" paradigm pushed from the North, the route to development is seen to be the route of liberalization and unmediated integration into the world economy, supplemented by domestic institutional reforms to make deep integration viable. As Dani Rodrik observes, "Global integration has become, for all practical purposes, a substitute for a development strategy" despite its "shaky empirical ground" and the serious distortion it gives to policymakers' priorities (Rodrik 2001).

Taken together, the three agreements greatly restrict the right of a government to carry though policies that favor the growth and technological upgrading of domestic industries and firms. The sanction is market access: a country that implemented such policies can now be legally handicapped in its access to developed country markets, and the United States and the European Union do not even have to provide serious evidence in the Dispute Settlement Mechanism that a developing country's use of specific industrial policy instruments is "trade distorting." To quote Dani Rodrik again,

> The rules for admission into the world economy not only reflect little awareness of development priorities, they are often completely unrelated to sensible economic principles. For instance, WTO agreements on anti-dumping, subsidies and countervailing measures, agriculture, textiles, and trade-related intellectual property rights lack any economic rationale beyond the mercantilist interests of a narrow set of powerful groups in advanced industrial countries. (Rodrik 2001)

With a touch of hyperbole the agreements could be called a slow-motion Great Train Robbery.

How Do We Know that the Agreements Are, on the Whole, Bad for Development?

Seen in the round the agreements are bad for development for at least two reasons. One is that they are vague at points where vagueness benefits the developed countries, and precise at points where precision works against developing countries. Vagueness allows the developed countries to raise the level of threat to developing countries – threats to bring a case before the DSM and threats to take other punitive actions justified on the claim that the developing country is breaking the (vaguely defined) rules of the WTO.

The second reason concerns the gulf between the agreements' constraints on public policies in developing countries and the public policies adopted by the successful developers (Kozul-Wright 1995). Almost all now-developed countries went through stages of protectionist policy before the capabilities of their firms reached the point where a policy of (more or less) free trade was declared to be in the national interest. Britain was protectionist when it was trying to catch up with the Netherlands. Germany was protectionist when it was trying to catch up with Britain. The United States was protectionist when trying to catch up with Britain and Germany. Japan was protectionist for most of the twentieth century right up to the 1970s, Korea and Taiwan to the 1990s. And none of them came close to matching our criteria for "democracy" till the late stages of their catch-ups.[15]

Today's fast growers – including China, India, and Vietnam – began their fast economic growth well before their fast trade growth and even longer before their trade liberalizations. They have constrained their trade liberalization by considerations of the capacities of domestic firms to compete against imports. But today the World Bank would be first to denounce the amount of protection in their current trade policies – if they were not growing so fast. If nothing else, their experience shows how little we understand the root causes of economic growth.

On the other hand, the development experience of Latin America and Africa over the whole of the twentieth century shows that regions that integrate into the world economy as commodity supply regions – in line with their "comparative advantage" – and that rely on "natural" import replacement in response to transport costs, growing skills, and shifting relative costs, are only too likely to remain stuck in the role of commodity supply regions, their level of prosperity a function of access to rich country markets and terms of trade for their commodities.

When Latin American countries did go beyond "natural" import replacement during the post-Second World War "import substituting industrialization" decades, their growth performance was in fact better by several measures than it has been during the subsequent era of liberalization and privatization.

As for the argument that the agreements benefit developing countries by raising the inflow of FDI, the share of developing countries in world FDI is small and falling (from the 1990s' peak of 40 per cent in 1994 to less than 20 per cent in 2000), and the concentration of FDI on a very small number of developing countries remains as high as in 1980, meaning that there has been no "evolutionary" spreading out to more and more countries (see Wade 2003b). Moreover, there is no evidence that GATS has lifted the inflow, as noted earlier.

Bilateral investment treaties, which have been proliferating since the early 1990s (the United States has now signed forty-two) take the TRIPS, TRIMs and GATS obligations of host governments as merely the starting point. They require the host government to lift even more restrictions on foreign firms hoping to operate in their territory, to give even more concessions, in return for better access to the US or other powerful-party market. And they establish firm-state arbitration boards, which allow a private firm to take a government to arbitration by a body dominated by private-sector adjudicators naturally sympathetic to the needs of the firm, using private contract law rather than public law, which allows damages against the government to be levied retroactively. The WTO's dispute settlement mechanism, where states deal with states under public law, looks evenly balanced by comparison.

Why Are Developed Country States Pushing this Agenda?

In the light of this evidence we should be skeptical of claims by representatives of developed countries that "ever-freer trade and investment benefit just about everybody." The claims are better understood in the light of Friedrich List's observations about how states with head-start advantages behave. Writing in the 1840s and generalizing from the behavior of first the Netherlands and then Britain in the face of manufacturing competition from elsewhere, he observed:

> It is a very clever common device that when anyone has attained the summit of greatness, he kicks away the ladder by which he has climbed up, in order to deprive others of the means of climbing up after him.... Any nation which by means of protective duties and restrictions on navigation has raised her manufacturing power and her navigation to such a degree of development that no other nation can sustain free competition with her, can do nothing wiser than to throw away these ladders of her greatness, to preach to other nations the benefits of free trade, and to declare in penitent tones that she has hitherto wandered in the paths of error, and has now for the first time succeeded in discovering the truth. (List 1966: 368)

Perhaps the starkest example of developed countries precluding developing countries from using an array of measures that they themselves used to protect themselves from unwanted competition is the Multi Fiber Agreement (MFA). The developed countries through the MFA put quotas on the import of textiles and apparel in order to protect their own – employment-intensive, therefore voter-sensitive – textile industries. Developing countries that tried to do something similar today would face serious trade sanctions under WTO rules. Moreover, even though the MFA has been abolished, Western textile and apparel markets remain heavily protected through both tariffs and quotas. And agricultural subsidies remain infamously high. Each EU cow receives an average net subsidy of $2.50 per year, while European wheat farmers derive half of their income from subsidies, thanks to which they are able to cripple the export prospects of rivals like Argentina, which has defaulted on its debt because it cannot export enough to keep to its repayment schedule.

The apparatus of economic analysis has been deployed to affirm that largely free and open markets work best for all – which from a Listian perspective amounts to legitimizing the kicking away of the ladder. But there is an odd twist. Since the 1980s much work on the frontiers of economics investigates the heterodox world of increasing returns, linkages, technological learning, oligopolistic pricing, herding behavior, irrational exuberance and the like, which at least in principle provide justifications for governments to implement industrial policy measures and restrictions on capital flows. On the other hand, the dominant "structural adjustment" prescriptions of the World Bank and the IMF assume orthodox decreasing returns, stable equilibria, and no significant non-market linkage effects. Sometimes the same economists straddle both worlds, setting aside their knowledge of the heterodox world when they deal with development policy in order to hammer home the orthodox "fundamentals."

The efforts of developed country states to hard-wire in the head-start advantages of their firms through the WTO agreements have been complemented by efforts to establish open capital accounts and free capital mobility as a principle of participation in the world economy. Notwithstanding all the evidence of the huge costs that free capital mobility can inflict on developing countries, especially after the East Asian financial crisis of 1997–98 (Wade 1998, 2000b, 2001; Wade and Veneroso 1998b), IMF Managing Director Michel Camdessus said in 1999, "I believe it is now time for momentum to be re-established.... Full liberalization of capital movements should be promoted in a prudent and well-sequenced fashion ... the liberalization of capital movements [should be made] one of the purposes of the Fund" (Camdessus 1999).[16] US Undersecretary of the Treasury John Taylor declared in 2003 that the free transfer of capital in and out of a country without delay is a "fundamental right" (Taylor 2003).

What Is To Be Done?

The new trade and investment rules and the old techniques of legitimation – "preach to other nations the benefits of free trade" – join with other features of the world system to tip the playing field even more against most developing countries. One instance is China's surging manufactured exports, which are hurting exporters in most other developing countries and sending a deflationary impulse through the world economy. Another is the skill-biased immigration policies of developed countries, which erode production and governance capabilities in many developing countries. And in a class of its own is HIV/AIDS, which is destroying lives, communities, economies, and governments across Africa, South Asia and parts of East Asia, with no end in sight (Putzel 2003).

If the world is probably not moving in the right direction, as trends in world poverty and inequality suggest,[17] then the precautionary principle – applied to the likely costs to the world of having a large proportion of the world's population still at a small fraction of the living standards of North America and Western Europe half a century from now – suggests the need for non-market measures of intervention and for refocusing international cooperation around "development" principles rather than "reciprocity" and "no distortions" principles. Concretely, this would entail stronger one-way trade preferences for poor countries, and more legitimate scope for protection.[18] This was List's central prescription for a catch-up country like Germany. "In order to allow freedom of trade to operate naturally, the less advanced nation must first be raised *by artificial measures* to that stage of cultivation to which the English nation has been artificially elevated" (List 1966: 131, emphasis added).

Of course, there is plenty of evidence of import substitution going awry in Latin America, Africa, South Asia, and Australasia. But this no more discredits import replacement as a principle than the failure of democracy in many developing countries discredits the principle of democracy. The policy response should be to do import replacement better, not do it less (Bruton 1998).

It is clear from post-Second World War experience that protection alone is not enough. Protection has to be made part of a larger industrial strategy to nurture the capabilities of domestic firms and raise the rate of domestic investment, in the context of a private enterprise, market-based economy. And as part of this larger strategy, government-led import replacement has to go with government-encouraged export development. The East Asian experience shows that trade policy restrictions on some imports need not stop the fast growth of other imports – and hence raise the demand for foreign exchange. Trade protection, in other words, need not be "anti trade" (Wade 1991, 2003a; Jacobs 1984).

The problem in many developing countries – in Latin America and South Asia, for example, and also in the formerly heavily protected economies of Australasia – has been the absence of this larger industrial strategy and implementing organizations, and the unwillingness of the "aid" community, including the World Bank, to help them do industrial strategy sensibly.

The standard dismissal from economists is that even if protection and other forms of industrial policy could be justified in some circumstances, developing country states do not have the capacity to implement them effectively. This response rests on an unexamined assumption about low "state capacity" in developing countries. But, ironically, the world is proceeding on the assumption, in the TRIPS agreement, that developing country states do have a considerable capacity to enforce patents and copyrights. It is not obvious that a state that can do this would not also be able to implement effective protection and other forms of industrial policy.[19]

Rearticulating 'articulation'

Today we use the word "integration" to refer exclusively to integration into the world economy, and we assume that more integration is always good for development. One of the strangest silences of development thinking is the silence about internal integration. We should distinguish between "external integration" and "internal integration" (or articulation), and recognize that the development of a national economy is more about internal integration than about external integration.

An internally integrated economy has a dense set of input–output linkages between sectors (a high level of sectoral articulation between, for example, rural and urban, and consumer goods and intermediate goods), and a structure of demand such that a high proportion of domestic production is sold to domestic wage earners (a high level of social articulation between wages, consumption, and production). Export demand is not the main source of economic growth. Robust political coalitions between capitalists and employees become possible in this type of economy, because capitalists, employees, and the government recognize a common interest in wages as a source of sales and economic growth, not just as a cost of production.

In unarticulated economies, by contrast, wages are viewed simply as a cost, not also a source of demand. Domestic production is not well connected to domestic consumption, leaving exports as the main stimulus to economic growth. Industrial and agricultural sectors producing for foreign markets remain enclaves. This socially and sectorally unintegrated structure limits the creation of class alliances, which handicaps democratic regimes.

The key question, then, is how can developing countries create more articulated economies? The starting point is to recognize that more external integration does not automatically generate more internal integration; on the contrary, it can erode internal integration. But it is also true that more internal integration, if fostered by high and unstrategic protection, can undermine external integration, at the cost of future internal integration at higher income levels.

Development strategy has to operate in the zone where the two forms of integration reinforce rather than undermine each other. But the fact is that the issues of internal integration – including practical nuts-and-bolts issues like nurturing supply links between domestic firms and the subsidiaries of multinational corporations, and designing arrangements to protect exports from protection – have largely dropped out of the development agenda as promulgated by Western development organizations. And the WTO agreements make it much more difficult than in the past for development strategy to capture the synergies between internal and external integration.

To put the same point in more familiar terms, today's development theory assumes that the principle of comparative advantage – specialization between countries in line with the location preferences of firms in free and competitive markets – should be the principal goal of development policy. Conversely it assumes that the principle of import replacement – government encouragement of local production of some items currently imported – is not to be followed, because such policies have seemingly been discredited by the evidence of what happens when it guides the policy framework. In fact, the central challenge of national development strategy is to combine the principle of comparative advantage with the principle of import replacement in a way that generates pressure for upgrading and diversifying national production. This does not always imply protection. Strategic economics prescribes free trade, protection, subsidies, or some combination, depending on a country's circumstances and level of industrialization. In some sectors and at some times, a country should give little weight to import replacement and a lot to comparative advantage, and vice versa. There are a number of small and non-growing countries which, even if untrammeled by international rules, could not hope in the foreseeable future to do more than provide a low-wage platform for rich-country outsourcing, and whose domestic markets are too small to offer more than very limited possibilities for import replacement. There are others, particularly in Latin America, where the scope for import replacement is much bigger but where rapacious oligarchs have long used import replacement policy as yet another means of monopolizing opportunities and exploiting their populations. Here, more trade liberalization and more foreign direct investment can plausibly be seen as a way to force the oligarchs to cede their control over the economy – after which it may make sense to promote another round of concerted import replacement. Meanwhile, China is currently doing both at once, aggressively exporting in line with changing comparative advantage and aggressively replacing some current imports, following in the footsteps of Japan, Korea, and Taiwan.

Re-tooling multilateral and regional economic organizations

A more development-friendly environment requires changes in the mandate and procedures of the multilateral economic organizations. The question is how to reconceptualize and legitimize expanded "special and differential treatment" for developing countries and dilute requirements for "reciprocity," "national treatment," and "international best practice." The balance needs to be shifted away from the drive to homogenize trading commitments to other states towards granting states reasonable scope to choose appropriate levels of national protection (including for health, safety, working conditions, and the environment).

More specifically, the rules of the international economic regime should allow developing countries to accelerate import replacement by measures such as tariffs and subsidies (preferably made conditional on improved performance of the assisted industries). The rules should allow developing countries to give less scope for intellectual property protection than the current TRIPS standards, and assistance in enforcing those lower standards. As a specific example of what should be changed, Article 27.1 of the TRIPS agreement says that a "patent shall be available and patent rights enjoyable without discrimination as to … whether products are imported or locally produced." Developing countries should have the right to discriminate against patent rights when − after an appropriate period of years − the product is not locally produced. This is a key to import replacement, which is a key to industrial transformation.

Furthermore, international rules need to grant countries the right to use forms of capital controls in order to maintain the stability of their economies and protect trade flows (Bhagwati and Tarullo 2003). The standard reply from economists is that global financial markets are now much too big and digitized to be subject to any form of cross-border controls. But the regime for tracing drug money and terrorist money across borders has proven to be quite effective; this suggests that unauthorized capital movements could be subject to the same sort of penalties as tax evasion.

Economists also qualify their recommendation by saying that the capital account should be liberalized *pari passu* with "sound" or "prudent" regulation. But in truth we do not have good measures for judging the soundness of financial regulation. The World Bank published in April 1997 a list of countries whose capital market regulation was strong enough safely to support an open capital account: South Korea, Malaysia, Thailand, "with Indonesia and the Philippines not far behind," Chile, Mexico, "with Brazil also ranking well" (World Bank 1997). The East Asian financial crisis began three months later.

Suppose that the IMF had the authority of its Articles of Agreement to pressure countries to open their capital accounts on a timetable that it deemed appropriate. It would almost certainly underplay the dangers to the countries, both because of our lack of knowledge of how to gauge the "strength" of a country's system of financial regulation and because the IMF is highly attentive to the preferences of Wall Street and the City of London as mediated by the US Treasury and the UK Treasury.

Arrangements for debt-repayment standstills also have to be part of the arsenal. They would require an international organization (perhaps the IMF) being authorized to support them and the major industrial countries recognizing the authority of the organization so that bondholders would be prevented from asserting claims in court.[20]

The rules of the system should encourage countries to maintain a "positively correlated" capital structure, such that the cost of borrowing is higher when ability to repay is higher and the cost is lower when ability to repay is lower. At present, developing countries tend to have "inversely correlated" capital structures, where they borrow cheaply when times are good and borrow expensively when times are bad. This is a recipe for volatility, financial crisis, slower long run growth, higher poverty, and higher inequality (Pettis 2001).

Finally, internationally agreed standards should be cast in terms which allow considerable leeway for national governments to interpret them. Committees of unaccountable experts, as in the WTO Dispute Settlement Mechanism, should have limited powers to constrain the role of democratically accountable national bodies.

All these changes would give more room for different forms of national capitalisms to flourish, with the international framework designed to maximize international economic stability rather than maximizing the free movement of goods and capital (Rodrik 1998). If this sounds pie in the sky, recall that the Bretton Woods system did meet these criteria and delivered magnificent economic performance through the 1950s to the 1970s.

As part of this policy-non-convergence scenario, we need to build up regional-level organizations, so that markets can be embedded not only nationally but also in regionally distinct configurations, with policy solutions tailored to the different vulnerabilities of different countries and regions. This is the point that the two Korean labor federations had in mind in their remarkable statement to US Treasury Secretary Rubin in July 1998:

The Asian development model, while containing some of the key elements which gave rise to the current crisis, also contains the very dynamic elements which made the "miraculous" growth over such a short period.... The IMF policy regime, however, has overlooked ... the positive and dynamic elements in its virtual blanket disavowal of the Asian economy.... It may be necessary, therefore, for Asian nations to build a body ... which can serve as an Asian monetary fund. (KCTU–FKTU 1998)

The unpromising politics

It is easy to say that "the international economic regime must be changed, developing countries should be given..." The politics are another matter. The developed country negotiators and the 500-strong WTO staff are being driven by a mixture of ideological conviction and intense corporate lobbying. A former WTO negotiator commented that, "without the enormous pressure generated by the American financial services sector ... there would have been no [GATS] services agreement." The pressure came especially from the US Coalition of Service Industries, the European Services Forum, and the UK's Liberalization of Trade in Services (LOTIS) group (World Development Movement 2002). The TRIPS agreement was propelled by a few industries – mainly pharmaceuticals, software, and Hollywood – that stand to gain a lot from the protections, whose interests the US government championed. It is not obvious that agreements written to suit Western pharmaceuticals companies, software companies, the Motion Picture Association, and Wall Street/City of London are good for the world (see Kwa 2002).

On the other hand, developing country governments are not cooperating closely enough to push for the sorts of changes suggested here. For the most part their trade negotiators accept the legitimacy of the idea that "market access" is the key to development – but they emphasize their access to the North's markets, while the North's "market access" agenda emphasizes the North's access to their markets, presented as being in *their* own best interest. They negotiate for better market access (for their exports) as an end in itself, not for "development space." And they do not see the critical importance of retaining the policy option of being able to constrain the inflow and outflow of capital by means of quantitative restrictions.

The vested interests are so strong, the legitimacy of the "globalization plus" paradigm so well defended in the centers of power, that only economic crisis is likely to shift thinking. How many more crashes like those of the 1990s and the early 2000s will the world endure before we conclude that the project of constructing a single integrated world market with universal standards – the culmination of the European Enlightenment ideal – is a mistake? Many, quite likely, provided that the populations of the G7 states are not seriously affected. But small changes are possible even outside of crisis conditions, generated by some combination of global social movements of NGOs, companies slowly expanding their social responsibility charters, "epistemic communities" of scholars rethinking development strategies, and developing country governments pushing quietly ahead to encourage new activities (import replacement, new exports) in ways that bypass or go under the radar of the international agreements.[21] From among these various entities it may be possible to organize coalitions for a determined push to revise specific and harmful clauses in existing agreements, such as article 27.1 of TRIPS.

And now that the WTO has come to affect central aspects of people's lives around the world, we should work right now to make it more open. At present the negotiations to create new trade agreements are opaque, and disputes about existing rules are mostly resolved in secret. Governments of developing countries are often left out of the horse-trading sessions and presented with faits accomplis. We should press the WTO to reduce the current vagueness of the capstone agreements, which rebounds to the advantage of the developed countries; to adopt clearer operating rules and procedures; to publish a record of voting and discussions; to require the chairs of negotiating committees to explain why they include some proposals and reject others from the text of the draft declaration, rather than, as at present, being able occultly to make a "magic text."[22] After all, several monetary authorities, including the Bank of England and the Federal Reserve, have started to publish full minutes soon after decision-making meetings, and the experience is generally considered to be successful; and judges in many countries are required to give reasons for their decisions. We need the WTO to be subject to much closer scrutiny by NGOs, in much the way that the World Bank is watched by the Bank Information Center (BIC), an NGO based in Washington DC, and by the Bretton Woods Project, based in London.[23] And it would surely help if the WTO – which is an active policymaker, far from a mere facilitator of negotiations among representatives of member states – was more representative. Some 80 per cent of the staff are nationals of developed countries, whose populations comprise less than 20 per cent of the population of the member states (Kwa 2002). As what the Bush administration calls the United States' "strategic competitor," China, begins to inject its nationals into the WTO and other international organizations, and as China acquires the technological and even military capacity to be a competitor to the dominance of the West, it will be interesting to see how the international development agenda changes.

Notes

I thank Mark Blyth, Carolyn Deere, Ronald Dore, Devesh Kapur, Michael Pettis, and Ken Shadlen for comments on an earlier draft; and to participants in the Rockefeller/ Bellagio workshop on technology transfer and human development, 5–17 November 2002. See also UNDP 2002.

1. For an account of the dominance of the G7 (Group of Seven) states inside the WTO, see Kwa 2002.

2. These commitments were made in the Uruguay Round of 1986–94, and re-made in the Doha agreement of November 2001 to start a new round of multilateral trade talks.

3. The United States has raised its agricultural and steel subsidies since the Doha agreement, and is more likely to raise trade barriers for textiles and garments, footwear, and several farm products than to lower them. These are sectors that are vulnerable to import competition from developing countries and important for the US political support system. The European Union deploys protection about as much as the United States, and has flouted its Doha commitments even more blatantly than the United States by failing to commit to a timetable for reducing its subsidies.

4. Tariff escalation refers to higher tariffs on imports of more highly processed commodities.

5. The section on TRIPS is co-written with Kenneth Shadlen; see Shadlen 2002.

6. Compulsory licensing laws allow states to sidestep patents, to insist that a firm holding a patent on a technology or product of general importance license it to other firms.

7. For example, the TRIPS agreement gives a precise and narrow scope for states to limit patent rights for public purposes (for example, to limit patents on community knowledge), but gives wide and vaguely defined scope for granting private patent rights (for example, over naturally occurring micro-organisms and micro-biological processes). So a state that refuses to allow patenting of micro-organisms is liable to a complaint, whereas a state whose firms take out patents on community knowledge in another country is not.

8. For example, the draft bilateral treaties (such as those with Singapore, Chile, Jordan, the Free Trade Area of the Americas (FTAA) negotiating text) further reduce exceptions to patentability, further limit the other government's ability to sidestep patents with compulsory licenses, and in pharmaceuticals make the other government commit to the same provisions for easy extension of the patent beyond twenty years, as in the United States. The United States in the FTAA negotiations is pressing for patents as the only method for protecting plant varieties.

9. The scope for sweet deals is enhanced by the "single undertaking" nature of the WTO. Countries may decide that they have to accept a bad deal on some matters (e.g., TRIPS) in order to get what they want on other issues (e.g., agriculture). US appeals to the agriculture minister may elicit governmental pressure on the Geneva ambassador to give way on TRIPS.

10. Dickens was so angry about American infringement of copyright on *A Christmas Carol* that he toured the United States in 1842 urging adoption of international copyright protection in the long-term interests of American authors (Lohr 2002). See

also Kozul-Wright 1995 and Chang 2002.

11. TRIPS relates mainly to patentable or copyrightable activity.

12. Performance requirements cover not only obligations but also incentives for investors/producers to do certain things. For example, the government might offer a tax incentive in return for a certain proportion of "local content," locally procured inputs; or in return for "trade balancing," exports worth a certain proportion of imports; or in return for exporting a certain proportion of total production; or joint venturing with a local firm.

13. See further, Raghavan 2002; and Sinclair 2002.

14. South Africa's awarding of telecommunications contracts to Malaysian companies on the grounds that they had experience of handling problems of racial access to telephone networks could be challenged on most-favored-nation grounds.

15. Hong Kong and Singapore are the great exceptions on the trade front, in that they did have free trade and they did catch up – but they are city-states and not to be treated as countries. In any case Singapore did place performance requirements/incentives on foreign subsidiaries and mounted an industrial policy to provide them with needed factor inputs.

16. But a recent paper by IMF staff economists, including Chief Economist Kenneth Rogoff, finds no evidence that opening the capital account is good for growth and good evidence that it raises the volatility of national consumption (Prasad et al. 2003).

17. I spell out the grounds for this contentious conclusion in Wade 2004.

18. The effectiveness of nonreciprocal trade preferences for poor countries is suggested by Andrew Rose's finding that, contrary to general assumption, being a member of the GATT/WTO as such made no statistical difference to how much trade a country did with others, but receiving trade preferences under GATT's Generalized System of Preferences (GSP) – preferences that rich countries gave to poor ones – roughly doubled a poor country's trade compared to what it would have been otherwise (Rose 2002).

19. My thanks to Ken Shadlen for this point.

20. For more radical proposals, see D'Arista 2000; Wade 2000a, 2002.

21. As Korea and Taiwan beefed up covert trade controls even as they announced bold trade liberalizations.

22. A South Asian delegate said about the process of formulating the Draft Declaration for Doha, "In the process of negotiations, we would object to a text, but it would still appear. We would state we wanted a text added in, and still it would not appear. It was like a magic text" (quoted in Kwa 2002: 21).

23. A small WTO-watching NGO called the International Center for Trade and Sustainable Development (ICTSD) already exists, now in its sixth year. It publishes a regular bulletin of WTO news of particular interest to developing countries, *Bridges*. Others include WTO WATCH, Our World Is Not For Sale Network, Third World Network, and the Trade Information Project, which focus on getting information to NGOs and social movements to enable them to engage in advocacy with their governments and with the WTO. On WTO openness, see *Washington Post* 2002. For a different view, see Walter 2001. On international organizations more generally, see Wood 2003. For UK-based NGOs' opposition to a new investment agreement at the WTO, see Oxfam 2003.

6

Kicking Away the Ladder: "Good Policies" and "Good Institutions" in Historical Perspective

Ha-Joon Chang

There is currently great pressure on developing countries from the developed countries and the international development policy establishment (IDPE) that they control to adopt a set of "good policies" and "good institutions" to foster their economic development.

As we are all aware, the "good policies" that they want are basically conservative macroeconomic policy, liberalization of international trade and investment, privatization, and deregulation. The emphasis on "good institutions" is more recent. This has come about because of the recognition on the part of the IDPE that what they see as "good policies" have failed to produce good economic results in most developing countries because of the absence of supporting institutions. So, for example, it is said that if private property rights are not well protected, price deregulation will not lead to greater investment and higher growth, because the potential investors cannot be sure of reaping the gains from their investments. As a result of this new thinking, the IFIs and many donor governments are increasingly attaching "governance-related conditionalities" to their loans and grants. The key institutions they recommend include democracy, "good" bureaucracy, an independent judiciary, strongly protected private property rights (including intellectual property rights), and transparent and market-oriented corporate governance and financial institutions (including a politically independent central bank).

As we know, there have been heated debates on whether these recommended policies and institutions are appropriate for developing countries. However, curiously, even many of those who are skeptical of the applicability of these policies and institutions to the developing countries take it for granted that these were the policies and the institutions that were used by the developed countries when they themselves were developing countries.

However, this cannot be further from the truth. As we shall show later in the chapter, when they were developing countries themselves the developed countries used virtually none of the policies and institutions that they are recommending to developing countries.

History of Economic Policy

The official history of capitalism

According to what I call "the official history of capitalism" that informs our debate on development and globalization, the world has developed in the following way over the last few centuries.

From the eighteenth century, the industrial success of laissez-faire Britain proved the superiority of free-market and free-trade policies by beating interventionist France, its main competitor at the time, and establishing itself as the supreme world economic power. Especially once it had abandoned its deplorable agricultural protection (the Corn Laws) and other remnants of old mercantilist protectionist measures in 1846, it was able to play the role of the architect and hegemon of a new "liberal" world economic order. This liberal world order, perfected around 1870, was based on: laissez-faire industrial policies at home; low barriers to the international flows of goods, capital, and labor; and macroeconomic stability, both nationally and internationally, guaranteed by the gold standard and the principle of balanced budgets. A period of unprecedented prosperity followed.

Unfortunately, according to this story, things started to go wrong with the First World War. In response to the ensuing instability of the world economic and political system, countries started to erect trade barriers again. In 1930, the United States also abandoned free trade and raised tariffs with the infamous Smoot–Hawley tariff, which the famous free-trade economist Jagdish Bhagwati called "the most visible and dramatic act of anti-trade folly" (Bhagwati 1985: 22 n10). The world free-trade system finally ended in 1932, when Britain, hitherto the champion of free trade, succumbed to the temptation and reintroduced tariffs. The resulting contraction and instability in the world economy and then finally the Second World War destroyed the last remnants of the first liberal world order.

After the Second World War, so the story goes, some significant progress was made in trade liberalization through the early GATT (General Agreement on Tariffs and Trade) talks. However, unfortunately, dirigiste approaches to economic management dominated the policymaking scene until the 1970s in the developed world, and until the early 1980s in the developing world (and the Communist world until its collapse in 1989). According to Sachs and Warner (1995), a number of factors contributed to the pursuit of protectionism and interventionism in developing countries (Sachs and Warner 1995: 11–21). There were "wrong" theories, such as the infant industry argument, the "big push" theory, and Latin American structuralism, not to speak of various Marxian theories. There were also political dividends to protectionist policies, such as the need for nation building and the need to "buy off" certain interest groups. And there were legacies of wartime control that persisted into peacetime.

Fortunately, it is said, interventionist policies have been largely abandoned across the world since the 1980s with the rise of neoliberalism, which emphasized the virtues of small government, laissez-faire policies, and international openness. Especially in the developing world, by the late 1970s economic growth had begun to falter in most countries outside East and Southeast Asia, which were already pursuing "good" policies (of free market and free trade). This growth failure, which often manifested itself in economic crises in the early 1980s, exposed the limitations of old-style interventionism and protectionism. As a result, most developing countries have come to embrace "policy reform" in a neoliberal direction.

When combined with the establishment of new global governance institutions represented by the WTO, these policy changes at the national level have created a new global economic system, comparable in its (at least potential) prosperity only to the earlier "golden age" of liberalism (1870–1914). Renato Ruggiero, the first director-general of the WTO, argues that thanks to this new world order we now have "the potential for eradicating global poverty in the early part of the next [twenty-first] century – a utopian notion even a few decades ago, but a real possibility today" (1998: 131). As we shall see later, this story paints a fundamentally misleading picture, but a no less powerful one for that. And it should be accepted that there are also some senses in which the late nineteenth century can indeed be described as an era of laissez-faire.

To begin with, there was a period in the late nineteenth century, albeit a brief one, when liberal trade regimes prevailed in large parts of the world economy. Between 1860 and 1880, many European countries reduced tariff protection substantially (see Table 6.1). At the same time, most of the rest of the world was forced to practice free trade through colonialism and through unequal treaties in the case of a few nominally "independent" countries (such as the Latin American countries, China, Thailand [then Siam], Iran [then Persia], and Turkey [then the Ottoman Empire], and even Japan until 1911). Of course, the obvious exception to this was the United States, which maintained a very high tariff barrier even during this period. However, given

Table 6.1 Average tariff rates on manufactured products for selected developed countries in their early stages of development (weighted average; % of value)

	1820[2]	1875[2]	1913	1925	1931	1950
Austria[3]	R[1]	15–20	18	16	24	18
Belgium[4]	6–8	9–10	9	15	14	11
Denmark	25–35	15–20	14	10	n.a.	3
France	R	12–15	20	21	30	18
Germany[5]	8–12	4–6	13	20	21	26
Italy	n.a.	8–10	18	22	46	25
Japan[6]	R	5	30	n.a.	n.a.	n.a.
Netherlands[4]	6–8	3–5	4	6	n.a.	11
Russia	R	15–20	84	R	R	R
Spain	R	15–20	41	41	63	n.a.
Sweden	R	3–5	20	16	21	9
Switzerland	8–12	4–6	9	14	19	n.a.
United Kingdom	45–55	0	0	5	n.a.	23
United States	35–45	40–50	44	37	48	14

1. R = numerous and important restrictions on manufactured imports existed and therefore average tariff rates are not meaningful.
2. These are very approximate rates, and give the range of average rates, not extremes.
3. Austria–Hungary before 1925.
4. In 1820, Belgium was united with the Netherlands.
5. The 1820 figure is for Prussia only.
6. Before 1911, Japan was obliged to keep low tariff rates (up to 5 per cent) through a series of "unequal treaties" with the European countries and the USA. The World Bank (1991: 97, Box table 5.2) gives Japan's unweighted average tariff rate for all goods (and not just manufactured goods) for the years 1925, 1930, 1950 as 13 per cent, 19 per cent, 4 per cent, respectively.

Source: Bairoch (1993), p. 40, table 3.3. World Bank (1991: 97, Box table 5.2) provides a similar table, partly drawing on Bairoch's own studies that form the basis of the above table. However, the World Bank figures, although in most cases very similar to Bairoch's figures, are unweighted averages, which are obviously less preferable to the weighted average figures that Bairoch provides.

that the United States was still a relatively small part of the world economy, it may not be totally unreasonable to say that this is as close to free trade as the world has ever got (or probably ever will).

More importantly, the scope of state intervention before the Second World War (or at least before the First World War) was quite limited by modern standards. States at the time had limited budgetary policy capability because there was no income tax and the balanced budget doctrine dominated. They also had limited monetary policy capability because many countries did not have a central bank, and the gold standard restricted their policy freedom.

They also had limited command over investment resources, as they owned or controlled few financial institutions and industrial enterprises. One somewhat paradoxical consequence of all these limitations was that tariff protection was far more important as a policy tool in the nineteenth century than it is in our time.

Despite these limitations, as we shall soon see, virtually all now-developed countries (NDCs) actively used interventionist industrial, trade, and technology (ITT) policies that are aimed at promoting infant industries during their catch-up periods. Moreover, when they reached the frontier, the NDCs used a range of policies in order to help themselves "pull away" from their existing and potential competitors. They used measures to control transfer of technology to their potential competitors (e.g. controls on skilled worker migration or machinery export) and made the less developed countries open up their markets by unequal treaties and colonization. However, the catch-up economies that were not (formal or informal) colonies did not simply sit down and accept these restrictive measures. They mobilized all kinds of different "legal" and "illegal" means to overcome the obstacles created by these restrictions, such as industrial espionage, "illegal" poaching of workers, and smuggling of contraband machinery.

In my book *Kicking Away the Ladder* I examine the historical experiences of a range of NDCs in relation to their "catching-up" and "pulling-away" experience and see what kinds of industrial, trade, and technology (henceforth ITT) policies they had used at the time. The countries I look at are Britain, the USA, Germany, France, Sweden, Belgium, the Netherlands, Switzerland, Japan, Korea, and Taiwan. This examination reveals a lot of myths that misinform today's policy debate, but there are particularly many myths about the economic policies of Britain and the USA – the two supposed homes of free-market, free-trade capitalism.

Britain

Contrary to the popular myth that depicts it as a country that developed on the basis of free market and free trade, Britain had been an aggressive user, and in certain areas a pioneer, of activist policies intended to promote infant industries.

Such policies, although limited in scope, date from the fourteenth century (Edward III) and the fifteenth century (Henry VII) in relation to woolen manufacturing, the leading industry of the time. At the time, England was an exporter of raw wool to the Low Countries (today's Belgium and the Netherlands), and Henry VII tried to change this by, among other things, taxing raw wool exports and poaching skilled workers from the Low Countries.

And between the 1721 trade policy reform of Robert Walpole, Britain's first prime minister, and the repeal of the Corn Laws in 1846, Britain implemented aggressive ITT policies. During this period, it actively used infant industry protection, export subsidies, import tariff rebates on inputs used for exporting, export quality control by the state – all policies that are typically associated with Japan and other East Asian countries. As we can see from Table 6.1, Britain had very high tariffs on manufacturing products even as late as the 1820s, some two generations after the start of its Industrial Revolution, and when it was significantly ahead of its competitor nations in technological terms.

Britain moved significantly, although not completely, to free trade with the repeal of the Corn Laws in 1846. The repeal of the Corn Laws is these days commonly regarded as the ultimate victory of the classical liberal economic doctrine over wrong-headed mercantilism (see e.g. Bhagwati 1985), but many historians see it as an act of "free trade imperialism" intended to "halt the move to industrialisation on the Continent by enlarging the market for agricultural produce and primary materials" (Kindleberger 1978: 196). Indeed, this is exactly how many key leaders of the campaign to repeal the Corn Laws, such as the politician Richard Cobden and John Bowring of the Board of Trade, saw their campaign.[1]

In short, contrary to popular belief, Britain's technological lead that enabled this shift to a free-trade regime had been achieved "behind high and long-lasting tariff barriers," as the eminent economic historian Paul Bairoch once put it (1993: 46). And it is for this reason that Friedrich List, the nineteenth-century German economist who is (mistakenly – see below) known as the father of modern "infant industry" theory, argued that the British preaching for free trade is equivalent to someone who has already climbed to the top "kicking away the ladder" with which he/she climbed. He is worth quoting at length on this point.

> It is a very common clever device that when anyone has attained the summit of greatness, he *kicks away the ladder* by which he has climbed up, in order to deprive others of the means of climbing up after him. In this lies the secret of the cosmopolitical doctrine of Adam Smith, and of the cosmopolitical tendencies of his great contemporary William Pitt, and of all his successors in the British Government administrations.
>
> Any nation which by means of protective duties and restrictions on navigation has raised her manufacturing power and her navigation to such a degree of development that no other nation can sustain free competition with her, can do nothing wiser than *to throw away these ladders* of her greatness, to preach to other nations the benefits of free trade, and to declare in penitent tones that she has hitherto wandered in the paths of error, and has now for the first time succeeded in discovering the truth. (List 1885: 295–6, emphasis added)

The United States

If Britain was the first country successfully to launch a large-scale infant industry promotion strategy, its most ardent user was the United States – Paul Bairoch once called it "the mother country and bastion of modern protectionism" (1993: 30).

Indeed, the first systematic arguments for infant industry were developed by American thinkers like Alexander Hamilton, the first Treasury Secretary of the United States, and Daniel Raymond, while Friedrich List, the supposed intellectual father of infant industry protection argument, first learned about the argument during his exile in the United States in the 1820s. Many US intellectuals and politicians during the country's catch-up period clearly understood that the free-trade theory advocated by the British Classical economists was unsuited to their country. List praises the Americans for not listening to influential economists like Adam Smith and Jean Baptiste Say, who had argued that infant industry protection would be a disaster for the resource-rich United States, and following "common sense" and "the instinct of what was necessary for the nation" and proceeding to protect their industries, starting from the new tariff act of 1816 (List 1885: 99–100).[2]

Between 1816 and the end of the Second World War, the United States had one of the highest average tariff rates on manufacturing imports in the world (see Table 6.1). Given that the country enjoyed an exceptionally high degree of "natural" protection due to high transportation costs at least until the 1870s, we can say that US industries were literally the most protected in the world until 1945.

Especially after the Civil War, protectionism became very strong. Notwithstanding the common view, the Civil War was *not* fought only on the issue of slavery – tariff was an equally, if not more, important issue.[3] It was only after the Second World War, with its industrial supremacy unchallenged, that the United States liberalized its trade (although not as unequivocally as Britain did in the mid-nineteenth century) and started championing the cause of free trade – once again proving List right on his "ladder-kicking" metaphor. The following quotation from Ulysses Grant, the Civil War hero and the president of the United States 1868–76, clearly shows how the Americans had no illusions about ladder-kicking on the British side and their side.

For centuries England has relied on protection, has carried it to extremes and has obtained satisfactory results from it. There is no doubt that it is to this system that it owes its present strength. After two centuries, England has found it convenient to adopt free trade because it thinks that protection can no longer offer it anything. Very well then, Gentlemen, my knowledge of our country leads me to believe that within 200 years, when America has gotten out of protection all that it can offer, it too will adopt free trade. (Ulysses S. Grant, president of the United States 1868–76, cited in Frank 1967: 164)[4]

Other countries

Leaving the interested reader to find out about other countries in my full-length treatment of the subject in the book *Kicking Away the Ladder*, we may say that the following points emerge from our historical examination.

First, almost all NDCs had used some form of infant industry promotion strategy when they were in catching-up positions. The exceptions to this historical pattern are Switzerland and the Netherlands. These, however, were countries that stood very close to (or even at) the world's technological frontier and therefore *did not need* much infant industry protection. Also, even these countries do not conform to modern-day neoliberal ideal, as they did not have patent laws until the early twentieth century and allowed their firms to "steal" technology freely from abroad.

Second, it was the United Kingdom and the United States – the supposed homes of free-trade policy – and not countries like Germany, France, or Japan – countries that are usually associated with state activism – that used tariff protection most aggressively. Tariff protection was relatively low in Germany (see Table 6.1), and Japan's tariff was bound below 5 per cent until 1911 due to a series of unequal treaties that it was forced to sign upon opening in 1853. Of course, tariff figures do not give a full picture of industrial promotion efforts. Germany and Japan actively used non-tariff measures to promote their industries. However, France, despite the fact that it is usually portrayed as the interventionist counterpoint to free-trade Britain, had lower tariff protection than that of Britain during the first three-quarters of the nineteenth century and also maintained a very non-interventionist stance throughout the nineteenth century and the first half of the twentieth century.

Third, tariff protection was in many countries a key component of the import promotion strategy, but was by no means the only, or even necessarily the most important, component in the strategy. There were many other tools, such as export subsidies, tariff rebates on inputs used for exports, conferring of monopoly rights, cartel arrangements, directed credits, investment planning, manpower planning, R&D supports, and the promotion of institutions that allow public–private cooperation. These policies are thought to have been invented by Japan and other East Asian countries after World War II or at least by Germany in the late nineteenth century, but many of them have a long pedigree.

Finally, despite the NDCs sharing the same underlying principle, there was a considerable degree of diversity among them in terms of the policy mix, suggesting that there is no "one-size-fits-all" *model* for industrial development.

Pulling-away exercises

As mentioned earlier, when they reached the top, the NDCs used all kinds of tactics to "pull away" from the follower countries. Policies deployed were, of course, different according to the political status of the latter – colonies, semi-independent countries bound by unequal treaties, and independent competitor countries.

Britain was particularly aggressive in preventing industrial development in the colonies. First, primary production in the colonies was encouraged through export subsidies ("bounties"), and import duties on raw materials produced in the colonies were abolished. Second, high-value-added manufacturing activities were outlawed in the colonies. Third, exports from the colonies that competed with British products were banned. For example, Britain put a ban on cotton textile imports from India ("calicoes") in 1700 and a ban on the export of woolen cloth from its colonies (e.g. Ireland and the United States) to other countries in 1699. Fourth, the use of tariffs by colonial authorities was banned or, if they were considered necessary for revenue reasons, countered in a number of ways. For example, when in 1859 the British colonial government in India imposed small import duties on textile goods (3–10 per cent) for purely fiscal reasons, the local producers were taxed to the same magnitude in order to provide a "level playing field."

As seen earlier, "unequal treaties" were used in order to deprive nominally independent weak countries of their tariff autonomy, with their tariff bound at a very low level (typically 3–5 per cent). All Latin American countries, starting with Brazil in 1810, China, Thailand (then Siam), Persia, the Ottoman Empire, and even Japan until 1911 were in this category.

Against the competitor nations, policies focused on restricting the out-flow of superior technologies through policies like a ban on skilled worker migration or a ban on exports of key machinery. The competitor nations countered these moves with industrial espionage, "illegal" recruitment of skilled workers, and violation of patents and other intellectual property rights. Most of these countries accorded only very inadequate protection to the intellectual property rights of foreign citizens (e.g. allowing the patenting of *imported inventions*). Switzerland did not have a patent system until 1907, and the Netherlands, although it introduced a patent law in 1817, abolished it in 1869 and did not reintroduce one until 1912. And as late as the latter part of the nineteenth century, when Germany was about to overtake Britain technologically, there was great concern in Britain over the widespread German violation of its trademarks.

Comparison with today's developing countries

Those few neoliberal economists who are aware of the records of protection-ism in the NDCs try to avoid the obvious conclusion (namely, it can be very useful for economic development) by arguing that, while some (minimal) tariff protection may be necessary, most developing countries have tariff rates that are much higher than those most NDCs used in the past. For example, the World Bank argues that "[a]lthough industrial countries did benefit from higher natural protection before transport costs declined, the average tariff for twelve industrial countries[5] ranged from 11 to 32 percent from 1820 to 1980.... In contrast, the average tariff on manufactures in developing countries is 34 percent" (World Bank 1991: 97, Box 5.2).

This argument sounds reasonable enough, but is actually highly misleading in one important sense. The problem with it is that the productivity gap between today's developed countries and the developing countries is much greater than what existed between the more developed NDCs and the less developed NDCs in earlier times. This means that the currently developing countries need to impose much higher tariff rates than those used by the NDCs in earlier times, if they are to provide the same degree of actual protection to their industries as that accorded to the NDC industries in the past.

For example, when the United States accorded over 40 per cent average tariff protection to its industries in the late nineteenth century, its per capita income in PPP terms was already about three-quarters that of Britain. And this was when the "natural protection" accorded by distance, which was especially important for the United States, was considerably higher than today. Compared to this, the 71 per cent trade-weighted average tariff rate that India used to have just before the WTO agreement, despite the fact that its per capita income in PPP terms is only about one-fifteenth that of the United States, makes the country look like a champion of free trade. Following the WTO agreement, India cut its trade-weighted average tariff to 32 per cent, bringing it down to the level below which the US average tariff rate never sank between the end of the Civil War and World War II.

To take a less extreme example, in 1875 Denmark had an average tariff rate around 15–20 per cent, when its income was slightly less than 60 per cent that of Britain. Following the WTO agreement, Brazil cut its trade-weighted average tariff from 41 per cent to 27 per cent, a level that is not far above the Danish level, but its income in PPP terms is barely 20 per cent that of the United States.

Thus seen, *given the productivity gap*, even the relatively high levels of protection that had prevailed in the developing countries until the 1980s do not seem excessive by the historical standards of the NDCs. When it comes to the substantially lower levels that have come to prevail after two decades of extensive trade liberalization in these countries, it may even be argued that today's developing countries are actually even less protectionist than the NDCs in earlier times.

Institutional Development in Historical Perspective

As mentioned at the beginning, there is a great pressure on developing countries to improve the quality of their institutions to conform to "global standards." Naturally, there is a lot of unease about this attempt. One obvious reason is that the IFIs and the donor governments do not have the mandate to intervene in many of these areas (democracy, corporate govern-ance, etc.). Taken to the extreme, the push for the adoption of institutional global standards amounts to neo-imperialism. Another is that the standards demanded from developing country institutions seem to be too high – many developing countries, often justly, say that they simply cannot "afford" the high-quality institutions that are demanded of them. They have an important point to make, but in the absence of some idea as to which institutions are necessary and/or viable under what conditions, they are in danger of justifying whatever institutional status quo exists in developing countries. But what is the alternative?

One obvious alternative is for us to find out directly which of the "best practice" institutions are suitable for particular developing countries by transplanting them and seeing how they fare. However, as the failures of "structural adjustment" in many developing countries and of "transition" in many former Communist economies show, this usually does not work and can be very costly. Another alternative is for the developing countries to wait for spontaneous institutional evolution. It may be argued that the best way to get the institutions that suit the local conditions is to let them evolve naturally. However, such spontaneous evolution may take a long time, and there is no guarantee that the outcome will be optimal, even from the local point of view. The third, and my preferred, alternative is to learn from history by looking at institutional development in the developed countries when they were "developing countries" themselves. Therefore, below I try to draw lessons from the *history*, as opposed to the *current state*, of the developed countries in terms of institutional development.

The history of institutional development in developed countries

In this section I discuss the evolution of six categories of institutions that are widely regarded as essential components of a "good governance" structure in the developed countries during the period between the early nineteenth century and the early twentieth century. They are: democracy, bureaucracy (including the judiciary), property rights, corporate governance institutions, financial institutions (including public finance institutions), and welfare and labor institutions. Let us summarize the main findings.

Democracy

There is currently a lively debate on whether democracy is good for economic development. Whatever one's position is in this regard, it is clear that the NDCs did not develop under democracy.

It was not until the 1920s that most NDCs had adopted even universal male suffrage for the majority white population (see Table 6.2). Genuine universal suffrage was adopted in all NDCs only during the late twentieth century (Spain restored democracy only in the 1970s; votes were granted to ethnic minorities in Australia and the United States in 1962 and 1965, respectively; votes were granted to women in many countries after the Second World War and in Switzerland as late as 1971). Moreover, until the Second World War, even when democracy formally existed, its quality was extremely poor. Secret balloting was introduced only in the early twentieth century even in France and Germany, and corrupt electoral practices (such as vote buying, electoral fraud, and legislative corruption) lasted in most countries well into the twentieth century.

Bureaucracy and judiciary

Sales of offices, the spoils system, and nepotism abounded in early bureaucracies (some countries even had official price lists for government jobs). Modern professional bureaucracies first emerged in Prussia in the early nineteenth century, but much later in other countries. Even Britain got a modern bureaucracy only in the mid-nineteenth century. Until 1883, none of the US federal bureaucrats was competitively recruited, and, even at the end of the nineteenth century, less than half of them were competitively recruited.

Judiciaries often lacked professionalism and independence. For example, in Italy, at least until the late nineteenth century, judges did not usually have a background in law, and, according to one historian, "could not protect themselves, let alone anyone else, against political abuses" (Clark 1996: 54). Until the early twentieth century, the judiciaries in many countries were prone to dispensing "class justice."

Table 6.2 Introduction of democracy in NDCs

Country	Universal male suffrage	Universal suffrage
Australia	1903[1]	1962
Austria	1907	1918
Belgium	1919	1948
Canada	1920[2]	1970
Denmark	1849	1915
Finland	1919[3]	1944
France	1848	1946
Germany	1849[2]	1946
Italy	1919[4]	1946
Japan	1925	1952
Netherlands	1917	1919
New Zealand	1889	1907
Norway	1898	1913
Portugal	n.a.	1970
Spain	n.a.	1977[7]
Sweden	1918	1918
Switzerland	1879	1971
UK	1918[5]	1928
USA	1965[6]	1965

1. With racial qualifications.   2. With property qualifications.   3. Communists excluded.
4. With restrictions.   5. All men and women over 30.
6. Universal male suffrage was introduced in 1870, but reversed between 1890 and 1908 through the disenfranchisement of the blacks in the Southern states. It was only restored in 1965.
7. Universal suffrage was introduced in 1931 but reversed by the military coup of General Franco in 1936. It was only restored in 1977, following Franco's death in 1975. See the text for details.

Source: Chang 2002: ch. 3, table 3.1.

Property rights

An attempt to chart the evolution of property rights regimes is *not* made in this section, since it involves an impossibly wide range of institutions (contract law, company law, bankruptcy law, inheritance law, tax law, land law, urban planning regulations, etc.). But one observation that needs to be made is that the current emphasis on strong protection of property rights is misplaced, as sometimes the preservation of certain property rights proved harmful for economic development. There are many historical examples where the violation of certain existing property rights, and the creation of new property rights, were actually beneficial for economic development (British enclosure, squatting in the US Midwest in the nineteenth century, East Asian land reform, nationalization in postwar Austria and France).

So in this section I will briefly comment on the element of the property rights system that is most easily tractable, namely intellectual property rights institutions. As mentioned above, intellectual property rights institutions in the NDCs fell acutely short of modern standards until well into the twentieth century.

Corporate governance institutions

Our study shows that, even in the most developed countries (the United Kingdom and the United States), many key institutions of what is these days regarded as a "modern corporate governance" system emerged after, rather than before, their industrial development.

Until the 1860s or the 1870s, in most countries limited liability, without which there would be no modern corporations based on stock ownership, was something that was granted as a privilege to high-risk projects with good government connections (e.g. the British East India Company), and was not a standard thing. Until the 1930s, there was virtually no regulation on company audit and information disclosure. Until the late nineteenth century, bankruptcy laws were geared more toward punishing bankrupt businessmen (typically involving a spell in a debtors' prison!) than giving them a chance to have a new start. Competition law did not really exist in any country until the 1914 Clayton Act in the United States (there was the 1890 Sherman Act, but this was mainly used against trade unions until President Theodore Roosevelt used it against J.P. Morgan in 1902).

Financial institutions

Modern financial systems with widespread and well-supervised banking, a central bank, and a well-regulated securities market did not come into being even in the most developed countries until the mid-twentieth century. For example, until the early twentieth century, countries such as Sweden, Germany, Italy, Switzerland, and the United States lacked a central bank (see Table 6.3). In the case of the United States, its central banking system, the Federal Reserve System, was established in 1913, but as late as 1929, 65 per cent of the banks, accounting for 20 per cent of banking assets, were outside the System.

A similar story applies to public finance. The fiscal capacity of the state remained highly inadequate in most NDCs until the mid-twentieth century, when most of them did not have income tax. Before Britain introduced a permanent income tax in 1842, countries used it only as an emergency measure during wartime. Even in Britain, as late as 1874, Gladstone was

Table 6.3 Development of central banking in the NDCs

	Establishment	Note issue monopoly gained
Sweden	1688	1904
UK	1694	1844
France	1800	1848[1]
Netherlands	1814	post-1860s
Spain	1829	1874
Portugal	1847	1891[2]
Belgium	1851	1851
Germany	1871	1905
Italy	1893	1926
Switzerland	1907	1907
USA	1913	post-1929[3]

1. Controlled by the bankers themselves until 1936.
2. Legally note issue monopoly was established in 1887, but de facto monopoly was achieved only in 1891 due to the resistance of other note-issuing banks. The bank is still 100 per cent privately owned and cannot intervene in the money market.
3. 65 per cent of the banks, accounting for 20 per cent of banking assets, were outside the Federal Reserve System until 1929.

fighting his election campaign with a pledge to abolish income tax. Even Sweden, despite its later reputation as a high-income-tax country, did not have income tax until 1932.

With limited taxation capability, local government finance especially was in a mess in most countries. A particularly telling example is the defaults by a number of US state governments on British loans in 1842. After these defaults, the British financiers put pressure on the US federal government to assume the liabilities (which reminds us of the events in Brazil following the default of the state of Minas Gerais in 1999). When this pressure came to naught, *The Times* poured scorn on the US federal government's attempt to raise a new loan later in the year by arguing that "[t]he people of the United States may be fully persuaded that there is a certain class of securities to which no abundance of money, however great, can give value; and that in this class their own securities stand pre-eminent" (cited in Cochran and Miller 1942: 48).

Welfare and labor institutions

Social welfare institutions (e.g. industrial accident insurance, health insurance, state pension, unemployment insurance) did not emerge until the last few decades of the nineteenth century, although once introduced they diffused quite quickly.

Effective labor institutions (e.g. regulations on child labor, working hours, workplace safety) did not emerge until around the same time even in the most advanced countries. Child labor regulations started emerging in the late eighteenth or early nineteenth century, but until the late nineteenth century or the early twentieth century most of these regulations were extremely mild and poorly enforced. Until the early twentieth century, in most countries regulation of working hours or working conditions for adult male workers was considered unthinkable. For example, in 1905 the US Supreme Court declared in a famous case that a 10-hour act for the bakers introduced by New York state was unconstitutional because "it deprived the baker of the liberty of working as long as they wished" (cited in Garraty and Carnes 2000: 607).

Institutional development in developing countries then and now

One important conclusion that emerges from our historical examination is that it took the developed countries a long time to develop institutions in their earlier days of development. The reasons behind such slow progress are varied and many, but institutions typically took decades, and sometimes generations, to develop. Thus seen, the currently popular demand that developing countries should adopt "global standard" institutions right away, or after very short transition periods of between five and ten years, is unrealistic.

Another important point emerges when we compare the levels of institutional development in the NDCs in the earlier period and those in today's developing countries.

For example, in 1820 the United Kingdom was at a somewhat higher level of development than that of India today, but it did not even have many of the most "basic" institutions that India has – universal suffrage (it did not even have universal *male* suffrage), a central bank, income tax, generalized limited liability, a generalized bankruptcy law, a professional bureaucracy, meaningful securities regulations, and even minimal labor regulations (except for a couple of minimal and hardly enforced regulations on child labor).

For another example, in 1875 Italy was at a level of development comparable to that of Pakistan today. However, it did not have universal male suffrage, a professional bureaucracy, an even remotely independent and professional judiciary, a central bank with note issue monopoly, and competition law – institutions that Pakistan has had for decades (except for periodic disruptions in democracy due to military intervention, but even then suffrage, when allowed, has remained universal).

For still another example, in 1913 the United States was at a level of development similar to that of Mexico today, but its level of institutional development was well behind what we see in Mexico today. Women were still formally disenfranchised and blacks and other ethnic minorities were de facto disenfranchised in many parts of the country. It had been just over a decade since a federal bankruptcy law was legislated (1898) and it had been barely two decades since the country recognized foreigners' copyrights (1891). A (highly incomplete) central banking system and income tax literally had only just come into being (1913), and the establishment of a meaningful competition law (the Clayton Act) had to wait another year (1914). Also, there was no federal regulation on securities trading or on child labor, with what few state legislations that existed in these areas being of low quality and very poorly enforced.

This kind of comparison can go on, but it seems clear that the developed countries in earlier times were institutionally *less advanced* than today's developing countries at similar stages of development, not to speak of the even higher "global standards" that the latter countries are forced to conform to these days.

Lessons for the Present

So what lessons can we draw from these historical examinations?

Rethinking economic policies for development

In relation to economic policies, the picture seems clear. When they were trying to catch up with the frontier economies, the NDCs used interventionist industrial, trade, and technology policies in order to promote their infant industries. The forms of these policies and the emphases among them may have been different across countries, but there is no denying that they actively used such policies. And, in relative terms (that is, taking into account the productivity gap with the more advanced countries), many of them actually protected their industries a lot more heavily than the currently developing countries have done.

If this is the case, the currently recommended package of "good policies," emphasizing the benefits of free trade and other laissez-faire ITT policies, seems at odds with historical experience, and the NDCs seem to be genuinely "kicking away the ladder."

The only possible way for the developed countries to counter this accusation of "ladder-kicking" will be to argue that the activist ITT policies that they had pursued used to be beneficial for economic development but are not so any more, because "times have changed." Apart from the paucity of convincing reasons why this may be the case, the poor growth records of the developing countries over the last two decades makes this line of defense simply untenable. It depends on the data we use, but roughly speaking per capita income in developing countries used to grow at 3 per cent per year between 1960 and 1980, but has grown only at about 1.5 per cent between 1980 and 2000. And it will be much lower than 1.5 per cent if we take out India and China, which have *not* pursued liberal ITT policies recommended by the developed countries.

So the neoliberal economist is faced with a "paradox" here. The developing countries grew much faster when they used "bad" policies during 1960–80 than when they used "good" (at least "better") policies during the following two decades. The obvious solution to this "paradox" is to accept that the supposedly "good" policies are actually *not* good for the developing countries and that the "bad" policies are actually good for them. The more interesting point is that these "bad" policies are also the ones that the NDCs had pursued when they were developing countries themselves.

Given these facts, we can only conclude that, in recommending the allegedly "good" policies, the NDCs are in effect "kicking away the ladder" by which they have climbed to the top beyond the reach of the developing countries.

Rethinking institutional development

When it comes to institutional development, the picture is much more complex than that for ITT policies, but the following may be said.

Most of the institutions that are currently recommended to the developing countries as parts of the "good governance" package were the results, rather than the causes, of economic development of the NDCs in earlier times. In this sense, it is not clear how many of them are indeed "necessary" for today's developing countries – so necessary, in the view of the IDPE, that they have to be imposed on these countries through strong bilateral and multilateral external pressures.

Moreover, even when we agree that certain institutions are "good" or even "necessary," we have to be careful in specifying their exact shapes. For just about every institution, there is a debate on what exact form it should take, and therefore the currently dominant view that there is only one set of "best practice" institutions (which usually, although not always, means Anglo-American institutions) that everyone has to adopt is highly problematic.

Arguing that many of the institutions currently recommended by the "good governance" discourse may not be necessary, or even beneficial, for the currently developing countries, however, should not be interpreted as saying that institutions do not matter or that developing countries do not need improvements in their institutions. On the contrary. Historically, improvements in the quality of institutions seem to have been associated with better growth performance, and we can easily support this with historical and contemporary evidence.

Annual per capita income growth rate among the eleven NDCs for which data are available during 1820–75 ranged between 0.6 per cent (Italy) and 2 per cent (Australia), with the unweighted average and the median values both at 1.1 per cent. Between 1875 and 1913, per capita income growth rates ranged between 0.6 per cent (Australia) and 2.4 per cent (Canada), with the unweighted average at 1.7 per cent and the median at 1.4 per cent. Given that the NDCs have seen a significant development in their institutions since the mid-nineteenth century, it is very plausible that at least a part of this growth acceleration was due to the improvements in the quality of their institutions.

The vastly superior economic performance of the NDCs during the so-called "golden age" of capitalism (1950–73) compared to those of the periods before or after it also highlights the importance of institutions in generating economic growth and stability. During the golden age, the NDCs typically grew at 3–4 per cent per annum in per capita terms, in contrast to the 1–2 per cent rate that had prevailed before it and also in contrast to the 2–2.5 per cent rate that has been typical since its end. Most commentators attribute the golden age in the NDCs to the institutional changes that were made following the Second World War, such as activist (Keynesian) budgetary institutions, a full-fledged welfare state, stricter financial market regulations, corporatist wage bargaining institutions, institutions of investment coordination, and in some cases nationalized industries (especially France and Austria).

The comparison of growth performance in the NDCs in earlier times with that of the developing countries during the postwar period also provides us with some important insights into the relationship between policies, institutions, and economic growth. Today's developing countries could grow faster in the early postwar period (1960–80) than the NDCs had done at comparable stages of development partly because they had much better institutions than the latter countries. During the 1960–80 period, in per capita terms, today's developing countries grew at about 3 per cent per annum. This is a growth performance that is far superior to what the NDCs managed during their "century of development" (1820–1913), when the average growth rates in the NDCs were around 1–1.5 per cent per annum.

All the above suggests that improving the quality of their institutions is an important task for the developing countries. However, two qualifications need to be made in relation to this statement. First of all, as argued earlier, in pushing for institutional improvement in developing countries, we should accept that it is a lengthy process and be more "patient" with the process, especially given that today's developing countries are already institutionally more advanced than the NDCs at comparable stages of development. The second qualification is that "good" institutions produce growth only when they are combined with "good" policies (good in my sense). The fact is that despite the continuous and presumably accelerating improvements in the quality of their institutions, today's developing countries have experienced marked slowdowns in growth during the last two decades. In my view, this was because the ability of the currently developing countries to pursue the (genuinely) "good" policies has been significantly curtailed due to the "policy reforms" during this period.

Possible objections

At least three objections can be raised against my argument. I examine them in turn. The first, and most obvious, objection is the argument that developing countries need to adopt the policies and institutions recommended by developed countries whether they like them or not, because that is how the world is – the strong calling the shots. At one level, it is difficult to deny the force of this argument. Indeed, my discussion on the "pulling away" tactics used by the NDCs in earlier times (e.g. colonialism, unequal treaties, bans on machinery exports) provides ample support for this argument. And even in the present age when colonialism and unequal treaties are not acceptable any more, the developed countries can exercise enormous influence on the developing countries through aid budgets and trade policies, as well as their influence on various international organizations.

However, at another level, this argument is beside the point. What I am arguing is precisely that these "new rules" should be changed. I do agree that the chance of these rules being changed in the near future is very low, but this does not mean that therefore it is not worth discussing how they should be changed.

The second possible objection to my argument is that the policies and institutions recommended to the developing countries have to be adopted because they are what the international investors want. It is not relevant, it may be argued, whether the developing countries like these "new rules" or not or even whether the IDPE is willing to change them, because in this globalized age international investors are those who are calling the shots. However, there are some serious problems with this argument. First, it is not clear whether international investors do necessarily care so much about the policies and institutions promoted by the IDPE. The massive inflow of foreign investments into China, despite its highly "deficient" policies and institutions, is a good example. Second, while increased conformity to international standards may increase foreign investment, increased foreign investment does not always bring net benefits. Third, even if certain "good" institutions get introduced under global pressure, they may not deliver the expected results, unless they can be effectively enforced. Fourth, contrary to the "follow the global norm or perish" argument, which assumes that the process of institutional evolution is beyond anyone's control, the donor governments and the IFIs are not weather vanes blindly following the winds of international investor sentiments, but they can, and do, actively decide to a large extent which institutions they push for and how strongly.

The third possible objection to my argument, which particularly concerns the issue of institutional development, is that the "world standard" in institutions has risen over the last century or so, and therefore that the current developing countries should not consider the NDCs of 100 or 150 years ago as their models. I wholeheartedly agree with this proposition. At one level, it is absurd to argue otherwise. Indeed the heightened global standard in institutions has been a good thing in many ways for the developing countries, or at least for the reformers in them. Unlike their counterparts in the NDCs of yesterday, the reformers in today's developing countries don't have to struggle (at least too hard) with the view that the introduction of things like female suffrage, income tax, restrictions on working hours, and social welfare institutions spells the end of civilization as we know it. They also don't have to reinvent certain institutions like central banking and limited liability, the logic behind which many people in the NDCs in earlier times had found difficult to understand. Therefore the developing countries should exploit to the maximum these advantages of being a latecomer and try to achieve the highest level of institutional development possible. What I am worried about, however, is the view that institutions are simply matters of choice and therefore all countries should try to reach the (quite high-set) "minimum global standard" right away or after a minimal transition period. While accepting that latecomer countries do not have to spend as much time as the pioneer countries had done in developing institutions (as they can import and assimilate, rather than invent, them), we should not forget that it took the NDCs typically decades, and sometimes even generations, to establish certain institutions whose need had already been perceived. In addition, we should not forget that, when compared to the NDCs in earlier times, today's developing countries *already* have high standards of institutional development.

Concluding Remarks

So back to the original question. Are the developed countries trying to "kick away the ladder" beyond the reach of the developing countries by insisting that the latter countries adopt policies and institutions that are *not* the ones that they had used in order to develop, but the ones that are beneficial for the developed countries themselves? The discussion in this chapter, and in my book, suggests that indeed they are.

I do accept that this "ladder-kicking" may be done genuinely out of (misinformed) goodwill. Some of those NDC policymakers and scholars who make the recommendations may genuinely believe that their own countries had developed through free trade and other laissez-faire policies and want the developing countries to benefit from the same policies. However, this makes it no less harmful for the developing countries. Indeed, it may be even more dangerous than "ladder-kicking" based on naked national interest, as self-righteousness can be a lot more stubborn than self-interest.

Whatever the intention is behind the "ladder-kicking," the fact remains that these allegedly "good" policies and institutions have not been able to generate the promised growth dynamism in the developing countries during the last two decades or so, when these policies and institutions have been strongly pushed by the IDPE. Indeed, in many developing countries growth has simply collapsed.

So what is to be done? While spelling out a detailed agenda for action is beyond the scope of this chapter, the following points may be made.

To begin with, the historical facts about the developmental experiences of the developed countries should be more widely publicized. This is not just a matter of "getting history right," but also of allowing the developing countries to make informed choices about policies and institutions that are appropriate for them.

In terms of policies, first of all, I would argue that policy-related conditionalities attached to financial assistance from the IMF and the World Bank or from the donor governments should be radically changed. These conditionalities should be based on the recognition that many of the policies that are considered "bad" are in fact not, and that there can be no "best practice" policy that everyone should use. Second, the WTO rules and other multilateral trade agreements should be rewritten in such a way that a more active use of infant industry promotion tools (e.g. tariffs, subsidies) is allowed.

In terms of institutions, their improvements should be encouraged, especially given the enormous growth potential that a combination of (truly) good policies and good institutions can bring about. However, this should not be equated with imposing a fixed set of (in practice, today's – not even yesterday's – Anglo-American) institutions on all countries. There also need to be more serious attempts to explore exactly which institutions are necessary, or at least beneficial, for what types of countries, given their stages of development and their economic, political, social, and even cultural conditions. Special care has to be taken in order not to demand excessively rapid upgrading of institutions by the developing countries, especially given that they already have quite developed institutions when compared to the NDCs at comparable stages of development, and given that establishing and running new institutions is costly.

Allowing the developing countries to adopt the policies and institutions that are more suitable to their stages of development and to other conditions they face will enable them to grow faster, as indeed it had done during the 1960s and the 1970s. This will benefit not only the developing countries but also the developed countries in the long run, as it will increase the trade and investment opportunities available to the developed countries in the developing countries. That the developed countries are not able to see this is the tragedy of our time. To use a classic Chinese adage, they may be "missing larger, longer-term gains by too eagerly seeking smaller, short-term ones." It is time to think again which policies and institutions will help the developing countries develop faster, which in the end will bring greater benefits to the developed countries as well.

Notes

1. Cobden argued:

The factory system would, in all probability, not have taken place in America and Germany. It most certainly could not have flourished, as it has done, both in these states, and in France, Belgium, and Switzerland, through the fostering bounties which the high-priced food of the British artisan has offered to the cheaper fed manufacturer of those countries. (cited in Reinert 1998: 292)

2. In his *Wealth of Nations*, Adam Smith wrote:

Were the Americans, either by combination or by any other sort of violence, to stop the importation of European manufactures, and, by thus giving a monopoly to such of their own countrymen as could manufacture the like goods, divert any considerable part of their capital into this employment, they would retard instead of accelerating the further increase in the value of their annual produce, and would obstruct instead of promoting the progress of their country towards real wealth and greatness. (Smith 1973: 347–8)

3. Lincoln thought the blacks racially inferior, was against giving them votes, and thought abolition of slavery an unrealistic proposition. In response to a newspaper editorial urging immediate slave emancipation, Lincoln wrote: "If I could save the

Union without freeing any slave, I would do it; and if I could save it by freeing all the slaves, I would do it; and if I could do it by freeing some and leaving others alone, I would also do that" (Garraty and Carnes 2000: 405).

4. I am grateful to Duncan Green for drawing my attention to this passage. Unfortunately, this happened only after *Kicking Away the Ladder* went to the printers, so this quotation does not appear in the book.

5. They are Austria, Belgium, Denmark, France, Germany, Italy, the Netherlands, Spain, Sweden, Switzerland, the United Kingdom, and the United States.

7

The TRIPS Agreement and Transfer of Technology

Carlos M. Correa

Ten years have elapsed since the adoption of the Agreement on Trade-Related Aspects of Intellectual Property Rights (TRIPS). Though its application in developing countries has only been mandatory since 2000, the Agreement has become one of the most controversial elements in the WTO system, particularly due to its broad implications in the area of public health and for the appropriation of biological resources.[1]

Developed countries prompted the negotiation of the TRIPS Agreement on the argument that an expanded and strengthened protection of IPRs would bring about increased flows of foreign direct investment (FDI) and technology transfer to developing countries, and that changes in IPRs would also stimulate local innovation. Even before the Agreement came into force, serious doubts about the extent to which such positive effects would take place were raised (see, e.g., Correa 1999).

Fears that the increased protection given to IPRs will not effectively promote the development process but will instead limit access to technology have been voiced by many developing countries. The North–South technological gap continues unabated and is likely to have grown since the adoption of the Agreement, except for those countries (such as South Korea) that have substantially enhanced their technological capacities on the basis of a significant domestic effort in research and development (Lall and Albaladejo 2002).

Many leading scholars and institutions have found those concerns justified and called for a fundamental rethinking of the IPR system from a North–South perspective soon after the adoption of the TRIPS Agreement. For Harvard economist Sachs, the global regime on intellectual property rights requires a new look. The United States prevailed upon the world to toughen patent codes and cut down on intellectual piracy. But now transnational corporations and rich-country institutions are patenting everything from the human genome to rainforest biodiversity. The poor will be ripped off unless some sense and equity are introduced into this runaway process. (Sachs 1999)

A similar view was expressed by Professor Barton (Stanford University), who noted that "the risk that intellectual property rights slow the movement of technological capability to developing nations, suggests that harmonization efforts might most wisely consider one common standard for developed nations and a different one for developing nations" (Barton 1999: 15). The UNDP *Human Development Report 1999* also stated that

The relentless march of intellectual property rights needs to be stopped and questioned. Developments in the new technologies are running far ahead of the ethical, legal, regulatory and policy frameworks needed to govern their use. More understanding is needed – in every country – of the economic and social consequences of the TRIPS Agreement. Many people have started to question the relationship between knowledge ownership and innovation. Alternative approaches to innovation, based on sharing, open access and communal innovation, are flourishing, disproving the claim that innovation necessarily requires patents. (UNDP 1999: 73)

This chapter examines the background and objectives of some WTO Member countries' proposals for review of the TRIPS Agreement, in particular as they relate to developing countries' concerns about transfer of technology.

Proposals for Review

Several proposals have been submitted to review the Agreement. Some of them belong to the "in-built agenda" (UNCTAD 1999b), such as issues relating to geographical indications (Article 23.4) and the patentability of biological inventions (Article 27.3(b)). Other proposals go beyond such limited review and suggest more substantive changes to the Agreement. Despite the broad coverage of the Agreement, patents and geographical indications are the only areas for which amendments have been suggested by developing countries – in the latter case with the aim of expanding rather than reducing protection.

Developed countries

Despite the criticism of the unequal impact of the elevation of standards of IPR protection, in the years following the adoption of the TRIPS Agreement, developed countries showed the desire to build thereon to obtain even higher standards of protection.[2] Thus the European Community (EC) pointed out that the TRIPS Agreement would not be the end of demands for increasing levels of IPR protection:

> It should of course be kept in mind that the TRIPS *acquis* is a basis from which to seek further improvements in the protection of IPR. There should therefore be no question, in future negotiations, of lowering of standards or granting of further transitional periods. (WGC 1999d)

For Japan, implementation of the Agreement was a priority, but discussions on new standards would have to continue:

> first and foremost, every Member should ensure the full implementation of the TRIPS Agreement and effective operation of the domestic legislation.... We should not discuss the TRIPS Agreement with a view to reducing the current level of protection of intellectual property rights. To the contrary, the TRIPS Agreement should be improved properly in line with new technological development and social needs. (WGC 1999f)

These statements illustrate that developed countries did not consider the TRIPS Agreement the end point of a process of strengthening and expansion of IPR protection. After the success achieved in GATT, they strategically moved back to the World Intellectual Property Organization (WIPO) – which was deemed a less effective organization when IPR issues were brought to GATT in 1986 – and, in a short period of time, they engineered two new international conventions (WIPO Copyright Treaty and WIPO Performance and Phonograms Treaty), while failing in their attempt to get agreement on a third one.[3]

The WIPO Copyright Treaty (1996) reconfirmed the provisions of the TRIPS Agreement on copyright, but its basic objective was to include new standards relevant to the generation and use of works in a digital environment. It introduced a "right of distribution" (Article 6) and the "right of communication to the public," including when "members of the public may access these works from a place and at a time individually chosen by them" (Article 8). It also prohibited conduct aimed at circumventing the technological protection of works. The WIPO Performance and Phonograms Treaty (1996) strengthened the protection available under the TRIPS Agreement with regard to the moral and rental rights of performers. It also improved the protection for phonogram producers (Reinbothe et al. 1997).

The United States and the European Union were quick to propose the absorption by the TRIPS Agreement of these WIPO treaties.[4] Japan also preferred that the TRIPS Agreement "deal with higher protection of intellectual property rights which has been achieved in other treaties or conventions in other fora appropriately," an obvious reference to the 1996 WIPO Treaties (WGC 1999f).[5]

The possibility of transferring the results achieved in WIPO to the TRIPS Agreement gave WIPO the opportunity to regain part of its lost role in the development of new international standards on IPRs. Such an opportunity also raised strategic issues for developing countries. Negotiations in WIPO are generally conducted without a quid pro quo concept: that is, there is no broad negotiating package within which to ask for concessions in other areas (as typically occurs in the framework of the WTO) as a "price" for the concessions given in IPRs. The organizations that represent the interest of corporate IPR holders are active in WIPO and are able to influence the negotiations. In addition, the WIPO Secretariat considers as its normal function the promotion of increased levels of IPR protection and is more activist than its WTO counterpart (see Musungu and Dutfield 2004.)

In the context of the mandated review of Article 27.3(b), the United States and the European Communities also made proposals for the substitution of the general concept of "effective *sui generis* regime" contained in that article for a specific obligation to comply with UPOV 1991.[6] Developing countries, however, have consistently opposed any attempt to limit the flexibility offered by the loose "*sui generis*" concept.

Whatever the merits of the WIPO Treaties[7] and of UPOV,[8] the reformist attempts in the WTO by developed countries cooled down. This was probably associated with the growing controversy that emerged around the effects of the TRIPS Agreement on public health and with the offensive that developing countries launched to obtain recognition of the flexibility incorporated into the Agreement, which concluded with the adoption of the Doha Ministerial Declaration on the TRIPS Agreement and Public Health (hereinafter the Doha Declaration) (WMC 2001).

Some contentious North–North issues also arose as candidates for a possible review of the TRIPS Agreement. The EC and Japan addressed the issue of the "first-to file" versus the "first-to-invent" systems for patent application. This latter system, practiced only in the United States, is claimed to burden inventors, particularly foreign applicants, the majority of whom are of European and Japanese origin. According to the EC, this issue was "left aside because of lack of consensus at the end of the Uruguay Round" (WGC 1998a). Japan also requested that the introduction of "an early publication system of filed patent applications" be considered.[9]

Developing countries

Developing countries have voiced the need to make the TRIPS Agreement more balanced with regard to the promotion of intellectual property rights, on the one hand, and the realization of development objectives, on the other (see WGC 1999h). One of the important goals of those countries has been to operationalize Article 7 (Objectives) and Article 8 (Principles) of the Agreement (see WGC 1998b). However, little progress has been made on this general front.

With the adoption of the Doha Declaration, these countries were successful in confirming the interpretation of a number of flexibilities present in the TRIPS Agreement (Correa 2002). They have also made some specific proposals for the review of substantive aspects of the TRIPS Agreement despite the fear that, given the power asymmetries and the way in which decisions are reached in the WTO, a possible reopening of the Agreement might allow developed countries to push for and impose higher standards of protection in certain areas.

Exceptions to patentability

Some proposals relating to exclusions from patentability have been submitted. Venezuela has advocated the exclusion of essential drugs as listed by the World Health Organization (WGC 1999j). In the context of the so far unproductive review of Article 27.3(b), the African Group proposed to exclude from patentability living matter. The Group held that

> There is lack of clarity on the criteria/rationale used to decide what can and cannot be excluded from patentability in Article 27.3(b). This relates to the artificial distinction made between plants and animals (which may be excluded) and micro-organisms (which may not be excluded); and also between "essentially biological" processes for making plants and animals (which may be excluded) and microbiological processes.
>
> By stipulating compulsory patenting of micro-organisms (which are natural living things) and microbiological processes (which are natural processes), the provisions of Article 27.3 contravene the basic tenets on which patent laws are based: that substances and processes that exist in nature are a discovery and not an invention and thus are not patentable. Moreover, by giving Members the option whether or not to exclude the patentability of plants and animals, Article 27.3(b) allows for life forms to be patented. (WGC 1999j)

Based on these and other considerations, the African Group proposed that the review process clarify that plants and animals, as well as micro-organisms and all other living organisms and their parts, cannot be patented, and that natural processes that produce plants, animals, and other living organisms should also be unpatentable. This Group has also suggested the incorporation (after the sentence on plant variety protection in Article 27.3(b)) of a footnote stating that any *sui generis* law for plant variety protection can provide for:

(i) the protection of the innovations of indigenous and local farming communities in developing countries, consistent with the Convention on Biological Diversity and the International Undertaking on Plant Genetic Resources;

(ii) the continuation of the traditional farming practices including the right to save, exchange and save seeds, and sell their harvest;

(iii) preventing anti-competitive rights or practices which will threaten food sovereignty of people in developing countries, as is permitted by Article 31 of the TRIPS Agreement. (WGC 1999j)

Finally, for the purposes of achieving the harmonization of the TRIPS Agreement with the Convention on Biological Diversity (CBD), India has proposed the incorporation of a provision establishing that patents inconsistent with Article 15 of the CBD must not be granted (WGC 1999h).

These proposals were never formally considered; they would have certainly found fierce opposition from the US pharmaceuticals industry and government, as illustrated by their position against the much less radical proposals for a waiver to allow the supply of drugs to countries without manufacturing capacity in pharmaceuticals (see WGC 2003).

Geographical indications

Another front of negotiations was opened by developing countries in relation to geographical indications in the context of Article 24.2 of the TRIPS Agreement. Unlike other issues, this one has been divisive among the developing countries themselves.

Some developing countries have sought the expansion of the product areas that can benefit from the higher level of protection presently required under the TRIPS Agreement for wines and spirits to include other agricultural and handicraft products, such as rice, tea, beer, and so on (Vandoren 1999: 30). A distinct advantage of such protection is that there is no need to prove unfair commercial practices or that the public has been misled (as is the case under Article 22). Any person or entity that does not produce within the territory alluded to by a geographical indication could be prevented from using the corresponding denomination. This, of course, greatly facilitates the enforcement of rights, though right holders must still face the substantial costs that litigation in the intellectual property area generally entails. A further advantage of that "absolute" protection is that it would permit ex officio action by WTO Members against false indications of origin, thus reducing the cost of protection in foreign markets.

Egypt proposed that the additional protection conferred for geographical indications for wines and spirits (Article 23.1) be extended to other products,

Table 7.1 Arguments for and against increased protection to products other than wines and spirits

For increased protection	Against increased protection
(a) additional protection of geographical indications for all products adds value for exports because it increases the chances of market access for such goods;	(a) the legal and administrative costs associated with extending the scope of Article 23.1 would be significant;
(b) without the additional protection, free-riding (unauthorized use by third parties) is possible and there is a risk that geographical indications will become generic over time;	(b) there is no evidence of failure of Article 22 to protect geographical indications for products other than wines and spirits;
(c) the test contained in Article 22, which currently applies to products other than wines and spirits, leads to legal uncertainty in the enforcement of protection for geographical indications;	(c) there is no evidence to indicate whether extending the scope of Article 23.1 to products other than wine and spirits would result in more effective protection than is already afforded to those products under Article 22;
(d) Article 22 places a costly burden of proof on the producer entitled to use a geographical indication to show that the public has been misled, or that there has been an act of unfair competition.	(d) additional protection could close off future market access opportunities for emerging industries and result in uncertainty concerning the continued use in existing markets;
	(d) consumer confusion would be caused through the disappearance of terms customarily used to identify products, which will, in turn, increase transaction costs for consumers and potentially prices as well.

Source: De Sousa 2001: 8–9.

particularly those of interest to developing countries (WGC 1999e). This idea was supported by a number of developing countries, such as Cuba, the Dominican Republic, Honduras, Indonesia, Nicaragua, and Pakistan (WGC 1999c), the African Group (WGC 1999j), and Venezuela (WGC 1999i).

The Indian delegation elaborated on this issue. It argued that

it is an anomaly that the higher level of protection is available only for – wines and spirits. It is proposed that such higher level of protection should be available for goods other than wines and spirits also. This would be helpful for products of export interest like basmati rice, Darjeeling tea, alphonso mangoes, Kohlapuri slippers in the case of India. It is India's belief that there are other Members of the WTO who would be interested in higher level of protection to products of export interest to them like Bulgarian yoghurt, Czech Pilsen beer, many agricultural products of the European Union, Hungarian Szatmar plums and so on. There is a need to expedite work already initiated in the TRIPS Council in this regard, under Article 24, so that benefits arising out of the TRIPS Agreement in this area are spread out wider. (WGC 1999g)

Turkey (WGC 1999b) and the Czech Republic have also joined the demand for additional protection for specific foodstuffs and handicraft products and, particularly in the case of the latter, "for beers which are particularly vulnerable to imitation, counterfeit and usurpation and whose protection of such indications against consumer deception is insufficient and trademark protection is not satisfactory due to its formal requirements such as registration and the use requirement" (WGC 1999a).

However, the proposal to increase the protection of geographical indications has been opposed by many developing (notably Argentina) and developed (e.g. Australia and the United States) countries. Table 7.1 summarizes the arguments for and against the reform.

The outstanding differences on this issue are deep and unlikely to be easily overcome in the short term. While some developing countries expect to benefit from the extension of protection, if it occurred, European countries (including Switzerland) that are in possession of a large number of geographical indications[10] may ultimately benefit the most. There are also fears that geographical indications might be used as a substitute for other protectionist measures that developed countries apply in agriculture.

Disclosure of origin[11]

Several WTO Members[12] have made submissions discussing the possible introduction into the TRIPS Agreement of a requirement to disclose the origin of biological materials (and the associated knowledge) claimed in patent applications. According to some proposals, such an obligation should include information not only about origin but also about compliance with national access laws, as well as benefit-sharing under relevant national regimes (WCTRIPS 2002c: para. 10).

The disclosure of origin obligation may help address the problem of "biopiracy" of biological materials and traditional knowledge (TK), and constitute a first step in the development of a misappropriation regime for TK. The disclosure of origin may fulfill three main functions relevant for the operation of the patent system. It would improve:

1. the substantive examination of patent applications involving biological materials and knowledge by facilitating the determination of prior art and simplifying searches with the databases on TK currently being established;
2. the determination of inventorship by the patent office or courts;
3. the disclosure of knowledge needed for the actual execution of the

invention, such as where a biological material is endemic to a specific location.

In addition, a disclosure obligation may have a significant role outside the patent system, notably to promote compliance with access legislation, where applicable, and to keep track of the commercial exploitation of such materials for the purposes of benefit-sharing.

The discussions on this issue still lack precision about the scope of the obligation to be established. The terminology used in different proposals varies: "country of origin"; "origin of genetic resources"; "source and country of origin"; "sources of any biological material"; "geographic origin"; "source of origin"; "source of a specific genetic resource" (WCTRIPS 2000a: 16; WCTRIPS 2000b; WCTRIPS 2002c: para 10; WCTRIPS 2003c: para. II (c); WCTRIPS 2002a: para. 54; WCTRIPS 2003b: para. 5,10; WCTRIPS 2003a). It should be recalled, in this regard, that the "country of origin" of genetic resources has a specific meaning according to the CBD[13] and that, although in some cases biological materials are directly obtained from the countries of origin, they are often supplied by sources that conserve such materials in *ex situ* conditions (such as in gene banks). Moreover, the determination of the "country of origin" of a biological material may sometimes be difficult or impossible, particularly in the case of plant varieties that have acquired distinctive characteristics in different countries.

All the submissions to the Council for TRIPS on this subject suggest that the disclosure obligation should encompass biological "materials" or "resources" *and* the associated *traditional knowledge*. In addition, developing countries propose that the obligation include information about compliance with prior informed consent and evidence of fair and equitable benefit sharing under the relevant national regimes (WCTRIPS 2002c: para 10).

The submissions so far made (with the exception of the Swiss proposal mentioned below) are broadly worded with regard to the relationship between the biological material used and the invention. Cases where the use of a biological material in an invention would trigger the disclosure requirement are an issue to be carefully addressed.

Another important issue relates to the consequences of the failure to comply with an obligation to disclose the origin (including the intentional submission of false information). Some proposals suggest the rejection of the application, the invalidation of the patent, or its non-enforceability as determined, for instance, under the doctrine of "inequitable conduct" in the United States (WCTRIPS 2003b: para. 14). In contrast, the EC and its member states have held that failure to disclose or the submission of false information should not stand in the way of granting the patent, and should have no effect on the validity of the patent once it is granted (see WCTRIPS 2002a: para. 55).

The incorporation of a disclosure of origin obligation would require a modification of the TRIPS Agreement in the context of Article 29.[14] As noted by the African Group,

> compared to other alternatives, Article 29 of the TRIPS Agreement seems to be the most suitable for an appropriate modification to contain these rights and obligations by including the requirements for equity, disclosure of the community of origin of the genetic resources and traditional knowledge, and a demonstration of compliance with applicable domestic procedures. (WCTRIPS 2003c: para. III (D))

The issue of disclosure of the origin of biological materials and associated TK has also arisen in discussions of Article 2 of the Draft Substantive Patent Law Treaty (SPLT) and in the Working Group on Patent Cooperation Treaty (PCT) Reform. The Swiss delegation presented a proposal[15] to allow PCT members to require such a disclosure at the national level in line with a submission on the matter made to the Council for TRIPS (WCTRIPS 2003a: n5).

Supply of drugs to countries without pharmaceuticals manufacturing capacity

An important development that may lead to an amendment of the TRIPS Agreement relates to the implementation of paragraph 6 of the Doha Declaration, which instructed the Council for TRIPS to address how WTO Members lacking or with insufficient manufacturing capacity in pharmaceuticals can make effective use of compulsory licensing. An agreement to address this problem was reached after considerable debate on 30 August 2003 (see WGC 2003, hereinafter "the Decision"), based on a compromise developed by the chair of the TRIPS Council and on a "Statement" by the chair of the General Council that "represents several key shared understandings of Members regarding the Decision to be taken and the way in which it will be interpreted and implemented" (see WGC 2003).

The Decision of the General Council implements *interim waivers* with regard to the obligations set out in paragraphs (f) and (h) of Article 31 of the TRIPS Agreement. The Council for TRIPS shall review annually the functioning of the system set out in this Decision "with a view to ensuring its effective operation and shall annually report on its operation to the General Council." These waivers shall terminate on the date on which an amendment to the TRIPS Agreement replacing its provisions takes effect for a Member.[16] The TRIPS Council was mandated to initiate, by the end of 2003, work on the preparation of such an amendment with a view to its adoption within six months, "on the understanding that the amendment will be based, where appropriate, on this Decision" (paragraph 11).

Transfer of technology

Developing countries have also voiced their concerns in relation to access to technology, which they feel is increasingly difficult to obtain from commercial sources. Such concerns are justified: while developing countries have been required to expand and enhance their intellectual property regimes, there is very little in the WTO agreements to facilitate effectively and promote access to technology. The distribution of capabilities to generate science and technology gives rise, in fact, to the most dramatic North–South asymmetry. World R&D expenditures are very unevenly distributed between developed and developing countries (UNDP 1999). These expenditures are increasingly concentrated in a few countries and firms and, though the apparent "globalization" of R&D activities has created some expectations as to the transfer of R&D capabilities to developing countries, decentralization of R&D is mainly taking place in other developed countries (Callan et al. 1997).

In addition, large firms from developed countries have been able to develop a complex network of technological cooperation through "strategic alliances" that further enhance their dominant role in technology generation and use (Chesnais 1996).

As developing countries reach higher levels of technological development, they have a more sophisticated demand for technologies that have not yet reached the "mature" stage. Unlike mature technologies, which are relatively easy to acquire, technology that is still changing and profitable is increasingly difficult to obtain (Correa 1994). A decline in the importance of contractual or non-equity modes of technology transfer has been observed in several studies (Kumar 1997). Internalized forms of technology transfer (i.e. those taking place intra-firm) are more likely to be preferred by technology holders when the technology changes rapidly and when potential recipients may pose competitive threats in world markets as future competitors (Lall 1992a: 4–6; UN/TCMD 1992: 154–5).

Some of these problems were reflected in submissions made by developing countries in the preparatory process of the WTO Seattle Ministerial Conference. In the most elaborate submission on this matter, India noted the relative decline in arm's length licensing of technology and the preference of technology suppliers for internalized forms of transfer.[17] It stated that

> One of the important objectives of the WTO Agreement, as mentioned in its preamble, is the need for positive efforts designed to ensure that developing countries secure a share in the growth in international trade commensurate with the needs of their economic development. However, the TRIPS Agreement in its current form might tempt IPR holders to charge exorbitant and commercially unviable prices for transfer or dissemination of technologies held through such IPRs. It is important, therefore, to build disciplines for effective transfer of technology at fair

and reasonable costs to developing countries so as to harmonize the objectives of the WTO Agreement and the TRIPS Agreement. (WGC 1999g)

India has, more generally, noted the difficulties faced by developing countries in obtaining access to foreign technology and has indicated the need to address that issue under the several provisions of the TRIPS Agreement, such as articles 7, 8, 30, 31, 40, 66.2, and 67.[18] It has argued that

> prospective technology seekers in developing countries face serious difficulties in their commercial dealings with technology holders in the developed countries. These difficulties are basically of three kinds: those which arise from the imperfections of the market for technology; those attributable to the relative lack of experience and skill of enterprises and institutions in developing countries in concluding adequate legal arrangements for the acquisition of technology; and those government practices, both legislative and administrative, in both developed and developing countries, which influence the implementation of national policies and procedures designed to encourage the flow of technology to, and its acquisition by, developing countries ... In addition, the transfer and dissemination needs of the developing countries have to be seen from the point of view of the capacity of those in need of accessing technologies, particularly where the cost of technology may be prohibitive due to economies of scale and other reasons. In such cases, in order to implement the related provisions of the TRIPS Agreement, commercially viable mechanisms need to be found.
>
> The high cost of technology makes it difficult for the smaller, poorer developing countries to acquire appropriate technology on commercial terms. Such countries may be able to acquire appropriate technology critically needed for their development only through government to government negotiations and with the financial assistance provided by government and other institutions in developed countries or inter-governmental organizations. For those enterprises and institutions in developing countries, which will not have the benefit of external financing, the acquisition of appropriate technology on international commercial terms will impose a burden on the local economy unless the price of the technology can be brought within manageable limits.
>
> The denial of dual-use technologies, even on a commercial basis, to developing countries is another aspect that leads to widening of the technology gap between developed and developing countries. Under this guise a variety of technologies and products are being denied to developing countries which could otherwise have helped to accelerate their growth process. This issue needs to be carefully examined and seriously dealt with as a trade distorting and restrictive measure. (WGC 1999g)

As a result of this analysis, India concluded that "the TRIPS Agreement may be reviewed to consider ways and means to operationalize the objective and principles in respect of transfer and dissemination of technology to developing countries, particularly the least developed amongst them" (WGC 1999g).

Upon demand by developing countries, the WTO Doha Ministerial Conference (2001) established a Working Group on Trade and Transfer of

Technology. Developing countries noted at the Working Group that most provisions in WTO agreements relating to transfer of technology were of "best endeavour" nature rather than binding obligations and that they should be made operational. Developed countries, however, have argued that the WTO provisions were underpinned by several priorities such as integrating countries into world trade, protecting IPRs, increasing the flow of investment, and promoting sustainable development. They also observed that some of these provisions identified technical assistance, training, provision of information and other forms of developmental cooperation as the principal means of promoting Transfer of Technology (TOT). They were reluctant to introduce any negotiating aspect into the Working Group (see WGTTT 2003).

A communication by a group of countries to the Working Group identified the following agreements as having an influence on transfer of technology: the TRIPS Agreement, the Agreement on the application of Sanitary and Phytosanitary (SPS) Measures, the Agreement on Technical Barriers to Trade (TBT), the General Agreement on Trade in Services (GATS), the GATS Annex on Telecommunications, and the Agreement on Subsidies and Countervailing Measures (SCM) (WGTTT 2002). As the TRIPS Agreement determines the modes of appropriation of technology, its implications for transfer of technology are critical.

As examined elsewhere, the TRIPS Agreement leaves WTO Members some space to adapt national legislation to their particular needs and policy objectives (see, for instance, Correa 1997, 1998; Reichman 1996–97). In implementing the Agreement, therefore, it is important to take into consideration those aspects that may promote technology transfer and development. The following aspects may be considered along those lines:

Patents   Member countries have flexibility to decide on such aspects as:

- the provision of an exception for experimental use, including for commercial purposes, of an invention;
- the establishment of compulsory licenses on various grounds;
- the granting of improvement patents;
- the protection of "minor" innovations through utility models;
- the definition of the scope of claims and of non-literal infringement;
- the determination of the scope of the disclosure requirement.

Some of the flexibilities referred to would evaporate if the initiative to adopt a Substantive Patent Law Treaty in WIPO were successful (see Correa and Musungu 2002). Legislation on these aspects may be adopted in the context of the existing rules of the TRIPS Agreement. However, the impact of some of these provisions on technology development and transfer could be enhanced with some changes in the current text. Article 31(g) may be revised in order to increase the incentives to use the compulsory license system. The obligation established by that article to terminate a compulsory license when the reasons that justified its granting have ceased to exist, if literally applied, may constitute a strong disincentive to request a compulsory license.

Restrictive business practices   Article 40 of the TRIPS Agreement permits Members to apply competition rules to restrictive business practices in voluntary licensing agreements.[19] Some examples of restrictive business practices are given in that article (exclusive grant-back conditions, conditions preventing challenges to validity and coercive package licensing). One of the purposes of Article 40 was to restrict the possible ways in which Member countries could control restrictive business practices and, in particular, to prevent developing countries from applying a "development test" to judge such practices, as proposed during the unsuccessful negotiations of an International Code of Conduct on Transfer of Technology.[20]

Article 40 provides for a "positive comity": that is, the obligation by a Member to consider requests for consultations by another Member relating to such practices. The Member to which a request has been addressed has, however, the "full freedom of an ultimate decision" on the action to be taken.

Future negotiations in this area may aim to clarify and expand the rules relating to restrictive business practices in licensing agreements. It should be borne in mind that, despite the failure of the initiative to establish an International Code on Transfer of Technology, in December 1980 the UN General Assembly adopted by Resolution 35/63 a "Set of Multilaterally Equitable Agreed Principles and Rules for the Control of Restrictive Business Practices."

The Set is applicable to all transactions in goods and services and to all enterprises (but not to intergovernmental agreements). It deals with horizontal restraints (such as price-fixing agreements, collusive tendering, and market or customer allocation agreements), and with the abuse of dominant position or market power through practices such as discriminatory pricing, mergers, joint ventures, and other acquisitions of control (Section D, paragraphs 3 and 4).

At the five-yearly Review Conferences of the Set of Principles and Rules, developing countries have actively promoted the upgrading of the Set to a binding instrument and of the Intergovernmental Group of Experts to a "committee." Developed countries, however, repeatedly turned these initiatives back.

The possible development of multilateral rules on competition in the WTO (one of the so-called "Singapore issues"), championed by the European

Union, has so far found no enthusiasm on the part of the United States and resistance on the part of most developing countries. The opposition to developing competition rules in the WTO by developing countries does not mean a denial of the benefits that competition laws may bring at the national level, but rather resistance to being burdened further by obligations that may lead to trade sanctions under the WTO dispute settlement system if breached.

Transfer of technology to LDCs   According to Article 66.2, developed Member countries are obliged to provide incentives under their legislation to enterprises and institutions in their territories for the purpose of promoting and encouraging the transfer of technology to LDCs "in order to enable them to create a sound and viable technological base."

At its meeting of September 1998, the Council for TRIPS agreed to put on the agenda the question of the review of the implementation of Article 66.2 and to circulate a questionnaire on the matter in an informal Council document.

On 19 February 2003, the Council for TRIPS adopted a Decision on the Implementation of Article 66.2 of the TRIPS Agreement that establishes mechanisms for "ensuring the monitoring and full implementation of the obligations in Article 66.2," including the obligation to "submit annually reports on actions taken or planned in pursuance of their commitments" under said article and their review by the Council at its annual year-end meeting. The reports on the implementation of Article 66.2 shall, subject to the protection of business confidential information, provide, *inter alia*, the following information:

1. an overview of the incentives regime put in place to fulfill the obligations of Article 66.2, including any specific legislative, policy, and regulatory framework;
2. identification of the type of incentive and the government agency or other entity making it available;
3. eligible enterprises and other institutions in the territory of the Member providing the incentives;
4. any information available on the functioning in practice of these incentives, such as:
    - statistical and/or other information on the use of the incentives in question by the eligible enterprises and institutions;
    - the type of technology that has been transferred by these enterprises and institutions, and the terms on which it has been transferred;
    - the mode of technology transfer;

- the least-developed countries to which these enterprises and institutions have transferred technology, and the extent to which the incentives are specific to least-developed countries;
- any additional information available that would help assess the effects of the measures in promoting and encouraging technology transfer to least-developed country Members in order to enable them to create a sound and viable technological base.

The issue of transfer of technology was also addressed in paragraph 7 of the Doha Declaration, which reaffirmed "the commitment of developed-country Members to provide incentives to their enterprises and institutions to promote and encourage technology transfer to least-developed country Members pursuant to Article 66.2." Though the wording in paragraph 7 is broad, its inclusion in the Doha Declaration indicates that effective incentives should be granted in developed countries in order specifically to foster the transfer to LDCs of health-related technologies, including pharmaceutical technologies. An interesting aspect of the Declaration is that it refers to "commitments of developed-country Members," thereby suggesting that this is not merely a "best effort" obligation.

The Decision of 19 February 2003 and the Doha Declaration are steps forward, but concrete measures to facilitate access to technologies by LDCs are still non-existent or insufficient. Given that Article 66.2 belongs to a treaty specifically dealing with technologies protected under IPRs, a logical interpretation is that developed countries are obliged to transfer IPR-protected technologies, and not only those that are already in the public domain.

Future negotiations on this provision may aim at further specifying the obligations of developed countries under Article 66.2, for instance, in respect of the transfer of environmentally sound technologies and other "horizontal" technologies that may contribute to develop a solid and viable technological base. LDCs may also aim to review other WTO agreements such as the Agreement on Subsidies and Countervailing Measures in a manner that facilitates compliance with Article 66.2.

Environmentally sound technologies A topic of particular importance, as mentioned before, is the impact of the WTO rules on the transfer of environmentally sound technology (EST). Chapter 34 of Agenda 21 recognized the need for favorable access to and transfer of EST, in particular to developing countries, including on concessional and preferential terms. That Chapter also incorporates a detailed provision on action to be undertaken to support and promote the access to and use of EST.

Despite the clear justification and purposes of these provisions, little has been done to implement them. Moreover, the strengthening of IPRs in accordance with the TRIPS Agreement has reinforced the power of private parties to control the use and eventual transfer of ESTs. The Agreement has set forth high standards of protection for patents and "undisclosed information" under which titleholders may retain their technologies or charge high royalties for allowing access to them.

Under Multilateral Environment Agreements (MEAs), obligations have been adopted to phase out the use of certain substances or technologies. Despite some measures to support developing countries in that process, technologies remain under the control of patent holders. Similarly, there are standards adopted at the national level that ban imports not complying with certain environmental requirements. Here again, the lack of access to relevant EST poses an additional barrier to exports from developing countries. A good example is provided by the case of a substitute to chlorofluorocarbons (CFCs). India has encountered difficulties in getting access to technology for HFC 134A, which is considered the best available replacement for certain CFCs. That technology is covered by patents and trade secrets, and the companies that possess them are unwilling to transfer it without majority control over the ownership of the Indian company.

As recommended by Agenda 21, compulsory licenses based on the protection of the environment may be specified in national legislation. These measures, however, may be insufficient to ensure the transfer of EST needed by developing countries. In line with the proposals made by India at the WTO Committee on Trade and the Environment, the TRIPS Agreement may require changes in order actually to promote the transfer and use of ESTs.

Despite possible changes in the TRIPS Agreement to favor the transfer of technology, the IPR framework is too limited to address the complex issues involved in the technology transfer process, including the creation of a local infrastructure able to absorb the transferred technologies. Technology transfer policy should aim for the absorption of foreign technologies and the building of local capabilities (UNCTAD 1993).

Conclusions

Developing countries reluctantly agreed to enter into negotiations for an agreement on IPRs during the Uruguay Round. Their concerns, particularly with respect to access to technologies necessary for development, were dismissed at that time. The proponents of an international agreement anticipated benefits for such countries in terms of increased flows of capital and technology, which have not materialized.

The strengthening and expansion of intellectual property rights have reinforced the technology owners' capacity to control the use of their intangible assets, including whether or not to transfer them to third parties. The access to technologies developed with public funding may also be limited in the case of foreign parties.

While developing countries seem more eager than their developed counterparts to review the TRIPS Agreement, developing countries' proposals generally aim to balance the agreement rather than to question its basic foundations, except (as in the case of the African Group) with respect to the patentability of living matter.

Developing countries seem to be better prepared for future negotiations on IPRs at the WTO than they were on the occasion of the TRIPS negotiations. IPR issues, which, for the most part, were new and generally unknown for trade negotiators of developing countries during the Uruguay Round, have become an important part of their concerns and negotiating strategies. However, since the Decision on the implementation of paragraph 6 of the Doha Declaration was adopted, the Council for TRIPS seems to be in a phase of hibernation, as the United States is actively pursuing TRIPS-plus protection through bilateral agreements (Okediji 2003–04) and negotiations on all pending issues are blocked in the WTO.

Notes

This chapter updates and elaborates on the article published by the author under the same title in the *Journal of World Intellectual Property*, vol. 2, no. 6, 1999.

1. With the sole exception of the patentability of certain products as allowed by Article 65.4 of the Agreement, all developing countries became bound by the provisions of the TRIPS Agreement as of 1 January 2000. Least developed countries (LDCs) can, however, delay the implementation of the Agreement until 2006. For pharmaceutical patents this period extends until 2016 (see WCTRIPS 2002b).

2. See also Thurow 1997: 103; Scherer 1998; CIPR 2001; World Bank 2001. For Abbott, "[T]hough industrialized country producers have at least a short-run interest in imposing high levels of IPRs protection on the developing countries, there is no convincing evidence that these high levels of IPRs protection will enhance economic development where it is most urgently required" (Abbott 1998: 520).

3. The initiative to adopt a treaty for the *sui generis* protection of databases following the European approach on the matter collapsed in 1996, largely due to the internal opposition in the United States by the scientific and librarian communities (see, e.g., Reichman and Samuelson 1997).

4. Article 71.2 of the TRIPS Agreement provides that:

II. amendments merely serving the purpose of adjusting to higher levels of protection of intellectual property rights achieved, and in force, in other multilateral agreements and accepted under those agreements by all Members of the WTO may be referred to the Ministerial Conference for action in accordance with paragraph 6 of Article X of the WTO Agreement on the basis of a consensus proposal from the Council for TRIPS.

5. Japan openly advocated a "further international harmonization" of IPR systems, since "differences in fundamental rules for protection of intellectual property rights still exist, which remain as obstacles for trade and investment" (WGC 1999f).

6. See WGC 1998a and European Commission 1999: 16.

7. According to Reichman, these treaties "represent a balanced and reciprocally beneficial set of foundational rules, with which each state can adapt its Internet policies to its own needs" (Reichman 1999: 21). For a different view, see CIPR 2002.

8. A significant number of developing countries have adhered to UPOV in the last ten years. 34 out of a total of 54 UPOV members (as of 15 January 2004) acceded after 1995.

9. The target of this proposal also was the United States, where patents were only published after granting. Subsequently, the United States reformed its patent law and now requires publication of patent applications, except those that are filed only in the United States.

10. In addition to the 118 geographical indications already registered for agricultural products and foodstuffs, there might be at least 3,558 products in Italy that may potentially seek recognition under geographical indications (interview with the Italian Minister of Agriculture and Forestry Policy, reported by Pinna 2002: 46).

11. The following analysis is partially based on Correa 2003.

12. See WCTRIPS 2002a, 2002c, 2003a, 2003b.

13. It is "the country which possesses those genetic resources in in-situ conditions." "In-situ conditions" means, in turn, "conditions where genetic resources exist within ecosystems and natural habitats, and, in the case of domesticated or cultivated species, in the surroundings where they have developed their distinctive properties" (article 2 of the CBD).

14. Article 27.1 lays down the three requirements for patentability (novelty, inventive step, industrial applicability). The obligation to disclose may affect how such requirements are applied in a particular case but would not create a new patentability requirement.

15. The Swiss submission suggests a requirement to be voluntarily established by national laws in relation to PCT procedures (see WCTRIPS 2003a and PCT Union 2004).

16. The purpose of this linkage has been to provide legal certainty and encourage countries to implement the Decision as soon as possible. So far only a handful of countries are reported to have taken action in order to amend national laws and allow exports under the Decision.

17. See also the proposals by Dominican Republic and Honduras (WGC 1998b) and Venezuela (WGC 1999i).

18. India also made a detailed proposal on 20 June 1996 to the Committee on Trade and Environment in relation to the transfer of environmentally sound technologies, so as to ensure that such technologies are made available at fair and most favorable terms and conditions upon demand to any interested party, which has an obligation to adopt these under national law of another country or under international law. India has suggested that an obligation is cast upon the WTO to bring about easy access to

and wide dissemination of technology relevant for sustainable development, and has suggested an examination of article 31 relating to compulsory licenses and article 33 relating to duration of patent rights

19. For an analysis of this article, see Roffe 1998.

20. Chapter IV of the draft Code contained detailed provisions on restrictive practices in technology transfer arrangements.

8

Will Investment Rules Shrink
Policy Space for Sustainable Development?
Evidence from the Electricity Sector

Albert H. Cho and Navroz K. Dubash

Will the emergent international framework of investment rules unduly constrain national governments' ability to make policy and, ultimately, to govern? Critics of the World Trade Organization (WTO) and other multilateral economic arrangements argue that internationally negotiated disciplines shrink the "policy space" for development and, by extension, undermine national democratic processes (Sinclair 2000). Proponents of an international investment regime, by contrast, contend that such disciplines are necessary for expanded trade and investment, economic growth, and development. Moreover, they argue that current and proposed policy instruments provide adequate flexibility to satisfy domestic political preferences.

Though negotiations on a multilateral investment framework were jettisoned from the Doha Development Agenda after the Cancún Ministerial in September 2003, the issue of policy space remains salient. Bilateral and regional trade and investment agreements continue to proliferate, and members of the World Trade Organization continue to discuss investment-related provisions in the context of the General Agreement on Trade in Services. And in the future, the ever-present pressure for investment disciplines may succeed in resurrecting multilateral negotiations.

In this chapter we seek to inform this debate by asking, what sorts of policies could national governments reasonably seek to pursue but for hindrance by international investment disciplines? By "investment disciplines" we mean not only a multilateral investment framework, but also negotiations on GATS rules, since the GATS affects certain kinds of investment through the inclusion of commercial presence as a mode of supply. We examine this question in the specific context of the electricity sector, with a particular emphasis on the social and environmental dimensions of electricity policies.

The electricity sector represents a particular challenge because it is in considerable flux. Electricity has long been managed as a public service, one with great social significance and a large environmental footprint.[1] In recent years the dominant model of a public vertically integrated utility has given way to a more fluid mix of public and private approaches, which includes a considerable role for private investment. Due to the central role of electricity in industrial economies, its networked characteristics, and its substantial social and environmental impacts, there remains a strong public stake in the terms and conditions under which the sector is owned and managed. Consequently, liberalization of investment in the electricity sector must address the continuing public interest in the sector and the current context of uncertain and rapidly shifting national regulatory environments.

In this chapter, we draw on experiences in the electricity sector to develop illustrative cases of innovative national policymaking that have aroused discussion among electricity professionals, and then examine these through the lens of international investment rules – in particular in the context of the General Agreement on Trade in Services (GATS) and the Multilateral Investment Framework that was unsuccessfully advanced as part of the Doha Round of multilateral trade negotiations. The proposals discussed in these arenas have a great deal of relevance not only for negotiations in the WTO but also for the rapidly expanding web of bilateral and regional trade and investment agreements. Given the shifting nature of what is considered good practice in electricity and the scattered, amorphous and incomplete body of international investment rules, this exercise necessarily involves extrapolation. Our goal is to identify potential points of friction in the application of innovative policies, with a view to informing the debate on trade, investment, and policy space for sustainable development. Our discussion hinges on two avenues of inquiry that are implicit in our central question. First, how broad is the set of policies that governments might reasonably wish to pursue? A second and related question is, how much room do investment negotiations provide in practice for governments to pursue pragmatic and innovative policies? These two questions, we believe, shed important light on the conceptual and practical importance of "policy space" in the context of the WTO.

The discussion of policy space echoes recent debates over the "Washington Consensus" package of macroeconomic stability and liberalization associated with the Bretton Woods institutions (Williamson 1994). An emerging literature now advocates a heterogeneous and strategic set of development policies used by East Asian countries and today's industrialized nations (see Rodrik 1997; Chang and Green 2003). From the latter perspective, stimulating successful economic development requires freedom to experiment and selectively intervene. While the debate remains unresolved, recent economic events, notably the collapse of the Bretton Woods institutions' most willing adherent, Argentina, suggest that it is premature to close the door to policy innovation.

The cases developed in this chapter support the conclusion that in order to create a socially progressive and environmentally sustainable electricity sector, countries may reasonably wish to pursue heterodox policies that run counter to investment disciplines. Specifically, these cases demonstrate how both industrialized and developing countries have used available policy space to build a domestic political consensus around environmental policies, to direct foreign capital to needed social and environmental ends, to address long-standing social inequalities, and to deal with external shocks. This chapter further argues that proposed extensions to international investment rules are likely to shrink policy space for sustainable development, and that measures designed to provide flexibility, such as the "positive list" approach whereby countries gradually schedule commitments over time, may nonetheless prove to be unduly limiting in practice.

In the following section we describe the concept of "policy space" and discuss its connection to investment rules. The next section provides a brief introduction to recent electricity policy debates and their relation to the World Trade Organization. This is followed by a section discussing key disciplines in investment rules that may affect the electricity sector. The bulk of the chapter is devoted to case studies of electricity policy; these are followed by a synthesis, and then by some concluding observations.

Investment Rules and Policy Space for Sustainable Development

Investment rules span a wide range of agreements between governments, including bilateral, regional, and multilateral arrangements. This chapter addresses investment-related disciplines in several policy arenas but focuses on negotiations for a multilateral investment framework and investment-related aspects of the General Agreement on Trade in Services (GATS).[2]

Advocates for international investment rules argue that such rules will "secure transparent, stable and predictable conditions for long-term cross-border investment, especially foreign direct investment, that will contribute to the expansion of trade" (WGTI 2002a). In particular, investment rules will reduce the scope for arbitrary, capricious, and economically pernicious government actions, providing investors with greater certainty and guarantees against risk. Likewise, supporters of stronger GATS rules propose that more stringent disciplines on trade-distorting policies related to services will reduce discrimination, facilitate domestic policy reform, and generate economy-wide gains (Adlung 2000). Those who promote deeper and more rapid liberalization voice their support in the language of benefits: more integration means more stability, more efficiency, and more growth.

New investment rules may indeed deliver some of these benefits, although recent World Bank research suggests that investment treaties may not substantially increase investment flows (World Bank 2003a). However, benefits are only one side of the equation; the costs that accompany increasingly stringent rules also merit closer examination. Resistance to international rules frequently stems from a desire to protect socially, politically, and environmentally sensitive spaces for domestic policy. By construction, international commitments encroach upon domestic policy autonomy; hence arguments that multilateral investment rules may infringe upon "policy space."

In one revealing exchange in the Working Group on Trade and Investment (WGTI), India noted that developing countries need "policy space" because there is "no single formula" for economic growth. Since multilateral disciplines reduce investment-related policy options as a means of promoting development, developing countries "must never subscribe to any doctrine that would limit policy flexibility in this important area" (WGTI 2002b). In response, the European Community argued that investment rules would leave sufficient "policy space for development," since policies addressing basic structural deficiencies in national economies would be left unaffected (WGTI 2003: paras 6 and 7; WGTI 2002d: para. 65). Moreover, should countries choose to implement measures inconsistent with investment rules, they would be able to do so by scheduling exemptions in advance. While this may be true in theory, in practice investment rules are unlikely to afford countries the flexibility to experiment with unorthodox but potentially effective policies, for a variety of reasons (Hardstaff 2003; Sinclair 2000). These include:

- *Limited ex ante knowledge* Requiring all exemptions to be scheduled at the time of commitment presumes an inconceivable degree of *ex ante* knowledge about an infinite range of policies.
- *Limited capacity* Capacity restrictions, particularly in the countries of the South, exacerbate the *ex ante* knowledge problem.
- *Technological change* Technological change can quickly change industry fundamentals such that the assumptions underlying initial policy orientations are dramatically altered.
- *Changing political contexts* Governments and political preferences change over time, but the international commitments and schedules they create do not automatically change with them. If one government liberalizes by scheduling a range of sectors with few protective exemptions, subsequent governments with contrasting but legitimate views about social policy may find it difficult to cultivate space for inconsistent investment policies.

- *Domestic policy coherence problems* Limited communication or consultation between various parts of governments means that commitments may not reflect the full range of possible concerns, particularly those articulated by ministries responsible for social and environmental issues.
- *Inflexibility* Once made, commitments are extremely difficult to reverse. While this certainly helps create a stable policy environment, it also means that governments are locked into potentially damaging policy commitments even if unforeseen crises or developments arise.

These arguments suggest that adopting new international investment rules may result in a de facto loss of policy space. To ground this debate in concrete examples, we turn next to the case of the electricity sector.

Electricity Sector Reform and the WTO

The decade of the 1990s witnessed dramatic changes in what had long been a stodgy, static industry. Around the world, governments began reconsidering their ownership of and control over large, monopolistic electricity systems. Over the preceding four decades, these systems had worked reasonably well in the industrialized world (although less well in the developing world), providing safe, reliable, and increasingly cheap power. This model was challenged by technological change, higher risks, stagnant demand, and an ideological predisposition toward markets and competition. Reformers aimed to increase efficiency by subjecting the sector to competition. Despite the lack of a blueprint on how to achieve competition in the technologically complex and heavily networked electricity industry, the United Kingdom and Chile were quick to "unbundle" the various components of the electricity system, privatize generation and distribution businesses, and establish a market for upstream and downstream electricity services.

The approach spread rapidly, but for reasons not always related to a coherent vision of change for the electricity sector. Developing countries unbundled and privatized electricity utilities in order to shed debt-ridden public enterprises or to satisfy lending conditions imposed by multilateral donor agencies. In some cases, particularly in Latin America, economic performance in the sector has improved, but in others these changes have produced political unrest without measurable improvements in the sector. Critics of liberalization have questioned its applicability to developing countries, where the most pressing problems are ensuring broad access to electricity and providing adequate and transparent regulation, rather than squeezing additional efficiency gains from a mature and established market. The disastrous collapse of California's electricity market also cast doubt on the long-term wisdom of power sector reform. These doubts were amplified by the dramatic implosion of the Enron Corporation, which pointed to underlying regulatory failures in the world's most sophisticated electricity market. At a minimum, these experiences suggest that kinks persist in the market-led model, and that countries with less regulatory capacity would be well advised to proceed with caution, if at all.[3]

Perhaps most problematic for the new model, a host of studies have documented that markets, left to their own devices, are unlikely to address legitimate social and environmental concerns in the electricity sector (Dubash 2002; Wamukonya 2003; World Bank 2003b).

For example, the rural poor are unlikely to be attractive customers for private operators, since remote locations and low population densities make them costly to serve, and their low consumption does not facilitate adequate returns. From an environmental perspective, while the electricity sector has a large and dirty footprint, an effective transition to a clean energy future may have to move beyond end-of-smokestack regulation toward creative strategies of energy transformation. A recent World Bank review of a decade of private-sector-led strategies for electricity concludes that poverty reduction and environmental objectives deserve considerably more importance in policymaking for the sector than has been the case thus far. For this reason, as well as because of uncertainties in the underlying model, the study concludes that "there is no 'one-size-fits-all' reform model and each approach should be country-specific" (World Bank, 2003b: ix). In short, experimentation and heterogeneity are important ingredients of successful electricity sector policies.

When the electricity sector was run as a vertically integrated, state-owned monopoly, questions of governing international private investment and cross-border trade in electricity did not arise. The recent emergence of electricity and electricity services as tradable products has brought the sector within the ambit of the WTO, but in ways that remain unclear. The implications of WTO rules for electricity policy depend on whether electricity is a good or a service. Under the asymmetric trade rules of the World Trade Organization, the classification of electricity has serious implications for investors and policymakers alike. As a tradable commodity but one that cannot be stored, electricity shares some qualities with both goods and services. The World Customs Organization (WCO), to pick one widely cited authority, classifies electrical energy as a commodity, although this is an optional heading, and countries are free to classify it as a service if they so choose (WCTS 1998). In the WTO context, some parties maintain that electricity is a commodity subject to rules under the General Agreement on Tariffs and Trade (GATT). The parties to NAFTA explicitly classified electricity as a commodity.

Many countries have unbundled the electricity sector into constituent parts: generation, transmission, distribution, and supply. Each of these functions requires classification. Even if electricity is a commodity, transmission and distribution qualify as services subject to the General Agreement on Trade in Services (GATS). Particularly relevant is Mode 3 of the GATS, which covers "commercial presence" and hence a range of investment activity. Since generating electricity may be a manufacturing process, however, it may or may not fall within the ambit of the GATS. According to an UNCTAD report, "most agree that the production of primary and secondary energy does not constitute services subject to the GATS, but that it results in goods whose trade is regulated by GATT rules. Transportation and distribution, on the other hand, are commonly regarded as services" (Zarrilli 2002).

Despite this seemingly clear distinction, these classifications remain ambiguous, even to experts. In the same UNCTAD publication, the author notes that "Mode 3 [of the GATS] is of paramount importance since it covers all different forms of foreign commercial presence, such as BOT and IPP." Both of these models – build–operate–transfer and independent power producers, respectively – refer to aspects of power generation, which would not fall under the GATS if electricity is strictly defined as a commodity. Whether or not GATS applies to power generation is at once a definitional and a political issue that is difficult to resolve, particularly since the GATS offers no definition of "services" (Evans 2002; Tacoa-Vielma 2002).

The classification of electricity is an evolving – and extremely political – issue. GATS and GATT rules offer very different kinds of protection to investments, so classification is of great economic importance to foreign investors (WCTS 1998). Clearly, evolving trade and investment rules will have significant implications for the future development of the electricity sector. In the following section, we will explore key components of international trade and investment rules that may have implications for sustainable development policies in the electricity sector.

Investment Rules and Sustainable Development in the Electricity Sector

Investment-related disciplines can be found in three parts of the World Trade Organization: in the Working Group on Trade and Investment (WGTI), which is spearheading preparations for negotiations on a multilateral framework for investment; under the Agreement on Trade-Related Investment Measures (TRIMs); and under the General Agreement on Trade in Services (GATS) as part of Mode 3, supply through commercial presence.[4] While discussions in the Working Group on Trade and Investment have been suspended due to decisions taken since Cancún, Members of the Committee on Trade in Services have many issues to resolve with respect to the depth and breadth of GATS rules, as well as ongoing negotiations on specific commitments.

Progress in both arenas raises a set of issues directly relevant to policy space for sustainable development. In the multilateral framework on investment, four issues of special importance stand out: commitments on pre-establishment national treatment; prohibitions on performance requirements; guarantees against indirect expropriation; and the imposition of international dispute arbitration. In continuing discussions on GATS rules, issues of importance include disciplines on monopolies and policies related to market size and structure, domestic regulation, services subsidies, and government procurement. As the case studies that follow will demonstrate, negotiations on each of these issues may have serious implications for the electricity sector.

Issues in a Multilateral Investment Framework

- *National treatment* Should the principle of national treatment apply to investment, and, if so, should it apply at the pre-establishment or post-establishment phase? (UNCTAD 1999a).
- *Performance requirements* Should performance requirements, which are conditions that countries attach to inward investment in order to maximize host-country benefits, be permitted or prohibited under investment rules?
- *Indirect expropriation* Should governments be liable for measures that are "tantamount"[5] or "equivalent"[6] to expropriation?
- *Dispute settlement* Should treaties provide foreign investors with recourse to international arbitration if they are dissatisfied with the results of domestic dispute resolution procedures? (WGTI 2002c)

Issues in the General Agreement on Trade in Services

- *Monopolies and market access* How restrictive will GATS market access disciplines restricting the creation of monopolies and exclusive service providers become?
- *Subsidies* How will Article XV negotiations influence the use of targeted subsidies as a public policy tool?
- *Government procurement* How will Article XIII negotiations affect government's ability to use procurement as an instrument to achieve national sustainable development objectives?

Negotiations on these new disciplines touch upon economically significant and politically sensitive policy measures, and they could significantly encroach upon policy space necessary to achieve sustainable development. Supporters of new disciplines argue that conflict can easily be avoided because countries can schedule unlimited exemptions for policies inconsistent with investment rules. Critics respond that forward-looking exemptions alone do not sufficiently protect policy space. Determining who is right, however, requires more than conjecture. The case studies that follow attempt to add to the debate by highlighting reasonable sustainable development policies in the electricity sectors of both industrialized and developing countries. By analyzing provisions that could violate norms of existing and proposed trade and investment rules, the cases demonstrate that conflict between sustainable development policies and the emerging global trade and investment regime is a potentially significant cause for concern.

Case Studies from the Electricity Sector

Access

Electricity delivers new benefits and opportunities, but only to those who are fortunate enough to be plugged in. For the 2 billion people around the world who lack access to modern electricity services, however, dung, scrapwood, and kerosene are among the only ways to cook dinner and illuminate the darkness. Expanding access to electricity improves health, local environmental conditions, and educational opportunities, not to mention the fact that it frees people from the ceaseless, onerous task of gathering material to burn each day (UNDP 2000b).

An overwhelming proportion of households without electricity live in rural areas. Rural electrification offers new opportunities and capabilities to isolated communities, but it is unlikely to occur without government intervention because remote, sparsely populated regions are technically difficult and expensive to electrify. Laying new infrastructure in isolated areas requires large initial investments that pay off only in the long run, a fact that deters investors with little patience or appetite for risk. Finally, rural populations are disproportionately likely to be poor and use relatively little electricity in the early stages of development. With low aggregate demand, they do not promise rapid and steady profits for utilities.

To surmount the difficulties inherent in rural electrification, governments and communities have developed a wide range of innovative – and often interventionist – tactics. Successful programs and policies have frequently involved unorthodox solutions, ranging from subsidizing non-profit cooperatives to bundling monopoly concessions across utility sectors. Many of these policies have departed from market-based intuition, and, though they may not have been the only or the best solutions available to governments, they have achieved some measure of success. The case studies in this section, which discuss rural electrification in the United States and Gabon, suggest that countries potentially require more space for policy innovation than emerging rules on services trade and investment may allow.

Rural electrification in the United States

Today's developed countries historically made use of interventionist and discriminatory policies to achieve rural electrification. In the late 1930s, urban Americans had modern amenities like pumped water and electric refrigerators, but their rural counterparts suffered from poor sanitation, poor diets, and the drudgery of endless manual labor. Then, at the height of the Great Depression, rural electrification programs successfully employed community-organized cooperatives to extend services to isolated areas through a mixture of government support and local initiative. This massive push toward state-led infrastructure development provided relief to Depression workers, laid the foundation for balanced regional development in the United States, and brought modern services to some of the most underserved families in the country.

Under the aegis of the Rural Electrification Administration (REA), the American government created a system of subsidized loans and financial guarantees available on preferential terms to members of co-operatives. To facilitate the extension of service to rural areas, funds earmarked for rural electrification projects were disbursed on a priority basis to public agencies and co-operatives. These funds were loaned at subsidized interest rates to make repayment less burdensome. Private companies and investors were eligible for these funds only after public bodies and co-operatives had borrowed what they needed. Since the scheme was regularly oversubscribed, the REA scheme was in practice a discriminatory measure that subsidized non-profit domestic service providers over their commercial counterparts. The REA measure was wildly successful, involving over 1,000 co-operatives that extended service to over 5 million households across the country (Brown 1980).

In recent years, subsidizing rural co-operatives has also emerged as an effective strategy for extending access in developing countries. For example, one highly successful rural electrification scheme in Bangladesh provides concessionary financing to electric co-operatives in addition to outright grants (Khan 2003). However, such programs could become more difficult to implement under increasingly stringent investment rules. While some international investment agreements "carve out" space to implement government grants and subsidy programs by exempting these instruments from national treatment obligations,[7] subsidy programs could face challenges in the future, either under new investment agreements or under the General Agreement on Trade in Services. Subsidies are already considered "measures" affecting trade in services under the GATS (Sinclair 2000),[8] and Article XV of the GATS instructs governments to develop further multilateral disciplines on subsidies affecting trade. Disciplines on subsidies apply equally to for-profit enterprises and non-profit organizations like electric co-operatives (Jackson and Sanger 2003).

Though discussions on services subsidies are still at an embryonic stage, these negotiations could have considerable implications for programs such as the credit subsidy to rural electrification co-operatives. Since co-operatives are generally owned and operated by the residents who consume the product, they are intrinsically domestic providers of potentially tradable services, and they therefore fall under commitments undertaken under the GATS.[9] As negotiators commence discussions on subsidy disciplines in the service sector, the potential for conflict with targeted subsidy policies could increase.

Rural electrification in Gabon

Due to unfavorable conditions, modern electricity services may take decades to reach isolated communities. In Gabon, Chile and Argentina, however, preliminary experience with power sector reform suggests a possible model for successful rural electrification – and demonstrates the need for careful attention to the provisions of the General Agreement on Trade in Services (GATS).

Gabon has a per capita income of about \$4,378, but much of the population lacks access to basic services like piped water or electricity (World Resources Institute 2003). This has started to change since 1997, when the government of Gabon concluded a competitive bidding cycle that awarded a twenty-year exclusive concession to a consortium of French and Irish investors, Société d'Energie et d'Eau du Gabon (SEEG). Competition for the contract was intense because Gabon's water and electricity utilities were relatively well-run with bill payment rates approaching 93 per cent, a rarity in the developing world (International Trade Finance 1997). The contract gives SEEG a geographically delimited monopoly over the provision of certain infrastructure services in parts of Gabon and is linked to a strict set of performance criteria that include extending water and electric power to previously unserved households.

Under the competitively bid contract, which promised a 17.25 per cent reduction in tariff rates relative to the previous service delivery regime, SEEG must invest a minimum of \$135 million in infrastructure rehabilitation. It must also meet stringent performance criteria for expanding the coverage of water and electricity services. SEEG is contractually committed to increase water coverage in one district from 37.7 per cent to 63 per cent by 2015;

during the same period, it is obligated to increase electricity coverage in underserved isolated regions from 0 per cent to 54 per cent. If it fails to meet these targets, SEEG faces stiff financial penalties equivalent to 25 per cent of the investment shortfall in addition to the costs associated with meeting its contractual commitments (FT Energy Newsletter 1997).

The concessionaire has so far met or exceeded its obligations. SEEG has outperformed its coverage targets and has made excellent progress toward meeting its investment obligations (Tremolet and Neale 2002). Supply losses have diminished, while investment planning has increased in efficiency. Careful planning and execution of the infrastructure concession seems to have produced extremely promising results.

Chile and Argentina have also successfully utilized variations on the monopoly concessionaire model. In Argentina, where over 90 per cent of the population already has access to electricity, franchise rights for unserved rural areas are distributed through competitive bidding, with contracts awarded to companies willing to accept the lowest subsidy to electrify rural areas (Covarrubias and Reiche 2000). Likewise, distributors in Chile have been granted exclusive concessions to serve unconnected jurisdictions (Basanes et al. 1999).

The monopoly concession model encourages rural electrification by offering the exclusive right and obligation to serve all households in a particular geographic area. By bundling high-cost and low-cost connections together, monopoly concessions can make the overall concession package profitable even if connecting some of the constituent households would be cost-prohibitive on a case-by-case basis. Without exclusivity, private firms would evaluate each connection individually and "cherry-pick," connecting only households where expected returns were high, making the remainder even less attractive to serve.

Policies like monopoly concessions can be accommodated within the framework of the GATS, but only by defending space for policy autonomy. Policy space can be preserved either by avoiding specific commitments in infrastructure services or by carving out specific exemptions in committed sectors. Given the built-in mandate to pursue progressively higher levels of liberalization in services (GATS Article XIX.1), the former approach will become less effective over time. As more sectors are committed in progressive rounds of negotiations, the ability to derogate from the GATS will require increasingly extensive and rigorous *ex ante* attention to detail.

The importance of this concern is evident in the case of monopoly concessions. Article VIII of the General Agreement on Trade in Services disciplines the creation of new monopolies in all committed sectors.[10] Concessions granted by local municipalities and local concessions granted by a central government are also subject to these disciplines. Under the conditions of GATS Article VIII(4), any new monopoly granted in a committed sector is subject to a notification process that can lead to arbitration and compensatory adjustment if other Members choose to challenge the measure.[11] The GATS is silent on the question of whether or not competitive bidding for the monopoly concession exempts countries from Article VIII provisions, but a strict interpretation of definitions suggests that it does not.

The implications of these rules are readily apparent in Gabon. If Gabon had made specific commitments on its electricity transmission or its water delivery sectors without scheduling exemptions, it could have been subject to onerous, time-consuming, and potentially costly arbitration procedures that might have complicated efforts to pursue sectoral reforms. Even though bidding procedures for the concession were competitive, transparent, and nondiscriminatory, the privatization process would essentially have been subject to external review and approval. Though the Gabonese authorities had not made specific commitments in this area, their experience is still instructive for other countries facing pressure to undertake new obligations.

The Gabonese experience demonstrates that countries can introduce structural reforms and private-sector participation without making binding commitments that constrain future policy options. SEEG was willing to invest in Gabon because it saw a profitable opportunity and coordinated closely with authorities to create a secure climate for operations. Even without specific commitments in the GATS, Gabon was able to attract world-class consortia to its competitive bidding process. Furthermore, the concession in Gabon bundled together two separate infrastructure sectors to attract well-qualified investors with whom to cooperate. Had commitments been undertaken in either sector, the entire process could have become more difficult or stalled altogether.

Many Gabonese have lived their entire lives without reliable access to electricity. Due to the successful auction of the monopoly concession, however, many will enjoy the benefits of electric heat and light within the next decade. Successful reform in Gabon depended largely on the government's freedom to structure foreign investment in ways consistent with its development priorities. The Gabonese experience suggests that countries should exercise great caution during the request-offer process to preserve the autonomy needed to pursue policies that work for them.

Crisis management

When crises occur, they require prompt and decisive government action. Investment agreements that constrain government action, however, can make countries pay twice for crises: first to solve the crisis, and again to compensate international investors on terms decided not through renegotiation, but through compulsory international arbitration.

Financial crisis in Argentina

After years of being the 'poster child' of the Washington Consensus, Argentina's economy imploded in 2001. Hordes of people found themselves scrounging for food and other essentials, many resorting to a barter system to replace liquid assets that had evaporated overnight (BBC News 2002). Buenos Aires erupted in violent protests that killed twenty-eight and forced the successive installation of three presidents (*Daily Telegraph* 2001). Between 2000 and 2001, per capita income fell from $12,377 to $7,327, and investments rushed out of the country, creating a severe balance of payments crisis from which the country has only now begun to recover (*Daily Telegraph* 2002). Since the financial crisis, Argentina's citizens suffered three years of negative economic growth, increasing unemployment, cuts in public services, and tight restrictions on their ability to access deposits (Roubini 2001). Now taxpayers face yet another potential blow: payouts to foreign investors who are using bilateral investment treaties to recover the losses they incurred during the crisis.

The financial crisis left many scars in Argentina, but one of its legacies was especially bitter: a groundswell of litigation before the International Center for the Settlement of Investment Disputes (ICSID), an organization closely tied to the World Bank. In July 2003, Argentina was named in 20 of the 58 investor–state disputes pending at ICSID; of the 17 energy-related cases, Argentina was named in 12.[12] The claims for all the suits *in toto* are said to exceed $17 billion (*The News Says* 2003), an amount that exceeds 5 per cent of annual GDP in Argentina (authors' calculations, based on WRI 2003). These numbers represent a lower bound, since there may also be cases brought under United Nations Commission on International Trade Law (UNCITRAL) rules, which do not require public disclosure.

At the height of the meltdown, Argentina took decisive action to avert the onset of total chaos. In January 2002, the government passed a suite of emergency legislation, including Law No. 25561, the Public Emergency and Foreign Exchange System Reform Act. Provisions in this law eliminated dollar-denominated tariff regimes for public utilities, struck out provisions pricing government contracts in foreign currencies, and imposed sweeping rate freezes across utilities sectors. All prices were automatically translated into pesos at an exchange rate of US$1 to 1 Argentine peso prior to a devaluation of the currency (M. & M. Bomchil Abogados 2002). This policy was intended to reduce foreign exchange obligations, implicitly shifting some of the burden of the crisis onto private investors and their investments.

Investors claim that these actions violated guarantees made in bilateral investment treaties (BITs) signed by Argentina. The US–Argentina BIT, signed in 1991, guarantees American investors "fair and equitable" as well as national treatment in Argentina. Other treaties, including the Argentina–France BIT, provide similar assurances. These BITs provide guarantees against direct and "indirect" expropriation and offer recourse to international arbitration if disputes between parties arise (United States 1991). Immediately after the imposition of Law No. 25561, international law firms began issuing advisories encouraging investors to explore litigation under the US–Argentina treaty (Coudert Brothers LLP 2002; Miller & Chevalier Chartered 2002). Soon enough, suits against Argentina began appearing on ICSID's register of pending cases, with sources indicating that many of them arose directly in response to emergency measures taken during the financial crisis (Peterson 2002). Some companies were even more explicit, issuing press releases to inform their shareholders that they would initiate arbitration to deal with the aftermath of the crisis (SUEZ International 2002).

These lawsuits involve alleged violations of "fair and equitable treatment," non-discrimination, and indirect expropriation without compensation. According to one law firm, "the elimination of the peso/dollar parity ... may amount to a breach of Argentina's obligations under applicable BITs, for which the investor may be entitled to compensation." Likewise, "the repeal of adjustment and indexation clauses in government contracts ... may also furnish the investors with a claim under international law" (Freshfields Bruckhaus Deringer 2002). Central to the issue is the claim that Argentina's foreign exchange policy and freeze on electricity rate hikes amounted to unfair treatment and indirectly expropriated investors without compensation.

Some 60 per cent of the suits against Argentina deal with the energy sector, and half of these specifically involve electricity services and concessions. Due to an unusually permissive foreign investment regime, the majority of privatized electricity assets went to foreign companies during Argentina's recent experience of rapid privatization (US Department of Energy 1997). These firms claim injury from the rate freezes mandated by law, as well as from the financial impact of "pesofication." Law No. 25561 provides provisions for comprehensive renegotiations with the government, but foreign firms have used bilateral investment treaty provisions to sidestep this process. Though domestic courts have repeatedly rejected proposed tariff increases because the law allows rate hikes only through renegotiation (Kerr 2003), foreign investors hope to recoup their losses through recourse to international arbitration – an option that domestic investors do not have.

The option of pursuing international arbitration sharply alters the playing field, since foreign investors can choose to involve ICSID if they believe they can extract more compensation by circumventing domestic renegotiation. Foreign investors have sued the Argentine government to reclaim losses incurred during an economy-wide disaster. However, since domestic investors do not have recourse to ICSID, the reparations paid to foreign and domestic investors via their respective arbitral and negotiating channels could be wildly different. Under the terms of the BITs, foreign investors can claim full compensation from the Argentine government even though Argentine citizens and companies have borne the full brunt of the crisis without compensation for the losses they have sustained (Roubini 2001).

Negotiating an international investment agreement at the World Trade Organization will raise complicated issues related to dispute settlement. Though most countries agree that an investor–state dispute settlement would be impracticable in the WTO context, there remains strong pressure for dispute settlement rules that could open similar avenues for arbitration (WGTI 2002c). Regardless of the specific details that emerge from negotiations, the case of Argentina powerfully demonstrates the potential dangers of providing foreign investors with privileged access to supranational arbitration.

Environment

Most traditional forms of electricity generation emit greenhouse gases, particulates, and other pollutants, compounding the environmental costs and dangers associated with the extraction and transport of fossil fuels. Recognizing the need for a transition to sustainable energy sources, governments at the 2002 World Summit on Sustainable Development called for a shift to more environmentally sustainable sources of energy (United Nations 2002).

Because they are relatively new, many renewable energy technologies are more costly than traditional fuels, which often benefit from substantial government subsidies. Sustainable energy technologies remain caught in a chicken-and-egg trap: cost-cutting technological advances will only develop if there is more demand for renewable energy, but demand will only develop if prices fall. To break out of this equilibrium, governments have used innovative public policies to drive the market forward. On the demand side, countries have established "feed-in" laws guaranteeing minimum prices for renewable energy, as well as renewable portfolio standards (RPS) requiring that a certain proportion of energy distributed comes from renewable sources. On the supply side, countries have subsidized research and development, as well as investments in generation equipment.

Creating an industry that many believe to be essential for our future survival has required substantial doses of political intervention. Building support for renewable energy in communities that must bear the cost of subsidizing new technologies has frequently required complex political compromises. The cases in this section, which describe policies in Arizona and Denmark, suggest that supporting green markets for electricity may require close attention to political, environmental, and economic interests, and that international rules on investment may infringe upon the space governments need to make trade-offs among the three.

Renewable portfolio standards in Arizona

Renewable portfolio standards (RPS) are an increasingly popular way for governments to encourage renewable energy use. Through an RPS, governments mandate that a certain proportion of the energy distributed in an area be derived from renewable sources. According to industry leaders, RPS policies significantly promote the use of renewable energy technologies (NACEC 2003). While renewable portfolio standards can effectively stimulate the development of a local market for sustainable energy, these policies could become a victim of investment-related disciplines undertaken at the national level.

Some believe that RPS standards could be challenged under NAFTA trade rules because they may constitute a de facto form of market access discrimination between suppliers who deliver like goods.[13] Others believe that RPS measures discriminate based on non-product-related process and production methods (PPMs), and therefore violate the GATT (Campbell 2002). Still others dismiss these claims and argue that there may still be space for properly designed renewable portfolio standards because renewable energy falls into a distinct and legitimately separate category of electricity (Hempling and Rader 2002).

There are good reasons to believe that investment rules, existing and future, may constrain governments' ability to design and implement effective, politically feasible RPS measures. The case of Arizona demonstrates that international investment rules may encroach upon sub-national regulatory autonomy, making it increasingly difficult to achieve consensus around sometimes costly environmental policies.

Arizona boasts some of the best sites in the United States for solar energy development, and the state recently implemented a portfolio standard mandating that 0.2 per cent of total energy distributed in 2001 come from renewable sources, of which 60 per cent must be new solar capacity. This relatively small percentage is scheduled to grow to 1.1 per cent by 2007 (Arizona Corporation Commission 2001). Because solar photovoltaic generation is not yet a mature technology, investing in solar energy can involve significant costs to communities that enter the market early.

To finance the development of renewable energy facilities in Arizona, utilities currently levy a surcharge on retail consumers. During the policy-making process, some observers argued that financing renewable energy would put Arizona's industry at a competitive disadvantage (Associated Press 2000). Consequently, the framers of the RPS tried to maximize the benefits the state receives from promoting renewable energy technology development by creating a "solar development strategy."

Arizona's "solar development strategy" is a striking attempt to integrate environmental and economic development concerns into the RPS. Enacted in 2001, the RPS provides incentives for the development of a strong and robust renewable energy technology sector in Arizona. These incentives include a two-layer "extra credit" scheme of incentives for power sourced from solar facilities located in Arizona, in addition to further credits awarded for locally sourced manufacturing and installation content. These incentives have helped stimulate the growth of a dynamic renewable energy industry in Arizona.

The Arizona RPS, however, may be inconsistent with investment provisions in the North American Free Trade Agreement. While RPS measures may be discriminatory in the sense described above, national treatment is not the issue in this particular case. Rather, the conflict arises due to performance requirements attached to the portfolio standard. NAFTA Article 1106(b) explicitly prohibits governments from making the "receipt or continued receipt of an advantage" conditional upon the use of goods produced in its territory.[14] Since the Arizona RPS conditions the receipt of bonus portfolio credits upon the use of in-state inputs, it could reasonably be argued that the RPS violates NAFTA's prohibition on performance requirements.[15]

This does not mean that the RPS – with its performance requirements – is not a good or an effective policy. From the perspectives of technology development and political economy, the provisions of the solar development strategy are defensible. Arizona consumers pay surcharges to foster the development of a new and environmentally friendly technology, and they hope to channel much of these resources into the development of local jobs and industries. Indeed, the renewable portfolio standard and the rate hikes that would accompany it were sold to the public explicitly on the basis of job creation and local economic development (Grand Canyon Trust 2000). Investing in technological innovation involves financial commitments and complex political compromises. Constraining the capacity to make these trade-offs may inhibit the development of innovative and environmentally friendly policies.

The Arizona case demonstrates that international investment rules can constrain electricity policies at all levels of government. Furthermore, they may inhibit the development of environmentally friendly policies by complicating communities' efforts to capture the economic benefits of investments in innovative technologies. By shrinking the room for compromise between political, economic, and environmental interests, investment agreements that straitjacket industrial policy could make it more difficult for governments to integrate a sustainable development agenda into the electricity sector.

Industrial policy for technology development

With 60 per cent of the world's wind turbine manufacturing capacity and a 50 per cent global market share, Denmark is a big player in renewable energy markets. In 1980, Denmark had 5 megawatts of installed wind energy capacity; by 2000, that figure had swelled to over 2,300 megawatts – equivalent to almost 20 per cent of the country's annual energy consumption. The Danish government now expects to produce 50 per cent of its energy consumption from renewable sources by 2030 (Sawin 2001; Krohn 2002). Denmark's successful transformation from a fossil-fuel-dependent economy to one of the world's most dynamic producers of wind power exemplifies the potentially positive role of a politically and environmentally sensitive industrial policy. It also demonstrates that international investment rules could restrict some of the instruments that made the country's energy revolution possible.

Denmark has committed itself to reduce greenhouse gas emissions by 22 per cent between 1988 and 2005 (Moore and Ihle 1999). Early on, the government decided that environmentally friendly energy technologies would play a critical role in achieving this target by replacing coal-fired power plants with non-polluting energy sources. Using a mix of taxes, subsidies, and other economic incentives, the Danish government stimulated the growth of a thriving and dynamic wind turbine export industry. These incentives successfully balanced social and economic objectives in a politically and environmentally sensitive industrial policy.

Shifting Denmark to wind energy faced both economic and political challenges. Initially, wind energy had to be made economically competitive to induce producers to set up wind turbines. In 1980, this was a major challenge, since the available technology could not compete with traditional generation methods. At the same time, there were political obstacles to overcome. Achieving the kind of coverage the government envisioned required wind turbines – lots of them. However, planners quickly realized that wind farms, though renewable, were far from perfect neighbors. Their large size, noise, and visibility have sometimes caused communities to resist wind energy development. The task of creating a wind energy industry therefore required building political consensus around a technology that needed government support to become competitive.

Denmark used a wide array of taxes and subsidies to deliver economic incentives for renewable energy.[16] These policies operated both on the demand side by encouraging utilities to purchase renewably generated electricity, and on the supply side by subsidizing research and development, investment, and production. To make the diffusion of wind energy politically feasible, the government drew upon a long-standing set of social institutions: local guilds and co-operatives. Denmark's long history of co-operatives had accustomed Danish citizens to controlling local affairs, and the government tapped into existing cooperative arrangements by encouraging co-operatives to invest in wind turbines and farms (Tranæs 2003). It also offered capital grants for the installation of wind turbines to Danish citizens amounting to $44 million. The theory was that cooperative ownership would facilitate local acceptance of wind turbines and energy self-sufficiency. To make installation economically attractive, the Danish government required utilities to buy wind-generated energy at 85 per cent of the utility's net cost but restricted these payouts to members of co-operatives (Sawin 2001). While it was in place, this policy simultaneously met two objectives: it provided economic incentives for environmentally friendly technologies while at the same time encouraging local ownership and acceptance.[17] Today, 100,000 Danish families own wind turbines or shares in wind co-operatives, a formidable constituency with a stake in sustainable energy development.

While it is difficult to isolate the impact of this particular policy from the broader impact of Denmark's supportive framework for renewable energy promotion, the outcomes speak for themselves. Denmark is a world leader in terms of installed capacity, and about three-quarters of this capacity is locally owned by individuals and co-operatives (Tranæs 2003). Widespread ownership and acceptance of wind technology have reduced fossil fuel dependence, helped cement political support for further development of wind energy sources, and stimulated the development of vibrant firms to export home-grown technology.

Yet some of the incentives Denmark used to launch its path-breaking renewable energy industry may be inconsistent with rules emerging in international investment agreements. Policies like a discriminatory tariff that privileges purchases from locally owned co-operatives could conflict with national treatment provisions of the General Agreement on Trade in Services (GATS), which specify that foreign service providers should receive treatment no less favorable than that accorded to domestic industries. Though co-operatives are non-profit entities, they are nonetheless part of the electricity market and may fall within the ambit of international trade agreements (Jackson and Sanger 2003).

To get to where it is today, Denmark had to tackle a problem of industrial policy and a problem of political economy. Creating a new industry based on immature technology required substantial investments in research and development, as well as market-based incentives to increase supply and demand. At the same time, Denmark needed to find ways to make potentially intrusive wind farms politically acceptable. Cooperative ownership of renewable energy systems simultaneously revitalized co-operatives in Denmark and led them to embrace the rapid development of wind energy. By tailoring its policies to local conditions, Denmark successfully developed both a constituency and a market for environmentally friendly technology.

Equity

With an annual turnover of over $1.7 trillion, energy is one of the largest industries in the world, and the electricity sector is a major part of it (Zarrilli 2002). The electricity industry employs workers, illuminates communities, and encourages entrepreneurship and skill development. Between 1990 and 1999, private investment in the electricity sector totaled over $160 billion, representing over 600 private electricity projects in 70 developing countries (World Bank 2000). Due to its importance, electricity is frequently seen as a public service, and even where privatization is most advanced, the industry is regulated in the public interest.

Given that electricity plays such a central role in the economic life of many countries, it is natural that governments have paid close attention to ownership and equity issues in the sector. Implementing ownership constraints may introduce economic inefficiencies, but ownership is a complicated concept that involves identity politics, status, and perceptions of social equity. Who owns what is economically irrelevant so long as competition induces firms to offer services efficiently to consumers. But in the world we inhabit, subjective identities and group affiliations matter a great deal, and governments ignore these social and political forces at their peril.

Imperialism and decolonization created countries whose boundaries included ethnic groups that competed for control of the post-colonial state. Where ethnic identities coincided with employment patterns or economic advantages, conflict frequently ensued. In countries like Malaysia, riots inspired policies designed to empower disadvantaged ethnic groups by encouraging property ownership; in South Africa, the government is attempting to redress the legacy of apartheid by actively promoting black economic empowerment in the electricity sector. Though unpopular with economists, such policies may help integrate the electricity sector into a stable social compact capable of delivering sustainable public benefits. As the following case study suggests, however, these socially integrative policies could conflict with emerging rules on international investment.

Black economic empowerment in South Africa

Apartheid dehumanized everyone it touched. It also destroyed economic opportunities for black South Africans. Democratic government in South Africa, however, has brought a new willingness to address the inequities of the past by pursuing Black Economic Empowerment (BEE), which encourages the transfer of skills and other productive assets to companies run by black entrepreneurs. The BEE agenda in South Africa suggests that socially integrative policies may require precisely the kind of government autonomy that binding investment norms may effectively eliminate.

As befits a program that aims at fundamentally changing ownership patterns, the Black Economic Empowerment agenda is comprehensive. It aims to leverage state resources to increase black economic participation through preferential procurement programs, financial incentives, and other forms of state aid (South African Department of Trade and Industry website). The South African government is also developing a multi-sectoral program of black empowerment, including a specific set of objectives for the electricity sector (Eberhard 2003). An initial glance at the framework of BEE reveals several potential conflicts between empowerment policies and the kinds of disciplines that have been promulgated in bilateral and regional investment treaties.

South Africa's government has identified reform in the power sector as a critical component of its BEE agenda. Broad-based access to electricity carries symbolic weight in a country where access to modern services was once restricted on the basis of race. In the near future, parts of Eskom, South Africa's electric utility, will be unbundled and privatized, and the government intends to integrate equity issues into the restructuring process (Philpott and Clark 2002). Discussions have focused on broadening ownership patterns within the sector by mandating that 10 per cent of generation assets be transferred to BEE-eligible groups, with a further 20 per cent open to general private-sector participation (Scott 2003).

Other BEE provisions require companies to make progress on black empowerment as a condition of eligibility for government contracts (Mortished 2003). The overall framework for the Black Economic Empowerment program involves a 'scorecard' system in which enterprises receive points for black ownership, preferential procurement from BEE enterprises, and employment equity. Whenever the government "engages in any economic activity," whether procurement, a concessionary arrangement, or a divestment, it will award contracts or shares on a preferential basis to companies that achieve high scores according to these criteria (South African Department of Trade and Industry website).

Though controversial, BEE is seen by many South Africans as an integral piece of post-apartheid reconciliation and development (Oppenheimer 2003; *Financial Times* 2003). Policies like BEE, however, require space for political flexibility in design and implementation – space that can shrink under investment disciplines without careful planning and scrutiny. BEE could be seen as inconsistent with the general principle of national treatment because it discriminates against investors who are not black South Africans. A total of 10 per cent of divested Eskom assets must by definition go to South African nationals, a reservation that is facially inconsistent with many interpretations of national treatment, particularly those that apply to the pre-establishment phase of investment. If sectoral commitments covering power generation and distribution were made under the GATS, this requirement could conflict with national treatment provisions unless specific exemptions were made *ex ante*.[18]

Several elements of BEE could also be inconsistent with proposed trade and investment rules. If services negotiations were to bring public procurement under GATS disciplines and countries made commitments without exhaustively scheduling *ex ante* exemptions, then conflict could emerge due to violations of national treatment.[19] Alternatively, under an investment regime similar to the North American Free Trade Agreement, BEE policies could conflict with the prohibition on performance requirements (Peterson 2003).[20]

Programs like BEE may be legitimate social policies, but they are incompatible with basic principles of non-discrimination. Yet history suggests that the need for balanced social and economic development may justify derogations from non-discrimination. In 1971, the Malaysian government adopted a "New Economic Policy" (NEP) that favored members of the disaffected and disadvantaged Bumiputera[21] population to quell persistent ethnic tensions in the wake of decolonization. The NEP aimed to reorganize the Malaysian economy by restructuring employment and ownership in various economic sectors. Under the terms of the NEP, Bumiputeras were to hold 30 per cent of corporate sector assets by 1990, other Malaysians were to hold 40 per cent, and the foreign share was to plummet from 65 per cent to 30 per cent (Snodgrass 1995).

Despite sparking controversy, the NEP managed to achieve many of its goals, sustaining a climate of political compromise and economic growth. The NEP deployed a wide range of unorthodox policies, including conditioning industrial licenses upon compliance with NEP guidelines of 30 per cent Malay ownership (Biddle and Milor 1999). Official figures indicate that Bumiputera ownership increased from 2.4 per cent of assets in 1970 to over 20 per cent in 1990; non-Bumiputera ownership increased from 32.3 per cent to 46.2 per cent over the same period. This redistribution occurred against a backdrop of rapid economic growth averaging 4.2 per cent per annum between 1970 and 1990. It is certainly possible that Malaysia would have grown more quickly without interventionist, redistributive policies. Yet the converse might also be true, for "if Malaysia had gone full-tilt for growth and not undertaken an affirmative action program like the NEP, it might have suffered other violent political blow-ups" (Snodgrass 1995). The merits of the NEP as an economic policy are certainly open to debate, but what is clear is that government flexibility was required to implement its provisions.

While there is room in WTO agreements to accommodate socially integrative policies if countries specify exemptions in advance, the exemption process presumes a depth of *ex ante* knowledge that is both theoretically and practically unreasonable. Had the pre-apartheid regime in South Africa signed investment agreements that included national treatment provisions without making exemptions for programs targeting socio-economically disadvantaged groups, the post-apartheid regime could have found itself facing insuperable barriers to programs resembling BEE. Moreover, even democratic governments find it difficult to predict in advance what sorts of derogations might one day become necessary to advance social, political or economic objectives. If the first ANC government had signed bilateral investment treaties with stringent language on non-discrimination, the ability to launch BEE-type initiatives could have been greatly reduced.

Removing government capacity to confront polarizing social divisions does little to help advance the causes of social or economic development. The South African and Malaysian cases illustrate the importance of protecting the public sector's ability to develop active social policies for development.

Synthesis and Conclusions

The debate over policy space is more than academic: it is highly relevant to proposals about a new multilateral investment framework. Discussions in the Working Group on Trade and Investment (WGTI) and the Working Party on GATS Rules (WPGR) have advanced proposals that would impose increasingly stringent disciplines on investment policies. In the former body, a proposed multilateral framework on investment could create new international rules affecting pre-establishment conditions, performance requirements, and dispute settlement. In the latter, future discussions on government procurement and subsidies may well result in further disciplines.

These developments are significant because new disciplines and further liberalization often come at the price of policy space. While few would dispute that removing the capacity of governments to pursue perverse or ill-advised policies can improve country performance, adopting new commitments without due regard for policy space risks throwing the proverbial baby out with the bathwater. In an international context where economic considerations are often privileged above space for environmental planning, policies for achieving sustainable development require a great deal of innovation and flexibility. Governments currently retain some degree of freedom to pursue heterodox investment policies, though these are already somewhat constrained by the Agreement on Trade-Related Investment Measures (TRIMs), the General Agreement on Trade in Services, and bilateral and regional investment treaties. Further movement toward stronger GATS rules or a multilateral framework on investment needs to be weighed against the possible costs of diminished policy space for sustainable development.

The cases discussed here show how governments have used non-conformist policies, which would likely fail to pass muster among practitioners of neoliberal orthodoxy, to advance social and environmental goals in the electricity sector.

To support access to electricity:

- The Government of Gabon instituted a monopoly concession that bundled together the electricity and water sectors with incentives for service expansion.
- The US government provided subsidies for rural co-operatives to promote grid expansion, paving the way for universal electrification in the United States.

To help resolve a financial crisis:

- The Government of Argentina imposed an electricity rate freeze and mandated renegotiation of utility contracts to spread the burden of crisis resolution to all participants in an economy, including foreign investors.

To promote innovative renewable energy technologies:

- The US state of Arizona provided competitive advantages to locally sourced solar power manufacturers in the form of a performance requirement to guarantee local economic benefits from renewable energy.
- The government of Denmark introduced a discriminatory tariff that privileged purchases of electricity from locally owned co-operatives.

To mitigate a history of inequitable treatment:

- The government of Malaysia conditioned industrial licenses on ownership guidelines, potentially diffusing political conflict among communal groups.

- The Government of South Africa mandated ownership shares for black populations as part of public asset sales, and conditioned eligibility for government contracts on black ownership as part of a larger policy of "Black Economic Empowerment."

These policies, which represent only an illustrative subset of approaches to internalizing environmental and social considerations in the electricity sector, can and should be subject to debate. Specifically, critics might argue that there are alternative means of reaching the same policy goals that are less trade restrictive, and less likely to conflict with trade and investment disciplines. There are at least two responses to this charge.

First, many of the policies above illustrate that heterodox efforts at steering and channeling investment can indeed be successful, reinforcing recent work that emphasizes the importance of domestic institutional innovation. For example, by privileging local co-operatives, Denmark has spurred creation of the world's most successful wind power equipment export industry, which also generates 20 per cent of national electricity needs.

Second, the need to balance economic, political, and social or environmental considerations in particular national contexts may require heterodox policies of the sort described here. For example, a neoliberal approach to rural electrification in Gabon might have dictated open access to the rural electricity market and the introduction of competition. However, the regulatory burden of a truly competitive market would likely have been beyond the capacity of the Gabon government at the time; a monopoly service provider was better suited to meet the needs of rural electricity expansion in the context of limited state capacity. Similarly, while South Africa's efforts at Black Economic Empowerment depart from market orthodoxy, the potential political and social gains from post-apartheid reconciliation may make the experiment worthwhile. In specific national contexts, the best economic policies may well be second- or third-best from a political economy perspective.

This is not to suggest that policy heterodoxy and experimentation always or even mostly result in positive change. Advocates for constraining policy space justifiably argue that policy heterodoxy can serve as a cover for arbitrary, capricious, and even venal government policies. However, since the use of institutional mechanisms to discipline governments is not without cost, ensuring responsible use of policy space is a task better addressed at the national level through transparent governance and accountability. International investment negotiations are unlikely to be an appropriate instrument to address venal domestic politics – and, indeed, they may exact a substantial price in forgone ability for future policy experimentation.

The policy case studies described in this chapter strongly suggest that investment rules would shrink available policy space. For example, Arizona's efforts at promoting renewable energy development, which also stimulates local industry, may violate prohibitions on performance standards that are present in many investment agreements. Subsidies to rural electricity co-operatives formed the backbone of a highly successful policy that turned on the lights across Depression-era America. Developing countries today could be hard-pressed to deploy similar instruments if GATS negotiations on subsidies prohibit favoring domestic providers.

The degree to which investment and trade rules shrink policy space lies in the details of the negotiated rules. We return to specific elements of what would constitute a more open policy space in the following section.

Supporters of investment rules often contend that fears of restrictions on policy flexibility are overblown and stem from a failure to understand the flexibility structured into investment rules. Specifically, they argue that under the "positive list" approach used by the GATS, and favored for an investment agreement, countries can choose whether or not to subject sectors to disciplines, and can further choose to schedule exemptions. Consequently, there is no conflict between strong investment rules and policy space. Critics counter that, in practice, governments face serious obstacles to utilizing these mechanisms. In the introductory section of this chapter, we developed a taxonomy of reasons to suspect that even a positive list approach could make comprehensive exemptions difficult to implement. The cases we have discussed support the view that the ability to retain policy space exists more in theory than in practice.

The flexibility afforded by the ability to choose which sectors to commit in a positive list approach is limited by two factors: the mandate for progressive liberalization and the increasingly ambitious scope of requests made by Members. Under the GATS, there is an explicit call for regular and progressive liberalization, and such a mandate would likely be incorporated into any new policy on investment. Even without such a mandate, however, a structure akin to the GATS provides the framework for comprehensive requests for liberalization. Both the European Union and the United States have made substantial requests for commitments in energy services, which encompass a broad array of functions and activities in the sector. Through the bilateral request-offer process, countries with less negotiating capacity and leverage may face substantial informal pressure to acquiesce.

Second, for the reasons enumerated in the introductory section, proponents of investment rules tend to overstate the amount of policy space that can be preserved through exemptions. Requiring that exemptions be scheduled at the time of commitment presumes that governments have an improbable degree of *ex ante* knowledge. Capacity constraints in the developing world further limit the likelihood of adequately scheduling exemptions in order to preserve policy space.

For example, to address rural electrification under an investment regime, energy or rural development authorities in Gabon would have had to identify first the range of policies available to promote access to electricity, including monopoly concessions. They then would have had to persuade their trade counterparts of the need to include the necessary exemptions when scheduling the energy sector. This sequence of actions stretches credulity, particularly since social and environmental ministries are hardly influential in dictating trade positions. To urge countries that have only achieved minimal levels of rural electrification to endorse an investment framework that limits their policy options to current policy knowledge is irresponsible.

The loss of policy space can limit the capacity for effective governance. When governments bind sectors of the economy on their behalf, citizens lose the ability to redirect their governments in keeping with changing political preferences and contexts. Had an earlier government in South Africa subjected itself to national treatment obligations in the electricity sector, the current government would have faced greater challenges in implementing Black Economic Empowerment. Finally, investment rules limit governments' ability to react to changing external circumstances. For example, Argentina's rapid privatization meant that its utility policies affected foreign investors, who are now deluging the government with lawsuits under bilateral investment treaties to avoid bearing any of the adjustment burdens following the crisis.

Reductions in policy space can have real consequences for the ability to govern the electricity sector in a socially and environmentally responsible way. To crystallize the points relevant for international investment negotiations in various arenas, we conclude with a few issues for further discussion.

Final points for consideration

The cases developed in this study are animated by potential friction between reasonable electricity policies and the principles inherent in international investment rules. Our analysis of these studies has identified several potential areas of conflict, including pre-establishment non-discrimination, performance requirements, indirect expropriation, dispute settlement, and disciplines on government procurement and subsidies for services. These studies suggest that the costs of investment negotiations, in terms of policy space forgone, may be underappreciated. Analysis of the cases in this chapter suggests several areas of particular concern:

- *Specific commitments* Many disciplines under the GATS, and potentially under an investment agreement organized on a positive list basis, apply only to sectors that have been bound during negotiations. Only eight countries made specific commitments in "services incidental to energy distribution" during the Uruguay Round, which means that other countries have until now retained substantial autonomy in the electricity sector (Evans 2002). Making commitments in electricity services when the scope and definition of these services remains relatively unclear may lead to unpleasant surprises in the future.

- *Pre-establishment national treatment* Disciplines on the admission and establishment of investments from abroad can have serious implications for national policy autonomy. As the cases in this study suggest, adopting the principle of pre-establishment national treatment could make it more difficult for governments to manage or attach conditions to the entry of investments, significantly reducing space for social and environmental policies.

- *Performance requirements* Prohibitions on performance requirements have appeared in several recent investment agreements and may constrain measures necessary to achieve consensus around policies for sustainable development. Economic historians have demonstrated that performance requirements played an important role in the development trajectories of today's industrialized nations, and we have seen that they can play a part in encouraging states to adopt stronger environmental policies. While some performance requirements are not helpful, others can help harness the power of foreign investment to achieve better environmental and development outcomes. These should continue to be permissible components of country sustainable development strategies.

- *Indirect expropriation* Indirect expropriation is an expansive concept that can include regulatory actions and judicial decrees. In Argentina, the government found that its crisis management strategy of pesofication and electricity rate freezes spawned a wave of lawsuits even though no actual expropriation had taken place. The concept of creeping expropriation may unduly infringe upon governments' ability to promulgate legislation in the public interest by extending to private investors an implicit guarantee that their assets will retain full value.

- *Dispute settlement* Experience with bilateral investment treaties demonstrates that investors have circumvented contractually specified dispute resolution methods by invoking BIT provisions that permit international arbitration. Providing foreign investors with privileged access to supranational arbitral bodies can result in severe inconsistencies in the treatment of national and foreign investors. Furthermore, the threat of recourse to international arbitration can produce a chilling effect that effectively reduces policy space.

- *Government procurement in services* The Working Party on GATS Rules (WPGR) is beginning to address the question of government procurement in services under Article XIII. While government procurement is already being addressed in other WTO bodies,[22] some countries have expressed a desire to move forward autonomously on services procurement in negotiations under the GATS. National treatment obligations in government procurement could block an important channel for policies supportive of social and environmental ends. Even a positive list for disciplines on government procurement could pave the way for progressive liberalization and the contraction of policy space for sustainable development.

- *Subsidies* Article XV of the General Agreement on Trade in Services requires countries to discuss new disciplines on subsidies for services. Subsidies are one of the most flexible policy tools available to governments, and they can be targeted to meet specific social and environmental goals. Because they apply to the supply of services via commercial presence, new disciplines on services subsidies could limit the use of innovative policies for sustainable development.

Limiting electricity policy options with new disciplines would stifle experimentation at precisely the historical moment at which policy innovation is most necessary. Electricity restructuring is bringing sweeping changes to institutions, patterns of investment, and technological development in the sector. Governments will need real ingenuity, flexibility and policy space to integrate public benefits into a new and largely uncharted economic environment. Investment rules provide stability for investors, but they may ultimately limit governments' ability to integrate social and environmental concerns into their governance of the sector. Unless more attention is paid to the potential costs of new rules, the inclusion of such disciplines may be a poor investment in the future.

A positive agenda for investment?

The preceding analysis gives rise to an important set of questions. Should governments merely adopt a defensive stance on investment negotiations, or is there room for investment rules that would strengthen and revitalize the policy space for sustainable development? Addressing these issues is beyond the scope of this chapter, but they should form the heart of any future research agenda.[23] It is difficult to meet demands for investment negotiations with a strictly defensive posture, and the refusal to negotiate is a tactic that may miss potential opportunities for integrating investment into a sustainable development agenda. Defining the contours of such an agenda will require further research, creativity, and political will, but it remains crucial to the pursuit of sustainable development.

Notes

We would like to thank: Mamadou Diarrasouba for research assistance, as well as Kevin Baumert, Anton Eberhard, Kevin Gallagher, David Jhirad, Rashid Kaukab, Tony La Vina, Aaditya Mattoo, Crescencia Maurer, Smita Nakhooda, Luke Peterson, Janet Sawin, Christiane Schuchhardt, Frances Seymour, Robert Stumberg, Elisabeth Tuerk, Scott Vaughan, David Waskow, and Jacob Werksman and Vice Yu for their helpful comments on earlier drafts of this chapter. Responsibility for the views expressed in this chapter and the errors that remain rests solely with the authors. We would also like to thank participants in the Cancún Trade and Development Symposium (12 September 2003) and the Concerted Action on Trade and Environment Conference (30 October 2003) for their helpful comments and feedback.

1. Indeed, as this chapter is being written, we are reminded of this fact by reports of a power failure across the northeast United States, resulting in the breakdown of transport and communication networks.

2. While the GATS is generally considered a trade agreement, in practice its inclusion of commercial presence as a mode of supply introduces investment disciplines into the World Trade Organization.

3. Indeed, this is the view of a World Bank study on the California experience (Besant Jones and Tenenbaum 2001).

4. See www.wto.org/english/tratop_e/invest_e/invest_e.htm.

5. See Article 1110.1 of the North American Free Trade Agreement.

6. See Article 15.6.1 of the US–Singapore Free Trade Agreement.

7. See, for example, NAFTA Article 1108.7.

8. Also see the schedule of commitments under the GATS, in which several countries schedule exceptions for subsidy programs.

9. GATS Article XVII suggests that national treatment applies to policies "according to services and services suppliers of any other Member, either formally identical treatment or formally different treatment to that it accords to its own like services and service suppliers." Subsidies to co-operatives may not on the face of it be discriminatory, but such subsidies make de facto distinctions between domestic and foreign suppliers, since co-operatives tend to be composed almost entirely of domestic residents who own and operate the investments they fund. Moreover, such treatment could be challenged on the grounds of "non-violation" in Article XXIII.3 of the GATS, which allows affected Members recourse to dispute settlement if expected benefits are nullified as the result of measures that do not otherwise conflict with the provisions of the GATS.

10. Article XXVIII (h) defines a "monopoly supplier of a service" to include "any person, public or private, which in the relevant market of the territory of a Member is authorized or established formally or in effect by that Member as the sole supplier of

that service," which can include exclusive concessions granted even under competitive and non-discriminatory bidding procedures.

11. According to Section 4 of GATS Article VIII, "if, after the date of entry into force of the WTO Agreement, a Member grants monopoly rights regarding the supply of a service covered by its specific commitments, that Member shall notify the Council for Trade in Services no later than three months before the intended implementation of the grant of monopoly rights and the provisions of paragraphs 2, 3 and 4 of Article XXI shall apply." Article XXI introduces language subjecting the approval of monopolies to international negotiation. According to Article XXI, Section 1(b), Members must notify the Council for Trade in Services if they wish to modify commitments, a phrase that includes the creation of sub-national concessionary arrangements. In Article XXI, Section 2(a), WTO rules state that,

> At the request of any Member the benefits of which under this Agreement may be affected (referred to in this Article as an "affected Member") by a proposed modification or withdrawal notified under subparagraph 1(b), the modifying Member shall enter into negotiations with a view to reaching agreement on any necessary compensatory adjustment. In such negotiations and agreement, the Members concerned shall endeavor to maintain a general level of mutually advantageous commitments not less favorable to trade than that provided for in Schedules of specific commitments prior to such negotiations.

Sections 3(a) and 4(a) of Article XXI specify that affected Members can refer the matter to arbitration if they are unhappy with the compensation offered. Until arbitration and the compensatory adjustments that ensue are resolved, the monopoly concession may not go forward.

12. For a current list of pending cases at ICSID, consult www.worldbank.org/icsid/cases/pending.htm.

13. See Horlick et al. 2002. The authors argue that RPS standards may constitute a de facto form of discrimination between power sources located in different countries. For example, definitions of renewable energy that exclude large hydro sources may discriminate against Canadian hydropower sources.

14. NAFTA Article 1106(c):

> No Party may condition the receipt or continued receipt of an advantage, in connection with an investment in its territory of an investor of a Party or of a non-Party, on compliance with any of the following requirements: (b) to purchase, use or accord a preference to goods produced in its territory, or to purchase goods from producers in its territory.

This language is stronger than provisions in other bilateral investment treaties. The OECD's draft Multilateral Agreement on Investment (MAI) explicitly exempted the conditioning of advantages on similar criteria in its section on performance requirements. The draft text of the FTAA includes separate bracketed elements that embrace both interpretations.

15. It is possible that other provisions in the RPS violate the same language in NAFTA. Arizona's experience with ravaging forest fires has led it to pursue forest-management techniques that generate wood waste, and the state's numerous golf courses and other open spaces also tend to generate large quantities of biomass that require disposal. In a landfill, these wastes would generate methane, a dangerous greenhouse gas. Arizona's RPS includes locally sourced biomass as a renewable energy

source. By incinerating organic wastes that would otherwise require costly disposal, biomass incineration closes a circle and generates useful thermal and electrical energy. But the requirement of local sourcing clearly violates NAFTA rules on performance requirements.

16. For a comprehensive discussion of these instruments, see Sawin 2001.

17. According to Sawin, Denmark imposed limitations on co-operative membership and benefits. For years, only people living within the district where turbines were located could join wind co-operatives and benefit from the advantages accorded to private generators.

18. GATS Article XVI(e) prohibits "measures which restrict or require specific types of legal entity or joint venture through which a service supplier may supply a service"; and Article XVI(f) prohibits "limitations on the participation of foreign capital in terms of maximum percentage limit on foreign shareholding or the total value of individual or aggregate foreign investment."

19. Bound sectors under the GATS are subject to national treatment requirements. If government procurement is incorporated into the GATS, then public authorities no longer have the authority to discriminate between enterprises on the basis of their ownership. See WPGR 2003 for a discussion of a GATS-style positive list approach to non-discrimination in government procurement of services.

20. The BEE scorecard's proposed inclusion of benefits for firms that purchase from BEE enterprises implicitly imposes a domestic content standard upon investors, potentially violating Chapter 1106(b) of the NAFTA.

21. *Bumiputera* literally means "sons of the soil," and refers to ethnic Malays.

22. Government procurement is currently governed by the voluntary, plurilateral Agreement on Government Procurement, and the issue of transparency in government procurement is currently being addressed in the Doha Development Agenda process.

23. For an initial analysis of these issues, see Cosbey et al. 2003.

9

Performance Requirements as Tools of Development Policy: Lessons from Developed and Developing Countries

Nagesh Kumar

There is currently a lot of discussion on the relevance of performance requirements as tools of host governments' development policy in the context of the ongoing debate over the emerging WTO regime on investment (UNCTAD 2001b; WTO and UNCTAD 2001). It is argued that performance requirements as policy tools may help to maximize the benefits of foreign direct investment (FDI) inflows for developing host countries. However, critics contend that performance requirements are inefficient and distort the patterns of trade and investment.

Generally FDI flows are expected to facilitate industrialization and development of host countries by enabling them to tap the resources of multinational enterprises (MNEs), such as production technology, organizational and managerial skills, marketing know-how, and even marketing networks. Host countries also expect to benefit from knowledge spillovers and other favorable externalities from FDI. However, there is considerable variation in the 'quality' of FDI inflows and not all of them benefit their host countries equally (Kumar 2002). Recent empirical studies have shown that knowledge spillovers may not take place, especially in developing countries, and domestic enterprises may actually be affected adversely (Haddad and Harrison 1993; Kokko et al. 1996; Aitken and Harrison 1999; De Mello 1999; Xu 2000). Recent empirical literature has also presented evidence that by crowding out domestic investment, FDI in some cases may thus be immiserizing (Fry 1992; Agosin and Mayer 2000; Kumar and Pradhan 2002; Carkovic and Levine 2002). There could also be possibilities of divergence between MNE interests and the host country's developmental objectives, arising from the MNE's strategy to pursue the objective of global profit maximization. In order to maximize global profits, the interests of certain affiliates may be compromised and sourcing decisions may not be taken on the basis of efficiency considerations alone. There is also evidence of widespread manipulation of transfer prices in intra-firm trade.

Given the possibility of conflicts of interest, performance requirements have been employed by the host governments, among other policy instruments (such as trade policy, screening mechanisms and incentives, etc.) to maximize the contribution of FDI to the process of development. These objectives include deepening of the domestic industrial base, generation of employment and local linkages, development of export capability and improvement of balance of payments, and the development of local technological capability through transfer and diffusion of technology, among others.

Besides helping in industrial development and managing the balance-of-payments objectives, it has been argued that trade-related investment measures (TRIMs) have been employed by host countries to deal with the restrictive business practices (RBPs) pursued by MNEs (Puri and Brussick 1989). For instance, MNEs may engage themselves in importing more to provide markets to related companies or may indulge in manipulation of transfer prices of imports from related sources to transfer profits. Local content requirements (LCRs) or foreign exchange neutrality could moderate the effect of such RBPs.

Many governments – in developed and developing countries alike – have imposed extensive performance regulations on FDI at the time of entry, in order to pattern their operations in consonance with the country's development objectives (see Guisinger et al. 1985; UNCTC 1991; UNCTAD 2001b). Commonly employed performance requirements include various forms of local content requirements (LCRs) and export performance requirements (EPRs); indirect export performance requirements in the form of trade balancing or dividend balancing, or foreign exchange neutrality requirements; requirements to establish a joint venture with domestic participation or for minimum level of domestic equity participation; employment performance requirements; requirement to transfer technology; production processes or other proprietary knowledge; and research and development requirements (see UNCTAD 2001b for a more complete list).

In this context, this chapter reviews the experiences of developed and developing countries to draw implications for the current debate on the relevance of performance requirements (PRs). The next section summarizes the evidence on use of PRs in developed countries. The following section reviews theoretical, cross-country and case evidence on effectiveness of PRs in meeting their stated policy objectives in developing countries. This is followed by an examination of the evidence of the effect of PRs on the magnitude of FDI inflows. The final section concludes the chapter with some policy remarks.

Evidence on the Use of Performance Requirements by Developed Countries

Today's developed countries employed PRs extensively in their process of development, especially when they were net importers of capital. For instance, Chang (2002, 2003a) documents how the United States had all kinds of performance requirements on foreign investors when it was a capital-importing country in the nineteenth century. The federal government had restrictions on foreigners' ownership in agricultural land, mining, and logging. It discriminated against foreign firms in banking and insurance, prohibited foreign investment in coastal shipping, reserved the directorships of national banks for American citizens, deprived foreign shareholders of voting rights in the case of federally chartered banks, and prohibited the employment of foreign workers by foreign firms. Chang also shows that major European countries that were originally capital exporting, such as the United Kingdom, France, and Germany, turned to adopting formal and informal measures to protect domestic enterprises from growing American companies after the Second World War. These included foreign exchange controls and regulations against foreign investment in sensitive sectors, promotion of state-owned enterprises, restrictions on takeovers, performance requirements (or undertakings), and voluntary restrictions on MNEs.

More evidence on the use of PRs by developed countries in the post-World War II period is available. Countries like Australia, Canada, France, and Japan, among others, have made extensive use of PRs (Safarian 2002; WTO and UNCTAD 2001). Australia (and New Zealand) imposed 50 per cent domestic ownership requirements in natural resource projects and also employed an offsets policy, under which larger government contracts required new domestic activity of 30 per cent of their import content. Canada enacted a Foreign Investment Review Act (FIRA) in the early 1970s under which an extensive set of PRs (called undertakings) were imposed to ensure that 'significant benefit' is reaped by Canada from the operations of FDI. Norway and Sweden also imposed PRs for natural resource concessions. France has imposed an extensive set of PRs on foreign investors, depending upon the nationality of the investor; economic growth effects including employment, regional balance and promotion of local R&D; competition with French enterprises; balance of payments, etc. Japan also imposed PRs at the time of approvals. These depended on the contribution to technology development, exports, or import substitution; competition with Japanese industry; 50 per cent foreign ownership; and a requirement that the president of the joint venture be Japanese. In the United States, CFIUS, under the Exxon–Florio Amendment, has rejected some proposed takeovers and also at times imposed what amount to PRs (Safarian 2002).

Among the specific types of performance requirements, local content requirements have been employed by most of the developed countries and developing countries at one time or other (see Sercovich 1998; Low and Subramanian 1995; and WTO and UNCTAD 2001, for illustrations). In particular, governments have employed LCRs in the auto industry to promote backward integration and localization of value-added production. Many of the developed countries imposed LCRs in the auto industry until recently. For instance, Italy imposed a 75 per cent local content requirement on the Mitsubishi Pajero; the United States imposed a 75 per cent rule on the Toyota Camry; and the United Kingdom imposed a 90 per cent rule on the Nissan Primera (Sercovich 1998). Australia imposed a 85 per cent local content rule on motor vehicles until 1989 (Pursell 1999).

The form of the PRs employed by developed countries in the 1990s was, however, changed in favor of trade policy measures that achieve objectives similar to those of PRs but are consistent with the provisions of TRIMs. These include rules of origin, screwdriver regulations, voluntary export restraints (VERs), and anti-dumping (Belderboss 1997; Moran 1998; Safarian 2002). The US government employed VERs against Japanese exports of cars in 1981. Subsequently the European Union imposed VERs on Japanese exports of consumer electronics. The European Union countries have also extensively used the screwdriver regulations, which are, in effect, like local content regulations to deepen the local commitment of Japanese corporations in consumer goods industries in the past. EU countries have also used anti-dumping measures to regulate imports of cars and other products from Japan and Southeast Asia, and the United States has aggressively used similar measures in attempting to achieve reciprocity (i.e. 'substantially equivalent competitive opportunities') in trade and investment with Japan and other countries (Safarian 2002). In the United States, provisions of the Buy American Act have also been used as local content requirements. For instance, in order to qualify as a domestic product to claim a 25 per cent price preference under the Buy American Act, a Hungarian manufacturer of buses had to buy US-made engines, transmissions, axles, and tires (Krugman and Obstfeld 2000: 205).

Even now, the industrialized countries – especially the EU and NAFTA member countries – taking advantage of RTA exceptions that are available under Section XXIV of GATT, are effectively using rules of origin

Box 9.1 Rules of origins imposed by NAFTA and the EU to increase local content: select case studies

NAFTA rules of origin

The objective of the US effort in NAFTA through rules of origin has been to prevent "screwdriver" assembly operations from being set up within the region to utilize low-cost inputs from outside. NAFTA rules of origin require that a substantial portion of inputs originate within the region for automobiles, electronic products (printers, copiers, television tubes), textiles, telecommunications, machine tools, forklift trucks, fabricated metals, household appliances, furniture, and tobacco products. For example:

- *Telecommunications* The NAFTA rule requires that nine out of every ten printed circuitboard assemblies, the essential component of office switching equipment, be packaged within the NAFTA countries. In response, AT&T shifted some production from Asia to Mexico, and Fujitsu and Ericsson brought new investments to Mexico.
- *Color televisions* NAFTA requires that television tubes be produced within the region to qualify for preferential status. Prior to NAFTA, there was no North American manufacturer of television tubes; in the first two years after NAFTA's passage, five factories took shape within the NAFTA region, with investments from Hitachi, Mitsubishi, Zenith, Sony, and Samsung.
- *Computers* US negotiators proposed a rule that would have required two of the three key components (motherboard, flat panel display, and hard disk drive) to be North American in origin. With forceful opposition from IBM and other companies that wanted to maintain their more flexible international sourcing patterns, the negotiators settled on a final rule requiring at least the motherboard to be North American.
- *Office equipment* NAFTA tightened origin rules for printers, photocopiers, and fax machines, requiring more components to be manufactured locally. For printers and photocopiers, all major subassemblies have to be produced in North America (equivalent to an 80 per cent domestic-content requirement). Apparently this rule was instrumental in motivating Canon to construct a plant costing more than $100 million in Virginia, rather than somewhere in Asia where the production costs would be lower.
- *Automobiles* The domestic content rule was raised from 50 per cent in the United States–Canada Free Trade Agreement to 62.5 per cent in NAFTA. It required Japanese and European firms to replace imports from their home countries.

EU rules of origin

The European Union has adopted high domestic-content rules of origin in automobiles and other industries such as photocopiers, and has also entertained proposals for even tighter requirements for printed circuit boards and telecoms switching equipment. The European Union also established product-specific rules that require printed circuit board assembly within Europe. It has negotiated association agreements in Central and Eastern Europe that require 60 per cent domestic content for products to qualify for entry into the European Union. Select examples are as follows:

- *Semiconductors*   In 1989, the European Union abruptly changed the rule of origin to require that wafer fabrication for semiconductors be done within Europe to avoid a 14 per cent semiconductor tariff. Whereas US companies performed most of their diffusion operations in the United States prior to the decision, seven of the largest ten US producers built fabrication facilities in Europe following the rule change. Citing the need to comply with the new rule of origin, for example, Intel invested $400 million in Ireland for wafer fabrication and semiconductor assembly. Even though wafer fabrication was not cost-competitive in Europe, compared to Asia or the United States, twenty-two new fabrication facilities were set up in Europe within two years of the change in the rule of origin.
- *Automobiles*   The United Kingdom and France proposed an 80 per cent local content rule for the Nissan Bluebird to qualify as an EC product. In the end, they backed down in the face of Italian and German opposition and decided to rely on quantitative restrictions to protect against Japanese imports. The 60 per cent domestic-content rule in the automotive sector has forced the General Motors engine plant in Hungary to use high-cost German steel as an input, preventing utilization of cheaper locally available steel.
- *Textiles and apparel*   The near 100 per cent domestic-content requirement in textiles and apparel has forced the German partner in the Brinkmann–Prochnik joint venture in Poland to load a truck with cotton fabrics, thread, buttons, and even labels in Germany; transport it to Lodz for stitching into trench coats; and re-import it for sale in the European Union – rather than allow the Polish partner to source from cheaper local supplies.

Source: Kumar 2001 on the basis of Moran 1998; Belderboss 1997; and other sources.

to increase domestic value added. Rules of origin determine the extent of domestic content a product must have to qualify as an internal product in a preferential trading agreement. Hence, they have the same effect as the local content requirements. By now considerable evidence is available on the use of rules of origin by EU and NAFTA countries to increase the extent of localization of production by MNEs supplying to them (see Box 9.1 for illustrations).

Therefore the low incidence of PRs in developed countries in the recent period is deceptive, as they extensively employ measures that achieve similar objectives as the PRs that are currently inconsistent with the obligations of TRIMs. Developed countries have extensively employed policies such as PRs throughout their period of development in one form or another. In contrast, developing countries have only recently started to use these policy tools to foster their industrialization and development. Developed countries have striven to take these valuable policy tools away from developing countries under the TRIMs Agreement. An attempt is being made by developed countries to expand the scope of WTO rules beyond what is covered under TRIMs to restrict further the policy space for developing countries.

Effectiveness of PRs in Meeting Developmental Objectives: Lessons from Developing Countries

Policy objectives and arguments against

Local content requirements (LCRs) are employed by host governments to deepen the commitment of foreign investors to the host economies and maximize their contribution to income and employment generation and hence the transfer of technology and other externalities. It has been argued that under conditions of perfect competition, LCRs reduce host country welfare in cases where the prices of local inputs are higher than world prices. Therefore an increased use of domestic inputs imposes a tax on the foreign producers, necessitating the need for protection (Moran 1998; WTO and UNCTAD 2001). However, this contention is not valid as the assumption of perfect competition hardly prevails in a real-life situation. Price competitiveness of local supplies may not be the only reason for an MNE not to obtain intermediates in the domestic markets. In many cases, local components required by an MNE may be of specifications and designs that are proprietary or patented. Hence, they would not be available in the host country unless the MNE licenses their manufacture to some local vendor and passes on the designs and drawings. There may be other considerations for not licensing local production of components, such as to utilize more fully production capacities created elsewhere in the world. Studies have shown that MNE affiliates in developing countries tend to buy the bulk of their inputs from their parents or other associated suppliers and hence generate few domestic linkages (UNCTAD 2002b; Lipsey 1998; Manifold 1997). Local content regulations play a useful role in prompting the MNE to consider licensing the local manufacture of such components, which it may not otherwise do because of such considerations. LCRs, therefore, may force MNEs to identify nascent local capabilities and provide them with the know-how and technology.

Similarly export performance requirements (EPRs) are imposed by host governments to prompt foreign investors to integrate the affiliates in the host countries into their global/regional production networks and also create other favorable externalities of export-oriented production. It has been argued that if a firm is able to export competitively, it would do so on its own to maximize its profits. Hence, requiring it to export beyond what is commercially viable will be a loss-making activity (WTO and UNCTAD 2001). Again, this observation is based on the assumption of perfect competition, which hardly prevails. As argued earlier, MNEs maximize their global profits, not the profits of individual affiliates. They practice market segmentation and product mandating strategies to maximize their global profits. They are known to impose export restrictions on their subsidiaries (see Kumar 2001 for evidence). Full exploitation of a host country's potential as an internationally competitive location for export-oriented production may also be prevented by information asymmetry.

Evidence from theoretical studies

A number of theoretical studies have shown LCRs to have favorable developmental effects and to be welfare improving for host countries. For instance, Davidson et al. (1985) show that within a duopolistic model local content and export requirements can increase the host country's welfare and employment at the cost of the source country and world welfare. McCulloh (1990) argues that in the presence of tariffs, LCRs may actually improve host country welfare. Balasubramanyam (1991) argues that the dynamic benefits resulting from LCRs – such as the development of local supplier capabilities – far outweigh the short-run welfare losses that they may impose. Richardson (1993), using a general equilibrium model, shows that an effective LCR will induce foreign firms to increase their own domestic production of the component input and will induce capital flows, thus furthering the process of industrialization of the host country. Lahiri and Ono (1998) develop a partial equilibrium model of an oligopolistic industry and show that LCRs imposed on foreign firms raise employment in host countries. Yu and Chao (1998) have shown (using earlier work of Chao and Yu 1993) that LCRs may be put to good use to improve allocative efficiency and enhance host country welfare. Rodrik (1987) argues that in the presence of oligopolistic behavior and tariff distortions, EPRs can benefit host countries by reducing payments to foreign owners, reducing output in excess supply, and shifting profits to locally owned firms. Greenaway (1991) comes to similar conclusions.

Evidence from cross-country studies

An attempt was made by the present author in a study conducted at the UNU Institute for New Technologies (UNU/INTECH) to examine empirically the effectiveness of performance requirements such as LCRs and EPRs in meeting their objectives (see Kumar 1998, 2000, 2002 for more details). The analysis was conducted with the help of an exclusive data set covering overseas operations of US and Japanese corporations in a sample of seventy-four countries in seven branches of manufacturing over the 1982–94 period. The effectiveness of LCRs was evaluated in terms of the proportion of domestic value-added generation in sales of foreign affiliates. Effectiveness of EPRs was evaluated in terms of the extent of export-orientation of sales of foreign affiliates. Furthermore, it was possible to split the direction of export-orientation – whether to the home country or to a third country. Simulating the patterns observed with the dataset for the seventy-four sample countries in the framework of an extended model of production location, the study found LCRs to favor the extent of localization of MNE affiliates' production in the host countries. Therefore the study argued that LCRs could be an important means of deepening the commitment of MNEs entering an economy and of generating local value added, with the resulting improvements in employment and the related knowledge spillovers. Similarly, the study found export performance requirements to be effective in increasing the export orientation of MNE affiliates to third countries (Kumar 1998, 2000, 2002).

Another recent empirical study has corroborated that LCRs were effective in raising local content of affiliates of Japanese electronics MNEs in twenty-four countries (Belderbos et al. 2001).

Therefore the cross-country evidence now available shows that performance requirements could be useful tools for development policy. A further understanding of the manner in which PRs could serve development policy objectives can be found in case-study evidence now available for several countries, as summarized below.

Case study evidence

The available evidence suggests that a number of countries have been able to build internationally competitive industrial capabilities using PRs. For instance, Brazil, Mexico, and Thailand have built internationally competitive auto industries by enforcing LCRs and export performance requirements on foreign auto MNEs (Moran 1998: 53–62). Taiwan has also emerged as a major supplier of auto parts in the world following similar policies (Gee 1997). Furthermore, it has been argued that export performance requirements have prompted MNEs to establish world-scale plants incorporating best-practice technology and have generated significant knowledge spillovers for local firms of the type reported by Aitken et al. (1994) and Moran (1998). Further case studies are summarized below.

PRs and the development of Thailand as Southeast Asia's auto hub

Thailand has extensively used different performance requirements in the automotive industry. To encourage domestic production, the government resorted to the policy of selective high tariff and import bans during the 1960s. However, the recurrence of weak domestic demand and continued deterioration in the trade balance because of importation of auto parts forced the government to impose minimum local content requirement on automotive assembly and continually pushed it upward, from 25 per cent in 1969, to 50 per cent in 1977, to 54 per cent in 1983 (see Damri 2000; Nippon 1999). Imposition of LCRs in 1970s and early 1980s did create domestic production capacities but exports by foreign auto producers remained "practically nil," blamed on the "inferior quality" of Thai component producers. However, domestic component enterprises that had emerged thanks to LCRs launched themselves in international markets by obtaining OEM status with external buyers (Moran 1998: 60). To persuade the Japanese auto companies to incorporate their Thai affiliates into their global production networks, the government has employed export performance requirements since 1985. The foreign enterprises selling their output, primarily in the domestic market, were required to have at least 51 per cent domestic ownership. However, those exporting more than 50 per cent of their output could have foreign majority ownership (until 2000). That prompted the Japanese auto makers to think of integrating Thailand into their global production networks. The development of an internationally competitive auto parts industry in the country also attracted global auto majors such as GM, Daimler–Chrysler and Ford to announce plans to set up auto plants in the country. Thailand has emerged as Southeast Asia's main auto hub with a production capacity of 1 million vehicles. It exported 1.7 million vehicles in 2001, making it the third largest exporter of automotives in Asia after Japan and Korea. Automotive exports earned 154 billion baht, and auto components an additional 60 billion baht, in 2001. Honda and Toyota have added a second shift, with Honda announcing the sourcing of the Honda City for the Japanese market from Thailand, and Toyota making Thailand a global production base for pick-up trucks (*Financial Times* 2002).

PRs and building competitive manufacturing capabilities in the auto industry in India

Like other developing countries, India also employed PRs to build domestic manufacturing capability in the auto industry. The Indian government entered into a joint venture agreement with Suzuki Motor Corporation (SMC) of Japan to set up a manufacturing facility in Gurgaon near Delhi in the early 1980s for the production of small passenger cars. The Maruti–Suzuki joint venture, in which both the government of India and Suzuki were equal partners, had imposed on it a phased manufacturing program where it was required to increase local content to 75 per cent within five years. In order to comply with the requirement, Suzuki started a program of vendor development in India. Suzuki assisted Indian manufacturers of auto components in producing components to its designs and specifications. It also set up joint ventures with a number of them that involved technology transfer. Furthermore, a number of Japanese OEM suppliers of SMC were prompted to license technology or set up joint ventures with Indian component manufacturers to be able to supply to its Maruti venture. As a result, a cluster of auto component manufacturers emerged around the Maruti plant in Gurgaon and the proportion of local value added steadily increased. However, exports of cars or components were relatively insignificant. In the 1990s, as a part of the measures taken to deal with the foreign exchange crisis of 1991, the government imposed a condition of foreign exchange neutrality and dividend balancing on consumer goods industries, including passenger car manufacturers. These obligations pushed Maruti to obtain a product mandate from its Japanese partner for exporting compact cars to Europe following the phasing out of the production of its Alto model in Japan.

The extensive network of auto component manufacturers created as a result of the phased manufacturing programs imposed on Maruti has laid down the foundations of an internationally competitive auto component industry. The subsequent entrants to the industry in the wake of liberalization of the FDI policy in the 1990s not only found a good base for their indigenization efforts but were also able to fulfill their export obligations easily, as is evident from case studies of Ford, GM and Daimler–Chrysler (see Kumar and Singh 2002). The export obligations prompted them to consider buying some components from India for export to their operations in other countries. As the Ford case shows, they were initially hesitant to import components from India, fearing poor quality, apprehensions that were belied. Hence, following a visit in 2000 by a Ford team to components' suppliers in India, a joint program was launched with the Automotive Component Manufacturers Association (ACMA) for sourcing components from the country for Ford. Ford set up two dedicated ventures in India to handle component sourcing. Ford has also undertaken growing exports of Ikon CKD kits to Mexico and South Africa. Thus while export obligations prompted Ford to discover an important sourcing base of quality components, from the host country point of view, they helped the country's auto component manufacturers develop their linkages with one of the world's largest manufacturers of automobiles, which could be of long-term interest. Similarly, General Motors India (GMI) Ltd claims to have helped its parent source components from India, including a major export order from GM Europe that also helped GMI to meet its export obligation. GMI is also pursuing partnerships with Indian component suppliers for worldwide sourcing of components for GM overseas units. Daimler–Chrysler India has developed more than twenty joint ventures for the manufacture and export of auto components to Daimler–Chrysler plants in Germany to fulfill its export obligation.

The export of components by these major producers has prompted interest by other auto producers in Indian supply capabilities, even though the PRs have been abolished. According to recent reports, about fifteen of the top auto majors have already set up international purchasing offices in India. In May 2003, CEOs of thirty Indian auto component producers were invited by Navistar, Caterpillar, Ford, and Delphi to visit the United States to discuss global outsourcing possibilities. The auto components exports from India earned US$375 million in 2002–03. Following the sudden interest of auto majors in sourcing from India, the exports are likely to increase by nearly four times to $1.5 billion in the current year (*Economic Times* 2003).

Therefore PRs until recently imposed on the auto industry in the form of export obligations and phased manufacturing programs have been successful in meeting government policy objectives with respect to development of the local manufacturing base while preventing a heavy drain of foreign exchange from imports. Even though the PRs have been abolished, the export and import figures in the car industry in March 2002, for instance, were balanced at around Rs 21 billion. In addition, most manufacturers had achieved high levels of localization of production. For instance, as of March 2002, Ford had achieved an indigenization level of 74 per cent, GM had 70 per cent and 64 per cent for the Astra and the Corsa respectively, Mercedes and Toyota had close to 70 per cent, and Honda had reached a level of around 78 per cent indigenization, given the development of a local base of OEM suppliers (*Economic Times* 2002). Furthermore, the export obligations helped to overcome the information asymmetry regarding the host country capabilities and led to a fuller realization of the export potential through MNEs with the establishment of vendor–OEM linkages between Indian component producers and global auto majors that would be of long-term value.

PRs and the development of export-oriented manufacturing in China

Chinese regulations stipulate that wholly owned foreign enterprises must undertake to export more than 50 per cent of their output. Enterprises producing import substitutes, as well as those producing high-technology goods, may be exempted from export performance requirements. Sometimes the targets may be in the form of foreign exchange neutrality. Chinese authorities also require that the establishment of foreign enterprises should encourage the transfer and acquisition of technology from abroad. There are guidelines to facilitate technology transfer, regarding, for instance, management control in joint ventures (Rosen 1999: 63–71). As a result of these policies, the proportion of foreign enterprises in manufactured exports steadily increased over the 1990s to 45 per cent. MNE affiliates account for over 80 per cent of China's high-technology exports (UNCTAD 2002a).

Domestic equity requirements and technology transfer and competitiveness: Korean and Indian cases

Joint venture requirements or domestic ownership requirements are employed by host governments to achieve several possible objectives, including the promotion of absorption of knowledge brought in, the development of local entrepreneurship, and the enhancement of the host country's share in the distribution of gains from the productive activity generated by the venture. Indian case studies have shown that domestic equity requirements have promoted the formation of joint ventures that, in turn, have generated favorable externalities in the form of substantial local learning and quick absorption of knowledge brought in by the foreign partners (Kumar and Singh 2002). Some have expressed the view that domestic equity requirements may adversely affect the extent or quality of technology transfer (Moran 2001). However, it has been shown that MNEs may not transfer key technologies even to their wholly owned subsidiaries abroad, fearing the risk of dissipation or diffusion through mobility of employees (see Kumar and Singh 2002 for a case study). Furthermore, even if the content and quality of technology transfer are superior in the case of a sole venture than in the case of a joint venture, from the host country's point of view the latter may have more desirable externalities in terms of local learning and diffusion of the knowledge transferred. In this context, the experiences of countries like South Korea are illustrative. As is well documented, Korea imported the bulk of its technology during the 1960s–1980s, using licensing contracts, minority foreign ownership, and joint ventures, and did not allow majority ownership by foreign investors. Yet Korean chaebol such as Samsung, LG, Hyundai, and Kia have emerged as internationally competitive suppliers in a large number of industries where they are represented (see Kim 1997 for a number of case studies).

Do PRs Affect the Magnitude of FDI Inflows?

It has been argued that imposition of PRs may adversely affect the magnitude of inflows by making the conditions of investment appear restrictive. While it would appear plausible that PRs may affect the quantity of FDI adversely, the evidence is mixed.

A USITC study based on a survey reported that PRs had only a marginal effect on the location of investment (cited in UNCTC 1991). An empirical study found PRs to have a significant negative effect on US investment abroad in 1977 but not in 1982 (Loree and Guisinger 1995). Our own cross-country study of US and Japanese affiliates (referred to earlier) found PRs to affect FDI in the case of US but not Japanese FDI (Kumar 2000, 2002). The finding of Kumar on the differential effect of PRs on US and Japanese FDI is corroborated by another study. Hackett and Srinivasan (1998) found for a sample of foreign subsidiaries over the period 1982–88 that the imposition of LCRs (and EPRs) had a negative but not statistically significant effect on US investments but a significant positive effect on Japanese investments. It would appear that Japanese investors do not perceive PRs negatively for the investment climate in a particular country.

The effect of PRs on the investment climate is to be viewed in the context of the other advantages the potential host country has. In a country offering a large and expanding domestic market and having other advantages, MNEs may want to invest in spite of PRs and other restrictions. Thus, China has managed to attract a huge volume of inflows despite stringent PRs enforced with respect to exports, ownership, and local content (Rosen 1999). Similarly, the Indian auto industry attracted nearly all global auto majors to set up their plants in the country despite many PRs imposed on them during the 1990s (Kumar and Singh 2002). In Malaysia FDI grew by 26 per cent on average per year compared to only 4.8 per cent growth of domestic investment, despite PRs (Pao Li and Imm 2002).

Furthermore, even if there is a slight dissuading effect on the magnitude of FDI inflow, the developmental benefits accruing to the PR-imposing host country may greatly outweigh the adverse effects on magnitudes. In the cases where PRs may affect the magnitude of FDI inflows due to poor locational advantages, host governments have generally used a combination of PRs and fiscal incentives to neutralize the potentially adverse effect of PRs on FDI inflows while improving their quality to meet development policy objectives.

Concluding Remarks

To sum up the above discussion, PRs have been employed extensively by developed countries to improve the quality of FDI and to maximize its contribution to the process of their development. The current low incidence of PRs in developed countries is deceptive because they have evolved new forms of policy interventions to achieve the objectives of PRs. They continue to use policy measures such as screwdriver regulations, "buy local" provisions, anti-dumping, and rules of origin that have effects similar to those of PRs. The same developed countries argue against the use of such policies by developing countries on efficiency grounds.

The evidence presented from developing countries on the effectiveness of PRs suggests that well-conceived PRs that have clear objectives and are effectively enforced are not only able to meet their objectives, but may also bring significant favorable externalities to the host countries. The effectiveness of PRs in meeting their policy objectives depends on the clarity of objectives, the policy capability of the governments, market size, absorptive capacity in terms of skills of the workforce and strength of domestic enterprises, and other locational advantages and policies. The available evidence also does not suggest a significant adverse effect of PRs on FDI inflows, which are governed more by the overall economic potential of the host countries than by such policies. In any case, the developmental benefits accruing as a result of the impact of PRs on the quality of inflows may outweigh any potential adverse effect on the magnitudes. FDI inflows in developing countries, after all, are the "means" for achieving development and not the "ends" in themselves.

The above findings have implications for the ongoing discussion on the relevance of PRs in the context of the Review of the TRIMs Agreement and the debate on the desirability of a possible multilateral framework on investment. It is clear that PRs serve a useful purpose as development policy tools. Hence, they should continue to be available to countries. Given the importance of PRs as instruments of development policy, there is a need for invoking Special and Differential Treatment (SDT) of developing and least developed countries in respect of this. In the TRIMs Agreement, developing countries, in the name of SDT, obtained a transition period for phasing out TRIMs only three years longer than that applying to developed countries. The vast development gap between developed and developing countries cannot be bridged in three years.

Therefore developing countries should seek exceptions based on a low level of industrialization at the TRIMs Review. Article 5(3) of the Agreement could be amended to provide this exception, linked to a per capita manufacturing value-added (MVA) threshold. All the countries with MVA per capita below that threshold level should qualify for exemption from the provisions of TRIMs. The Agreement would, in this way, have taken care of the development dimension as well as the graduation.

The Review of TRIMs should also be used to address other asymmetries present in the TRIMs Agreement. One such asymmetry pertains to its failure to curb trade related restrictions imposed by MNEs on their subsidiaries that are as trade-distorting as the government-imposed restrictions. Given the trade-distorting effect of these restrictions, developing countries should seek in the TRIMs Review to discipline the restrictive conditions that MNEs impose on their foreign affiliates.

Yet another asymmetry in the TRIMs Agreement is its failure to discipline the investment incentives given by host governments to attract FDI inflows. The empirical evidence has shown that these incentives tend to distort investment patterns in much the same way as export subsidies do patterns of trade (see Kumar 2002). Industrialized countries have largely indulged in the incentive wars to attract foreign investments to particular locations and have been offering substantial subsidies to MNEs to attract investments.

Finally, and more importantly, developing countries should resist the attempt of developed countries to expand the list of TRIMs that are proscribed under the Agreement.

10

Neoliberalism as a Political Opportunity: Constraint and Innovation in Contemporary Development Strategy

Peter Evans

Analyses of the developmental consequences of the current neoliberal global regime correctly emphasize the ways in which global ideology, legal rules, and economic power structures limit and distort the policy options available to the global South. Yet global neoliberalism[1] is not likely to be an exception to the rule that any system of domination contains opportunities for challenge and transformation. Identifying these opportunities is, if not logically prior, still just as important as critiquing the regime. Seized creatively, such opportunities have the potential not just to improve the circumstances of the less privileged, but to transform the global system itself.

Anti-developmental Effects

Setting out neoliberalism's anti-developmental effects makes the importance of the opportunities it creates all the clearer. A variety of other negative aspects of the current global system could be highlighted. A hegemonic cultural/ideological paradigm proffers theoretically and historically unfounded prescriptions that reduce the likelihood of policy success while simultaneously stifling developmentally promising local institutional innovation (see Chang 2003a; Evans 2004). The current behavior of the United States as an irresponsible and crassly self-seeking hegemon dramatically exacerbates the negative structural features of the global system. A variety of other effects could be highlighted. Since the primary purpose of this chapter is to focus on positive possibilities, I will restrict my critique to a quick look at three negative aspects of the current global political economy: the simultaneously fragile and oppressive character of the global financial system; the "rigged rules" of the global trading system (see Oxfam 2002); and, perhaps most important, the political enforcement of the economic privilege of transnational corporations based primarily in the rich countries of the North, as epitomized by recent policies with regard to "intellectual property rights."

The International Monetary Fund (IMF) provides a good centerpiece for a sketch of the simultaneously fragile and oppressive character of the international financial system. Staffed by one of the largest concentrations of economic expertise on the planet, the IMF has, nevertheless, been guilty of imposing policies on the countries of the global South that have increased rather than reduced their vulnerability. Admonitions to open capital markets in the absence of an adequate regulatory framework are perhaps the most clear-cut example (Singh, in this volume; Stiglitz 2002b).[2]

While the oppressive aspects of the IMF's role are the usual focus of its critics, they are ultimately less threatening to the long-term interests of the global South than the Fund's weakness. The IMF's resources are far too small in relation to current global levels of capital flows to stabilize the system or serve as a true lender of last resort (Kelkar and Chaudhry 2004; Rubin and Weisberg 2003). The absence of global capacity to dampen volatility and protect markets from crisis raises the cost of capital to all, but particularly to capital-starved countries of the global South.

Real power in the current international financial system lies with the perhaps 200 private financial firms that dominate international capital markets. These firms have an undeniable collective interest in maintaining the stability of the global financial system, but their behavior is much more irresistibly shaped by short-run pressures to achieve profit rates at least equal to those of their competitors. This, combined with powerful tendencies toward herd behavior, generates a structural bias toward volatility and crisis that is potentially disastrous (Wade and Veneroso 1998a).

Even if crises are averted, the assessments of the most powerful global financial actors are systematically biased in a way that stifles developmental initiatives in the global South. The plummeting value of the Brazilian *real* during the run-up to Brazil's 2002 elections offers a dramatic case in point. As the Worker's Party (PT) gained electoral strength, the major banks' aversion to the possibility of redistributive developmentalism was translated into negative recommendations with regard to Brazil's currency (Martínez and Santiso 2003). Having experienced a 40 per cent fall in the value of Brazil's currency in the course of a few months, the Worker's Party (PT) "learned its lesson" and, once elected, pursued only the most timid macroeconomic policies for the next two years. The PT chose to suffer low growth, high unemployment and flat levels of social expenditure rather than risk retribution from the global financial actors who constitute "the markets."

The current international financial system forces developing countries to conform to the strictly limited set of developmental strategies that meet the approval of international bankers, none of whom is likely to have any direct experience confronting the challenges of development on the ground. At the same time, neoliberal financial arrangements foster a level of volatility and systemic risk that limits capital flows and increases the vulnerability of the global South to destructive financial crises. The South suffers from both national-level constraints and global fragility.

Like the rules of the international financial system, current trading rules have been crafted to reflect the interests of politically powerful constituencies in the global North. As Singh (in this volume) points out, there are powerful arguments, theoretical as well as historical, for "special and differential treatment" of the South with regard to trading rules. Instead, neoliberalism preaches the false universalism of "free trade" for all, while, in reality, the contemporary neoliberal trading system does not even offer the South a "level playing field." Oxfam (2002: 98) estimates losses to poor countries resulting from developed country trade barriers of over US$100 billion a year. Subsidies and tariffs protections to agricultural producers in the North are the most obviously hypocritical violations of the North's supposed principles, with supports for corporate agribusiness in the United States being the most difficult to defend.[3]

Nor is agriculture a unique aberration. Even in manufacturing, local industrialists in the South are likely to find themselves confronting tariff "peaks" located in exactly the areas in which they have managed to become competitive (Abreu 2004: 432).[4] Likewise, when confronted with the possibility that WTO rules might prevent the US from protecting its manufacturers from China's new manufacturing prowess, US policymakers' immediate response is to threaten to stop playing by the rules (see, for example, Bradsher 2004). Such blatantly self-interested definitions of what constitutes "free trade" make it extremely difficult to defend the proposition that neoliberal practice is aimed at maximizing global welfare.

While unfair trade rules hit immediate incomes, neoliberalism's equally unfair political construction of property rights may end up having a larger long-run effect on the North–South income divide. This is most clear in the case of so-called "intellectual property rights," whose inviolability over time and space are one of the most stoutly defended principles of the neoliberal global regime. The right of the owners of ideas and images (primarily large corporations in the North) to continue to appropriate returns not only from the sales of the ideas and images themselves but from any associated product or activity has now become enshrined in the global trading system.

From the point of view of neoclassical theory, the status of intellectual property rights (like the status of knowledge itself) is quite ambiguous (see

Lall, Stiglitz, in this volume). In principle, "free trade" would best be embodied in a regime that restricted monopoly returns on ideas to the minimal degree necessary to reward invention. In practice, the corporations whose returns are based on their monopoly control of intangible assets are the most powerful non-financial actors in the global political economy, and maximal rather than minimal protection reflects their interests.[5]

The most salient and outrageous case is the stubborn resistance of US pharmaceuticals companies to allow producers in the global South to provide more reasonably priced drugs to the victims of AIDS. This particular example is useful, not only because it makes it clear that Northern property rights take precedence over Southern health and well-being, but also because it underlines the fact that neoliberal rules are written not primarily to benefit ordinary citizens in the North but rather to benefit the corporate capital that is disproportionately housed in the North. Global availability of inexpensive, non-proprietary life-saving drugs produced in the South would be a benefit, not a cost, to ordinary citizens in the North.

Whether we look at finance, trade, or property rights, there is a strong case to be made that the global neoliberal regime is anti-development, protecting entrenched interests at the expense of both economic dynamism and equity, yet failing to construct a sufficiently robust institutional structure to protect even the privileged against volatility and the threat of economic crisis. At the same time, highly selective and distorted invocations of economic theory are used to portray the regime as being in the general interest.

Critics of neoliberalism have made these points many times before. What is more politically interesting is to look at the potential for change that is contained in neoliberal rules and institutions. Any set of theories and institutions designed to preserve privilege creates opportunities for the less privileged, which, if effectively exploited, can transform the existing order into one that is more just, equitable, and supportive of innovation. Invocations of the "end of history" aside, neoliberalism is as vulnerable to being changed from below as any previous global regime. I will focus here on potential opportunities at two levels.

First, I will argue that the rules and institutional structures that neo-liberalism has generated at the global level are double-edged: they provide potential sources of political leverage for the unprivileged at the same time that they serve as institutional and organizational instruments for the defense of privilege. Compared to the anarchy of "might makes right" relations among nations, even biased efforts to establish some sort of "rule of law" have advantages from the point of view of the unprivileged. Most important, the current neoliberal regime creates powerful incentives for the nations of the South to act collectively.

Current institutions of global economic governance might be compared to early governance institutions at the national level, which were also designed to favor oligarchic control by the privileged. If intense political mobilization and long years of struggle at the national level could turn institutions dominated by property qualifications, racial exclusion, and gender privilege into the means of defending minority rights and constructing welfare states, then the transformation of global governance institutions should also be possible.

At the national level, I will agree with Amsden and Lall that while neo-liberal constraints impede a variety of valuable instruments for industrial policy, they do not exclude a range of equally useful innovation-oriented policies. Insofar as crude versions of industrial policy become more difficult, "smart" industrial policy becomes relatively more attractive, which may, in the long run, benefit the South. Perhaps even more important, by providing ideological (and structural) impetus for loosening the developmentally burdensome hold that uninnovative and ineffectual industrial elites have often had on the political allocation of rents in the South, neoliberalism may actually help states achieve the "reciprocal control mechanisms" that Amsden (2003b: 87 and in this volume) advocates as central to effective development strategies. Finally, and most speculatively, I will argue that neoliberal constraints may lead states in the South in the direction of "capability-centered" development strategies that would imply a broader distribution of public investments and greater returns to ordinary citizens than current "accumulationist" strategies.

Let me begin with the opportunities created by global rules and global economic governance organizations like the WTO, returning later to the ways in which neoliberal constraints might turn out to be political springboards for more progressive development trajectories.

The Double-edged Potential of Global Governance

The rule of law has important generic advantages for the powerful. Most important, it protects them from each other, or at least increases the probability that they will be able to call on their confrères when a rogue rival violates shared norms. It also diminishes the cost of disciplining the less privileged. Once social organization has grown beyond the most minimal scale, obedience to established general rules (whether in the form of informal norms and traditions or formal legal strictures) is more reliable and less costly than conformity based coercion applied individually.

Current global rules are no exception. Even for a global hegemon like the United States, an endless series of bilateral trade agreements are a second-best solution compared to first negotiating a single global trade agreement through the WTO and then being able to rely on the WTO itself to organize enforcement. Bilateral bullying is likely to produce more favorable agreements (especially with small, poor countries) but the overall transaction costs are very high. The gains from general agreements apply much more unequivocally to other, smaller, and less powerful countries in the North, which lack the economic (and potentially military) clout necessary to bully bilateral partners effectively.

Yet the rule of law, even when the law is designed by the powerful to suit their own interests, has costs. In principle, even the powerful themselves are subject to the law, and, even when this principle is honored primarily in the breach, it is still a source of constraint. Recent US experience with respect to the WTO offers a number of examples. In 2003, the WTO ruled that President Bush's 2002 special 30 per cent increase in steel tariffs violated WTO rules. In June of 2004, the WTO decided in favor of a group of cotton-producing countries from the global South, ruling that US cotton subsidies were in violation of GATT rules. In August of 2004, the WTO panel favored Brazil's brief against sugar subsidies (the case targeted the EU but has ominous implications for US sugar subsidies). This is not to say that either the WTO dispute settlement mechanism process or the GATT rules on which cases must be based are a "level playing field" – far from it. Nonetheless, the fact remains that small, poor countries can occasionally win significant rulings against large powerful ones, in contrast to their virtually zero chance of securing redress on the basis of bilateral bargaining. Even more important, since all poor countries confront the same set of rules and the same global institutions, there is a clear incentive to develop a collective response.

Neoliberalism's avowed goals of building a global economic system based on universalistic rule of law has advantages for the global South relative to the obvious alternative of unconstrained realpolitik, but getting the North to live by its own rules is only a first step. Winning disputes in the WTO may help curb the most blatant and capricious Northern abuses of economic power, but it won't change the biased character of the rules themselves. The bigger issue is whether there is any possibility of generating more democratic rule-making processes that would reflect the interests of the majority of the world's citizens rather than the interests of Northern corporations. Recent experience suggests that the system is obdurate but not impervious to change.

The WTO is the most obvious target. Preserving informal oligarchic control in an organization with formally democratic procedures – one country, one vote in this case – requires that the unprivileged accede to their own exclusion, or at least be willing to sacrifice common interests in return for individual "deals." Over time, the North's control of WTO politics has become increasingly precarious. In 1998, the South stubbornly refused to let the North continue the tradition of WTO directors automatically coming from the North. The North backed down, leading to the appointment of the current WTO director, Supachai Panitchpakdi (Evans 2003). In 1999, the struggle moved from organizational form to policy substance as the South blocked the initiation of a new trade round in Seattle. At the fifth Ministerial meetings in Cancún in 2003, the South was able to move further, from simple blockage to pushing collective demands for more equitable trading rules. This process continued in Doha, and there is every reason to believe that collective action from the South will increasingly become a characteristic of future WTO negotiations, especially if, as expected, the North continues to drag its heels on agriculture while pushing its own interests with respect to services and intellectual property.[6]

The claims to universalism put forward by neoliberal institutions create both incentives for collective action and potential political leverage that the global South would lack in an anarchic international arena. Overcoming collective action problems, developing common positions, and sticking to them in the face of real threats require immense political determination and consummate consensus-building skills. Long-run success can by no means be assumed. Nevertheless, neoliberalism has proved to be the most effective system to date in teaching the South how to work together to defend its interests.

This conclusion still leaves the ominous question, "Would the democratization of neoliberal governance institutions simply result in their abandonment by the North?" Would the "takeover" of the WTO and the IMF be a pyrrhic victory? The recent international behavior of the Bush administration has made this specter more concrete. At the same time, US actions have had the effect of discrediting unilateralism, dramatically among the broader international community and significantly even within the United States. At home, would-be empire builders have been forced to recognize that ceding some power to the UN might have advantages after all. Abroad, the value of being able to subject the United States to collective constraints is apparent to even the staunchest US allies. Threatening to opt out of the WTO or the IMF would be extremely damaging to US international alliances, even if it were in response to the reduced economic usefulness of these organizations to the North as a result of an increasingly organized South. From the point of view of the smaller countries of the North, the case against pulling out is unequivocal.

It is entirely plausible that the South will succeed in increasing its collective power at the global level, but the politics of such a process will involve more then simply resolving collective action problems at the international level. International negotiations are a "2-level game" (Evans et al. 1993). Northern negotiators traditionally invoke their inability to counter politically powerful domestic constituencies (classically agriculturalists) to make their positions credible. If negotiators from the South begin to experience more success, invoking engaged domestic constituencies is likely to become more important to them as well.

Indeed, popular mobilization has already played an important role in the South's limited victories. The South was successful both in Seattle and in Cancún in part because business as usual at the WTO was made more difficult by social movement activists with roots in both North and South. In the same way, a highly organized network of civil society organizations in both North and South America have helped to keep the Northern corporate agenda at bay in the ongoing FTAA (Free Trade Area of the Americas) negotiations (Anner and Evans 2004). To the degree that the character of the political process of global negotiations continues to evolve in the direction of greater popular involvement, the content of the negotiations is likely to change as well.

The economic officials who currently do the negotiating at the global level are likely to share similar economic assumptions whether they represent the South or the North. Indeed, they all are likely to have studied in the same elite economic departments. Southern officials may be counted on to defend their countries' interests in the face of blatant Northern departures from standard economic theory – as in the case of agricultural subsidies – but when it comes to challenging more fundamental propositions, such as the value of allowing free rein to investors or the value of unrestricted corporate claims to returns from intellectual property, they will start from the same assumptions (if not the same corporate pressures) as the Northern officials with whom they are bargaining. Insofar as popular involvement becomes part of the process of winning basic nationalist victories, there is also likely to be pressure to expand the negotiating agenda.

It would be truly ironic if the North's "over-reaching" by trying to enforce rules that violate the basic free-trade principles it claims to defend and reconstruct property rights in an obviously self-interested manner ended up creating a global politics that began to question corporate prerogatives more generally. Even more ironic would be neoliberalism's contributing to the expansion of public investment in capability-enhancing public goods in the South. Such a result is unlikely, but the connections are less implausible than they might at first appear.

Development Politics at the National Level

One of the most persistent critiques of neoliberalism is that it has robbed governments in the South of a set of tools – roughly dubbed "industrial policies" – that are of proven historical effectiveness and are amply justified by modern economic theory. Chang, Cho and Dubash, Kumar, Lall, and Wade all make the point forcefully in this volume. Policies that have produced positive developmental results – in the now developed countries as well as in the South – are now proscribed. These restrictions present another opportunity for collective organization at the international level. There is no reason why Northern hypocrisy with regard to industrial policy should be any less subject to attack than Northern hypocrisy with regard to trade policy. At the national level, another strategy is also available. As Amsden (2003b and in this volume) and Lall (in this volume) emphasize, "smart" industrial policies, which focus on national systems of innovation, have largely been exempted from neoliberal proscriptions. Neoliberalism is not just constraining industrial policy, it is redirecting it.

The current redirection of industrial policy is not just driven by regulatory policy. It reflects the changing face of the global economy, created in part by neoliberal policy and ideology, but also by technology-driven changes in the nature of production and consumption. Interpreting this redirection and its implications requires reflection, not just on the successes of past industrial policy, but also on its failures.

Starting from the political underpinnings of the failures of past industrial policy, I would like to offer a series of arguments suggesting that there may be some non-obvious progressive opportunities associated with neoliberal constraints at the national level. The first step in my case is to suggest that the roots of traditional industrial policy failures – and by extension the limits of traditional developmentalism – were political, reflecting the excessive political and ideological privilege granted local elites, particularly industrial elites. The larger and more controversial step is to suggest that contemporary changes in the nature of "industry" have political as well as economic implications. As the physical transformation of goods cedes its primacy in the process of economic growth to the manipulation of bits of information, it should become more difficult for owners of capital to retain the same level of political privilege, especially in the global South.

The final positive leap is to raise the possibility that there is an "elective affinity"[7] between these same economic changes and the potential for shifting development policy toward investments in collective goods with widespread benefits in terms of both economic dynamism and well-being, which I have labeled, following Sen (1999), "capability-centered" development. Then, in the last substantive section of the chapter, I will explore the ambiguous, but unfortunately on balance negative, relation between neoliberalism and the possibility of capability-centered development. First, let me take the easiest step, a brief retrospective look at the political problems of developmentalist industrial policy.

The failures of traditional industrial policies were often failures of what Amsden (2003b: 87) calls "reciprocal control mechanisms." It is definitional of entrepreneurship that some proportion of the undertakings fostered by successful state policies will be mistakes that end up absorbing resources without contributing to development, growth, or the national welfare. "Negative value-added" assembly industries in Latin America are a notorious case in point. Unfortunately, even in such extreme cases it takes an unusually disciplined and effective state apparatus to be able to withdraw subsidies and protection from the mistakes and refocus resources on the successes. In short, the failures of traditional industrial policy flow not primarily from the predictive inability to pick winners, but from the political inability to jettison losers.

To enjoy such "failures" would, of course, be a privilege for large areas of the South. A politically privileged industrial elite is vastly preferable to no industrial elite at all. Arguments about the "failures" of traditional industrial policy are primarily relevant to the South's more successful industrializers. Nonetheless, as industry spreads more widely in the South (Amsden 2001), the relevance of these arguments spreads with it. Even more important, these specific failures were symptomatic of a more general flaw in industrial successes in at least a number of countries in the South. Even in countries which succeeded in creating very sophisticated industrial sectors capable of competing with advanced industrial manufacturers in the North (such as Brazil and Mexico), the accumulation of industrial capital did not generate commensurate changes in the well-being for the majority of their populations.

Local industrialists managed to lay claims to politically allocated rents, even when these rents were diverted to consumption rather than invested in developmentally effective new productive endeavors. Their claims to be the main agents of welfare-enhancing economic progress went unquestioned even when they didn't deliver and absorbed public resources that could have been invested in collective goods with demonstrably superior returns – like basic education.

Defenders of a traditional focus on the accumulation of industrial capital can, of course, claim powerful empirical support in the form of the East Asian Tigers, but these claims only reinforce political conclusions derived from more flawed successes. Industrialization in East Asia unquestionably delivered improved general welfare, but the political relation between the state and the private sector was quite different. During the period of most rapid industrial transformation, states were able to enforce "reciprocal control mechanisms" making the privileges of local capitalist elites contingent on performance rather than taken for granted (Amsden 1989; Wade 1990; Evans 1995).

For other governments, too politically dependent on local capitalists to engage in the "reciprocal control mechanisms," neoliberalism could be an ally, allowing state officials to claim credibly, "We would like to support your ineffectual enterprise, but the Bank, the Fund, or 'The Markets' will punish us if we do." This neoliberal service is, of course, no advantage if neoliberalism prevents the state from fostering local enterprise to begin with. With no fledglings in the nest, increased ability to push them out of the nest and force them to learn to fly is superfluous. Reducing the cost of failures by eliminating the possibility of successes is not a winning strategy.

To evaluate the overall effects of neoliberalism on industrial initiatives in the South, three channels of influence must be considered. The first is the set of global regulatory constraints that have been enshrined in WTO rules. The second channel is the more diffuse cultural and ideological effects that shape the behavior of technocrats and state managers in the South. Third, and arguably most important of all, is the way in which the structure of the neoliberal global economy, which has been shaped by technological as well as political changes, has changed the opportunity set of new industrial ventures in the South.

Regulatory effects have already been discussed. The basic argument, following Amsden (2003b and in this volume), is that neoliberal regulatory rules push in the direction of "smart" industrial policy but still leave plenty of policy space. If local developmentalists maintain their intellectual independence, read the rules carefully, and exploit aggressive interpretations of what is allowed, they will find that there is still a gamut of policies open to them that avoid the regulatory restrictions imposed by the WTO and deliver more consistent results than old-style industrial policy.

Instead of picking sectors and ending up forced to support losers as well as winners, "smart" industrial policy tries to catalyze entrepreneurship at both a more general and a more specific level. At a general level it focuses on providing productivity-enhancing collective goods, education and research being the obvious examples. At a specific level it focuses on facilitating the innovative activities of individual firms with strategies ranging from science and technology parks (such as those Amsden describes in the Taiwanese case) to collective provision of information about international markets for local products.[8]

Even if neoliberalism's regulatory effects are supportive of smart industrial policy, its more diffuse cultural and ideological effects may still impede the effective implementation of even "smart" industrial policy. Local officials may "overconform" to the strictures of neoliberal ideology, failing to initiate efforts to stimulate transformative investments, not because they are prohibited from doing so, but because their own training and ideological presuppositions lead them to share the belief that any variety of industrial policy is not just ineffective but welfare reducing. Overcoming this kind of problem involves combining the compilation of evidence and logical arguments on the one hand with intra-elite ideological struggles on the other hand. It is a struggle against cultural/ideological hegemony rather than against coercive political and economic power, and the chapters in this volume suggest that it is eminently winnable.

The third of neoliberalism's effects – the structural pressures of the global economy in which neoliberal rules and ideology are embedded (and which they helped construct) – is consistent with the push toward smart industrial policy. These structural effects also complement the political effects discussed earlier, undercutting the claims of local industrialists to exceptional political privilege. Most interesting, they may be supportive of a policy shift in the direction of "capability-centered development."

The opportunity set currently available to entrepreneurs is dramatically different from the one that presented itself in the mid-twentieth century. As Stiglitz (in this volume) notes, contemporary entrepreneurs take advantage more easily of technologies generated elsewhere, depend less on local markets to provide demand for their products, and are correspondingly more subject to non-local competition. In part as a result of the imposition of neoliberal rules, but also as a result of revolutionary changes in technologies of communication and information processing (as well as technological progress in other areas), the nature of products and markets is radically different than it was a half-century ago, throughout the world.

To begin with, as Lall (in this volume) points out, even in industries where physical transformation is still central (from apparel to autos to electronic equipment), "larger parts of industrial value added consist of 'weightless activities' like research, design, marketing and networking." Intangible assets – ideas and images – are increasingly the most important source of returns for these "industries." For a growing set of sectors from software to entertainment, the physical transformation of products is only ancillary. Bits of information, not atoms, are what firms in these sectors rearrange. Overall, growth is "bit-driven" (Negroponte 1996).

These changes don't just privilege "high technology" manufacturing, they force acknowledgement that manufacturing in the sense of the physical transformation of goods may no longer play the central role in development that has been attributed to it for the past two hundred years. For two centuries, theorists of capitalist growth have assumed that the manufacturing sector was the primary driver of both technological change and the possibility of improved welfare. Now we are experiencing a sea change comparable to the earlier shift from agriculture to industry.

Some of the eighteenth century's most brilliant economists, the physiocrats, were convinced that land was the only source of wealth and only agriculture could yield a surplus. To the physiocrats, industry was at best an auxiliary to agriculture, a subsidiary branch of the economy which could never be the primary driver of developmental transformation. The nineteenth and twentieth centuries showed how wrong the physiocrats were. The twenty-first century is likely to be equally unkind to those who remain fixated on manufacturing as the essential driver of changes in wealth, incomes, and welfare.

For one thing, it is clear that manufacturing will only provide employment for no more than a small minority of the world's workers. As a source of employment, manufacturing is following the path that agriculture has already traversed in the developed North. As agriculture becomes more capital-intensive in the South, the overwhelming majority of the world's people will be paid for delivering services, not making goods. In addition, it is becoming ever clearer that the historic association of high, stable incomes with manufacturing employment was the product of political struggle as much or more than it was the product of technologically determined "higher productivity." The ability of manufacturing workers to organize collectively at the industry level and gain political power at the national level was essential to making manufacturing employment synonymous with high standards of living.

In the current century, it will take more than locating an ever larger number of the machines that transform physical goods in your national territory to deliver higher levels of income and welfare. Indeed, many argue that manufacturing had already ceased to be a generalized vehicle for reducing the North–South income gap by the end of the twentieth century. Arrighi, Silver, and Brewer (2003) point out that if simply shifting an economy toward a greater reliance on manufacturing were sufficient to generate increased levels of wealth and income, the North–South income gap would have closed dramatically instead of remaining at the same glaring level. The share of manufacturing as a proportion of GDP has actually increased in the global South to the point where, by their calculations, it has now exceeded the share of manufacturing in GDP in the North, while overall levels of income in the South remain a persistently small fraction of those in the North (see Figure 10.1).[9]

A less manufacturing-centric vision of development is consistent with a move toward "smart industrial policy," but it has implications that go well beyond it. So far, the sea change in the character of production and consumption has yet to be reflected in politics and ideology. Owners of capital

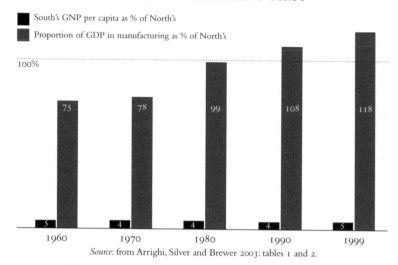

Source: from Arrighi, Silver and Brewer 2003: tables 1 and 2.

Figure 10.1   Industrial catch-up and the persistence
of the North–South income divide

continue to receive the same privileges that they did in the "age of the
machine." In the longer run, however, the shift should undercut the most
long-standing and well-established claims of local capitalists – those based
on their role in industrialization – to being the most important agents of
improved economic well-being. The question remains how the increased
political autonomy relative to local elites that should follow from this undercutting will be used by political leaderships in the South.

Has the world wrought by technological change and neoliberalism helped
create an opportunity for states, political leaderships, and policymakers in the
South to gain greater independence from the industrial elites that were the
principle beneficiaries of earlier developmentalism? The answer may well be
"yes." Might the current neoliberal political economy turn out to have an
"elective affinity" with a shift toward "capability-centered" development? Sadly,
the answer is probably "no." While the changing dynamics of global economic
growth may favor "capability-centered" development, the political prejudices
of neoliberalism are likely to undercut the public investment necessary to
make it possible. Even so, the possibility is worth exploring.

Capability-centered Development

The idea of capability-centered development draws on Sen's (1999) thesis
that the expansion of human capabilities is definitional of development and
that expanding capabilities requires, in turn, provision of capability-enhancing

infrastructure – primarily health and education, broadly defined – to the citizenry as a whole. Freedom from oppression and access to income-producing activities are central to the possibility of exercising capabilities, but it is the expansion of human capabilities themselves rather than the accumulation of capital that define development.

In nineteenth- and twentieth-century developmentalism, the road to capabilities led through machines and the technology they embodied. Crudely put, "If there is enough technologically up-to-date machinery available, both widely-shared incomes and resources for investing in social infrastructure will follow naturally." Bestowing political privilege, including the allocation of politically created rents, on those who owned the machines was a logical corollary. If we now live in a world in which manufacturing, like agriculture, has become only a key element in economic growth, no longer either the central driver of growth or the main source of employment, then, logically, the political calculus should change along with the economic one. The political implications of "bit-driven" growth are still seen through a glass darkly at best, but there would seem to be a connection between "bit-driven growth" and capability-centered development strategies.

Especially when the ultimate outputs are likely to be intangible, maximizing the rate of innovation depends on developing the capabilities of the broadest possible set of potential innovators. What is somewhat misleadingly called "human capital" takes priority over physical and financial capital. If the ownership of machines is a relatively straightforward concept, the idea of owning knowledge is more problematic, and owning the knowledge that sits in other people's heads more problematic still.

Unless people can be compelled to focus on the most commercially rewarding implementations of the knowledge they hold and prevented from taking their knowledge from one firm to another, assets that are located in people's heads are hard to capitalize fully. Consequently, capitalists on their own will underinvest in human capital. The innovative activities of traditional corporations are obviously essential to bit-based growth, but focusing too heavily on traditional corporate forms is likely to be insufficient if not counterproductive. Maximizing the rate of innovation is likely to require a combination of organizational forms of which the traditional firm is only one.[10]

All of this implies that neoliberalism, in its efforts to enthrone markets and privilege capital, may have facilitated "behind its own back" an economic transformation that undercuts the basis of capital's political privilege. In the North, these tendencies may be counterbalanced by the fact that neoliberalism has simultaneously opened up global opportunities for profit and correspondingly enhanced corporate economic power. In the South, neoliberal policy reinforces the decentering of local capital's political position. Neoliberalism's bias toward the rights of Northern corporations undercuts capital in the South, as does its regulatory proscription of the traditional relations of subsidy and protection that connected local capital to the state. In short, neoliberalism may have inadvertently created an opportunity to diminish the political power of capital relative to other social groups in the global South.

Unfortunately, this does not in itself expand opportunities for capability-centered development and the political inclusion of a more encompassing set of social groups. If capitalists are likely to underinvest in human capital, collective investment must compensate. Public investments in capability-enhancing collective goods must move to center stage. Education is central and the provision of information infrastructure – traditionally the public library, now high-speed Internet access – also becomes a key public good. Childcare and health services can be seen as underlying supportive investments in future "human capital."

Such a scenario is quite consistent with the success of East Asia, where the foundations of success lay in a potent combination of income spreading, productivity-enhancing interventions in agriculture (primarily land reform), and massive public investment in education and knowledge production. One way of reading the lessons of the East Asian cases is to focus on the question, "How might 'reciprocal control mechanisms' be established in countries where the political privilege of private elites has not already been jarred loose by war or revolution?" An alternative reading might focus on the centrality of "capability-enhancing" public policies to creating the foundation for successful development in East Asia.

Unfortunately, it is at this point in the process that neoliberalism's positive potential is likely to disappear. Neoliberalism may favor Northern over Southern capital but it unquestionably favors any kind of capital relative to the state. If increased public investment in collective goods that expand human capabilities is the essence of capability-centered development, then neoliberalism is a problem. There are two axes along which neoliberalism is likely to have an effect on possibilities for the expansion of capability-enhancing public investments. The first is the allocation of whatever public expenditures is allowed. The second is the overall level of public resources.

On the allocation question, neoliberal "rules of the game," by impeding direct subsidies to local capital, may actually facilitate a larger share of government expenditures being allocated to capability-enhancing infrastructure. Insofar as the neoliberal global economy makes it structurally harder for states to deliver jobs and incomes by supporting local manufacturers, it may reinforce the effects of policy prescriptions in making subsidies to local capital less politically attractive. Collective goods like health and education have, after all, the peculiar quality of being both immediately satisfying consumption goods and growth-producing investment goods. In a neoliberal world, this combination may begin to trump the old winning combination of politically rewarding subsidies to capital universalistically justified by prospective increases in gainful employment. Insofar as the connection between knowledge-based (or "bit-driven") economic growth and capability-enhancing collective goods becomes "common sense," investments in capability-enhancing infrastructure become even more attractive.

The effects of more general neoliberal ideological opposition to the state's role and the strictures on fiscal deficits that are enforced by international financial markets are harder to paint as positive. Their practical effect to date has been to make valuable investments in collective goods more difficult and to push governments to privatize delivery of services, even when private delivery involves higher overheads and lower quality. At the same time, neoliberalism's ideological assault on the state exacerbates inherent tendencies to underinvest in collective goods by helping to destroy confidence in the ability of public institutions to deliver.[11]

It is true that by introducing politically exogenous constraints on fiscal deficits, neoliberalism may make two potential contributions (beyond the vaunted benefits of such constraints in terms of macroeconomic stability). Most conventionally, "fiscal discipline" should encourage state agencies to think carefully about how to get the most "bangs for their buck" and avoid undertakings that are beyond their capacity (organizationally as well as fiscally). As long as the state is careful to avoid cuts that undermine its long-run institutional capacity (for example, by cutting public-sector salaries and driving away competent civil servants), fiscal discipline could help stimulate the efficiency of public institutions, which would increase the state's ability to deliver collective goods in the long run.

Equally important, credible exogenous constraint on deficit spending provides both an incentive and a rationale for taking tax collection seriously. In the end, increased revenues are the only solution to the problem of under-investment in collective goods. "Soft budget constraints" give incumbents a way to avoid tackling the revenue side of the equation. Neoliberalism could help focus the attention of state elites on the fundamental problem of getting elites to contribute to the provision of collective goods at a level commensurate with the services that they receive.

Does neoliberalism expand political opportunities to move in the direction of capability-centered development? The effects are mixed and depend on the response of local political leadership. Undercutting the relative political privilege of local capital could push political elites to form more encompassing alliances with civil society and reallocate expenditures in the direction of capability-enhancing infrastructure, but it by no means assures that they will do so. Developing dependent relationships with global capital would be an equally rational response. The effects of overall constraints on state spending are also contingent on local political response. If political leaders use the existence of credible external constraints to argue for the necessity of increased revenues, effects could be positive. If not, negative effects of neoliberalism's anti-state ideology will dominate. It short, trying to extend the argument for neoliberalism as a political opportunity to the construction of capability-centered development is a useful exercise, but one whose results are tenuous and contingent at best.

Neoliberalism's Political Opportunities

The global South (and ordinary citizens in the North) could benefit immeasurably from an alternative global political and economic regime that was more democratic, less driven by the particular interests of Northern corporations, more in tune with contemporary economics (particularly with regard to the central role of knowledge and other collective goods), and based on recognition that the essential foundations of development are social and institutional. Compared to the potential of such a regime, the current global hegemony of neoliberalism is a disaster. Be this as it may, looking for opportunity makes more sense than lamenting disaster.

Precisely because it is a global system, the most important contribution of neoliberalism may well be that it will succeed in convincing the states (and, even more importantly, the citizens) of the global South that their struggles can't be fought simply on the basis of nationalism but must be fought globally and collectively by all the nations of the South. Rhetorical solidarity must be superseded by carefully organized concrete political actions, focusing first of all on the transformation of neoliberalism's own institutions of global economic governance.

By trying to construct a global system of economic governance based on a supposedly universalistic set of rules, neoliberalism has made the case for collective action obvious and compelling. The recent evolution of global trade negotiations suggests that the South is beginning to respond. If the South continues to develop its ability to surmount collective action problems and uses what it learns to expand the fight from trade and the WTO to finance and the IMF, neoliberalism will have helped generate unprecedented changes in the organization of international politics.

What is involved in these changes should not be seen as gains by one set of parochial interests vis-à-vis another set of parochial interests. It is rather an opportunity to create a global system in which the political construction of economic rules is more democratic, rule of law at the global level is more genuinely universalistic, and the fruits of global productivity are most justly distributed. In short, the South's victories will move the global political economy forward from everyone's (or almost everyone's) point of view.

At the national level, as at the international level, the primary thrust of neoliberal policies is to strengthen the hand of Northern corporations, especially financial corporations, by expanding their legal rights and using international financial markets to punish nations that interfere with those rights, while at the same time impeding the possibility of using public policy tools that we have solid historical and theoretical reasons to believe would help accelerate development and circumscribing the state's ability to act on behalf of development. Nonetheless, at the national as at the international level, neoliberalism creates certain kinds of political space.

Neoliberalism does help insulate states from the more irrational (negative value-added) sorts of excesses that were part of earlier efforts to industrialize and pushes them in the direction of "smart" industrial policy. Neoliberalism may also provide leverage for diminishing the disproportionate political privileges of local elites. In much of the South, local elites have managed in the past to use state support to enhance their own returns and consumption without generating commensurate returns for society as a whole. If used strategically by local political leaders, the exogenous constraints imposed by neoliberalism could allow states to gain more policy autonomy vis-à-vis local elites.

The question is whether this space will be used to spread the benefits of development and create more encompassing political alliances. Here the association of neoliberalism falters. Important features of the neoliberal global political economy open a path toward "capability-centered" development that would spread returns more widely, while at the same time enhancing the South's ability to take advantage of the possibilities for "bit-driven" growth. Where neoliberalism fails to support new political opportunities is in its inadequate appreciation of the importance of public investment in collective goods and its consequent failure to support the necessity of increasing public revenues. When the political debate over development policy in the South reaches this point, political leaders will have to create their own opportunities.

The positive possibilities that have been raised here, at both national and global levels, are no more than possibilities, contingent on the imaginative and determined exercise of political entrepreneurship. Nonetheless, there is no reason to believe that the South is politically hamstrung as long as the global structure of power that sustains neoliberalism remains in place. Promising paths for political action are not only available but beckoning.

Notes

1. "Neoliberalism" is an ill-defined term. The more formal and easily specified side of "neoliberalism" is simply the set of trade and regulatory rules that have prevailed in the world since the formation of the WTO. The economic policy prescriptions that the US Treasury, the IMF, and, to a lesser extent, the World Bank have attempted to impose on the world's nations (particularly in the South) represent a less consistent complement to the WTO rules. More amorphous, but equally powerful, are the ideological presumptions and preferences that prevail in both global policymaking circles and among elite private financial actors. Opinions in these circles are far from homogeneous, but certain basic assumptions, such as the generalized superiority of markets over allocational systems rooted in political decision-making, are widespread. Weeding out anachronisms and inconsistencies in the current ideological and policy environment in order to distill the precise topology of the rules, policy prescriptions, and ideology that epitomizes "neoliberalism" is a worthwhile project that this chapter does not pretend to embark on. Here, I examine the impact of rules, policy prescriptions, and ideology that prevail in the currently hegemonic global regime, using "neoliberalism" as an admittedly crude, but still useful, cover term.

2. It is worth noting that the IMF's own research is not very supportive of aggressive generalized rules forcing the South to open their capital accounts (see Prasad et al. 2003).

3. While Japan and the European Union are at least equally guilty of depriving the global South of the markets for agricultural products that they would enjoy under "free market" trade rules, at least in these cases the protection of agriculture is in some measure in the service of social and cultural protection of agrarian communities, as opposed to primarily enhancing the profits of large corporations as in the United States (see Losch 2004).

4. As Cho and Dubash, Chang, and Kumar all note in this volume, a similar hypocrisy prevails in the area of industrial policy, with the official global policies of the North condemning policies that have already been used to good development effect in the North.

5. As Wade (in this volume) points out, "the TRIPS agreement was propelled by a few industries – mainly pharmaceuticals, software and Hollywood." One of the baldest illustrations of the extent to which intellectual property rules are interest-based artifices was the recent move of the US Congress to extend for additional decades the Disney Corporation's monopoly over the economic returns from the images of Mickey Mouse and Donald Duck, from which the company had already extracted more than half a century of monopoly profits. Only the most tortured rendition of neoclassical theory could justify such blatant disregard for the positive externalities created by initiating normal market rules.

6. The case of the IMF, which can only be noted here, is more complicated. Its "historic property rights" system of voting means that even full-fledged unity on the part of the South could not generate sufficient votes to push through any significant changes in policy. At the same time, the actual practice of decision-making in the Executive Board is one of consensus. Any substantial coalition of Southern countries would be sufficient to destroy the appearance of consensus. The greater salience of individual country interests on a day-to-day basis and the consequently greater difficulty of building consensus across countries may in the end be as much of a problem

as the "democracy deficit" in the formal voting rules. Even so, collective action on the part of the South is much more likely in relation to the Fund than in relation to the private financial corporations that now control the overwhelming bulk of the capital flowing to the South (see Evans and Finnemore 2001).

7. The term evokes Guillermo O'Donnell's (1973) famous hypothesized "effective affinity" between capitalist industrialization and authoritarianism in Latin America in the 1970s.

8. For an interesting analysis of possibilities of "smart" industrial policy in one of the South's more complex industrial environments, see Castro and Ávila 2004. Castro and Ávila emphasize that the heterogeneity of Brazilian firms dictates an equally diverse set of policies but that stimulating and supporting efforts at various kinds of innovation are an overarching theme.

9. Obviously these statistics require careful interpretation. The category "manufacturing" is sufficiently heterogeneous that increased share of manufacturing in Africa may mean something entirely different than increased share of manufacturing in Korea. Arrighi, Silver, and Brewer themselves acknowledge that East Asia, the region of the global South in which income growth has made the most progress in catching up to Northern income levels, is also the region with the highest share of manufacturing in GDP. Obviously manufacturing remains a key element in any successful development strategy. What Arrighi, Silver, and Brewer's analysis underlines is that increased reliance on manufacturing per se is no panacea. See Amsden 2003b; Firebaugh 2004 for further discussion.

10. One of the best examples of the efficacy of radically different organizational forms is the surprising commercial success of open source software, whose production is based on networks that don't subject individual workers to the control of traditional hierarchies and that locate the ownership of the resulting intangible assets with a diffuse collectivity rather than allowing a single owner to claim the returns (see Weber 2004).

11. Less central to the current argument, though perhaps more important in terms of overall economic effects, is the most hypocritical form of neoliberal constraint on state expenditures: the opprobrium from both the IMF and private markets directed at standard Keynesian counter-cyclical deficit spending during downturns in the business cycle. While governments in the North continue to avail themselves of this tried and true strategy (most notably the Bush administration in 2003), governments in the South are expected to respond to cyclical crises by cutting government expenditures rather than increasing them. The only reasonable response to these strictures would seem to be a collective political campaign for IMF endorsement of counter-cyclical strategies. Private financial markets might, of course, still choose to punish counter-cyclical strategies but the markets' response would certainly be dampened if the IMF were on the other side of the issue.

Promoting Industry under WTO Law

Alice H. Amsden

For nearly half a century after World War II, many countries that were outside the main orbit of world manufacturing nonetheless experienced rapid industrial expansion under old General Agreement on Tariffs and Trade (GATT) law (see Table 11.1).[1] These, and other latecomers, must now build their manufacturing sectors under a new trade regime. This new regime is allegedly more liberal than the previous one, which operated from the time of the Bretton Woods Agreement in 1944 to the formation of the World Trade Organization (WTO) in 1994.

The challenge is indeed great because, historically, relatively high tariffs have accompanied major waves of industrialization: the first industrial revolution in the United Kingdom from about 1770 to 1830; the second industrial revolution in the North Atlantic from about 1873 to 1914; and "late" industrialization from about 1950 to 1995. In broad terms, tariffs fluctuated in a downward direction from 1830 to 1873, and then went up again between 1873 and 1914, and still further up during the interwar years (O'Brien 1997). After World War II, tariffs were again high and then gradually diminished, first in the North Atlantic and then, in a more desultory fashion, in latecomer countries.

This raises the question of how less industrialized countries, with only modest manufacturing experience, are to continue to move into mid-technology industries if the WTO forbids infant industry protection and subsidization. This chapter provides an answer to this question.

The Flexibility of WTO Law

The WTO, like the GATT, enables members to protect themselves from two types of foreign import competition: competition from aggregate imports that destabilizes their balance of payments (Article XVIII); and competition that threatens their individual industries, due either to an import surge (Article XIX on temporary safeguards) or to an unfair trade practice (Article VI on anti-dumping and countervailing duties). GATT placed no formal limits on the duration of safeguards, whereas the WTO limits their duration to eight years and improves their transparency.

Under GATT, voluntary export restraints (VERs) were the premier safeguard. While they had been used most extensively by the North Atlantic economies of Europe, Canada, and the United States, they had also been relied upon by "the rest" to protect strategic industries.[2] The Republic of Korea, for example, used a form of VER to ban imports of automobiles and electronics from Japan, its most serious competitor. This "agreement" (to which Japan was not even a consenting party) began to function in the 1980s and remained in effect until 1999 – long enough to allow these industries to build up their knowledge-based assets (Taiwan Province of China and mainland China were neither GATT members nor signatories to the WTO, and thus may protect these and other industries more openly; the electronics industry in Taiwan Province of China is a case in point). The new WTO bans VERs because they are discriminatory; that is, their effect varies by country. The advantage of eliminating VERs was that they were nontransparent. The disadvantage was that they served a useful purpose, and "unless a superior means of serving that purpose is provided, then countries will find ways of their own to do it, and those ways are likely to be even worse" (Deardorff 1994: 57).

As predicted, countries in "the rest" have raised tariffs in lieu of using VERs or other cumbersome safeguards. Despite the fact that the level of tariffs fell after the Uruguay Round of trade negotiations, developing countries have bound many of their tariffs at fairly high levels (or have left them altogether unbound) as the starting point for their entry into the WTO (see Table 11.2). In the event of an import threat, they can raise their tariffs to these high levels and keep them there for at least eight years:

> While developing countries have committed to a significant increase in their tariff bindings in the Uruguay Round (albeit at levels generally well above currently applied rates), they are still unlikely to invoke Article XIX (on safeguards) because they have both the unfettered right to raise tariffs to their bound levels and virtual carte blanche authority to impose new tariffs or quotas for balance of payments reasons. (Schott 1994: 113)

Raising tariffs in an emergency has become the recourse even of countries whose policy regime has been liberalized; for example, when a new "free-trade" Mexico confronted stiff foreign competition in 1995 tariffs were increased from the prevailing rates of 20 per cent, or less, to 35 per cent on

Table 11.1   Real annual average growth rates of GDP in manufacturing latecomer countries, 1960–95 (%)

Country	1960–70	1970–80	1980–90	1990–95	1960–95
Argentina	5.4	0.9	−1.4	11.6	2.1
Brazil	8.0	9.0	0.15	25.2	8.5
Chile	9.4	1.8	2.9	10.4	5.5
China	n.a.	8.4	9.6	13.5	9.9
India	3.1	4.0	7.4	2.3	4.5
Indonesia	6.4	14.2	7.4	15.1	10.1
Republic of Korea	17.7	16.0	12.0	10.9	14.6
Malaysia	10.9	11.8	9.5	19.8	12.0
Mexico	9.7	7.2	2.2	8.4	6.6
Taiwan	15.0	12.6	7.2	4.8	10.6
Thailand	9.1	10.1	9.6	13.2	10.1
Turkey	8.1	5.1	7.1	4.7	6.5
Prime 12: mean	**9.7**	**9.1**	**6.8**	**11.7**	**9.0**
Egypt	4.8	9.7	n.a.	8.3	7.9
Tunisia	7.8	11.9	6.8	5.6	7.6
Pakistan	9.4	8.4	2.2	6.4	6.7
Philippines	6.7	7.0	1.1	9.5	6.6
Nigeria	9.1	14.8	−8.8	14.8	6.4
Venezuela	6.4	5.2	1.1	7.1	5.8
Colombia	5.7	5.7	3.0	9.1	5.7
Ecuador	4.9	9.6	0.5	11.7	5.7
Kenya	6.5	5.7	4.8	2.4	5.2
Honduras	4.5	5.7	3.0	3.4	4.9
Second 10*: mean	**6.6**	**8.4**	**1.4**	**7.8**	**6.2**

Note: Statistics for each column represent averages of real annual growth rates for all available years. An entry was deemed unavailable (n.a.) if growth rates were not available for seven out of ten possible years. Growth rates are calculated using inflation-adjusted current market prices. Comparability is not ensured because sometimes manufacturing includes some combination of mining, construction, and/or utilities. The definition of manufacturing may also vary across countries depending on the coverage of firms below a minimum employment level.

* average 1960–95.

Source: 1990–95 data adapted from UNIDO 1997 and earlier years. All other data adapted from World Bank, various; cited in Amsden 2001.

Table 11.2   Tariffs before and after liberalization (pre- and post-Uruguay Round)

	Pre-Uruguay	Post-Uruguay
Argentina	38.2	30.9
Brazil	40.7	27.0
Chile	34.9	24.9
India	71.4	32.4
Indonesia	20.4	36.9
Republic of Korea	18.0	8.3
Malaysia	10.0	10.1
Mexico	46.1	33.7
Thailand	37.3	28.0
Turkey	25.1	22.3
European Union	5.7	3.6
Japan	3.9	1.7
United States	5.4	3.5

Note: The pre-Uruguay Round duties refer to 1994 bound duties or, for unbound tariff lines, to duties applicable as of September 1986. The post-Uruguay Round duties refer to the concessions listed in the schedules annexed to the Uruguay Round Protocol to the GATT (1994). As import statistics refer in general to 1988, trade-weighted duties using post-Uruguay Round import data may be slightly different. The data are preliminary and may be revised to reflect the final schedules annexed to the Final Act of the Uruguay Round, although as of April 1999 no changes were registered, except for Thailand. The changes for Thailand appear above.

Source: Hoda 1994.

clothing, footwear, and manufactured leather products imported from non-preferential sources. These sectors were already protected to a certain degree through anti-dumping duties and a relatively restrictive use of marking and origin requirements (OECD 1996a: 106).

Marking and origin requirements are forms of non-tariff measures (NTMs) that restrict trade. In the Uruguay Round of negotiations, however, "achievements in the area of NTMs had been less than had been expected" (Raby 1994). Mexico's affiliation to the North American Free Trade Agreement (NAFTA) is in itself a form of managed trade that violates orthodox free-market principles. Members of free-trade agreements can protect themselves against all other countries except one another, and, unlike members of customs unions, they need not have common external tariffs. Of one hundred or so regional trade agreements notified to the WTO since its inception, only one was approved by the end of 1999 (that between the Czech Republic and Slovakia). Others, such as NAFTA, were not forbidden; WTO members simply agreed not to take action on them.

Anti-dumping duties have emerged as another way to protect trade in an emergency, supposedly when competitors engage in "dumping," or selling below costs. In the late 1980s, the United States, the European Union, Australia, and Canada accounted for about four-fifths of all anti-dumping cases. However, by 1998 they accounted for barely one-third of the 225 cases opened in that year. Instead, the developing countries became leaders in anti-dumping initiatives, especially India (which also maintains almost permanent import surcharges to protect its balance of payments), Brazil, and Mexico. As other types of trade barriers decreased, anti-dumping suits rose in importance (data are from Rowand Maw Ltd, London). Thus Argentina's steel industry, a showcase of restructuring, cut tariffs unilaterally to within a range of 0 per cent to a "mere" 24 per cent. But when Brazilian steel started to flood the Argentine market in 1992, a tax on imports was "temporarily" increased by almost fourfold (Toulan and Guillen 1996).[3]

In response to United States pressure, the Uruguay Round of negotiations was extended to trade in services, which included foreign investment. The results of the Uruguay Round on trade-related investment measures (TRIMs), however, were "relatively modest" (Startup 1994: 189).[4] As a consequence of limited agreement in the area of TRIMs, developing countries are able to maintain or even strengthen local content requirements. They can also retain trade balancing stipulations and the 100 per cent export requirement of export processing zones, both of which are forms of export promotion. In 1995, for example, Brazil hammered out an agreement with the countries representing its major automobile assemblers, whereby all of them consented to export cars whose value equaled the imports of parts that components assemblers were bringing into Brazil. Countries that had notified the WTO of their local content and/or trade balancing programs under a new 1998 TRIMs Agreement include Argentina (automotive industry), Chile (automotive industry), India (pharmaceuticals and, in the case of "dividend balancing," twenty-two consumer goods industries),[5] Indonesia (selected products), Mexico (automotive industry), Malaysia (automotive industry) and Thailand (selected products) (UNCTAD 1998).

Thus, safeguards of various sorts enable countries to buttress their balance of payments and sustain an industry under siege. Safeguards can also be used to protect an infant industry, with eight years of protectionism virtually guaranteed. The major risk is that of triggering unilateral trade sanctions under Section 301 of the US Omnibus Trade Act, but not until a US industry is actually threatened by foreign competition are sanctions likely to be invoked (Low 1993).

Subsidies also receive relatively permissive treatment under WTO law. They fall into three categories. Some are prohibited (for exports and for domestic, rather than imported, inputs); others are "actionable" (they can be punished subject to proof of injury); and three are permissible (all heavily utilized in the North Atlantic). Permissible subsidies include those to promote (i) R&D, (ii) regional development, and (iii) environmentalism. Any high-tech industry, therefore, can receive unbounded subsidies for the purpose of strengthening S&T. Export subsidies are also permissible for countries with per capita incomes equal to or less than $1,000. As noted earlier, exports can be promoted indirectly through the establishment of science parks or export processing zones. Unfortunately, these once "non-actionable" subsidies are now sunsetted and developing nations no longer have the ability to perform such subsidization projects without being subject to penalty, at least in theory. However, such provisions are under review under the current round of negotiations. It is very unlikely that subsidies to R&D will be declared out of bounds by the WTO, because this would put the national innovation systems of all developed countries out of business; the American Department of Defense and the National Institute of Health, both of which transfer technology to the private business sector at below market prices, are prime examples. It would also be difficult to get rid of the regional development subsidies. Europe uses them extensively to help develop backward parts of southern regions, and all fifty American states use them to attract industry.

All in all, the liberal bark of the WTO appears to be worse than its bite, and "neodevelopmental states" in "the rest" have taken advantage of this, where necessary.

Performance Standards

Here we may distinguish among latecomer countries, between those with prewar manufacturing experience that were generally successful in introducing reciprocal control mechanisms ("the rest") and those with negligible prewar manufacturing experience whose reciprocal control mechanisms, if any, were weak or malfunctioning ("the remainder").[6]

Given their absence of rich knowledge-based assets, countries in "the remainder" may need to use subsidies in order to make mid-technology industries sufficiently profitable to attract enough resources to undertake a "three-pronged" investment: in managerial and technological capabilities; in plants of minimum efficient scale; and in distribution networks (Chandler 1990). Nevertheless, whereas subsidies continue to be sanctioned under WTO law, and may be a necessary condition for industrial expansion, they are not a sufficient condition. Countries must also allocate subsidies in a disciplined manner, under what may be called a "reciprocal control mechanism."

A control mechanism is a set of institutions that disciplines economic behavior based on a feedback of information that has been sensed and assessed.[7] The control mechanism of the North Atlantic countries revolved around the principle of *market competition*, which disciplined economic actors and allocated resources efficiently. The "invisible hand" thus transformed the chaos and selfishness of free-market forces into general well-being (Mandeville 1924). The control mechanism of "the rest" revolved around the principle of *reciprocity*, which disciplined subsidy recipients and thereby minimized government failures. Subsidies were allocated to make manufacturing profitable – to convert moneylenders into financiers and importers into industrialists – but did not become giveaways. Recipients of subsidies were subjected to monitorable performance standards that were redistributive in nature and result-oriented. The reciprocal control mechanism of "the rest" thus transformed the inefficiency and venality associated with government intervention into collective good.

In the cotton textile industry, for example, the privilege of selling in the protected domestic market was made conditional on the fulfillment of export targets. Later, other industries had to match imports with an equivalent value of exports (or comply with some sort of "trade-balancing" arrangement). In automobile assembly and consumer electronics, the right to sell locally under tariff protection was tied to the "localization" of parts and components manufacture. A condition for receiving the soft loans of development banks was the employment of non-familial professionals in responsible positions, such as chief financial officer and quality control engineer. Development bank credit for heavy industries committed borrowers to contributing their own capital (under debt–equity ratio requirements) and constructing plants of minimum efficient scale. In India, price controls in the pharmaceuticals industry encouraged cost-saving innovation and exporting in exchange for loosely enforced foreign patent laws. In the Republic of Korea, a lucrative license to establish a general trading company depended on exports meeting criteria related to value, geographical diversity, and product complexity. As industries in "the rest" were upscaled, performance standards increasingly pertained to research and development, as noted below. Chinese "science and technology enterprises" were granted a special legal status in exchange for performance standards with respect to technically trained employment and new products in total sales. The best small firms in Taiwan Province of China were specially picked to locate in science parks, which obliged them to spend a certain percentage of their sales on R&D and to employ advanced production techniques.

"The rest" rose, therefore, in conjunction with getting the control mechanism right. No matter what prices existed – whether as a consequence of market forces, technocratic choice, or political intervention – they were taken as given by policymakers concerned with industrial expansion. Around existing prices a set of rules and institutions was constructed to attract resources into manufacturing and to make those resources conform with performance standards that were result-oriented.

Development Institutions:
The Case of Thailand

We briefly review here the developmental institutions created by Thailand, a case of relative minimalism so far as government intervention is concerned (World Bank 1993). A country overview, based on information from high-ranking government officials, gives some sense of the depth and breadth of controls in Thailand.[8]

Selection by academic merit

Thailand's control mechanism was managed by civil servants selected by academic merit, as a result of a 1932 political movement that had led to civil service reforms. The Thai civil service thus became very well-educated in a society where social status came to depend on higher education. In 1963, as much as one-third of Thai students studying abroad were government officials on leave of absence (Evers and Silcock 1967). Thailand's Board of Investment (BOI), the overseer of industrial promotion, claimed that until the 1990s it had never faced a shortage of well-trained engineers, despite low school enrollments. In the early phase of industrialization, as most Thai manufacturing firms were first-generation family-owned enterprises, government officials tended to be better educated than private entrepreneurs.[9] Whatever the balance, the BOI attracted the brightest talents after World War II, as did elite bureaucracies in Meiji Japan and other countries in "the rest" (Daito 1986).

A permanent opposition to the developmental policies of the Thai civil service arose in the form of American-trained economists.[10] Officials in the BOI complained of constant criticism from the "pure economists" in the prime minister's office who "misunderstood the real world." Pure economists countercharged that private enterprise would have grown strong without BOI support, that power bred corruption, and that the BOI's methods of "picking winners" were arbitrary. The BOI responded by appointing its critics as advisers.

Coverage

A very large number of investment projects in Thailand grew up under the BOI's wing. A survey of Thailand's big businesses in the 1990s estimated that around 70 per cent of the manufacturing firms belonging to the largest industrial groups had received benefits and had fulfilled performance standards under contract with the BOI (Suehiro 1993). According to the BOI's own estimates, it was involved in about 90 per cent of Thailand's major manufacturing projects covering both private and public sectors and foreign and local firms, with investments totaling around $14 billion by 1990. Given Thailand's thin industrial base and BOI's relatively small staff, any official with the BOI for twenty-three years (1968–91) would know every major investor personally. In 1990, 70 per cent of the BOI's professional staff were engineers, and only 100 engineers were employed in total.

As it became clearer that manufacturing activity under the BOI's direction could generate profits, the government became more committed to industrialization. As such commitment from top political leaders strengthened, industrial promotion expanded and development flourished despite militarism and corruption. As one senior government official commented, "Everyone was nervous that rapid growth would end," and success itself helped keep corruption in check, at least through the early fast-growth years.

Thailand's real annual average growth rate of manufacturing output jumped from 5.6 per cent in the pre-plan period before 1960 to 9.1 per cent in the period 1960–70, and 10.1 per cent in the period 1970–80. The share of manufacturing in GDP rose from 12.5 per cent in 1960 to 18.3 per cent in 1975. The BOI's pervasive influence thus went hand in hand with sustained manufacturing expansion (Amsden 2001).

New rules

The BOI gave mainly tax breaks, protection (in consultation with the Ministry of Finance), subsidized credit (reserved for national firms by a development bank, the Industrial Finance Corporation of Thailand), entry restrictions (in consultation with the Ministry of Industry), and special benefits for foreign firms (permission to own land and to import labor). These benefits were exchanged for performance standards related to export targets, local content requirements, debt–equity ratio ceilings, national ownership floors, operating scale minima, investment timetable obligations, regional location criteria, and, eventually, product quality specifications and environmental rules. The government specifically promoted technology transfers from multinational firms by making the support of such firms contingent on their hiring local managers. The Foreigners' Occupation Control Law restricted the number of working visas issued to foreign personnel, thereby initiating the replacement of foreign managers and engineers with Thais.

In the 1960s, Thailand's corporate income tax was as high as 30 per cent and its import duties on inputs for finished manufactures were pervasive.

Import duties had been a major source of government revenue since before the eighteenth century. Despite Thailand's reputation for "openness," import duties around the time of the Third National Economic and Social Development Plan (1972–76) averaged 30–40 per cent, and 60 per cent on luxuries. In 1983 the average nominal tariff was 31 per cent in "open" Thailand, compared with 24 per cent in "fortress" Republic of Korea (James 1987). Therefore the right to a reduction in, or exemption from, import duties was a rich reward. To protect local industry, however, duty exemptions were only given for machinery and other inputs *not* made in Thailand (variants of this "law" of similars existed throughout "the rest," the first instance possibly dating back to the 1930s in Brazil). BOI staff argued that "tax benefits under the Investment Promotion Law were the beginning of business prosperity in this country."

All BOI projects followed the same procedure no matter who initiated them (missions abroad to court potential investors were usually BOI-initiated). Proposals were first subject to Project Analysis by engineers, who checked technical feasibility and capacity fit with related industries, and economists, who checked conformance with policy criteria specified in five-year plans. Viable proposals were then sent to a Decision Committee, whose members were from the BOI and private industry. Proposals approved by this committee then went to a Privileges Committee, which reviewed the benefits package involved. As a way to reduce corruption, Decision Committee meetings on major projects were open to all concerned ministries, and approved projects, no matter what their size, had to have a detailed Return Statement indicating the rationale for their acceptance. After approval, inspectors monitored performance (for instance, they checked to see if specified technologies had been bought and machinery installed). On average, the BOI annually withdrew benefits from 7 per cent of its clients for non-compliance with agreed terms.

Performance standards attached to tax breaks were designed to create new capacity in "targeted" industries based on modern, as opposed to second-hand, equipment. Firms that expanded their own capacity through acquisition of an existing firm or extension of an existing plant facility did not qualify (although new plants of existing firms did qualify). Additional performance standards were negotiated when projects were being screened. In the case of prescreened projects, performance criteria were laid down by the BOI. Cotton textile manufacturers, for example, had to export 50 per cent of their output after the first energy crisis in 1973 to qualify for new or continued support. This applied equally to foreign and national firms. Given this 50 per cent floor (which was determined after "detailed study"), a textile firm would be selected for promotion depending on how competitive its proposal was in terms of the additional performance standards it promised.

In the case of guided projects, the BOI divided all industries into three classifications with varying benefits lasting for a finite duration. As economists criticized this procedure, the BOI resorted to a case-by-case decision rule. However, as this was unworkable, in 1977 the BOI went back to a three-way classification, but used new criteria to select the industries for the largest privileges, such as export-intensity and regional location, rather than capital- or labor-intensity. On average, only 15 per cent of applications were rejected, but only companies that fitted BOI criteria tended to apply.

In the case of big projects, the BOI and potential clients engaged in intense bargaining. Major sticking points were the number of entrants to an industry that the BOI would promote (and the Ministry of Industry would license) and the amount of "own-capital" the firms would supply (which influenced a firm's debt–equity ratio). In the case of color television picture tubes, for example, considerations of scale economy led the BOI to offer privileges to only one player. Players in big projects were selected in a transparent process involving all ministers with economic portfolios.

Response to economic disequilibria

At critical turning points before the 1990s (defined by exogenous shocks, big new projects, or more foreign competition), the BOI responded by altering the scope and nature of support. Tariffs were the business of the Ministry of Finance, but a key section of a general tariff law gave the BOI power to impose surcharges on existing tariffs. When Thai industry faltered after the second energy crisis of 1979, twenty product groups were subjected to import surcharges ranging from 10 to 40 per cent on top of existing duties (Narongchai and Ajanant 1983). Likewise, extraordinary measures were taken in order to build major industries. In the case of automobiles, one of the most problematic industries in the BOI's portfolio, from 1978 to 1990 the BOI banned imports of small cars (below 2,400 cc) and limited the number of brands and models of automobiles that could be assembled or produced locally. A diesel engine project related to motor vehicles, which received competitive bids from three Thai–Japanese joint ventures, typified the BOI's non-bureaucratic side. On the issue of number of entrants to produce diesel engines in Thailand, the BOI's technical staff "fought hard" (in the words of a senior official) for a limit of one, at most two, but was overruled by the BOI's governing board, which wanted more competition and licensed "no more than three firms." On the issue of using Thailand's casting capacity to make engine blocks, the BOI supported local Thai casters against the Japanese claims of poor quality. In exchange, the BOI forced Thai casters to subcontract work to smaller Thai suppliers. Finally, with regard to exports, the BOI secured an export commitment from Japanese contenders (who had initially demanded export *restrictions)* by causing cut-throat bidding among them (Doner 1991).

All the BOI's daring-cum-bureaucratism may have reflected "culture" at work, but not necessarily Thai culture. Developmental bureaucracies throughout "the rest" exhibited similar behavior under conditions of economic disequilibria. The culture among all latecomers in the 1960s was "getting the job done." The problem by the year 2000 for latecomers trailing behind Thailand in manufacturing growth and industrial diversification was precisely the lack of a culture or vision to "get the job done." The constraint does not lie in the liberal machinery of the new "global" world order, as exemplified by the WTO. This machinery sanctions the use of reciprocal performance standards in exchange for (legal) subsidies and trade protection, as examined above.

Three major types of performance standard may be distinguished for purposes of assessing their legality. First, techno-standards tie subsidies (typically, subsidized credit offered by development banks) to the professionalization of managerial practices. Second, policy standards tie subsidies to the promotion of major national strategic priorities, such as maintaining price stability, increasing local content, raising the level of exports and not worsening income distribution. Third, both types of performance standards, as they operate in the area of science and technology, are designed to increase national skill formation and the generation of firm-specific knowledge-based assets. Possibly the only performance standard restricted by WTO law concerns exporting, insofar as direct export subsidies can no longer be offered by WTO members. Indirect requirements to export, however, are possible in the form of trade-balancing requirements, for example, as noted earlier.

Given this permissiveness, we turn now to the issue of vision.

Promoting Science and Technology

The principle of reciprocity has not died in "the rest" with the liberalization of markets, the privatization of state enterprises, and the deregulation of business. Instead, it has survived in the realm of science and technology, in the subset of countries in "the rest" that have invested heavily in national skill formation and proprietary knowledge-based assets — let us call these countries "the independents" (Amsden 2002). Industrial development, through means that also strengthen science and technology, based on a reciprocal principle, presents a possible vision or culture to energize industrialization in secondary or tertiary latecomers in "the remainder" countries (for the ten countries in "the remainder" whose manufacturing sectors grew the fastest after World War II, see Table 11.1).

The principle of reciprocity slowly pervaded the policies of "the independents" with respect to science and technology. Firm-level targeting in high-technology industries was typically transacted through public research institutes or science parks. Even when admission into such parks depended on a competitive process, picking winners was inherent in this process. Otherwise, given the benefits of locating in such parks, all firms would have wanted to operate in such a setting. To qualify for the benefits of a science park, a firm had to meet pre-screening criteria.[11] In Taiwan Province of China, for example, admission into Hsinchu Science Park depended on the evaluation of a committee that consisted of representatives from government, industry, and academia. The major criterion for admission was the nature of the technology a firm was developing. Tainan Science Industrial Park (TSIP), approved by the legislature in 1995, was designed to attract firms in the microelectronics, precision machinery, semi-conductor, agricultural, and biotechnology industries. Benefits for TSIP companies included grants of up to 50 per cent of necessary funds from government programs, tax exemptions, low interest loans, as well as special educational facilities. In exchange, companies seeking admission into TSIP had to meet criteria related to operating objectives, product technology, marketing strategy, pollution prevention, and management (Tainan Science-Based Industrial Park 1996).

In comparison with Europe, what appeared distinct about the science parks in Taiwan Province of China was their scope (measured in terms of sales and park employees) and the extent to which the neo-developmental state made park benefits conditional on innovative behavior. According to the Hsinchu Park Administration, "An existing company would be asked to leave if it changed to labor-intensive operations and no longer met the evaluation criteria (which the Park Administration specified)" (Xue 1997: 750–51).

Taiwan Province of China promoted S&T through science parks and related government research institutes, as well as spin-offs from such institutes in the form of "model factories" (such as United Microelectronics Corporation, which manufactures integrated circuits). The Republic of Korea promoted S&T by means of large national research projects. These expanded in the 1990s with a plan for Highly Advanced National Projects (RAN), or "G7 projects" as Koreans called them, in recognition of their aim to propel their country into the ranks of the world's top group of seven countries (the G7).[12] Both approaches involved targeting. The science park administrations of Taiwan Province of China and the Republic of Korea's G7 Planning Committee selected projects according to the criterion of how well they advanced "strategic industries," which were themselves selected at the highest political level of decision-making. By involving large-scale projects, however, the Korean approach also tended to involve participation by big firms.

By the 1990s, China had also moved away from the defense-oriented national innovation systems of the United States and the former Soviet Union toward a firm-focused system that emphasized industrial competitiveness.[13] The transition had come in 1985, when the Central Committee of the Chinese Communist Party and the national State Council had decreed that "economic construction should rely on science and technology," which was far richer in China than in equally poor developing countries, and "science and technology research should serve the needs of economic development" (Lu 1997: 17). To modernize S&T, China combined science parks and national R&D projects, tax breaks, and subsidized credit, playing a large role in both. The Beijing city government, for example, established a leading-edge R&D testing zone, dubbed "Beijing's Silicon Valley," with exports in 1998 of $267 million (expected to reach $1 billion by 2000). "In the enterprise zone, the Government adopted institutional devices nested in the taxation process and investment process that redistributed resources to strategic sectors." Targeted industries were given tax breaks, special loans from state banks with below-market interest rates, and permission to exceed normal debt–equity ratio ceilings (Lu 1997: 234). On the other hand, the Chinese government also emphasized national R&D projects and the formation of "science and technology enterprises" that were neither state-owned nor private. The State Planning Commission announced a policy to build approximately one hundred national key laboratories (analogous to corporate central R&D laboratories) in selected fields of basic science in which Chinese capabilities already excelled. "S&T enterprises" were spun off by city, provincial, or national governments to commercialize the knowledge of public labs (see, for example, the annual report of Stone Electronic Technology Ltd, one of China's most successful S&T enterprises). Although these enterprises were nominally independent,

> in granting S&T enterprises a special legal status, the government obliged them to meet certain requirements (analogous to performance standards under a reciprocal control mechanism). These requirements included the percentage of technology personnel, the percentage of sales contributed by new products, the percentage of products exported, the allocation of retained earnings, etc. (Lu 1997: 235)

Thus, to a greater or lesser degree, the neo-developmental state retained its conditionality-based form of subsidy allocation in the high-tech phase of industrial transformation.

Conclusion

Late industrializers may expect both discontinuity and continuity between GATT and WTO rules. The major difference between the two trade regimes from the viewpoint of late industrializers is the prohibition by the WTO of subsidies to exports. This prohibition terminates a very powerful developmental tool insofar as latecomers that made the transition from low technology into mid-technology industries after World War II made exporting, with subsidies, a condition for operating in protected domestic markets. Exporting was a performance standard that contributed to efficiency and growth. Continuity characterizes the two trade regimes insofar as most preferential measures to protect infant industries and to diversify manufacturing industry are still permissible, as is the reciprocal control mechanism that the most successful latecomers used to insure that subsidies to business were not given away for free.

WTO provisions related to science and technology enable developing countries to promote their mid-technology (and, especially, high-technology) industries through the medium of science parks, R&D national projects, as well as temporary and transparent barriers to imports. The major lesson from successful industrializers after World War II is that whatever the instrument of promotion, to be successful it must be tied to a monitorable performance standard and operate within a reciprocal control mechanism that disciplines all parties involved in industrial expansion. Given whatever prices exist as a consequence of market forces, technocratic decision-making, or political intervention, it is important to get the control mechanism right. Getting the control mechanism right, in conjunction with promoting science and technology, are twin pillars of a new industrial development strategy that may serve to energize still later industrializers.

Notes

1. To avoid the bias introduced by different levels of manufacturing activity among countries in 1950, it would have been preferable to examine manufacturing output per worker. However, the requisite data are not available to make this calculation for a sufficient number of countries. Table 11.1 is meant to suggest the wide variety of countries, if only in terms of geography, whose manufacturing sectors have grown rapidly over the past fifty or so years.

2. "The rest," or prime latecomers (as listed in Table 11.1), includes twelve econo- mies, most of which have well-developed control mechanisms (the major exception being Argentina): Argentina, Brazil, Chile, China, India, Indonesia, Malaysia, Mexico, Republic of Korea, Taiwan Province of China, Thailand, and Turkey.

3. The steel industry accounted for roughly 40 per cent of all anti-dumping cases in 1998 (data are from Row and Maw Ltd, London 1999).

4. Trade-related aspects of intellectual property rights (TRIPS) were a whole other new area of regulation, designed to protect rather than liberalize access to proprietary know-how. The United States placed TRIPS on the WTO agenda: "Just

before the Uruguay Round an American enquete among industries cited intellectual property rights as the biggest problem when investing in other countries" (Knutrud 1994: 193). The effect of TRIPS by the year 2000 is still unknown, but much feared by developing countries, especially those with large pharmaceuticals industries which circumvented patents to produce and deliver drugs locally at below-world prices (see Mourshed 1999). There was also a movement afoot among North Atlantic members of the WTO to regulate international business practices (Malaguti 1998).

5. Dividend balancing stipulates that during a period of seven years after the start of commercial production the amount of dividend that a firm can repatriate must be covered by the firm's export earnings (UNCTAD 1998: 58).

6. Economies comprising "the rest" are explained in note 2; "the remainder" includes secondary, tertiary, and still later industrializers, few of which had substantial prewar manufacturing experience (Amsden 2001).

7. The concept of a control mechanism was first applied to the animal and the machine, and adapted to cybernetics by a physicist (Wiener 1948). It also became an integral part of modern corporate management techniques (Merchant 1985). All control mechanisms share at least four elements: a detector or sensor, or a measuring device to identify what is happening in the process to be controlled; an assessor, or a device to determine the significance of what is happening (where significance is typically evaluated by comparing information on what is happening with a specified standard of what should happen); an effector, or a feedback device to alter behavior, if necessary; and a communications network, or a device to transmit information between the detector and assessor and between the assessor and effector (Anthony and Govindarajan 1995).

8. Information on Thailand is from interviews with Board of Investment officials, Bangkok: Deputy Secretary General Vanee Lertudumrikam, July 1991 and August 1993; Deputy Secretary General Khun Chakchai, July 1991 and April 1996; and Deputy Secretary General Chakramon Phasukavanich, April 1996. Shorter quotations in the text from Board of Investment officials are from one or another of these people.

9. This contrasted with a more even incidence of university education in the public and private sectors in India, Brazil, and Mexico, whose industries were more advanced than Thailand's in the late 1950, and hence more managerial. For the private sector, see CEPAL 1963 for Latin America, and Agarwala 1986 for India. For the bureaucracies responsible for economic policy in Brazil, see Willis 1990. For country examples, see Ross Schneider 1998.

10. For a comparable situation in the Republic of Korea, see Amsden 1994a.

11. "Because of the attractive investment policies in Hsinchu Science Industrial Park, HSIP could easily be filled with companies from various kinds of industries.... Should that happen, however, HSIP would simply become another industrial park or Export Processing Zone. It would not be able to achieve its main objective of developing high-tech industry. To prevent this from happening, the Park Administration (under the auspices of the National Science Council) has played an active role as the 'gatekeeper' to make sure that only firms which fit the target industry list are considered" (Xue 1997: 750).

12. Four HAN projects fell into the product technology category: new agrochemicals; broadband integrated service digital networks; high definition television; and next-generation vehicle technology. Seven projects fell into the fundamental technology category: next-generation semiconductors; advanced materials for information, electronics

and energy; advanced manufacturing systems; new functional bio-materials; environmental technology; new energy technology; and next-generation nuclear reactors. In
addition to these projects, S&T in the Republic of Korea in the 1990s involved more
centralized coordination (to avoid duplication by competing ministries), a 1997 law
("Special Law for the Promotion of S&T Innovation") to expedite R&D within a
five-year period, and the internationalization of R&D activity (see Cho and Amsden
1999; Cho and Kim 1997; Kim and Yi 1997; Lim 1999; and OECD 1996b).

13. For the old system, see Wang 1993, and Saich 1989, who also discuss reforms
in the 1980s.

Special and Differential Treatment: The Multilateral Trading System and Economic Development in the Twenty-first Century

Ajit Singh

The principle of "non-reciprocity" in international trade negotiations, and the concept of Special and Differential Treatment (S&DT) for developing countries (DCs), were considered by the latter at the time to have been some of their important achievements in the 1950s and 1960s. Non-reciprocity indicated recognition by the international community that playing fields between developed and developing countries are not level.[1] In order to provide some kind of parity, advanced countries (ACs) were urged to give access to their markets to DCs without requiring them to open their own markets to AC goods on a reciprocal basis.

The doctrine of S&DT is normally associated with the name of Raul Prebisch, the first secretary-general of UNCTAD, and with the establishment of UNCTAD itself in 1964 as an international organization.[2] S&DT was in keeping with the spirit of the age in that it was intended to promote the then widely favored strategy of import substitution industrialization. The acceptance by ACs of these concepts of non-reciprocity and S&DT permitted DCs to pursue their economic development under protection whilst enjoying all the privileges and advantages of the multilateral trading system.

S&DT was reaffirmed at the Tokyo meeting of GATT in 1973 and DCs took full advantage of it in the Tokyo Round of tariff cutting during 1974–79 – that is, they mostly did not cut their tariffs. However, in the 1980s, under the intellectual assault of neoliberalism, import substitution became a byword for inefficiency, and consequently S&DT for DCs fell from favor in the eyes of both the international financial institutions and developing countries themselves. Nevertheless, for various reasons, the S&DT principle was not abandoned in the subsequent multilateral trade negotiations. The

1986 Punta del Este Ministerial declaration inaugurating the Uruguay Round again reaffirmed this principle in the following terms:

> Contracting Parties agree that the principle of differential and more favorable treatment embodied in Part IV and other relevant provisions of the General Agreement … applies to the negotiations … [D]eveloped countries do not expect reciprocity for commitments made by them in trade negotiations to reduce or remove tariffs and other barriers to trade of developing countries. (GATT 1986: 7)[3]

The S&DT principle is therefore deeply embedded in the WTO Agreements that came into being in 1994 at the end of the Uruguay Round. It has been given a further fillip by the Doha Ministerial meeting in 2001. Paragraph 44 of the Ministerial declaration stated:

> We reaffirm that provisions for special and differential treatment are an integral part of the WTO Agreements. We note the concerns expressed regarding their operation in addressing specific constraints faced by developing countries, particularly least-developed countries. In that connection, we also note that some Members have proposed a Framework Agreement on Special and Differential Treatment (WT/GC/W/442). We therefore agree that all special and differential treatment provisions shall be reviewed with a view to strengthening them and making them more precise, effective and operational. In this connection, we endorse the work programme on special and differential treatment set out in the Decision on Implementation-Related Issues and Concerns.[4]

Paragraph 14 of the declaration also stipulated that "Modalities for the further commitments, including provisions for special and differential treatment, shall be established no later than 31 March 2003."

In February 2002, the Trade Negotiating Committee of the WTO agreed that the mandate from paragraph 44 (referred to above) of the Doha Ministerial Declaration should be negotiated in the Committee on Trade and Development (CTD) in Special Sessions. The CTD has, accordingly, met in such sessions but there has been a wide gulf and a deadlock between DCs and ACs. The deadline for completing these tasks has been repeatedly extended but there has been little progress in the negotiations. Serious commentators suggest that this deadlock threatens the entire negotiating process under the Doha Round.[5]

The main purpose of this chapter is to look afresh at the concept of S&DT and revisit its economic rationale in the current context of the world economy. Unlike many AC evaluations and studies, which take a generally negative view of S&DT in terms of its benefits either to the DCs or to the multilateral trading system, this chapter presents a rather different view. It acknowledges the failure of some current and previous approaches to S&DT but nevertheless argues that the unqualified endorsement of S&DT

by ministers at Doha provides a basis for working toward realizing the inherent potential of S&DT for economic development. Specifically it is argued here that important impediments to economic development are represented by certain articles and clauses of the WTO Agreements themselves. It is a strange irony that, apart from all the normal structural reasons for seeking special and differential treatment, parts of the Agreements now constitute an important additional reason for seeking S&DT for DCs. The chapter suggests, however, that in order for it to meet the developmental needs of DCs, a fresh and broader conceptualization of S&DT would be required than is available under the current Agreements of the WTO. It is further argued that this new S&DT conceptualization would not only be of benefit to developing countries but would also serve the long-term interests of developed countries. Such S&DT architecture would be Pareto optimal in the present and prospective circumstances of the world economy.

Apart from its significance for developing countries, S&DT also provides an opportunity for the multilateral trading system to regain the necessary public legitimacy that it has evidently lost in the recent period (Ricupero 2000). For this to happen, the fresh thinking on these issues should aim to bring to the forefront the overarching environmental and developmental goals of the multilateral trading systems.

The Agreement Establishing the World Trade Organization states at the very outset:

The *Parties* to this Agreement,

Recognizing that their relations in the field of trade and economic endeavour should be conducted with a view to raising standards of living, ensuring full employment and a large and steadily growing volume of real income and effective demand, and expanding the production of and trade in goods, and services, while allowing for the optimal use of the world's resources in accordance with the objective of sustainable development, seeking both to protect and preserve the environment and to enhance the means for doing so in a manner consistent with their respective needs and concerns at different levels of economic development. (WTO 1995: 9)

The above passage may be regarded as being effectively the mission statement of the WTO. The restoration of public confidence of civil society in the organization will only come if is seen to be actively engaged in fulfilling is own laudable mission objectives.

This chapter is in two parts. Part I discusses the analytical and policy issues which arise from examining S&DT provisions in WTO Agreements in the light of the Doha Declaration. This part of the chapter is structured as follows. The next section provides a brief history and legal basis of S&DT provisions in multilateral trade agreements. The following section outlines the main issues that arise in examining the economic case for S&DT in the contemporary international economy. In this and the following sections the claim that the best way to promote economic development is to integrate as quickly as possible with the multilateral trading system under the WTO Agreements is examined in some detail. The chapter puts forward the concept of the optimal degree of openness of an economy from a developmental perspective and argues that this varies between countries. It is suggested in that context that the "single undertaking" requirement of the WTO Agreements is not very helpful. Evidence from the historical experience of East Asian countries, China, India, Latin America, and Africa is analyzed to suggest the difficulties created by provisions of the WTO Agreements for economic development. It also examines *inter alia* the use of effective S&DT measures by several advanced countries during the period of the golden age of 1950 to 1973. The advanced country examples illustrate the inherent potential of S&DT for economic development. The final section of Part I sums up its main findings.

Part II considers issues of economic policy. It outlines alternative policy approaches to S&DT, and comments on the characteristics of a development-friendly WTO regime. It provides a detailed analysis of the vexed issue of graduation and differentiation. It finds the North's obsession with graduation and differentiation in relation to S&DT to be a mercantilist misconception with little economic justification. The next section considers the S&DT question within the broader context of the global economy and pays particular attention to the relationship between trade liberalization and financial liberalization. The last section outlines the main policy concerns of developing countries in relation to S&DT and the WTO Agreements.

I S&DT Provisions: Analytical and Policy Issues

The evolution of S&DT provisions and their legal basis

Over the years, there have been a whole plethora of S&DT provisions intended to help developing countries to benefit from the multilateral trading system. WTO (2000) records that there are 145 such provisions spread across the different Multilateral Agreements: Multilateral Agreements on Trade in Goods; the General Agreement on Trade in Services; the Agreement on Trade-Related Aspects of Intellectual Property; the Understanding on Rules and Procedures Governing the Settlements of Disputes; and various Ministerial Decisions. Of the 145 provisions, 107 were adopted at the conclusion of the Uruguay Round, and 22 apply to least-developed country Members only.

Whalley (1999) makes a useful distinction between S&DT provisions adopted before the Uruguay Round and those adopted subsequently. The former were crafted to provide market access for developing countries in advanced countries' markets on a preferential and non-reciprocal basis. The post-Uruguay Round S&DT measures have been of a different kind. Their main concern appears to be to assist developing countries in implementing the WTO disciplines. Thus developing countries were offered extra time, and technical assistance to enhance capacity, in order to facilitate their adjustment into the new World Trading System. The WTO secretariat has developed a sixfold typology to classify the existing S&DT provisions:

- provisions aimed at increasing the trade opportunities of developing country Members;
- provisions under which WTO Members should safeguard the interests of developing country Members;
- flexibility of commitments, of actions, and use of policy instruments;
- transitional time periods;
- technical assistance;
- provisions relating to least-developed-country Members.

GP and ICTSD (2003) suggest the following two dimensions for capturing the development concerns of S&DT:

- market access and fair competition in favor of developing countries;
- "spaces for development policies" – that is, the extent to which S&DT measures enhance the capacity and the policy autonomy of developing countries in meeting their developmental needs and potential through trade.

Table 12.1 illustrates the nature of the relationship between the WTO Secretariat's classification of S&DT provisions and how these might translate into the two important channels above for achieving economic development (Corrales-Leal et al. 2003).

However, it is interesting to observe that the WTO's categorization of S&DT measures has an extremely important omission. There are no S&DT provisions here that would enable DCs to overcome the anti-developmental impact of several parts of the WTO Agreements themselves. It will be difficult to maintain that the TRIPS, the TRIMs, and several other elements of the Agreements normally have, *ceteris paribus*, a positive impact on economic development (see further below). These provisions clearly should not have been accepted by DCs at the time of their accession. As explained in later sections, the acceptance reflects the economic and political weaknesses of DCs in the "lost decade" of the 1980s. These anti-developmental features of WTO Agreements need to be renegotiated and suitably amended if the

Table 12.1 Relationship between S&DT provisions and dimensions according to development criteria

WTO's sixfold typology	Dimension I: market access and trade fairness for DCs	Dimension II: space for development policies			
		Enabling framework for national development policies		Frameworks and actions for coherent multilateral policies	
		Active trade policies	Supply-side active policies	Positive international measures	Coherent multilateral institutions
Provisions aimed at increasing trade opportunities of DC Members	X				
Provisions under which WTO Members should safeguard the interests of DC Members	X				
Flexibility of commitments, of actions, and use of policy instruments		X	X		
Transitional time periods		X	X		
Technical assistance	X				
Provisions relating to LDCs	X	X	X		

Note: DC = developing country.

Agreements are to serve the cause of development. The means by which this can be done would constitute a most important S&DT provision.

WTO Agreements contain not only provisions that are not conducive to developmental interest of DCs but also a number of elements that can only be regarded as being S&DT in favor of ACs. Textile quotas and agricultural support schemes are obvious examples in this context. Less obvious are the provisions with respect to TRIPS and TRIMs. Restrictions on competition are accepted under the TRIPS Agreement, for example, in order presumably to promote technical change and long-term economic growth. However, since most patents are held by AC corporations and individuals, the Agreement promotes the interest of developed rather than developing countries.

Similarly, the notion of industrial policy that is implicit in the Agreement on Subsidies and Countervailing Measures does not prohibit government grants to private firms to promote R&D, subsidies granted to disadvantaged regions, or those relating to new environmental laws. This rule again favors industrial policy requirements of advanced countries; many of the subsidies of interest from the perspective of industrial policy in DCs are ruled out. For example, prohibited subsidies include those contingent on export performance or those given for the use of domestic in preference to imported products.

Turning to the legal basis for the evolution of the S&DT provisions, at the beginning in 1947, Article XVIII of GATT was the only provision available to developing countries for enhancing economic development. This was the infant industry protection clause. In 1954–55, this clause was modified to include XVIII:b on quantitative restrictions on imports in case of balance-of-payments difficulties encountered by developing countries. This provision was used by many developing countries until WTO Agreements came into force in the 1990s. In 1965, a new Part IV was added to GATT, which introduced the concept of non-reciprocity for developing countries. One of the most important results of the Tokyo Round in the 1970s was a framework agreement on "differential and a more favorable treatment, reciprocity and fuller participation of the developing countries." This is also known as the Enabling Clause, which provided a permanent legal basis for the GSP scheme.

One of the main difficulties in S&DT provisions in the WTO Agreements is that they are generally speaking voluntary and not legally binding. Part IV of GATT and most of the other S&DT measures in WTO Agreements are also voluntary and in the nature of "best endeavor" clauses. Kessie argues that "much of the WTO provisions dealing with S&D treatment could be said to be unenforceable, as they are expressed in imprecise and hortatory language" (2000: 15). This poses a challenge for the legal experts.[6] The nature of other legal and related political challenges that will follow from the substantive analysis of this chapter will become clear in the following sections.

Finally, it is important to note that a large number of regional trade agreements (RTAs) now exist side by side with the WTO Agreements. The former vary in their scope, in coverage, and in their provision of S&DT for DCs in their jurisdiction. The most well known RTA is NAFTA (the North American Free Trade Agreement comprising the United States, Canada, and Mexico), which has arguably more stringent disciplines for DCs than the WTO Agreements.[7]

The economic rationale for S&DT in the contemporary international economy: the main issues

A central analytical issue raised by the discussion so far of S&DT, the develop-mental objectives of the Doha Round as well as the Preambular paragraph of the WTO Agreements, is to what extent, if any, the multilateral trading system in its current form promotes or hinders economic development. The proponents of the WTO suggest that trade liberalization and integration into the world economy are the best way for DCs to achieve economic development, and this is exactly the path the multilateral trading system of the WTO has been following.

WTO adherents, which include not only the IFIs but also other influential globalizers, normally support their case with the following kinds of subsidiary arguments:[8]

- The rate of growth of world trade has been twice the rate of production in the postwar period and that trade is therefore the engine of growth.
- The failure of the Soviet Union indicates that dirigiste policies are inappropriate.
- On the positive side, the experiences of Japan and East Asia indicate that export orientation, greater openness, and integration with the world economy are the best means of achieving fast and equitable economic growth.

It is further suggested that developing countries would be better off abandoning S&DT altogether and integrating themselves quickly into the international economy. S&DT is regarded as being ineffective and, in any case, likely to delay the necessary market-oriented pro-competition economic reforms that are necessary. Essentially, the basic development philosophy of the WTO consists of two main elements: (a) trade liberalization and greater integration with the world economy; (b) increasing the role of the market and diminishing that of the state (as exemplified by TRIMs, abolition of state aid to subsidize industry, etc.).

Thus, the case of the proponents of the WTO and its current policies is multifaceted and seemingly formidable. However, on close examination, it will be seen to be deeply flawed. The reader will recognize that the above line of reasoning is enshrined in the Washington Consensus, which in recent years has lost much of its luster and is being rapidly abandoned even by former adherents. (However, this issue is discussed further in Part II.)

Nevertheless, in view of the hold of these arguments in influential circles in the WTO and elsewhere, these will be fully reviewed here in the light of the latest available research. It will be suggested that trade liberalization and globalization are far from being the best ways, let alone the only ways, of promoting economic development. From the perspective of economic development there is an optimal degree of openness for each country that does not necessarily coincide either with free trade or with free capital movements, and it is proposed that each country should have policy autonomy to choose its optimal level of openness. Indeed the intellectual case for suitable S&DT for countries at different levels of development and different circumstances is overwhelming. These propositions and proposals are systematically examined in the next three sections.

Liberal multilateral trading system and economic development: analytical considerations[9]

The traditional case for free trade can best be put in terms of the two fundamental theorems of welfare economics. According to the first welfare theorem, a competitive equilibrium in the absence of externalities and non-satiation constitutes a Pareto optimum. The second theorem, which is more relevant for present purposes, states that any Pareto optimum can be realized as a competitive equilibrium in the presence of all-around convexity, provided suitable lump-sum transfers can be arranged among the participants. Most of these assumptions are unrealistic in relation to the real world, which does not always display all-around convexity and where externalities do matter.[10] Nevertheless, neoclassical economists suggest that such considerations do not destroy the case for free trade but only change the nature of the argument. Thus Krugman (1987) concludes his classic defense of free trade in terms of modern theory as follows: "this is not the argument that free trade is optimal because markets are efficient. Instead it is a sadder but wiser argument for free trade as a rule of thumb in a world whose politics are as imperfect as its markets."

However, as Chakravarty and Singh (1988) suggest, the politics of a world of increasing returns to scale are more likely to make it gravitate towards "managed" rather than free trade. Instead of either free trade or autarchy, this would be a world in between: one in which there were trade restrictions, government assistance to favored industries, and a plethora of special arrangements between countries – in other words, the messy real world. In place of all-around convexity, this real world is characterized by learning by doing (Arrow 1962), dynamic economies, and cumulative causation (Young 1928; Kaldor 1978). This is, therefore, the world of second best and of multiple equilibria, and the purpose of policy is to move from a bad to a good equilibrium. The gains from such policy intervention have, however, to be balanced against the losses from government failure, and appropriate policy can therefore be prescribed only on a case-by-case basis (Ocampo and Taylor 2000; Gomery and Baumol 2000). Provided there is a mechanism for ensuring full employment of each nation's resources so that there are gains from trade to be realized, and if we abstract, for the moment, from the possibility of government failure, Chakravarty and Singh suggest that a policy of selective economic openness may be a source of great advantage for an economy for any one of the following reasons:[11]

- it may enable a country to concentrate its relatively specialized resources in areas of production where the world demand is highly income and price elastic;
- it may lead to diffusion of knowledge of a nature which can lead to considerable upgrading of the quality of local factors of production;
- it may lead to sufficient competitive pressure to eliminate X-inefficiency;
- trade may lead to changes in the distribution of income that can lead to a greater share of accumulation in national income;
- trade may facilitate what Schumpeter stressed so much: an accelerated process of creative destruction.

In general, such trade openness works positively if the phenomenon of "learning" from contacts with the rest of the world is institutionalized through suitable adaptations on the policy side involving appropriate government interventions that make the domestic economy more responsive to change. This is a main lesson that emerges from the outstanding industrial success of East Asian economies during the second half of the twentieth century, as we shall see in the next section (see further Freeman 1989; Chang 1994; Singh 1995b; and Amsden 2001).

To sum up, while neoclassical arguments for "free trade" suffer from serious conceptual and operational difficulties, there are indeed substantive benefits from selective trade or economic openness, which are more robust than the traditional neoclassical theory suggests. However, such benefits can be realized only in a world in which there is full employment in all trading nations, coupled with an appropriate set of domestic policies which go considerably beyond the limits of commercial policy as traditionally defined.

Strategic versus close integration with the world economy: the East Asian experience

It used to be customary for international financial institutions (IFIs) and orthodox economists to ascribe East Asia's outstanding economic success during the last four decades to (a) their close integration with the world economy; (b) competition and economic efficiency; (c) governments' market-friendly approach, which suggested that the government intervened in these countries sparingly, only to provide infrastructure and human capital for private enterprise to flourish. The export success of East Asian countries underlined their competitiveness. Overall, in the IFIs' view, the experience of these countries is thought to show how orthodox economic policies can bring fast GDP growth.[12]

Recently, the IFIs have re-evaluated their analysis of East Asian success in the wake of the Asian crisis. Their new conclusion is that the crisis was caused in part by too much government intervention in these economies and by the lack of competition, which led to over investment, to the collapse of profits, and ultimately to the crisis (see IMF 1997; Summers 1998).

The above version of the IFIs' East Asian analysis is comprehensively rejected by independent scholars. The broad consensus view is that the governments in East Asian countries did not intervene reluctantly or sparingly but followed a vigorous industrial policy by which they attempted to change the vectors of prices and costs facing enterprises in the direction desired by the planners. The government intervened not only at the broad sectoral levels but also at the level of the individual firm, favoring companies that accepted its strategic plans. These interventions were normally carried out by so-called administrative guidance rather than explicit legislation.[13]

To make the discussion more specific, the instruments of industrial and export promotion policies used either by Japan or by the Republic of Korea during their periods of rapid economic growth – the former country from 1950 to 1973 and the latter during the 1960s and the 1970s – can be summed up as follows:[14]

Export promotion and import restriction

- Import restrictions, both general and specific;
- favoring particular sectors for export promotion and in some cases particular firms for that purpose;
- seeking compliance for subsidies given to exporters by means of export targets for specific firms (the Korean case);
- interest rate subsidies and the availability of credit and foreign exchange to favored firms that meet export targets;
- general export promotion, in Japan through JETRO (Japan Export Trade Promotion Organization) and in the Republic of Korea via KOTRA (Korean Trade Promotion Organization);
- provision of infrastructure, including human capital, in support of exports;
- taxation relief on imported inputs and on R&D expenditures;
- allowing favored conglomerates to import capital goods and foreign technology and to raise cheaper finance on international markets.

Industrial policy measures

- Lax enforcement of competition policy, including the extensive use of cartels (see further Amsden and Singh 1994);

- government creation and promotion of conglomerates (in the Republic of Korea) (see Chang 1994);
- tax concessions to corporations to increase investment;
- promotion of a close, long-term relationship between finance and industry, which was critical to the implementation of the industrial policy (Johnson et al. 1989);
- labor repression to ensure labor peace in a period of massive structural change (this applies to Korea rather than to Japan);[15]
- establishment of state industries to enhance industrial development (this again applies to the Republic of Korea rather than to Japan);
- administrative guidance, used extensively in both countries.

Clearly, many of the above policies are *prima facie* in violation of the WTO Agreements, particularly in the areas of TRIMs, subsidies, and technology policy (TRIPS). It may be argued, however, that such policies had been implemented by many countries in Latin America as well but that they have not been successful. This is clearly an important issue and will be taken up below.

Apart from industrial policy, it is important to emphasize, in the context of this chapter, that the East Asian countries, contrary to the IFI view, did not have a close integration with the world economy. Rather, the degree of their integration can be regarded as being strategic but not close. Thus these countries had export orientation but they extensively used selective as well as comprehensive import controls during the course of industrialization. As Table 12.2 shows, as late as 1979, when Japan had been a member of OECD for nearly a decade and was therefore committed to more or less free trade, its manufactured imports as a proportion of GDP were just over 2 per cent. The corresponding imports of European countries were several

Table 12.2 Import penetration in manufactures in advanced industrial countries, 1961–79 (ratio of manufactured imports to GNP)

	1961	1965	1969	1973	1979
USA	1.5	2.1	3.4	4.0	4.5
UK	4.6	6.7	8.0	11.7	14.2
Rest of EEC (9)	6.1	7.6	10.1	13.0	15.8
Japan	1.8	1.5	2.2	3.0	2.4

Source: CEPG 1979.

orders of magnitude higher. Even the United States, which, because of its continental size, has traditionally been relatively closed, had manufacturing imports nearly twice as high as those of Japan, relative to the respective GDPs in the two countries. Clearly, Japan was using informal methods of controlling imports even well after it had become a leading world exporter of a whole range of manufactured products, including cars and electronic goods of various kinds.[16] Similarly, South Korea afforded protection to its fledgling car industry for nearly three decades to reach a stage where it too became a major exporter of cars.

East Asian countries' selective openness is indicated not just by their being open to exports but not imports; in a number of other relevant spheres a similar policy was also adopted. As is widely acknowledged, both Korea and Japan during their high-growth phases discouraged foreign direct investment. This didn't mean that they were averse to technical change but rather that they thought that foreign direct investment was more expensive than licensing or other means of obtaining technology from abroad. Thus they were more open to imports of technology through scientific and technical interchange and through licensing than through FDI.

The widely used policy of selective economic openness, which the East Asian countries followed with spectacular results, has been conceptualized by Chakravarty and Singh in the following terms. They suggest that economic openness is a multi-dimensional concept. A country can be open, or not so open, with respect to trade, to finance, to migration, to educational, scientific and cultural exchange. There is no economic theory that suggests that a country needs to be open in all dimensions at all times. A policy of strategic openness enables a nation to be open in areas where it is in its interest to do so. The optimal degree of economic openness will vary between countries depending on their previous history, level of economic development, size, institutional development, and on the nature of their comparative and competitive advantage.

A striking feature of the WTO multilateral regime is that it does not generally permit the kind of diversity in international economic arrangements between countries that would be required if each country were to have its own optimal degree of openness. Under the "single undertaking" arrangement, developing countries cannot opt out of some disciplines while accepting others: the Agreements as a whole have to be accepted by members. Although some concessions are given to developing countries under S&DT they tend to be grossly inadequate, and basically the same rules apply to countries at widely different levels of economic development and with widely different capabilities. Such rules are *prima facie* unfair and unjust, and, as we shall see below, also anti-development.

Economic openness and the experience of China, India, and other emerging countries

Some of the fastest growing economies in the world for the last two decades have been the world's most populous as well as among the world's poorest countries, namely India and China. The IFIs regularly claim credit for this fast economic growth on the basis of the alleged openness of the two countries to the world economy. Openness is measured here in terms of the rate of growth of exports and imports. It is argued that the fast economic growth in the two countries is due to their high rate of growth of trade, and that in the case of China is also caused by FDI, of which China has been a major recipient.

There are, however, important difficulties with this line of reasoning. First, it is not correct to infer openness from just the rate of growth of trade. This is because the growth of this variable does not just depend on import and export restrictions but also on the size of GDP and its rate of growth. Thus the causation could easily be the other way around: the faster the growth of GDP, the faster the growth of imports and exports.

Apart from the question of causation, to which we shall return soon in another context, the Indian and Chinese story does not support the claims of the IFIs and kindred globalizers in other respects as well. The Indian growth rate began to pick up in the 1980s whereas most of the "openness" reforms were not carried out until the early 1990s. Similarly, both China and India, despite their fast growth of exports and imports, continued to have extensive import controls and capital controls, notwithstanding the liberalization which these countries have carried out over the last two decades. Thus, India still has one of the highest rates of average protection in the world. Similarly, China, while being the largest recipient of foreign direct investment among developing countries during the last decade, maintains a wide range of capital controls (see further Rodrik 2001). Table 12.3 provides information on the relative openness of capital account regimes in China, India, and other selected DCs and ACs.

Apart from India and China, the case of Latin America is also relevant to the debate about the virtues of a free multilateral trading system versus those of selective economic openness, as well as to the broader discussion of the role of the state in the economy. The facts are that the Latin American countries from the end of the Second World War to 1980 generally followed dirigiste and import substitution policies. However, following the debt crisis in the 1980s, they were persuaded by the international financial institutions to bring about a fundamental change and to adopt instead Washington Consensus policies of privatization, deregulation, trade and financial

Table 12.3 Financial openness in selected developed and developing countries, 1977

Country	Index
Open	
Argentina	1.78
Australia	1.77
Canada	1.92
Egypt	1.81
France	1.73
Japan	1.73
Mexico	1.69
Sweden	1.86
United Kingdom	1.86
United States	1.85
Largely open	
Croatia	1.54
Honduras	1.56
Philippines	1.59
Turkey	1.52
Partially closed	
Chile	1.43
China	1.37
Czech Republic	1.48
Ghana	1.43
Indonesia	1.46
Republic of Korea	1.42
Mozambique	1.41
Russian Federation	1.43
South Africa	1.44
Thailand	1.46
Largely closed	
Brazil	1.19
Ethiopia	1.12
India	1.20
Malaysia	1.34
Pakistan	1.31

Note: The Financial Openness Index scoring draws on the methodology originally developed by Quinn and Inclan (1997), and is based on information contained in IMF 1998. *Open*: little or no regulation for outward or inward transactions, with a generally non-discriminatory environment. *Largely open*: some regulations are exercised on outward and inward transactions requiring documentary support but not governmental approval. *Partially closed*: regulation with governmental approval required for outward and inward transactions and usually granted. *Largely closed*: substantial restrictions, with governmental approval required but seldom granted for outward and inward transactions.

Source: Dailami 2000: 458.

liberalization.[17] However, these policies have not worked. The long-term trend rate of growth in Latin American countries during the last fifteen years is half that recorded by these countries during the bad old days of import substitution and interventionist industrial policy. In the wake of the Latin American experience under the Washington Consensus policies it is widely acknowledged that the liberalization of trade and capital movements does not by itself lead to long-term economic growth.

An important lesson from the experience of the Latin American countries during the dirigiste period and the East Asian countries (examined earlier) is that since developing countries have incomplete and missing markets, the state can play an important role in coordinating investment activity of firms through a robust industrial policy. It can also help build the capabilities of domestic firms and enterprises until they are ready to compete in the world markets. Amsden (2001), however, suggests that state-directed industrial policies have been successful only in those countries where the state has certain autonomy and has been able to set performance standards for the private sector in return for state aid. Many of the standards that developing countries have successfully used – for example, those relating to domestic content requirements and export targets – have unfortunately been specifically prohibited under the WTO Agreements. These prohibitions add to the disadvantages of developing countries.

Finally and briefly we turn to African countries. Broadly speaking, the experience of African countries that have followed the liberalization policies under structural adjustment has been, if anything, even worse than that of Latin America. Many of these countries have long been under the IFI structural adjustment programs, but these have not led to sustainable long-term economic development.

Econometric evidence on trade liberalization and long-term economic growth

There is a large literature that attempts to establish the nature of the causal relationship between trade liberalization and long-term economic growth. The literature is vast and highly contentious. However, it has recently been comprehensively reviewed by Rodriguez and Rodrik (1999). The two authors have analyzed some of the leading studies on the subject that have purported to show that trade liberalization causes long-term economic growth. Rodriguez and Rodrik's analysis indicates that the results of these studies are not at all robust and are indeed quite shaky. One general fault they find in this research is that openness is not measured directly but by a number of proxies, many of which are quite unsuitable. Specifically, measuring the degree of openness by a variable such as black-market premium (see Sachs and Warner 1995) is not legitimate. Black-market premiums reflect more the macroeconomic disequilibria in the economy than how open the trade regime is.

Dollar and Kraay's (2000) influential study, which purports to find a positive relationship between trade liberalization and economic growth, is subject to some of the same limitations as Rodriguez and Rodrik found in the earlier studies they analyzed. Dollar and Kraay measure openness by the growth of exports and imports rather than by the country's commercial policy. India, in this analysis, comes out as a liberalizer even though, as noted earlier, it has the highest average rate of protection in the world.

Rodriguez and Rodrik's other relevant result in the context of this chapter is that trade liberalization does not lead to convergence but rather to divergence between countries.[18]

The experience of advanced countries in the golden age 1950–73: S&DT on a grand scale[19]

In the debate on S&DT, it is usually forgotten that European economic recovery and prosperity following the end of the Second World War depended to a large degree on what can only be called special and differential treatment accorded by the United States to Germany, Italy, Japan, and other defeated as well as victor countries. The period 1950 to 1973 is rightly regarded as the golden age of world capitalism, for during this period the OECD economy grew at twice its historic trend rate over the last two centuries. Research suggests that an important element in this extraordinary epoch in economic history was the far-sighted international economic policies pursued by the United States. Analysis and evidence indicate that the United States, confronted with the challenge of a triumphant Soviet Union at the end of the war, adopted for strategic reasons long-term economic policies designed to build up the economies of Western countries rapidly so that they would not fall under Soviet influence. The net result was not only the Marshall Plan for Europe but also non-reciprocity in relation to US trade with the other now advanced countries. As Spero (1977) notes:

> In the *short-term*, it [the United States] dealt with its own huge balance-of-trade surplus and the European and Japanese deficits by foreign aid and military expenditures. In addition the *United States abandoned the Bretton Woods goal of convertibility and encouraged European and Japanese trade protectionism and discrimination against the dollar. For example, the United States absorbed large volumes of Japanese exports while accepting Japanese restrictions against American exports. It supported the European Payments Union, an intra European clearing system which discriminated against the dollar. And it promoted European and Japanese exports to the United States.* ... To encourage *long-term*

adjustment, the United States promoted European and Japanese trade competitiveness. Policies for economic controls on the defeated Axis countries were scrapped. Aid to Europe and Japan was designed to rebuild productive and export capacity. In the long run it was expected that such European and Japanese recovery would benefit the United States by widening markets for American exports. (Spero 1977: 37, emphasis added)

The challenge for the international community today is whether the advanced countries are willing to follow enlightened long-term international economic policies similar to those pioneered by the United States in the golden age. These policies were evidently highly successful both for the United States and for its allies and led ultimately to the demise of the Soviet Union. The important issue is whether advanced countries not faced with a strategic threat from another superpower are willing voluntarily to sacrifice short-term and transient trade advantages for long-term economic policy that would benefit developing countries as well as themselves.

The case for special and differential treatment for developing countries: a summary

The analysis of the previous sections has indicated that simply integrating developing countries with varying degrees of economic weaknesses in a multilateral world trading system is unlikely to lead by itself to economic development. Evidence from the developmental experience of various countries during the last half-century or more, as well as economic analysis, suggest that the optimal degree of openness from the perspective of economic development varies between countries. Moreover, as Rodrik rightly argues, capitalism may be the only viable system in the world, but a wide variety of institutional arrangements are compatible with capitalism. To bring about sustainable economic development, developing countries need to have policy autonomy so that they can create their own institutions best suited to their needs. This type of choice is precisely what effectively becomes seriously circumscribed under the multilateral trading arrangements of the WTO.[20]

Equally importantly, developing countries are unable to employ the variety of policy instruments used effectively (as seen above) by both developing and developed countries during the post-World War II period to enhance their economic development. These notably include industrial policies employed in many Asian countries with outstanding results. These restrictions on government policy space under the WTO Agreements might not be regarded as a handicap if it is maintained that in most developing countries government failure is more important than market failure and so countries are better off in a regime where their governments cannot intervene. This may appear to be a plausible argument but it is one that flies in the face of the evidence. Governments in China, India, Mexico, Brazil, Korea, Taiwan Province of China, and Malaysia and in many other developing countries have long overall records of successful government interventions, poverty reduction, and economic development.[21] These countries have effective governments that are involved in carrying out myriad developmental tasks.

At a developmental level, the WTO Agreements have arguably been a colossal mistake. Rodrik is rightly scathing in his indictment:

> The rules for admission into the world economy not only reflect little awareness of development priorities, they are often completely unrelated to sensible economic principles. WTO rules on anti-dumping, subsidies and countervailing measures, agriculture, textiles, trade related investment measures (TRIMs) and trade related intellectual property rights (TRIPS) are utterly devoid of any economic rationale beyond the mercantilist interests of a narrow set of powerful groups in the advanced industrial countries. The developmental pay-off of most of these requirements is hard to see. (Rodrik 2001: 27)

Moreover, developing countries had to pay heavily for the privilege of joining this anti-development club. The World Bank (2002b) estimates that it costs a typical developing country $US1.5 million in start-up costs and $US2 million in annual recurrent costs to implement a single WTO agreement, namely the TRIPS. These expenses are onerous for many developing countries.

Developing countries signed up to WTO Agreements on which they were evidently not properly consulted. The implications of the Agreements for economic development were not spelled out. The euphoria of developing countries over the demand for the New International Economic Order in the 1970s had given way in the 1980s to a debt crisis in Latin America and Africa that reduced many of these countries to the status of being supplicants before the IFIs. The political weaknesses of developing countries were also noted earlier. These, plus the pressure from IFIs under the structural adjustment programs, obliged these countries to accept what many of them knew to be development-unfriendly Agreements.

At a global level it is important to note that developing countries already suffer from an additional structural handicap compared with the pre-globalization period. Research indicates that, in part as a consequence of trade liberalization and lowered tariffs on imported foreign consumer goods, developing countries are experiencing surges in imports. This results in their becoming balance-of-payments-constrained at a systematically slower growth rate than was the case before (see further UNCTAD 2000b). To finance their current account deficits, countries often open up their capital account. This perhaps helps in the short term, but over the medium term many countries have unhappy results with these capital accounts openings. (The latter issue is discussed further below.)

Significantly, the current account disequilibria of the kind outlined above can be rectified in other ways, without resorting to premature capital account liberalization and risking financial fragility. One important trade- as well as development-friendly way to do this would be to allow DCs again to have a balance of payments let-out clause (as in GATT), which would permit them to control the level and growth rate of their imports directly (including the use of quantitative controls if necessary). Permitting DCs this additional measure of economic autonomy would mean that the affected country does not necessarily have to reduce its level or its rate of growth of GDP in order to reduce the level and the growth rates of imports. S&DT provisions of this kind in favor of DCs would thus benefit both the North and the South by reducing the costs of adjustments from temporary balance-of-payments disequilibria.

To sum up, in view of the evident anti-development bias of the many WTO Agreements, a very large degree of special and differential treatment would be needed to redress the balance. There is ample historical evidence, not least from developed countries themselves, that a reasonably high and predictable degree of special and differential treatment can assist economic development. Such S&DT could also be in the long-term interest of developed countries, as outlined below. This is in part because a prosperous developing world provides a greater market for advanced country goods, which in turn leads to higher incomes and production in the North. This generates a greater demand for imports from the South, a positive feedback loop, and a virtuous circle of cumulative causation and higher incomes in both North and South than would otherwise be the case. However, the resulting growth path is unstable, implying a fragility of the positive feedback loop. The latter could easily go into reverse in a vicious circle if, for example, higher incomes in both regions lead to an increase in commodity prices or there is a wage–price spiral in the labor markets in the North. To avoid this vicious circle, it will be necessary to establish long-term restraining institutions, both nationally (e.g. pay coordination policies) and internationally (e.g. commodity price stabilization policies) to deliver mutually supportive fast economic growth in both the North and the South, as occurred in the golden age.[22]

II   Alternative Policy Approaches to S&DT

The terms of paragraph 44 of the Doha Ministerial Declaration on S&DT as well as other references to the latter provisions elsewhere in the Declaration can be interpreted in two diametrically opposite ways. The first interpretation would take the text at its face value and regard the fulsome endorsement of the S&DT and the mandate to rationalize and operationalize the concept as indicating a real desire on the part of ACs to make S&DT the cornerstone of a Doha Developmental Round. In short, this interpretation would suggest a genuine call for new thinking on S&DT issues to address the developmental concerns of emerging countries in the WTO system.

The second and opposite interpretation of the references to S&DT in the Doha Declaration is to reject these as another cynical attempt by ACs to mislead DCs by putting before them the prospect of strengthened S&DT when they do not intend to do anything other than induce DCs to accept the full rigors of the WTO system, as well as to adopt the system of "graduation," which would be deeply divisive for DCs.

Although there is a considerable history in support of the second interpretation, this chapter takes the more optimistic first view so as to make a constructive contribution to the current North–South discussions on these issues, which are taking place in Geneva and elsewhere. This broader and positive approach to S&DT provisions has also been implicitly called for by the heads of governments or states of non-aligned countries, which met in Kuala Lumpur in February 2003. In relation to the current WTO negotiations, the heads were "particularly concerned that major trading partners have yet again sought to place the question of S&DT for developing countries at a level less than at par with the other aspects of the negotiations." They called for "immediate negotiations on the proposed Framework Agreement on Special and Differential Treatment[23] for developing countries during the course of the present negotiations and reaffirmed that S&DT applies to all developing countries" (Koh 2003).

Toward a development-friendly WTO regime

It would be useful to begin the policy analysis by considering, first, the most optimistic policy scenario from the perspective of DCs. In this hypothetical world, ACs decide to act in the anti-mercantilist mode of the post-World War II US economic policy described earlier. In this mode the anti-developmental aspects of TRIPS, TRIMs, subsidies, balance-of-payments provisions, as well as other relevant parts of WTO Agreements would be openly acknowledged and the DCs (but not the ACs) would be allowed to opt out of any of these components if desired. This may appear to be a huge change with respect to the current situation, but it is worth remembering that the hypothesized conditions represent in many ways no more than the GATT privileges and protections that were available to DCs in the pre-Uruguay round period.

During the 1960s and 1970s, as Hoekman et al. (2003) put it, DC members were able to enjoy GATT on an à la carte basis. Further, in this imagined development-friendly world, developing countries would have preferential access to advanced countries' markets without being obliged to open their own markets in return. Thus, under the assumed circumstances, S&DT provisions in different areas help create an environment conducive to economic development: DCs are provided with the policy autonomy and the means and instruments for achieving their developmental priorities.

Would such a world, where S&DT takes what some would regard as an extreme form, necessarily harm economic development in developed countries? The theoretical answer in terms of neoclassical analysis is to suggest that such asymmetric integration of developing countries with the world economy would not prejudice economic growth and jobs in ACs. However, such a theoretical response is unlikely to cut much ice with the advanced countries' policymakers, who would say that although in principle trade is not a zero-sum game, the presence of many advanced developing countries with low wages and poor working conditions provides unfair competition and threatens the survival of many of their industries. There can be sudden surges of imports from leading DCs that harm workers in ACs. Policymakers in ACs would go on to suggest that they may be willing to provide some or all of these concessions to the least developed countries but there has to be some progression, a "graduation" level, beyond which S&DT would no longer be appropriate. However, a contrary view is expressed in the NAM Declaration above, with the heads of governments or states of DCs reaffirming "that S&DT applies to all DCs." Hence the question of graduation is a major point of contention between ACs and DCs and it deserves careful examination.

Graduation and differentiation: a mercantilist misconception

It was suggested by the analysis in Part I that the optimal degree of openness differs between developing and developed countries, as well as within each of these country groups. In terms of the application of S&DT to DCs, that would suggest a case-by-case approach to each country. This, however, at the present stage of development of the multilateral trading system, would be extremely expensive either in terms of trust or in more orthodox financial terms of costs and is therefore likely to be impractical. Hence the South's view that all DCs should benefit from S&DT and there should be no "graduation." The significant issue here, which may help towards a resolution of this controversy, concerns how much extra cost, if any, developed countries would have to bear if the S&DT provisions were not confined to least developed countries but were given to all developing countries. Would the costs of greater universality of S&DT provisions be prohibitively high for developed countries?

In a recent important World Bank study (Hoekman et al. 2003) on the S&DT controversy, the distinguished authors argue:

> Defining (agreeing to) the criteria to determine eligibility for S&DT lies at the heart of the S&DT debate. The experience to date suggests that the depth of the differential treatment granted will be inversely related to the number of eligible countries. Eligibility for S&DT should be restricted to fewer WTO member countries than is currently the case under the self-declaration approach that is used to identify developing countries.

The authors, however, do not provide any economic justification for their advocacy of selection rather than universality in the granting of S&DT treatments to DCs. Yet this issue is central to the dispute. For if the cost of universality were zero or negative or even a positive number which was small, it would be difficult to maintain a case for selectivity in favor of simply the least developed countries and a small number of other similar countries, as suggested by Hoekman et al. (2003). For if universality has no net economic cost to the ACs, their insistence on selectivity would be regarded by DCs as simply a political device to create divisions among their ranks.

It is therefore important in relation to the "graduation" issue to estimate the net costs and benefits to ACs of the international trading system, which up to now has been working mainly on a universalist criterion of self-declaration as a DC in relation to S&DT matters.[24] There are no studies which directly compare a universalist S&DT regime with a selective one. There is, nevertheless, a large body of analysis and indirect evidence which bears on the issue of the costs and benefits of the present trading system to ACs. The relevant parts of this literature[25] concern the effects of North–South trade in manufactures on labor market outcomes (in terms of unemployment, wage dispersion, and deindustrialization) in the North. This literature is highly contentious, albeit more in terms of methodology than with respect to the results. Until recently, the general empirical conclusion of this body of research was that the ACs' manufacturing trade with DCs during the 1980s was responsible for about 20 per cent of the observed wage dispersion in the United States. It was also thought to contribute to deindustrialization and unemployment on a similar modest scale.[26] Most of the observed negative changes in the labor market outcomes in the North have been ascribed to technology.

Most researchers accept the view that the proximate cause of labor market outcomes in the North is the fall in the demand for unskilled labor, which is ascribed to either trade or technology. Prof. Sir Tony Atkinson (1999, 2000, 2001) refers to this common view as the transatlantic consensus, since it provides a unified explanation for both unemployment in Western Europe and inequality in income distribution in the United States. It does so by making the auxiliary assumption that labor markets in Western Europe are highly imperfect because of the welfare state, so that reduced demand for unskilled labor leads to unemployment rather than reduced wages. However, in the United States the flexible labor market prevents unemployment at the expense of unfavorable changes in wage distribution.

Be that as it may, the most recent research on the subject, which covers the data for the 1990s, produces radically different conclusions. It suggests that neither trade nor technology can explain the observed changes, either in income distribution in the United States or in unemployment in Europe. Macroeconomic factors, unionization, and variables such as social norms have been deemed to be more important than either trade or technology in explaining the observed changes in the 1990s.

Equally significantly, empirical studies of the effects of trade and technology on AC labor markets do not take into account changes in terms of trade, which are connected with the trade with the South and which have a highly positive effect on the welfare in the North. To illustrate, the large devaluations that occurred in the crisis-affected Asian countries as a consequence of the acute macroeconomic disturbances in the region in the period 1997 to 2000 did not cause serious difficulties for US industry as was expected. Instead, improvements in terms of trade helped reduce inflation in the United States, which enabled the Federal Reserve to run the economy at a higher level of output and employment than would otherwise have been the case.

The above analysis suggests that, provided import surges can be controlled by multilaterally agreed safeguard measures, there are unlikely to be significant net economic costs to ACs of allowing a universalist S&DT regime in DCs. In view of this, it is not surprising that the DCs view the AC emphasis on graduation and differentiation as being politically motivated and designed to create further divisions among the DCs. Since there is a vast gap between countries in their relative political and economic strengths, more divisions among developing countries would further reduce their bargaining power in a unipolar world and lead to even greater imbalances between the North and the South.

To sum up, the North's insistence on graduation and differentiation is a mercantilist misconception from which it needs to be weaned so that attention can be focused on the real and substantive issues relating to the kinds of S&DT that would best help emerging countries.

Trade, finance, and the global economy

While the attention of developing country policymakers is concentrated on the WTO and the Doha Round, much of the relevant action is taking place elsewhere – in the financial sphere. There is unfortunately no reprieve for developing countries in that sphere from the ACs' pursuit of short-term economic advantage and mercantilism. In some ways the situation is worse. As noted in Part I, in view of emerging markets' high propensity to import, relaxation of import controls via trade liberalization has been closely connected with balance-of-payments difficulties. These difficulties oblige these countries to seek financial liberalization. The experience of developing countries with financial liberalization during the last decade has been catastrophic. A vast literature has explored the theoretical and empirical reasons for the financial crises that have invariably followed financial liberalization rather than the consumption smoothing that textbook theory would predict.[27]

The Bretton Woods institutions were established following the end of World War II precisely in order to reduce such instability in the global and national economies. In practice, the International Monetary Fund has shown no stomach for disciplining its most powerful members, whose macroeconomic policies often do collateral damage in developing countries.[28] Indeed, the Fund has effectively been used by leading industrial countries exclusively as a way of disciplining the Third World. Advanced countries, over nearly the last two decades (specifically since the Plaza Agreement of 1985), have maintained the minimum degree of economic cooperation among themselves so as not to provoke the price wars through competitive devaluations and deflations that characterized the 1930s. This has left developing countries increasingly at the mercy of highly unstable financial markets. Recent research indicates that developing countries suffer from much greater instability than developed countries and, further, that this phenomenon is not due to greater labor market rigidities in developing countries (as economic theory would suggest), but rather to the nature of the financial systems in developing countries as well as fluctuations in developing countries' terms of trade (see further Easterly et al. 2000).

Hence, developing countries require special and differential treatment not just at the WTO but also at the IMF. Until the Asian crisis, what they were getting instead at the IMF were strong exhortations to liberalize not just their current accounts but also their capital accounts. In 1997, the IMF attempted to change its Articles of Agreement to make capital account liberalization one of the main objectives of the organization. The Asian crisis brought some restraint and pull-back from these proposals. Joseph Stiglitz, Nobel laureate and former chief economist of the World Bank, found striking the zeal with which the International Monetary Fund (IMF) had requested an extension of its mandate to include capital market liberalization a short two years earlier at the Annual Meetings in Hong Kong. It should have been clear then, and it is certainly clear now, that the position was maintained either as a matter of ideology or of special interests, and not on the basis of careful analysis of theory, historical experience or a wealth of econometric studies. Indeed it has become increasingly clear that there is not only no case for capital market liberalization, but that there is a fairly compelling case against full liberalization. (2000a: 1076)

It is therefore not surprising that although there has been an intellectual retreat from the Washington Consensus policies by the Fund and the Bank (as noted in Part I), in practice it is widely felt that these policies have not fundamentally changed but have simply been given a new name (for example, poverty reduction strategy).[29] Similarly, it is disappointing that, notwithstanding all the pious references to S&DT in the Doha Declaration, the on-the-ground reality is that any such considerations are being blatantly ignored in the negotiations on services modalities that have recently been agreed to. The WTO's press note of 10 March 2003 reports the following decisions of the Council for Trade and Services in relation to liberalization of services in developing countries:

13. Pursuant to the objectives of the GATS, as stipulated in the Preamble, *Article IV*, and *Article XIX:2*, and in line with *paragraph 2* of the Doha Ministerial Declaration, these modalities shall be used inter alia as a means of promoting the economic growth and development of developing countries and their increasing participation in trade in services.

14. In the application of these modalities, and in recognizing and granting credit pursuant to these modalities, Members shall take fully into account the flexibility provided for individual developing country Members under the provisions referred to in paragraph 13 above, as well as the level of development of developing country Members in relation to other Members. Special consideration shall be given to the least-developed country Members.

There is clearly no new concept of S&DT here. The juggernaut of precipitated liberalization rolls on regardless of the anti-developmental effects that such liberalization entails for developing countries, as suggested by the analysis in Part I of this chapter.

In endorsing S&DT in glowing terms, the Doha Ministerial Meeting provided the international community with an opportunity to make the concept of Special and Differential Treatment meaningful and use it as an instrument to correct the structural imbalances between developed and developing countries. However, as the example of services above shows, no such new thinking is actually permeating the normal WTO processes. Liberalization of trade, whether in goods or services, without any assessment of the developmental consequences of such liberalization, still seems to be the order of the day. However, unlike the trade in goods, precipitated liberalization in the banking and financial sectors of services carries with it serious dangers to the stability of the economy. Before a country undertakes such liberalization it requires a well-functioning regulatory mechanism to provide prudent regulations. Alexander (2003) has argued that in the rush to liberalize the banking and financial services of the WTO, these elementary but exceptionally important requirements of prudential regulation are being ignored.

This last point has recently been forcefully argued by Bhagwati and Tarullo (2003). They refer specifically to the US government's recent RTA with Chile and Singapore. The Bush administration has insisted that the two countries will not be permitted to use capital controls against American firms. This, the reader will recall, is the exact opposite of the effective Special and Differential Treatment that the United States offered after the war to the European countries. These countries, within the framework of the European payments union, were able to discriminate against the US dollar in favor of the local currency. Bhagwati and Tarullo observe:

> Since the Asian financial crisis of 1997–98 the IMF has changed its thinking and acknowledged the need for careful policies that monitor and, in some cases, regulate capital flows.
> Yet now, just as the world has become saner in these matters, the Bush administration has insisted that the free trade areas for Chile and Singapore include provisions penalizing them for the use of any controls on capital. This short-sighted view marks a discouraging triumph of ideology over experience and good sense. (Bhagwati and Tarullo 2003: 21)

The two authors are worried that the Bush administration may use these two agreements (with Chile and Singapore) as templates for other trade agreements, possibly including the Doha Round.

Conclusion: S&DT and economic development

The unequivocal endorsement of S&DT at Doha gives the international community a fresh chance to change course, to put economic development at the heart of the agenda for the current and future evolution of the multilateral trading system. In operational terms this would indicate not only that internationally agreed poverty reduction goals are met, but that a movement toward convergence in income and productivity levels with rich countries is regarded as a legitimate objective which poor countries shall have the right, and be provided with the opportunity and the ability, to pursue. Taking development goals seriously in this manner would require a new definition and a new conceptualization of S&DT than the narrow meaning given to it under the Uruguay Round and the WTO Agreements. This new conceptualization of S&DT should satisfy the following broad concerns of developing countries:

1. There are parts of WTO Agreements that do not advance the cause of development and, arguably, restrict it. Reference here is to TRIMs, TRIPS, subsidies and countervailing duties, anti-dumping and other similar measures.[30] These Agreements need to be renegotiated, and, if they cannot be satisfactorily amended, developing countries should have the right to opt out of these. Indeed, what is being suggested here is that, in terms of Hoekman et al. (2003), developing countries should be allowed to indulge in the cardinal sin of participating in the multilateral trading system on the basis of 'GATT à la carte' as it were.

2. It is not only necessary to recognize the imbalances and anti-development character of the existing WTO Agreements; equally importantly it is essential to ensure that S&DT of DCs is made a part and parcel of the liberalization of services and of other areas, as well as in the consideration of new disciplines (e.g. the Singapore issues) on which negotiations are taking place now or are likely in the foreseeable future. Again, if DCs' concerns on these issues cannot be met within the framework of existing Agreements they should be permitted to opt out.

The achievement of 1 and 2 above depends on the ACs being weaned away from their insistence on graduation and differentiation, which this chapter has argued is a mercantilist misconception. Indeed, this entire program of putting development center stage in WTO negotiations requires a sea change in the culture and conduct of such negotiations, which at present appear to be steeped in narrow mercantilism rather than any long-term vision of a trading system that benefits both rich and poor countries. The AC negotiators should not forget that trade is not a zero-sum game, and their countries themselves provide an outstanding example of the success of non-reciprocity in international trade and finance. As suggested in Part I of the chapter, in the golden age, 1950–73, the far-sighted economic policies of the United States, which sought long-term objectives rather than short-term gains, were spectacularly successful in building up most of Europe and Japan as showpieces of liberal capitalism.

The challenge that ACs face today is whether they are willing to take a similar long-term view in their trade and financial relationships with developing countries and whether or not they will be able to overcome the narrow mercantilist outlook that demands reciprocity. The ball is squarely in the court of the ACs, as only they have the economic power to determine the world's economic priorities and agenda.

Notes

I am grateful to Reinaldo Figueredo, Werner Corrales, Yilmaz Akyuz, Chakravarti Raghavan, Manuela Tortora, Mahesh Sugathan, David Primack, Eduardo Escobedo, and other colleagues at UNCTAD and ICTSD for their detailed comments on an earlier version of this chapter. I am particularly grateful to Werner Corrales and Manuela Tortora for their patient and careful reading of drafts. Although I did not have the opportunity to discuss this chapter with Dani Rodrik, it is a pleasure to acknowledge my intellectual debt to his writings on the subject. The usual caveat applies, more than ever in this case as I have not always followed the advice given to me.

1. Even large firms from DCs are severely handicapped when they compete with large AC firms, usually multinationals, many of which have long been active in international trade and investment. DC firms are subject to infrastructural deficits, many missing or incomplete markets, lack of integration with the small and medium-sized firms, and much higher costs of capital. It is important to note that a typical AC multinational's average costs of production may be lower than those of a DC large firm not because the former enjoys economies of scale and scope, but because it is a monopolistic buyer and seller in many of its markets. Similarly, DC firms do not have brand names or marketing infrastructure and skills compared with the giant AC firms. To compensate for such structural deficits of DC firms – and there are myriad such deficits in other areas as well that also impinge on competitiveness – they were given the privilege of preferential access to AC markets without being asked for reciprocal access in DC markets.

2. Many people identify the S&DT concept with the formulation of the General System of Preferences (GSPs), which was done at UNCTAD. However, the concept itself predates GSPs.

3. Quoted in Hoekman and Kostecki 2001. On the reasons for the reaffirmation of S&DT in the Uruguay round, see further South Centre 1999; Kessie 2000; and Fukasaku 2000. Tables 1–3 in Whalley 1999 provide an excellent account of the evolution of non-reciprocity and S&DT during the last four decades.

4. Paragraph 44 of the Doha Ministerial Declaration is the main, central mandate on S&DT, but it is not the only one. It is reinforced by paragraph 12 of the Ministerial Decision on Implementation Issues that defines: (i) what the CTD has to do – i.e. the scope of the mandate; (ii) the place of the S&DT issues in the single undertaking; and (iii) the crucial link between the S&DT issue and the pending implementation issues. Another key element of the Doha mandate on S&DT is contained in paragraph 50 of the Doha Ministerial Declaration, which sets the legal framework of the negotiation on S&DT; that is, it reiterates the legal (i.e. binding) value of the relevant WTO texts. The divergent interpretation of these three provisions altogether is what generates the obstacles in the current negotiations. There are other "S&DT-like" mandates in the Doha texts, expressed in a variety of S&DT or "pro-development" language: for instance, paragraphs 6 and 7 of the Declaration on TRIPS and Public Health; paragraphs 16, 19, 21, 24, 26–29, 32, 33, 35–43, 51, plus the Decision on Implementation. I am grateful to Werner Corrales and Manuela Tortora for this point.

5. For a review of the progress on S&DT following the Doha meeting, see Tortora (2002); Mangeni (2002a and 2002b); ICTSD BRIDGES Weekly Trade News Digest

(Various); ICTSD & IISD (2003); and Melamed (2003).

6. This chapter is primarily concerned with underlying economic issues rather than with legal principles. However, for an interesting recent paper on legal issues concerned with S&DT, see Mangeni 2002a.

7. On NAFTA and its implications for domestic policy autonomy in Mexico, see Oxfam 2002.

8. The classic reference here is Sachs and Warner 1995. For more recent studies, see Prowse 2002; Hoekman et al. 2003. See also Srinivasan and Bhagwati 1999; Rodrik 1999.

9. This section draws on Chakravarty and Singh 1988.

10. The traditional theory of comparative advantage assumes, *inter alia*, constant or decreasing returns to scale and full employment. There is, however, considerable evidence in the real world of increasing returns which arise from (a) the static textbook economies of scale; (b) Kaldorian dynamic economies of scale; and (c) Young's macroeconomic economies of scale. The "new" trade theory's response to these problems has been, as Ocampo and Taylor (2000) put it, "to muffle the impact of scale economies by 'convexifying' assumptions." They note, for example, the "Dixit and Stiglitz (1977) model of monopolistic competition, in which firms' profitability gains from returns to scale are strictly limited by consumers' desires for product diversity."

11. Such a mechanism, for example, existed in the "golden age" of the post-World War II era (1950–73) when, under the aegis of a single hegemonic economic power, namely the United States, European economies were able to maintain high levels of aggregate demand to ensure full employment (Glyn et al. 1990; Singh 1995a).

12. The classic references here are World Bank 1991 and 1993.

13. See Singh 1994, 1997, 1998; Amsden 1994b; Lall 1995; Singh and Weisse 1999. For differing perspectives on the causes, consequences and remedies of the financial crisis in East Asian countries, see three recent collections of articles published by National Bureau of Economic Research: Feldstein 2002; Dooley and Frankel 2002; Edwards and Frankel 2002.

14. For information on Japan, see, among others, Okimoto 1989; Tsuru 1993; Caves and Uekusa 1976. For the Republic of Korea, see Amsden 1989; Chang 1994; Singh 1998.

15. In the postwar period, Japan has cultivated an enterprise-based, in-house approach to labor unions, which has contributed to industrial peace. See further You and Chang 1993.

16. It is not unreasonable to infer informal import controls (possibly in the form of foreigners' access to the complex Japanese retail network) as being a cause of slow growth of Japanese imports. The Japanese GDP growth was, if anything, faster than that in the competitor countries. This factor should have increased the rate of growth and the level of imports and not lowered them. For a fuller discussion of these issues, see further Singh 1995b; Johnson et al. 1989.

17. The IFIs ascribed the debt crisis to macroeconomic mistakes on the part of the Latin American governments and to their microeconomic inefficiencies, rent seeking and inappropriate resource allocation. The latter were thought to arise from import substitution and the pervasive role of the state in the economy. Singh (1993), Taylor (1988), and Fishlow (1991), strongly contested this thesis. They pointed out that the debt crisis was due to international economic forces over which developing countries had no control. It was noted that the financial contagion played a major role in

the debt crisis. It was also observed that Brazil had a debt crisis even though it had better fundamentals than Korea, and Korea did not have such a crisis. Williamson (1985) suggested that if Korea had been a Latin American country it too would have succumbed to the contagion.

18. For other important contributions to the debate about the relationship between trade and economic growth, see Srinivasan and Bhagwati 1999; Rodrik 1999.

19. For a further analysis of the issues raised in this section, see Glyn et al. 1990; Kindleberger 1992.

20. Strictly speaking, WTO Agreements do not prohibit the establishing of new institutions as such. What they do is to place limitations on a country's policies and legal framework. The latter are compatible with some institutional arrangements and not with others, which unnecessarily restricts many DCs' policy autonomy and their ability to establish important development-friendly institutions.

21. See further Amsden 2001, for a discussion of why in some countries government interventions succeed and in other they do not.

22. For a more comprehensive discussion of these issues, see Kaldor's (1978) classic paper; Singh 1995a; Singh and Zammit 2000.

23. WT/GC/442.

24. There are parts of WTO agreements in addition to S&DT where a reference to least developed group is made, but such references are few and far between. Generally speaking, the statement in the text is correct that the main beneficiaries of S&DT are supposed to be DCs.

25. For review of this literature, see Slaughter and Swagel 1997; Atkinson 1999, 2000, 2001; Singh 2003; Gottschalk and Smeeding 1997.

26. However, Wood (1994) regards North–South manufacturing trade to be a major cause of the adverse labor market outcomes in the North. For alternative perspectives, see the references cited in note 25. See also Singh's (1995c) review of Wood.

27. For a fuller discussion and recent reviews, see Singh 2002; Stiglitz 2000b; Feldstein 2002. However, for a defense of capital account liberalization, see Summers 2000; Fischer 1997.

28. Consider, for example, the interest rate shock of the late 1970s, which was a consequence of major changes in US monetary policy in 1979 under the then chairman of the US Federal Reserve Paul Volker. This had devastating consequences for developing countries, leading eventually to the "lost" decade of the 1980s in Africa and Latin America. See further Fishlow 1991; Singh 1993.

29. For a strong reaffirmation of the Washington Consensus policies, see Aninat 2003.

30. For fuller discussion of how the various parts of the WTO Agreements disadvantage developing countries and discourage development, see Third World Network 2001; Oxfam 2002.

References

Abbot, F. (1998) "The enduring enigma of TRIPS: a challenge for the world economic system," Special Issue on Trade-Related Aspects of Intellectual Property Rights (TRIPS), *Journal of International Economic Law* 1:4.

Abreu, M. de P. (2004) "The political economy of economic integration in the Americas: Latin American interests," in A. Estevadeordal, D. Rodrik, A.M. Taylor and A. Velasco (eds), *Integrating the Americas: FTAA and Beyond*, 417–45. Cambridge, MA: Harvard University Press.

Adlung, R. (2000) "Services trade liberalization from developed and developing country perspectives," in P. Sauvé and R. Stern (eds), *GATS 2000: New Directions in Services Trade Liberalization*. Washington, DC: Brookings Institution Press.

Agarwala, P.N. (1986) "The development of managerial enterprises in India," in K. Kobayashi and H. Morikawa (eds), *Development of Managerial Enterprise*, 235–257. Tokyo: University of Tokyo Press.

Agosin, M.R., and R. Mayer (2000) *Foreign Investment in Developing Countries: Does it Crowd in Domestic Investment?* UNCTAD Discussion Paper, No. 146, Geneva: UNCTAD.

Aitken, B., G.H. Hanson and A.E. Harrison (1994) *Spillovers, Foreign Direct Investment, and Export Behaviour*, NBER Working Paper Series, Working Paper 4967, Cambridge, MA: NBER.

Aitken, B., and A.E. Harrison (1999) "Do domestic firms benefit from direct foreign investment?" *American Economic Review* 89:3, 605–18.

Akerlof, G.A., W.T. Dickens and G.L. Perry (1996) "The macroeconomics of low inflation," *Brookings Papers on Economic Activity* 96:1, 1–76.

Alexander, K. (2003) "The World Trade Organisation and financial stability: accommodating trade liberalisation with prudential regulation" (online), Working Paper 5, Cambridge Endowment for Research in France, University of Cambridge, www.cerf.cam.ac.uk.

Amsden, A.H. (1989) *Asia's Next Giant: South Korea and Late Industrialization*. Oxford: Oxford University Press.

———— (1994a) "The spectre of Anglo-Saxonization is haunting South Korea," in L.J. Cho and Y. H. Kim (eds), *Korea's Political Economy: An Institutional Perspective*, 87–125. Boulder, CO: Westview.

———— (1994b) "Why isn't the whole world experimenting with the East Asian model to develop?," *World Development* 22:4.

———— (2001) *The Rise of the "The Rest": Challenges to the West from Late-Industrializing Economies*. New York: Oxford University Press.

———— (2003a) "Good-bye dependency theory, hello dependency theory," *Studies in Comparative International Development* 38:1, 32–8.

———— (2003b) "Industrialization under new WTO law," in John Toye (ed.), *Trade and Development: Directions for the 21st Century*, 82–99. Cheltenham: Edward Elgar.

Amsden, A.H., and A. Singh (1994) "The optimal degree of competition and dynamic efficiency in Japan and Korea," *European Economic Review* 38:3/4, 941–51.

Anderson, K. (2004) "Subsidies and trade barriers," in B. Lomberg (ed.), *Global Crises, Global Solutions*. Cambridge: Cambridge University Press.

Aninat, E. (2003) "Aninat on Latin America," *IMF Survey* 32:4, 49.

Ann-Elliot, K. (2003) *Pitfalls in Asymmetric Negotiations: Will the U.S. be the Next Goliath?* (online), Washington, DC: Center for Global Development, www.cgdev.org/Publications/?PubID=58.

Anner, M., and P. Evans (2004) "Building bridges across a double-divide: alliances between US and Latin American Labor and NGOs," *Development in Practice* 14:1–2, 34–47.

Anthony, R.N., and V. Govindarajan (1995) *Management Control Systems*. Chicago: Irwin.

Arizona Corporation Commission (2001) Mandate R14–2–1618, February 2001.

Arrighi, G., B. Silver and B. Brewer (2003) "Industrial convergence, globalization, and the persistence of the North–South divide," *Studies in Comparative International Development* 38:1, 3–31.

Arrow, K. (1962) "The economic implications of learning by doing," *Review of Economic Studies* 29:1, 155–73.

Ashton, D., F. Green, D. James and J. Sung (1999) *Education and Training for Development in East Asia*. London: Routledge.

Atkinson, A.B. (1999) "Is rising inequality inevitable? A critique of the transatlantic consensus," *WIDER Annual Lectures 3*, World Institute for Development Economics Research, United Nations University.

———— (2000) "The changing distribution of income: evidence and explanations," *German Economic Review* 1.

———— (2001) "A critique of the transatlantic consensus on rising income inequality," *The World Economy* 24:4, 433–52.

Bairoch, P. (1993) *Economics and World History: Myths and Paradoxes*. Brighton: Wheatsheaf.

Balasubramanyam, V.N. (1991) "Putting TRIMs to good use," *World Development* 19:9, 1215–24.

Bank of International Settlement (BIS) (2001) "Central Bank survey of foreign exchange and derivatives market activity in April 2001: preliminary global data," press release, October.

Barenberg, M. (2004) "The FTAA's impact on democratic governance," in A. Estevade-ordal, D. Rodrik, A.M. Taylor and A. Velasco (eds), *Integrating the Americas: FTAA and Beyond*, 755–89. Cambridge, MA: Harvard University Press.

Barton, J. (1999) "Intellectual property, biotechnology, and international trade: two examples," paper prepared for Berne World Trade Forum, Berne University, 28–29 August 1999.

Basanes, F.C., E. Saavedra and R. Soto (1999) *Post-Privatization Renegotiation and Disputes in Chile*. Washington, DC: Inter-American Development Bank, IFM-116.

BBC News, "Argentines barter to survive," 9 May 2002.

Belderbos, R. (1997) *Japanese Electronics Multinationals and Strategic Trade Policies*. Oxford: Clarendon Press.

Belderbos, R., G. Capannelli and K. Fukao (2001) "Backward vertical linkages of foreign manufacturing affiliates: evidence from Japanese multinationals," *World Development* 29:1, 189–208.

Besant-Jones, J., and B. Tenenbaum (2001) "California power crisis: lessons for developing countries" (online), ESMAP Working Paper, http://rru.worldbank.org/Documents/PapersLinks/365.pdf.

Best, M. (2001) *The New Competitive Advantage*. Oxford: Oxford University Press.

Bhaduri, A. (2003) "Structural change and economic development: on the relative roles of effective demand and the price mechanisms in a dual economy," in H.J. Chang (ed.), *Rethinking Development Economics*. London: Anthem Press.

Bhaduri, A., and R. Skarstein, (2003) "Effective demand and the terms of trade in a dual economy: a Kaldorian perspective," *Cambridge Journal of Economics* 27:4, 583–95.

Bhagwati, J. (1985) *Protectionism*. Cambridge, MA: MIT Press.

Bhagwati, J., and D. Tarullo (2003) "A ban on capital controls is a bad trade-off," *Financial Times*, 17 March 2003.

Biddle, J., and V. Milor. (1999) *Consultative Mechanisms and Economic Governance in Malaysia*, World Bank PSD Occasional Paper No. 38. Washington, DC: World Bank.

Bradsher, K. (2004) "U.S. Weighs Import Limits on China," *New York Times*, September 11, 2004, C2.

Brown, D.C. (1980) *Electricity for Rural America: The Fight for the REA*. Westport, CT: Greenwood Press.

Bruton, H. (1998) "A reconsideration of import substitution," *Journal of Economic Literature* 36:2 (June), 903–36.

Callan, B., S. Costigan and K. Keller (1997) *Exporting U.S. High Tech: Facts and Fiction about the Globalization of Industrial R&D*. New York: Council of Foreign Relations.

Cambridge Economic Policy Group (CEPG) (1979) *Economic Policy Review* 5.

Camdessus, M. (1999) Speech, Hong Kong, 17 May 1999.

Campbell, Laura (2002) "Energy globalization and the environment: bridging the international governance gap," in M.C. Harris (ed.), *Energy Market Restructuring and the Environment*, Lanham, MD: University Press of America.

Carkovic, M., and R. Levine (2002) "Does foreign direct investment accelerate economic growth?" (online), www.worldbank.org/research/conferences/financial_globalization/fdi.pdf.

Castro, A.B. de, and J. de P. C. Ávila (2004) "Uma Política industrial e tecnológica voltada para o potencial das empresas," paper presented at XVI Fórum Nacional, Rio de Janeiro, Brazil.

Caves, R., and M. Uekusa (1976) *Industrial Organization in Japan*. Washington, DC: Brookings Institution.

Comisión Económica Para América Latina (CEPAL) (1963) "El empresario industrial en America Latina," document prepared for the CEPAL Executive Secretariat. Santiago, Chile: CEPAL.

Chakravarty, S., and A. Singh (1988) *The Desirable Forms of Economic Openness in the South*. Helsinki: WIDER.

Chandler Jr, A.D. (1990) *Scale and Scope: The Dynamics of Industrial Capitalism*. Cambridge, MA: Harvard University Press.

Chang, H.J. (1994) *The Political Economy of Industrial Policy*. London: Macmillan.

———— (2002) *Kicking Away the Ladder: Development Strategy in Historical Perspective*. London: Anthem Press.

———— (2003a) *Foreign Investment Regulation in Historical Perspective – Lessons for the Proposed WTO Agreement on Investment*. Cambridge: Cambridge University, mimeo.

———— (2003b) *Rethinking Development Economics*. London: Anthem Press.

Chang, H.J., and D. Green (2003) *The Northern WTO Agenda on Investment: Do As We Say, Not As We Did*. Geneva: South Centre and CAFOD.

Chang, H.J., and P. Evans (forthcoming) "The role of institutions in economic change," in G. Dymski and S. de Paula (eds), *Reimagining Growth: Institutions, Development, and Society*. New York: Edward Elgar.

Chao, C.C., and E.S.H. Yu (1993) "Content protection, urban unemployment and welfare," *Canadian Journal of Economics* 26, 481-92.

Cheng, T.J., S. Haggard and D. Kang (1998) "Institutions and growth in Korea and Taiwan: the bureaucracy," *Journal of Development Studies* 34:6, 87–111.

Chesnais, F. (1996) "Technological agreements, networks and selected issues in economic theory," in R. Coombs, A. Richards, P. Saviotti and V. Walsh (eds), *Technological Collaboration: The Dynamics of Cooperation in Industrial Innovation*. Cheltenham: Edward Elgar.

Cho, H.D., and A.H. Amsden (1999) *Government Husbandry and Control Mechanism for the Promotion of High-Tech Development*. Cambridge, MA: MIT, Materials Science Laboratory.

Cho, H.H., and J.S. Kim (1997) "Transition of the government role in research and development in developing countries: R&D and human capital," Special Issue on R&D Management, *International Journal of Technology Management* 13:7/8, 729–43.

Clark, M. (1996) *Modern Italy, 1871–1995*, 2nd edn. London and New York: Longman.

Cline, W. (2004) *Trade Policy and Global Poverty*. Washington, DC: Institute for International Economics.

Cochran, T., and W. Miller (1942) *The Age of Enterprise: A Social History of Industrial America*. New York: Macmillan.

Commission on Intellectual Property Rights (CIPR) (2002) *Integrating Intellectual Property Rights and Development Policy*. London: CIPR (online), www.iprcommission.org.

Corrales-Leal, W., M. Sugathan and D. Primack (2003) "Spaces for Development Policy," in *Revisiting Special and Differential Treatment*. Geneva: International Centre for Trade and Sustainable Development (ICTSD).

Correa, C. (1997) "New international standards for intellectual property: impact on technology flows and innovation in developing countries," *Science and Public Policy* 24:2.

———— (1998) "Implementing the TRIPS Agreement in the patents field – options for developing countries," *Journal of World Intellectual Property* 1:1.

———— (1999) *Intellectual Property Rights, the WTO and Developing Countries: The TRIPS Agreement and Policy Options*. London: Zed Books.

———— (2002) *Implications of the Doha Declaration on the TRIPS Agreement and Public Health* (online), Geneva: World Health Organization, www.who.int.

———— (2003) *Establishing a Disclosure of Origin Obligation in the TRIPS Agreement*, Occasional Paper No. 12. Geneva: QUNO.

Correa, C., and S. Musungu (2002) *The WIPO Patent Agenda: The Risks for Developing Countries*, Working Paper No. 12. Geneva: South Centre.

Correa, M. (1994) "Trends in technology transfer implications for developing countries," *Science and Public Policy* 21:6.

Cosbey, A., H. Mann, L. Peterson and K. von Moltke. "Investment, Doha and the WTO," background paper, Chatham House. Meeting convened by RIIA and IISD on Trade and Sustainable Development Priorities Post-Doha, London, 7–8 April 2003.

Coudert Brothers LLP (2002) "Argentina: should foreign companies shoulder the burden?," *Currents Latin America* 1:2 (June).

Council of Economic Advisers, Executive Office of the President (1995) "Supporting research and development: the federal government's role" (online), Washington, DC: Executive Office of the President, www.whitehouse.gov/WH/EOP/CEA/econ/html/econ-rpt.html.

Covarrubias, A., and K. Reiche (2000) "A case study on exclusive concessions for rural off-grid service in Argentina," in *Energy Services for the World's Poor*. Washington, DC: World Bank.

Dailami, M. (2000) "Managing risks of global financial market integration," in C. Adams, R.E. Litan and M. Pomerleano (eds), *Managing Financial and Corporate Distress: Lessons from Asia*, 447–80. Washington, DC: Brookings Institution Press.

Daily Telegraph (2001) "Argentina on the brink of collapse," 21 December.

D'Arista, J. (2000) "Reforming international financial architecture," *Challenge* 43:3 (May–June), 44–82.

Daito, E. (1986) "Recruitment and training of middle managers in Japan, 1900–1930," in K. Kobayashi and H. Morikawa (eds), *Development of Managerial Enterprise*, 151–79. Tokyo: University of Tokyo Press.

Damri, S (2000) "Building linkages for sustainable development in Thailand," in *TNC–SME Linkages for Development: Issues–Experience–Best Practices*, 99–104. New York and Geneva: UNCTAD.

Das, B.L. (2003) *WTO: The Doha Agenda: The New Negotiations on World Trade*. London: Zed Books.

Davidson, C., S.J. Matusz and M. Kreinin (1985) "Analysis of performance standards for direct foreign investments," *Canadian Journal of Economics* 18:4, 133–54.

Dasgupta, P., and J. Stiglitz (1985) *Learning by Doing: Market Structure and Industrial and Trade Policies*, CEPR Discussion Papers 80.

Deardorff, A.V. (1994) "Market access," in A.V. Deardoff (ed.), *The New World Trading System: Readings*, 57–63. Paris: OECD.

De la Cuadra, S., and S. Valdes (1992) "Myths and facts about financial liberalization in Chile: 1974–1983," in P. Brock (ed.), *If Texas Were Chile: A Primer on Banking Reform*, 11–101. San Francisco: ICS Press.

De Mello Jr., L.R. (1999) "Foreign direct investment-led growth: evidence from time series and panel data," *Oxford Economic Papers* 51, 133–54.

De Sousa, D. (2001) "Protection of geographical indications under the TRIPS Agreement and related work of the World Trade Organization (WTO)," Symposium on the International Protection of Geographical indications, WIPO/GEO/MVD/01/2, Montevideo, 28–29 November.

Diaz-Alejandro, C. (1985) "Good-bye financial repression, hello financial crash," *Journal of Development Economics* 19:1–2 (September–October), 1–24.

Dixit, A., and J.E. Stiglitz (1977) "Monopolistic competition and optimal product diversity," *American Economic Review* 67, 297–308.

Dollar, D., and A. Kraay (2000) *Trade, Growth, and Poverty*. Washington, DC: World Bank.

Doner, R.F. (1991) *Driving a Bargain: Automobile Industrialization and Japanese Firms in Southeast Asia*. Berkeley and Los Angeles: University of California Press.

Dooley, M., and J.A. Frankel (eds) (2002) *Managing Currency Crises in Emerging Markets*. Chicago: University of Chicago Press.

Dubash, N.K. (2002) *Power Politics*. Washington, DC: World Resources Institute.

Easterly, W., R. Islam and J.E. Stiglitz (2000) "Shaken and stirred: volatility and macroeconomic paradigms for rich and poor countries," speech given for Michael Bruno Memorial Lecture, 12th World Congress of IEA, Buenos Aires, 27 August 1999, in *Annual Bank Conference on Development Economics 2000*, 191–212. Washington: World Bank. Also in J. Drèze (ed.), *Advances in Macroeconomic Theory*, IEA Conference Volume 133, 352–72. London: Palgrave Macmillan.

Eberhard, A. (2003) "The political, economic, institutional and legal dimensions of electricity supply industry reform in South Africa," paper presented to conference on Political Economy of Power Market Reform, Stanford University, 19–20 February 2003.

Economic Commission for Latin America and the Caribbean (ECLAC) (2002) *Social Panorama of Latin America 2001–2002*. Santiago, Chile: ECLAC.

Economic Commission for Latin America and the Caribbean and United Nations Environment Program (ECLAC and UNEP) (2003) *The Sustainability of Development in Latin America and the Caribbean: Challenges and Opportunities*. Santiago: ECLAC/UNEP.

Edwards, S., and A.C. Edwards (1991) *Monetarism and Liberalization: The Chilean Experiment*. Chicago: University of Chicago Press.

Edwards, S., and J.A. Frankel (eds) (2002) *Preventing Currency Crises in Emerging Markets*. Chicago: University of Chicago Press.

Economic Times (2002) 2 September 2002.

———— (2003) 9 May 2003.

'Electricity providers face new mandate on renewable energy," Associated Press, 27 April 2000.

Elliot, K. (2003) *Pitfalls in Asymmetric Negotiations: Will the U.S. be the Next Goliath?* Washington, DC: Center for Global Development.

European Commission (1999) "The EU approach to the Millennium Round" (online), Communication from the Commission to the Council and the European Parliament, http://attac.org/fra/libe/doc/uedg1.htm.

Evans, P.B. (1995) *Embedded Autonomy: States and Industrial Transformation*. Princeton, NJ: Princeton University Press.

———— (1998) "Transferable lessons? Re-examining the institutional prerequisites of East Asian economic policies," *Journal of Development Studies* 34:6, 66–86.

———— (2003) "Economic governance institutions in a global political economy: implications for developing countries," in J. Toye (ed.), *Trade and Development: Directions for the Twenty-first Century*. Cheltenham: Edward Elgar.

———— (2004) "Development as institutional change: the pitfalls of monocropping and potentials of deliberation," *Studies in Comparative International Development* 38:4, 30–52.

Evans, P.C. (2002) *Liberalizing Global Trade in Energy Services*. Washington: American Enterprise Institute.

Evans, P., and M. Finnemore (2001) *Organizational Reform and the Expansion of the South's Voice at the Fund*, G-24 Discussion Paper Series, no. 15. UNCTAD and Harvard University Center for International Development.

Evans, P., H. Jacobson and R. Putnam (eds) (1993) *Double-Edged Diplomacy: International Bargaining and Domestic Politics*. Berkeley, CA: University of California Press.

Evers, H.D., and T.H. Silcock (1967) "Elites and selection," in T.H. Silcock (ed.), *Thailand: Social and Economic Studies in Development*, 84–104. Durham, NC: Australian National University Press in association with Duke University Press.

Feldstein, M. (2002) *Economic and Financial Crisis in Emerging Market Economies: Overview of Prevention and Management*, NBER Working Paper Series, Working Paper 8837. Cambridge, MA: NBER.

Ffrench-Davis, R. (2002) *Economic Reforms in Chile*. Ann Arbor: University of Michigan Press.

Financial Times (2002) 6 December 2002.

———— (2003) "Black empowerment," Editorial, 7 August 2003.

Firebaugh, G. (2004) "Does industrialization no longer benefit poor countries? A comment on Arrighi, Silver and Brewer, 2003," *Studies in Comparative International Development* 39:1, 99–103.

Fischer, S. (1997) "Capital account liberalisation and the role of the IMF," paper presented at the seminar Asia and the IMF, Hong Kong, 19 September 1997.

———— (2003) "Globalization and its challenges," *American Economic Review, Papers and Proceedings* 93:2.

Fishlow, A. (1991) "Some reflections on comparative Latin American economic performance and policy," in T. Banuri (ed.), *Economic Liberalisation: No Panacea*. Oxford: Clarendon Press.

Frank, A.G. (1967) *Capitalism and Underdevelopment in Latin America*. New York: Monthly Review Press.

Frankel, J.A., and D. Roemer (1999) "Does trade cause growth?" *American Economic Review* 89:3, 379–99.

Freeman, C. (1989) "New technology and catching up," *European Journal of Development Research* 1:1.

Freshfields Bruckhaus Deringer (2002) "The Argentine crisis – foreign investors' rights," *Briefing*, January 2002.

Fry, M.J. (1992) *Foreign Direct Investment in a Macroeconomic Framework: Finance, Efficiency, Incentives and Distortions*, PRE Working Paper. Washington, DC: World Bank.

FT Energy Newsletters – Global Water Report (1997) "French–Irish team to run Gabon's main utility," 26 March.

Fukasaku, K. (2000) *Special and Differential Treatment for Developing Countries: Does It*

Help Those Who Help Themselves? Working Paper 197. Helsinki: UNU World Institute for Developing Economics Research.

Gallagher, K.P., and L. Zarsky (2004) "Foreign direct investment and sustainable development," in L. Zarsky (ed.), *Rights without Rewards? Sustainability, Development, and the Governance of International Investment.* London: Earthscan Books.

Garraty, J., and M. Carnes (2000) *The American Nation – A History of the United States,* 10th edn. New York: Addison Wesley Longman.

Gee, S. (1997) "Taiwan Auto Parts Industry," in G. Felker et al. (eds), *Technology Development in the Auto Parts Industry: Japan, Korea, Taiwan, India and Hungary,* 73–84. New Delhi: Ramko Press.

General Agreement on Tariffs and Trade (GATT) (1986) *The Text of the General Agreement,* 7. Geneva: GATT.

Gereffi, G., J. Humphrey, R. Kaplinsky and T.J. Sturgeon (2001) "Introduction: globalisation, value chains and development," *IDS Bulletin* (Institute of Development Studies, Sussex University) 32:2, 1–8.

Gereffi, G., J. Humphrey and T. Sturgeon (forthcoming) "The governance of global value chains," *Review of International Political Economy.*

Global Programme for Globalization, Liberalization and Sustainable Human Development (GP) and the International Centre for Trade and Sustainable Development (ICTSD) (2003) "Making Special and Differential Treatment effective and responsive to development needs" (online), paper presented by UNCTAD–UNDP, GP, and ICTSD, March 2003, www.ictsd.org/dlogue/2003–05–06/06–05–03–desc.htm.

Glyn, A., A. Hughes, A. Lipietz and A. Singh (1990) "The rise and fall of the golden age," in S. Marglin and J. Schor (eds), *The Golden Age of Capitalism.* Oxford: Clarendon Press.

Gomery R.E., and W.J. Baumol (2000) *Global Trade and Conflicting National Interest.* Cambridge, MA: MIT Press.

Gottschalk, P., and T. Smeeding (1997) "Cross national comparisons of earnings and income inequality," *Journal of Economic Literature* 35:2, 633–87.

Grand Canyon Trust (2000)'Environmental organization comments on rulemaking before the Arizona Corporation Commission, October 3, 2000" (online), www.grandcanyontrust.org/ggc/grcanyon/air/energy/comments3.html.

Greenaway, D. (1991) "Why are we negotiating on TRIMs?," in D. Greenaway et al. (eds), *Global Protectionism,* 145–70. London: Macmillan.

Greenwald, B., and J.E. Stiglitz (1986) "Externalities in economies with imperfect information and incomplete markets," *Quarterly Journal of Economics,* May, 229–64.

Guisinger, S.E., et al. (1985) *Investment Incentives and Performance Requirements: Patterns of International Trade, Production and Investment.* New York: Praeger.

Hackett, S. and N. Srinivasan (1998) "Do supplier switching costs differ across Japanese and US multinational firms?" *Japan and the World Economy* 10, 13–32.

Haddad, M., and A. Harrison (1993) "Are there positive spillovers from direct foreign investment? Evidence from panel data for Morocco," *Journal of Development Economics* 42, 51–74.

Hardstaff, P. (2003) "The 'flexibility' myth: why GATS is a bad model for a new WTO investment agreement," World Development Movement paper, Seminar on WTO Investment Agreement, Geneva, 20 March.

Helpman, E. (1993) "Innovation, imitation, and intellectual property rights," *Econometrica* 61:6 (November), 1247–80.

Hempling, S., and N. Rader. (2002) "Comments of the Union of Concerned Scientists to the Commission for Environmental Cooperation in response to its 'NAFTA provisions and the electricity sector' background paper." Washington, DC: Union of Concerned Scientists.

Hinojosa-Ojeda, R., D. Runsten, F. Depaolis and N. Kamel (2000) "The U.S. employment impacts of North American integration after NAFTA: a partial equilibrium approach" (online), Los Angeles, CA: North American Integration and Development Center, School of Public Policy and Social Research, UCLA, http://naid.sppsr.ucla.edu/pubs&news/nafta2000.html.

Hoda, A. (1994) "Trade liberalisation," in A.V. Deardoff (ed.), *The New World Trading System: Readings*, 41–56. Paris: Organization for Economic Cooperation and Development.

Hoekman, B.M., and M.M. Kostecki (2001) *The Political Economy of the World Trading System: The WTO and Beyond*, 2nd edn. New York: Oxford University Press.

Hoekman, B., P. Messerlin, C. Michalopoulos, M. Pangestu, K. Saggi, J. Tybout and A. Winters (2003) "Differential and more favorable treatment, reciprocity and fuller participation of developing countries: objectives, instruments and options for the WTO," paper presented at the DFID Special and Differential Treatment Seminar, London, March.

Hoff, K., and J. Stiglitz (2001) "Modern economic theory and development," in G. Meier and J. Stiglitz (eds), *Frontiers of Development Economics*, 389–460. New York: Oxford University Press.

Horlick, G., C. Schuchhardt and H. Mann (2002) *NAFTA Provisions and the Electricity Sector*, CEC Background Paper. Montreal: North American Commission on Environmental Cooperation.

International Centre for Trade and Sustainable Development (ICTSD). *BRIDGES Weekly Trade News Digest* (various editions) (online), www.ictsd.org/weekly.

International Centre for Trade and Sustainable Development (ICTSD) and International Institute for Sustainable Development (IISD) (2003) *Doha Round Briefings: Special and Differential Treatment* 1:13.

International Monetary Fund (IMF) (1997) *World Economic Outlook: Interim Assessment*. Washington DC: IMF.

———— (1998) *Annual Report on Exchange Arrangements and Exchange Restrictions*. Washington DC: IMF.

———— (2003) *Effects of Financial Globalization on Developing Countries: Some Empirical Evidence*. Washington DC: International Monetary Fund.

International Trade Finance (1997) "Gabon selects French/Irish team for 20 year water and power concession," 28 March.

Jackson, A., and M. Sanger (2003) *When Worlds Collide: Implications of International Trade and Investment Agreements for Non-Profit Social Services*. Ottawa: Canadian Centre for Policy Alternatives and Canadian Council on Social Development.

Jacobs, J. (1984) *Cities and the Wealth of Nations: Principles of Economic Life*. New York: Random House.

James, W.E. (1987) *Asian Development: Economic Success and Policy Lessons*. Madison: University of Wisconsin, for the International Center for Economic Growth.

Johnson. C., L. Tyson and J. Zysman (1989) *Politics and Productivity*. New York: Harper Business.

Kaldor, N. (1978) *Further Essays on Economic Theory*. London: Duckworth.

Kanbur, R. (2001) "Economic policy, distribution, and poverty: the nature of disagreements" (online), http://people.cornell.edu/pages/sk145/papers/Disagreements. pdf.

———— (2002) "The case for cross-disciplinary approaches in international development," *World Development* 30:3.

KCTU–FKTU (1998) "The KCTU proposal," document presented at KCTU–FKTU meeting with US Treasury Secretary Rubin, 1 July.

Kelkar, V.L., P.K. Chaudhry and M. Vanduzer-Snow (2005) "A time for change at the IMF: an institution transformed to address new forces in the global economy," *Finance and Development* March.

Kerr, J. (2003) "Gas Natural takes legal action against Argentine government over frozen rates," *World Markets Analysis*, 3 June.

Kessie, E. (2000) "Enforceability of the legal provisions relating to special and differential treatment under the WTO agreements" (online), paper prepared for WTO Seminar on Special and Differential Treatment for Developing Countries, Geneva, 7 March, www.wto.org/english/tratop_e/devel_e/sem01_e/kessie_e.doc.

Khan, S.I. (2003) "Protecting the poor in the era of utility privatization," *Energy for Sustainable Development* 7:2 (June).

Kim, L. (1997) *Imitation to Innovation: The Dynamics of Korea's Technological Learning.* Boston, MA: HBS Press.

Kim, L., and G. Yi (1997) "The dynamics of R&D in industrial development: lessons from the Korean experience," *Industry and Innovation* 4:2, 167–82.

Kindleberger, C. (1978) "Germany's overtaking of England, 1806 to 1914," in *Economic Response: Comparative Studies in Trade, Finance, and Growth*, ch. 7. Cambridge, MA: Harvard University Press.

———— (1992) "Why did the golden age last so long?," in F. Cairncross and A. Cairncross (eds), *The Legacy of the Golden Age*, 15–44. London and New York: Routledge.

Knutrud, L.H. (1994) "TRIPS in the Uruguay Round," in A.V. Deardoff (ed.), *The New World Trading System: Readings*, 193–195. Paris: Organization for Economic Cooperation and Development.

Koh (2003) "TWN Info: NAM calls for WTO reforms." Kuala Lumpur: Third World Network, 25 February.

Kokko, A., R. Tansini and M.C. Zejan (1996) "Local technological capability and productivity spillovers from FDI in the Uruguayan manufacturing sector," *Journal of Development Studies* 32:4, 602–11.

Kozul-Wright, R. (1995) "The myth of Anglo-Saxon capitalism: reconstructing the history of the American state," in H.-J. Chang and R. Rowthorn (eds), *The Role of the State in Economic Change*, 81–113. Oxford: Clarendon Press.

Krohn, S. (2002) *Wind Energy Policy in Denmark: Status 2002.* Copenhagen: Danish Wind Industry Association.

Krugman, P. (1987) "Is free trade passé?," *Journal of Economic Perspectives* 1:2, 131–43.

———— (1990) *Strategic Trade Policy and the New International Economics.* Cambridge, MA: MIT Press.

———— (1996) *Pop Internationalism.* Cambridge, MA: MIT Press.

Krugman, P., and M. Obstfeld (2000) *International Economics*, 4th edn. New York: McGraw-Hill.

Kumar, N. (1997) *Technology Generation and Technology Transfer in the World Economy: Recent Trends and Implications for Developing Countries.* Maastricht: United Nations

University, Institute of New Technologies.

——— (1998) "Multinational enterprises, regional economic integration, and export-platform production in the host countries: an empirical analysis for the US and Japanese corporations," *Weltwirtschaftliches Archiv* 134:3, 450–83.

——— (2000) "Explaining the geography and depth of international production: the case of US and Japanese multinational enterprises," *Weltwirtschaftliches Archiv* 136:3, 442–76.

——— (2001) "WTO's emerging investment regime: way forward for Doha ministerial meeting," *Economic and Political Weekly* 36:33, 3151–8.

——— (2002) *Globalization and Quality of Foreign Direct Investment*. New Delhi: Oxford University Press.

Kumar, N., and J.P. Pradhan (2002) *Foreign Direct Investment, Externalities and Economic Growth in Developing Countries: Some Empirical Explorations and Implications for WTO Negotiations on Investment*, RIS Discussion Paper No. 27. New Delhi: Research and Information System for the Non-Aligned and Other Developing Countries.

Kumar, N., and N. Singh (2002) *The Use and Effectiveness of Performance Requirements: The Case of India*. New Delhi: Research and Information System for the Non-Aligned and Other Developing Countries and UNCTAD, mimeo.

Kwa, A. (2002) *Power Politics in the WTO*. Bangkok: Focus on the Global South, Chulalongkorn University.

Lahiri, S., and Y. Ono (1998) "Foreign direct investment, local content requirement, and profit taxation," *Economic Journal* 108:447, 444–57.

Lall, S. (1992a) *The Interrelationship between Investment Flows and Technology Transfer: An Overview of the Main Issues*. Geneva: UNCTAD, ITD/TEC/1.

——— (1992b) "Technological capabilities and industrialization," *World Development* 20:2, 165–86.

——— (1995) "Industrial strategy and policies on foreign direct investment in East Asia," *Transnational Corporations* 4:3.

——— (1996) *Learning from the Asian Tigers*. London: Macmillan.

——— (2001a) *Competitiveness, Technology and Skills*. Cheltenham: Edward Elgar.

——— (2001b) "Competitiveness indices and developing countries: an economic evaluation of the Global Competitiveness Report," *World Development* 29:9, 1501–25.

——— (2003) "Indicators of the relative importance of IPRs in developing countries," *Research Policy* 32.

Lall, S., and M. Albaladejo (2002) *Indicators of the Relevant Importance of IPRs in Developing Countries*. Geneva: UNCTAD/ICTSD.

——— (2003) *China's Export Surge: The Competitive Implications for Southeast Asia*, report for the World Bank East Asia Department. Oxford: Queen Elizabeth House.

Lall, S., and C. Pietrobelli (2002) *Failing to Compete: Technology Development and Technology Systems in Africa*. Cheltenham: Edward Elgar.

Lall, S., and M. Teubal (1998) "'Market stimulating' technology policies in developing countries: a framework with examples from East Asia," *World Development* 26:8, 1369–85.

Latin American Southern Cone Report (2002), "Argentina tops 'new' development report," 30 July.

Lim, Y. (1999) *Public Policy for Upgrading Industrial Technology in Korea*. Boston: MIT Press.

Lipsey, R.E (1998) "The internationalization of US MNEs and its impact in developing countries," in N. Kumar et al. (eds), *Globalization, Foreign Direct Investment and Technology Transfers: Impacts on and Prospects for Developing Countries*, 197–212. London and New York: Routledge.

List, F. (1885) *The National System of Political Economy*, translated from the original German edition (1841) by S. Lloyd. London: Longmans, Green.

———— (1966) *The National System of Political Economy* [1885]. New York: Augustus Kelley.

Loewendahl, H. (2001) "A framework for FDI promotion," *Transnational Corporations* 10:1, 1–42.

Lohr, S. (2002) "On intellectual property, U.S. forgets its own past," *International Herald Tribune*, 16 October.

Loree, D.W., and S.E. Guisinger (1995) "Policy and non-policy determinants of U.S. equity foreign direct investment," *Journal of International Business Studies* 26:2.

Losch, B. (2004) "Debating the multifunctionality of agriculture: from trade negotiations to development policies by the South," *Journal of Agrarian Change* 4:3, 336–60.

Low, P. (1993) *The GATT and US Trade Policy*. New York: Twentieth Century Fund Press.

Low, P., and A. Subramanian (1995) *TRIMs in the Uruguay Round: An Unfinished Business?* World Bank Conference Paper L6–27 95. Washington, DC: World Bank International Trade Division.

Lu, Q. (1997) *Innovation and Organization: The Rise of New Science and Technology Enterprises in China*. Cambridge, MA: Harvard University Press.

M. & M. Bomchil Abogados (2002) "Public Emergency Regulations on Public Works and Utilities Contracts and Licenses," Legal Updates from Argentina. Buenos Aires: M. & M. Bomchil Abogados.

Maddison, A. (1991) *Dynamic Forces in Capitalist Development: A Long Run Comparative View*. New York: Oxford University Press.

———— (2001) *The World Economy. A Millennial Perspective*. Paris: Development Centre Studies, OECD.

Malaguti, M.C. (1998) "Restrictive business practices in international trade and the role of the World Trade Organization," *Journal of World Trade* 32:3, 117–52.

Mandeville, B. (1924) *The Fable of the Bees: or, Private Vices, Public Benefits* [1714]. London: Oxford University Press.

Mangeni, F. (2002a) "The legal basis for a new regime of differential treatment," in *Bridges: Between Trade and Sustainable Development* (online), Geneva: International Centre for Trade and Sustainable Development, www.ictsd.org.

———— (2002b) *Strengthening the Special and Differential Treatment Provisions in the WTO Agreements: Some Reflections on the Priorities and Stakes for African Countries*. Geneva: International Centre for Trade and Sustainable Development.

Manifold, D.L. (1997) *Japanese Corporate Activities in Asia: Implications for U.S.–Japan Relations*. Office of Economics Working Paper No. 96–04–A. Washington, DC: US International Trade Commission.

Martínez, J., and J. Santiso (2003) "Financial markets and politics: the confidence game in Latin American emerging economies," *International Political Science Review* 24:3, 363–95.

Mathews, J.A. (2002) "The origins and dynamics of Taiwan's R&D consortia," *Research Policy* 31:4, 633–51.

Mathews, J.A., and D.S. Cho (1999) *Tiger Technology: The Creation of a Semiconductor Industry in East Asia*. Cambridge: Cambridge University Press.

McCulloh, R. (1990) "Investment policies in the GATT," *World Economy* 13:3, 541–53.

Melamed, C. (2003) "Doing 'development' at the WTO: the Doha Round and special and differential treatment," paper presented at DFID Special and Differential Treatment Seminar, Church House, London, 7 March.

Merchant, K. (1985) *Control in Business Organizations*. Marshfield MA: Pitman.

Mill, J. S. (1940) *Principles of Political Economy* [1848]. London: Longmans, Green.

Miller & Chevalier Chartered (2002) "The Argentina Meltdown, BIT by BIT," *International Alert*, 8 February.

Moore, C., and J. Ihle (1999) *Renewable Energy Policy outside the United States*, Issue Brief No. 14. Washington, DC: Renewable Energy Policy Project.

Moran, T.H. (1998) *Foreign Direct Investment and Development*. Washington, DC: Institute for International Economics.

—— (2001) *Parental Supervision: The New Paradigm for Foreign Direct Investment and Development*. Washington, DC: Institute for International Economics.

Mortished, Carl (2003) "Black empowerment hurdle for government contracts," *The Times*, 26 April.

Mourshed, M. (1999) "Technology transfer dynamics: lessons from the Egyptian and Indian pharmaceutical industries," *Urban Studies and Planning*, Cambridge MA: MIT.

Munk, K.J. (1990) "The use of general equilibrium models for the assessment of the impact of agricultural trade liberalization," in I. Goldin and O. Knudsen (eds), *Agricultural Trade Liberalization: Implications for Developing Countries*, 456–60. Paris and Washington DC: OECD and the World Bank.

Murthi, M., J.M. Orszag and P.R. Orszag (1999) *The Charge Ratio on Individual Accounts: Lessons from the UK Experience*. Birkbeck College Working Paper 99–2. London: University of London.

Musungu, S., and G. Dutfield (2004) *Multilateral Agreements and a TRIPS-Plus World: The World Intellectual Property Organisation*. Geneva: QUNO.

Nadal, A. (2003) "Macroeconomic challenges for Mexico," in K.J. Middlebrook and E. Zepeda (eds), *Confronting Development: Assessing Mexico's Social and Economic Policy*. Palo Alto: Stanford University Press.

Narongchai, A., and J. Ajanant (1983) *Manufacturing Protection in Thailand: Issues and Empirical Studies*. Canberra: ASEAN–Australia Joint Research Project.

Narula, R. (2003) *Globalization and Technology*. Cambridge: Polity Press.

Negroponte, N. (1996) *Being Digital*. New York: Vintage Books.

Nelson, R.R., and S.J. Winter (1982) *An Evolutionary Theory of Economic Change*. Cambridge, MA: Harvard University Press.

The News Says – Argentina (2003), "Private companies demand 17,000 million dollars," 3 August.

Nippon, P. (1999) *The Thailand Automotive Industry* (online), Bangkok: Thailand Development Research Institute, www.asean-auto.org/publication.htm.

Noland, M., and H. Pack (2003) *Industrial Policy in an Era of Globalization: Lessons from Asia*. Washington, DC: Institute for International Economics.

North American Commission on Environmental Cooperation (NACEC) (2003) "Proceedings: overcoming obstacles to renewable energy sources in Mexico: lessons from the NAFTA partners." Mexico City, 7 February.

O'Brien, P.K. (1997) "Intercontinental trade and the development of the third world since the industrial revolution," *Journal of World History* 8:1, 75–133.

Ocampo, J.A., and L. Taylor (2000) "Trade liberalization in developing economies: modest benefits but problems with productivity growth, macro prices, and income distribution," in H.D. Dixon (ed.), *Controversies in Macroeconomics Growth, Trade and Policy*. Cambridge, MA: Blackwell.

O'Donnell, G. (1973) *Modernization and Bureaucratic Authoritarianism*. Berkeley: University of California Press.

Okediji, R. (2003–04) "Back to bilateralism? Pendulum swings in international intellectual property protection," *University of Ottawa Law & Technology Journal* 1, 125–47.

Okamoto, Y., and F. Sjoholm (2000) "Productivity in the Indonesian automotive industry," *ASEAN Economic Bulletin* 17:1, 60–73.

Okimoto, D.I. (1989) *Between the MITI and the Market*. Palo Alto, CA: Stanford University Press.

Oppenheimer, N. (2003) "A fairer society needs faster growth," *Financial Times*, 15 August.

Organization for Economic Cooperation and Development (OECD) (1996a) *Trade Liberalization Policies in Mexico*. Paris: OECD.

——— (1996b) *Reviews of National Science and Technology Policy: Korea*. Paris: OECD.

Oxfam (2002) *Rigged Rules and Double Standards: Trade, Globalization, and the Fight against Poverty*. Oxford: Oxfam.

——— (2003) *Unwanted, Unproductive and Unbalanced: Six Arguments against an Investment Agreement at the WTO*, Joint Policy Paper. Oxford: Oxfam.

Pack, H., and L.E. Westphal (1986) "Industrial strategy and technological change: theory versus reality," *Journal of Development Economics* 22:1, 87–128.

Pangestu, M. (2002) "Industrial policy and developing countries," in B. Hoekman, A. Mattoo and P. English (eds), *Trade and the WTO: A Handbook*. Washington, DC: World Bank.

Pao Li, L., and A.O.C. Imm (2002) *Malaysian Case Study of the Use and Impact of Performance Requirements*. New York and Geneva: UNCTAD.

Pasinetti, L.L. (1981) *Structural Change and Economic Growth: A Theoretical Essay on the Dynamics of the Wealth of Nations*. Cambridge: Cambridge University Press.

PCT Union (World Intellectual Property Organization, International Patent Cooperation Union) (2004) Working Group on Reform of the Patent Cooperation Treaty (PCT), Sixth Session; Additional Comments by Switzerland on its Proposals Regarding the Declaration of the Source of Genetic Resources and Traditional Knowledge in Patent Applications, 21 April (online), PCT/R/WG/6/11, www.wipo.int/pct/en/meetings/reform_wg/doc/pct_r_wg_6_11.doc.

Peterson, L. (2002) *Investment Law and Sustainable Development Weekly*, 27 December.

——— (2003) "South Africa's black economic empowerment plans an obstacle to a US FTA?," *Investment Law and Sustainable Development Weekly*, 8 July.

Pettis, M. (2001) *The Volatility Machine: Emerging Economies and the Threat of Financial Collapse*. New York: Oxford University Press.

Philpott, J., and A. Clark. (2002) "South Africa: reform with a human face?," in N.K. Dubash (ed.), *Power Politics: Equity and Environment in Electricity Reform*. Washington, DC: World Resources Institute.

Pinna, G. (2002) "Che cosa bolle davvero in pentola," *Panorama* 40, 32.

Prasad, E., K. Rogoff, S.-J. Wie and M.A. Kose (2003) "Effects of financial globalization on developing countries," typescript.

Prowse, S. (2002) "The role of international and national agencies in trade-related capacity building," *The World Economy* 25:9.

Puri, H., and P. Brusick (1989) "Trade-related investment measures: Issues for developing countries in the Uruguay Round," in *Uruguay Round: Papers on Selected Issues*. New York: UNCTAD, UNCTAD/ITP/10.

Pursell, G. (1999) "The Australian experience with FDI and local content programmes in the auto industry," paper presented at the Conference on WTO, Technology and Globalization, Institute of Economic Growth, Delhi.

Putzel, J. (2003) "Governance and HIV/AIDS: institutionalising an emergency response in Uganda and Senegal," draft report to the Department for International Development, Government of the United Kingdom.

Quinn, D., and C. Inclan (1997) "The origins of financial openness: a study of current capital account liberalization," *American Journal of Political Science* 41, 771–813.

Raby, D. (1994) "Introduction," in A.V. Deardoff (ed.), *The New World Trading System: Readings*. Paris: OECD.

Radosevic, S. (1999) *International Technology Transfer and Catch-Up in Economic Development*. Cheltenham: Edward Elgar.

Raghavan, C. (2002) *Developing Countries and Services Trade: Chasing A Black Cat in a Dark Room, Blindfolded*. Penang: Third World Network.

Reichman, J. (1996/7) "From free riders to fair followers: global competition under the TRIPS Agreement," *New York University Journal of International Law and Politics* 29:1–2.

——— (1999) "The TRIPS Agreement comes of age: conflict or cooperation with the developing countries?," paper presented to the World Trade Forum, University of Berne, 28–29 August.

Reichman, J.H., and P. Samuelson (1997) "Intellectual property rights in data?," *Vanderbilt Law Review* 50:1, 51–166.

Reinbothe, J., M. Martin-Prat and S. Von Lewinski (1997) "The new WIPO treaties: a first resume," *EIPR* 4.

Reinert, E. (1995) "Competitiveness and its predecessors – a 500 year cross-national perspective," *Structural Change and Economics Dynamics* 6, 23–42.

——— (1998) "Raw materials in the history of economic policy – or why List (the protectionist) and Cobden (the free trader) both agreed on free trade in corn," in G. Cook (ed.), *The Economics and Politics of International Trade – Freedom and Trade*, Vol. 2. London: Routledge.

Rhee, Y., B. Ross-Larson and G. Pursell (1984), *Korea's Competitive Edge*. Baltimore: Johns Hopkins University Press.

Ricardo, D. (1817) *On the Principles of Political Economy and Taxation*. London: J. Murray.

Richardson, M. (1993) "Content protection with foreign capital," *Oxford Economic Papers* 45, 103–17.

Ricupero, R. (2000) *Rebuilding Confidence in the Multilateral Trading System: Closing the "Legitimacy Gap"*. New York and Geneva: UNCTAD.

Rodriguez, F., and D. Rodrik (1999) *Trade Policy and Economic Growth: A Skeptic's Guide to the Cross-National Evidence*. NBER Working Paper Series, Working Paper 7081. Cambridge, MA: NBER.

Rodrik, D. (1987) "The economics of export-performance requirements," *Quarterly Journal of Economics* 102, 633–50.

——— (1997) *Making Openness Work: The New Global Economy and the Developing Countries.* Washington: Overseas Development Council.

——— (1998) "The global fix," *The New Republic*, 2 November.

——— (1999) *The New Global Economy and the Developing Countries: Making Openness Work.* Washington, DC: Overseas Development Council.

——— (2001a) "Trading in illusions," *Foreign Policy* (online), March–April, www.foreignpolicy.com/issue_marapr_2001/rodrik.

——— (2001b) "The global governance of trade as if development really mattered" (online), Background paper for UNDP, http://ksghome.harvard.edu/~.drodrik.academic.ksg/papers.html.

——— (2004) *How to Make the Trade Regime Work for Development.* Cambridge, MA: Harvard University.

Rodrik, D., A. Subramanina and F. Trebbi (2004). "Institutions rule: the primacy of institutions over geography and integration in economic development." Cambridge, MA: Harvard University, mimeo.

Roffe, P. (1998) "Control of anticompetitive practices in contractual licenses under the TRIPS Agreement," in C. Correa and A. Yusuf (eds) *Intellectual Property and International Trade: The TRIPS Agreement.* London: Kluwer Law International.

Rose, A. (2002) *Do We Really Know that the WTO Increases Trade?* CEPR Discussion Paper 3538. London: Centre for Economic Policy Research.

Rosen, D. (1999) *Behind the Open Door: Foreign Enterprise Establishment in China.* Washington, DC: Institute for International Economics.

Ross Schneider, B. (1998) "Elusive synergy: business-government relations and development," *Comparative Politics* 31:1, 101–22.

Roubini, N. (2001) "Why should the foreign creditors of Argentina take a greater hit/haircut than the domestic ones?" Working paper. Stern School of Business, New York University.

Rubin, R., and J. Weisberg (2003) *In an Uncertain World: Tough Choices from Wall Street to Washington.* New York: Random House.

Ruggiero, R. (1998) "Whither the trade system next?," in J. Bhagwati and M. Hirsch (eds), *The Uruguay Round and Beyond – Essays in Honour of Arthur Dunkel.* Ann Arbor: University of Michigan Press.

Sachs, J. (1999) "Helping the world's poorest," *The Economist*, 14 August.

Sachs, J., and A. Warner (1995) "Economic reform and the process of global integration," *Brookings Papers on Economic Activity* 1 (1995), 1–118.

Safarian, A.E. (1993) *Multinational Enterprise and Public Policy: A Study of the Industrial Countries.* Aldershot: Edward Elgar.

——— (2002) *The Use and Impact of Performance Requirements in the Developed Countries.* Geneva: UNCTAD, mimeo.

Saich, T. (1989) "Reforms of China's science and technology organizational system," in D. Simon and M. Goldman (eds), *Science and Technology in Post-Mao China*, 69–88. Cambridge: Cambridge University Press.

Sawin, J. (2001) "The role of government in the development and diffusion of renewable energy technologies: wind power in the United States, California, Denmark, and Germany, 1970–2000," Ph.D. dissertation. Medford, MA: Fletcher School of Law and Diplomacy, Tufts University.

Scherer, F.M. (1998) *The Patent System and Innovation in Pharmaceuticals*. Cambridge, MA: Harvard University, mimeo.

Schott, J.J. (1994) "Safeguards," in A.V. Deardoff (ed.), *The New World Trading System: Readings*, 113–16. Paris: OECD.

Scott, N. (2003) "Eskom sets 2006 as privatization deadline," *World Markets Analysis* 4 (March).

Sen, A. (1999) *Development as Freedom*. New York: Alfred A. Knopf.

Sercovich, F. (1998) "Best practices, policy convergence, and the WTO trade-related investment measures," *CEPAL Review* 64, 93–112.

Shadlen, K. (2004) "Patents and pills, power and procedure: the North–South politics of public health in the WTO," *Studies in Comparative International Development* 39:3 (Fall 2004), 76–108.

Sinclair, S. (2000) *GATS: How the WTO's New "Services" Negotiations Threaten Democracy*. Ottawa: Canadian Centre for Policy Alternatives.

———— (2002) *Facing the Facts: A Guide to the GATS Debate*. Ottawa: Canadian Center for Policy Alternatives.

Singh, A. (1993) "Asian economic success and Latin American failure in the 1980s: new analyses and future policy implications," *International Review of Applied Economics* 7:3, 267–89.

———— (1994) "Openness and the market-friendly approach to development: learning the right lessons from development experience," *World Development* 22:12, 1811–23.

———— (1995a) "Institutional requirements for full employment in advanced economies," *International Labour Review* 134:4–5, 471–96.

———— (1995b) *The Causes of Fast Economic Growth in East Asia*. Geneva: UNCTAD.

———— (1995c) "Review of Wood, Adrian (1994), "North–South Trade, Employment and Inequality," *Economic Journal* 105:432, 1287–9.

———— (1996) "The post-Uruguay round world trading system, industrialisation, trade and development," in *Expansion of Trading Opportunities in the Year 2000 for Asia-Pacific Developing Countries*, 147–88. Geneva: UNCTAD.

———— (1997) "Catching up with the West: a perspective on Asian economic development and lessons for Latin America," in L. Emmerij (ed.), *Economic and Social Development into the XXI Century*, 222–72. Washington, DC: Inter-American Development Bank/Johns Hopkins University Press.

———— (1998) "Savings, investments and the corporations in the East Asian miracle," *Journal of Development Studies* 34:6, 112–37.

———— (2000) *Global Economic Trends and Social Development*. Occasional Paper No. 9. Geneva: UNRISD.

———— (2002) *Capital Account Liberalization, Free Long-Term Capital Flows, Financial Crisis and Economic Development*. CBR Working paper Series, WP 245.

———— (2003) "Income inequality in advanced economies: a critical examination of trade and technology theories and an alternative perspective," in J. Ghosh and C.P. Chandrasekhar (eds), *Work and Well-Being in the Age of Finance*, Muttukadu Papers 1. New Delhi: Tulia Books.

Singh, A., and B. Weisse (1999) "The Asian model: a crisis foretold," *International Social Science Journal* 51:160, 203–15.

Singh, A., and A. Zammit (2000). *The Global Labour Standards Controversy: Critical Issues for Developing Countries*. Geneva: South Perspectives, South Centre.

Slaughter, M., and P. Swagel (1997) *Does Globalization Lower Wages and Export Jobs?* Economic Issues Series, No. 11. Washington, DC: IMF.

Smith, A. (1937) *An Inquiry into the Nature and Causes of the Wealth of Nations* [1776], ed. E. Cannan and M. Lerner. New York: The Modern Library.

Snodgrass, D. (1995) *Successful Economic Development in a Multi-Ethnic Society: The Malaysian Case.* Harvard Institute for International Development Discussion Paper No. 503. Cambridge, MA: Harvard Institute for International Development.

South African Department of Trade and Industry. *South Africa's Economic Transformation: A Strategy for Broad-Based Black Economic Empowerment,* Strategy document (online), www.dti.gov.za/bee/complete.pdf.

South Centre (1999) *Special and Differential Treatment for Developing Countries in the WTO,* Trade-Related Agenda, Development and Equity (T.R.A.D.E.) Working Papers. Geneva: South Centre.

Spero, J.E. (1977) *The Politics of International Economic Relations.* London: George Allen & Unwin.

Srinivasan, T.N., and J. Bhagwati (1999) *Outward-Orientation and Development: Are Revisionists Right?* Economic Growth Centre Discussion Paper No. 806. New Haven, CT: Yale University.

Stallings, B., and W. Peres (2000) *Growth, Employment, and Equity: The Impact of the Economic Reforms in Latin America and the Caribbean.* Washington: ECLAC/Brookings.

Stanford, J. (1993) *Estimating the Effects of North American Free Trade: A Three-Country General Equilibrium Model with "Real-World" Assumptions.* Ottawa: Canadian Centre for Policy Alternatives.

Startup, J. (1994) "An agenda for international investment," in A.V. Deardoff (ed.), *The New World Trading System: Readings,* 189–92. Paris: OECD.

Stiglitz, J.E. (1996) "Some lessons from the East Asian miracle," *World Bank Research Observer* 11:2, 151–77.

——— (2000a) "Capital market liberalization, economic growth, and instability," *World Development* 28:6, 1075–86.

——— (2000b) "Quis custodiet ipsos custodes? Les defaillances du gouvernement d'entreprise dans la transition," *Revue d'Economie du Developpement,* 0:1–2 (June), 33–70.

——— (2000c) "Whither reform? ten years of transition," in B. Pleskovic and J.E. Stiglitz (eds), *Annual World Bank Conference on Economic Development,* 27–56. Washington, DC: World Bank.

——— (2001) "*Quis custodiet ipsos custodes?* Corporate governance failures in the transition," in P.-A. Muet and J.E. Stiglitz (eds), *Governance, Equity and Global Markets, Proceedings from the Annual Bank Conference on Development Economics in Europe, June 1999,* 51–84. Paris: Conseil d'Analyse economique.

——— (2002a) *Globalization and its Discontents.* London: Penguin Books.

——— (2002b) "Reforming reform: towards a new agenda for Latin America', 2002 Prebisch Lecture, 26 August. Santiago, Chile: ECLAC.

Stiglitz, J., and A. Charlton (2004) *An Agenda for the Development Round of Trade Negotiations in the Aftermath of Cancún.* Commonwealth Secretariat, Great Britain.

Stiglitz, J.E., and B. Greenwald (2003) *A New Paradigm for Monetary Economics.* Cambridge: Cambridge University Press.

Sturgeon, T.J. (2002) "Modular production networks: a new American model of industrial organization?' *Industrial and Corporate Change* 11:3, 2002.

Suehiro, A. (1993) "Capitalist development in postwar Thailand: commercial bankers, industrial elite, and agribusiness groups," in R. McVey (ed.), *Southeast Asian Capitalists*, 35–63. Ithaca NY: Southeast Asia Program, Cornell University.

SUEZ International (2002) "SUEZ invokes procedures provided under the French–Argentine bilateral investment treaty and books provisions to cover all its exposure in Argentina," press release, SUEZ International, 28 June.

Summers, L.H. (1998) "Opportunities out of crisis: lessons from Asia," remarks to the Overseas Development Council, from the Office of Public Affairs, 19 March.

——— (2000) "International financial crisis: causes, prevention and cures," *American Economic Review Papers and Proceedings* 90:2, 1–16.

Tacoa-Vielma, J. (2002) "Defining energy services for the GATS: an issue under discussion," in *Energy and Environmental Services: Negotiating Objectives and Development Priorities*, 70–83. New York and Geneva: UNCTAD.

Tainan Science-Based Industrial Park (1996) *Prospectus, Tainan*, Taiwan Province of China: Tainan Science-Based Industrial Park.

Taylor, J. (2003) Testimony before the Subcommittee on Domestic and International Monetary Policy, Trade and Technology, Committee on Financial Services, US House of Representatives. Washington, DC, 1 April.

Taylor, L. (1988) *Varieties of Stabilisation Experiences*. Oxford: Oxford University Press.

Third World Network (2001) *The Multilateral Trading System: A Development Perspective*, Background Paper, Third World Network and UNDP.

Thurow, L. (1997) "Needed: a new system of intellectual property rights," *Harvard Business Review*, September–October.

Tims, W. (1990) "Issues in modeling," in I. Goldin and O. Knudsen (eds), *Agricultural Trade Liberalization: Implications for Developing Countries*, 471–2. Paris and Washington, DC: OECD and the World Bank.

Tortora, M. (2002) *Special and Differential Treatment in the Multilateral Trade Negotiations: The Skeleton in the Closet*. Geneva: UNCTAD.

Toulan, O., and M. Guillen (1996) *Internationalization: Lessons from Mendoza*. Cambridge and Mendoza: CIT/MIT.

Tranæs, F. (2003) "Danish wind energy cooperatives" (online), Copenhagen: Danish Wind Industry Association, www.windpower.org/en/articles/coop.htm.

Tremolet, S., and J. Neale (2002) *Emerging Lessons in Private Provision of Infrastructure Services in Rural Areas: Water and Electricity Services in Gabon*. London: Environmental Resources Management.

Tsuru, S. (1993) *Japan's Capitalism: Creative Defeat and Beyond*. Cambridge: Cambridge University Press.

United Nations (1967) *The Growth of World Industry*. New York: United Nations.

——— (2002) *Report of the World Summit on Sustainable Development*. New York: United Nations, A/CONF.199/20.

United Nations Conference on Trade and Development (UNCTAD) (1993) *Fostering Technological Dynamism: Evolution of Thought on Technology Capacity Building and Competitiveness. Summary of the Review and Analysis of the Literature*, TD/B/WG.5/7. Geneva: UNCTAD Secretariat.

——— (1996) *The TRIPS Agreement and Developing Countries*. Geneva, United Nations.

——— (1997) *Trade and Development Report, 1997*. New York and Geneva: United Nations.

——— (1998) *World Investment Report*. Geneva and New York: United Nations.

———— (1999a) *National Treatment*, UNCTAD Series on Issues in International Investment Agreements, UNCTAD/ITE/IIT/11(Vol. IV). New York and Geneva: United Nations.

———— (1999b) *Preparing for Future Multilateral Trade Negotiations: Issues and Research Needs from a Development Perspective.* New York and Geneva: United Nations.

———— (1999c) *World Investment Report 1999.* Geneva: United Nations.

———— (2000a) *A Positive Agenda for Developing Countries: Issues for Future Trade Negotiations.* New York and Geneva: UNCTAD.

———— (2000b) *Trade and Development Report, 2000.* New York and Geneva: United Nations.

———— (2001a) *Host Country Operational Measures*, UNCTAD/ITE/IIT/26. New York and Geneva: UNCTAD.

———— (2001b) *World Investment Report 2001.* New York: United Nations.

———— (2002a) *World Investment Report 2002.* New York: United Nations.

———— (2002b) *Trade and Development Report 2002.* New York: United Nations.

———— (2003a) *Foreign Direct Investment and Performance Requirements: New Evidence from Selected Countries.* New York and Geneva: United Nations.

———— (2003b) *World Investment Report 2003.* Geneva: United Nations.

UNCTC (1991) *The Impact of Trade-related Investment Measures on Trade and Development: Theory, Evidence and Policy Implications.* New York: United Nations.

United Nations Development Program (UNDP) (1999) *Human Development Report 1999.* New York: Oxford University Press.

———— (2000a) *Millennium Development Goals.* New York: United Nations.

———— (2000b) *World Energy Assessment.* New York: UNDP.

———— (2002) *Making Global Trade Work for People.* London: Earthscan.

———— (2003) *Human Development Report 2003.* New York: United Nations.

United Nations Industrial Development Organization (UNIDO) (1997) *International Yearbook of Industrial Statistics.* Vienna: Edward Elgar.

———— (2002) *Industrial Development Report 2002/2003.* Vienna: United Nations.

UN/TCMD (1992) *World Investment Report 1992: Transnational Corporations as Engines of Growth.* New York: United Nations.

United States (1991) "US–Argentina Bilateral Investment Treaty. Signed November 14, 1991" (online), www.tcc.mac.gov/cgi-bin/doit.cgi?226:64:564161045:1:5.

United States, Energy Information Administration, US Department of Energy (1997) "The transformation of Argentina's electricity industry," in *Electricity Reform Abroad and U.S. Investment.* Washington, DC: Energy Information Administration.

Vandoren, P. (1999) "The implementation of the TRIPS Agreement," *Journal of World Intellectual Property* 2.

Wacziarg, R., and K.H. Welch (2003) *Trade Liberalization and Growth: New Evidence*, NBER Working Paper Series, Working Paper 10152. Cambridge, MA: NBER.

Wade, R.H. (1990) *Governing the Market.* Princeton, NJ: Princeton University Press.

———— (1991) "How to protect exports from protection: Taiwan's duty drawback scheme," *The World Economy* 14:3, 299–309.

———— (1996) "Globalization and its limits: Reports of the death of the national economy are greatly exaggerated," in S. Berger and R. Dore (eds), *National Diversity and Global Capitalism*, 60–88. Ithaca: Cornell University Press.

———— (1998) "From 'miracle' to 'cronyism': explaining the Great Asian Slump," *Cambridge Journal of Economics* 22:6.

——— (2000a) "Out of the box: rethinking the governance of international financial markets," *Journal of Human Development* 1:1, 145–58.

——— (2000b) "Wheels within wheels: rethinking the Asian crisis and the Asian model," *Annual Review of Political Science 2000* 3, 85–115.

——— (2001) "The US role in the long Asian crisis of 1990–2000," in F. Batista-Rivera and A. Lukauskis (eds), *The East Asian Crisis and Its Aftermath*. Cheltenham: Edward Elgar.

——— (2002) "On Soros: are special drawing rights the deus ex machina of the world economy?" *Challenge* 45:5, 112–24.

——— (2003a) *Governing the Market* [1990]. Princeton: Princeton University Press.

——— (2003b) "Reply," *Oxford Development Studies* 31:1, 8–14.

——— (2004) "Is globalization reducing poverty and inequality?" *World Development* 32:4, 567–89.

Wade, R., and F. Veneroso (1998a) "The Asian crisis: the high debt model versus the Wall Street–Treasury–IMF complex," *New Left Review* 228.

——— (1998b) "The gathering world slump and the battle over capital controls," *New Left Review* 231, 13–42.

Walter, A. (2001) "NGOs, business, and international investment: the Multilateral Agreement on Investment, Seattle, and beyond," *Global Governance* 7, 51–73.

Wamukonya, N. (ed.) (2003), *Electricity Reform: Social and Environmental Challenges*. Roskilde: UNEP.

Wang, Y.F. (1993) *China's Science and Technology Policy: 1949–1989*. Aldershot: Avebury.

Washington Post (2002) "Open up the WTO," (editorial), *Washington Post*, reprinted in *International Herald Tribune*, 23 December.

Weber, S. (2004) *The Success of Open Source*. Cambridge, MA: Harvard University Press.

Westphal, L.E. (1982) "Fostering technological mastery by means of selective infant-industry protection," in M. Syrquin and S. Teitel (eds), *Trade, Stability, Technology, and Equity in Latin America*, 255–79. New York: Academic Press.

——— (1990), "Industrial policy in an export-propelled economy: lessons from South Korea's experience," *Journal of Economic Perspectives* 4:3, 41–59.

——— (1997), "Government-business relations: experience of the Republic of Korea," background note prepared for UNCTAD Expert Group Meeting.

——— (2002) "Technology strategies for economic development in a fast changing global economy," *Economics of Innovation and New Technology* 11, 275–320.

Whalley, J. (1999) *Special and Differential Treatment in the Millennium Round*, CSGR Working paper No. 30/99.

Wiener, N. (1948) *Cybernetics: Or Control and Communication in the Animal and Machine*. New York: John Wiley.

Williamson, J. (1985) "Comment on Sachs," *Brookings Papers on Economic Activity* 2.

——— (1994) *The Political Economy of Policy Reform*. Washington, DC: Institute for International Economics.

Willis, E.I. (1990) *The Politicized Bureaucracy: Regimes, Presidents and Economic Policy in Brazil*. Boston, MA: Boston College.

Wong, P.-K. (2003) "From using to creating technology: the evolution of Singapore's national innovation system and the changing role of public policy," in S. Lall and S. Urata (eds), *Competitiveness, FDI and Technological Activity in East Asia*, 191–238. Cheltenham: Edward Elgar.

Wood, A. (1994) *North–South Trade, Employment and Inequality.* New York: Clarendon Press.

——— (ed.) (2003) "Symposium on infant industries," with contributions by J. Roberts, R. Wade and S. Lall, *Oxford Development Studies* 31:1, 3–20.

Woodroffe, J., and C. Joy (2002) *Out of Service: The Development Dangers of the General Agreement on Trade in Services.* London: World Development Movement.

Woods, N. (2003) "Holding intergovernmental institutions to account," *Ethics and International Affairs* 17:1, 69–80.

World Bank (1991) *World Development Report, 1991 – The Development Challenge.* New York: Oxford University Press.

——— (1993) *East Asian Miracle: Economic Growth and Public Policy.* New York: Oxford University Press.

——— (1997) *Private Capital Flows to Developing Countries: The Road to Financial Integration. A World Bank Policy Research Report.* Washington, DC: World Bank.

——— (2000) *Private Participation in Energy.* Public Policy for the Private Sector Note No. 208. Washington, DC: World Bank Group.

——— (2001) *Global Economic Prospects and the Developing Countries 2002.* Washington, DC: World Bank.

——— (2002a) "Intellectual property: balancing incentives with competitive access," in *Global Economic Prospects 2002.* Washington, DC: World Bank.

——— (2002b) *World Development Report 2002 – Building Institutions for Markets.* Washington, DC: World Bank.

——— (2003a) *Global Economic Prospects and the Developing Countries 2003.* Washington, DC: World Bank.

——— (2003b) *Private Sector Development in the Electric Power Sector.* Washington, DC: World Bank OED.

——— (various) *World Tables.* Washington DC: World Bank.

World Development Movement (2002) *Out of Service: The Development Dangers of the General Agreement on Trade in Services.* London: World Development Movement.

World Resources Institute (WRI) (2003) *World Resources 2002–2004.* Washington, DC: World Resources Institute.

World Trade Organization (WTO) (1995) *Agreement Establishing the World Trade Organization* (online), Geneva: WTO Information and Media Relations Divisions, www.wto.org/english/docs_e/legal_e/04–wto.pdf.

——— (1998) *World Trade Organization, Annual Report 1998.* Geneva: World Trade Organization.

——— (2000) *Implementation of Special and Differential Treatment Provisions in WTO Agreements and Decisions* (online), WTO, WT/ComTD/W/77, www.wto.org/english/docs_e/docs_e.htm.

——— (2003) "Negotiators agree on modalities for treatment of autonomous liberalization" (online), WTO Press Note 334, 10 March, www.wto.org/english/news_e/pres03_e/pr335_e.htm.

——— (2004) "Trade and investment" (online), www.wto.org/english/tratop_e/invest_e/invest_e.htm.

World Trade Organization and United Nations Conference on Trade and Development (WTO and UNCTAD) (2001) *Joint Study on Trade Related Investment Measures and Other Performance Requirements* (online), G/C/W/307, www.wto.org/english/docs_e/docs_e.htm.

World Trade Organization Council for Trade in Services (WCTS) (1998) "Energy services – background note by the Secretariat" (online), S/C/W/52, www.wto. org/english/docs_e/docs_e.htm.

World Trade Organization Council for Trade-Related Aspects of Intellectual Property Rights (WCTRIPS) (2000a) "Communication from India," 12 July (online), IP/C/W/195, www.wto.org/english/docs_e/docs_e.htm.

——— (2000b) "Communication from Norway, 29 June 2001" (online), IP/C/W/293, www.wto.org/english/docs_e/docs_e.htm.

——— (2002a) "Communication from the European Communities and Their Member States, 17 October 2002" (online), IP/C/W/383, www.wto.org/english/docs_e/ docs_e.htm.

——— (2002b) "Extension of the Transition Period under Article 66.1 of the TRIPS Agreement for Least-Developed Country Members for Certain Obligations with Respect to Pharmaceutical Products; Decision of the Council for TRIPS of 27 June 2002" (online), IP/C/25, www.wto.org/english/docs_e/docs_e.htm.

——— (2002c) "The Relationship between the TRIPS Agreement and the Convention on Biological Diversity and the Protection of Traditional Knowledge, Communication from the Permanent Mission of Brazil on behalf of the delegations of Brazil, China, Cuba, Dominican Republic, Ecuador, India, Pakistan, Thailand, Venezuela, Zambia and Zimbabwe" (online), IP/C/W/356, www.wto.org/english/ docs_e/docs_e.htm.

——— (2003a) Article 27.3(B), "The Relationship between the TRIPS Agreement and the Convention on Biological Diversity, and the Protection of Traditional Knowledge; Communication from Switzerland, 28 May 2003" (online), IP/C/ W/400, www.wto.org/english/docs_e/docs_e.htm.

——— (2003b) "The Relationship between the TRIPS Agreement and the Convention on Biological Diversity and the Protection of Traditional Knowledge; Submission by Bolivia, Brazil, Cuba, Dominican Republic, Ecuador, India, Peru, Thailand, Venezuela, 24 June 2003" (online), IP/C/W/403, www.wto.org/english/docs_e/docs_e.htm.

——— (2003c) "Taking Forward the Review of Article 27.3(b) of the TRIPS Agreement; Joint Communication from the African Group, 26 June 2003" (online), IP/C/W/404, www.wto.org/english/docs_e/docs_e.htm.

World Trade Organization General Council (WGC) (1998a) "Preparations for the 1999 Ministerial Conference, General Council Discussion on Mandated Negotiations and the Built-In Agenda; Communication from the United States, 23 November 1998" (online), WT/GC/W/115, www.wto.org/english/docs_e/docs_e.htm.

——— (1998b) "Preparatory Process for the 3rd Ministerial Conference of the WTO; Communication from the Dominican Republic and Honduras, 30 November 1998" (online), WT/GC/W/119, www.wto.org/english/docs_e/docs_e.htm.

——— (1999a) "Preparations for the 1999 Ministerial Conference, Agreement on TRIPS Extension of the Additional Protection for Geographical Indications to Other Products; Communication from the Czech Republic, 14 June 1999" (online), WT/GC/W/206, www.wto.org/english/docs_e/docs_e.htm.

——— (1999b) "Preparations for the 1999 Ministerial Conference, Agreement on TRIPS Extension of the Additional Protection for Geographical Indications to Other Products; Communication from Turkey, 13 July 1999" (online), WT/GC/ W/249, www.wto.org/english/docs_e/docs_e.htm.

———— (1999c) "Preparations for the 1999 Ministerial Conference, Agreement on TRIPS Proposal Regarding Extension of Protection of Geographical Indications under Paragraph 9(a)(i) of the Geneva Ministerial Declaration; Communication from Cuba, Dominican Republic, Egypt, Honduras, India, Indonesia, Nicaragua and Pakistan, 17 June 1999" (online), WT/GC/W/208, www.wto.org/english/docs_e/docs_e.htm.

———— (1999d) "Preparations for the 1999 Ministerial Conference, EC Approach to Trade-Related Aspects of Intellectual Property in the New Round; Communication from the European Communities, 2 June 1999" (online), WT/GC/W/193, www.wto.org/english/docs_e/docs_e.htm.

———— (1999e) "Preparations for the 1999 Ministerial Conference, General Council Discussion on the Built-In-Agenda; Communication from Egypt, 26 January 1999" (online), WT/GC/W/136, www.wto.org/english/docs_e/docs_e.htm.

———— (1999f) "Preparations for the 1999 Ministerial Conference, Proposal on Trade-Related Aspects of Intellectual Property; Communication from Japan, 6 July 1999" (online), WT/GC/W/242, www.wto.org/english/docs_e/docs_e.htm.

———— (1999g) "Preparations for the 1999 Ministerial Conference, Proposals on IPR Issues; Communication from India, 18 February 1999" (online), WT/GC/W/147, www.wto.org/english/docs_e/docs_e.htm.

———— (1999h) "Preparations for the 1999 Ministerial Conference, Proposals Regarding the TRIPS Agreement in terms of Paragraph 9(a)(i) of the Geneva Ministerial Declaration; Communication from India, 2 July 1999" (online), WT/GC/W/225, www.wto.org/english/docs_e/docs_e.htm.

———— (1999i) "Preparations for the 1999 Ministerial Conference, Proposals Regarding the TRIPS Agreement (Paragraph 9(a)(ii) of the Geneva Ministerial Declaration); Communication from Venezuela, 6 August 1999" (online), WT/GC/W/282, www.wto.org/english/docs_e/docs_e.htm.

———— (1999j) Preparations for the 1999 Ministerial Conference, The TRIPS Agreement; Communication from Kenya on behalf of the African Group, 6 August 1999" (online), WT/GC/W/302,www.wto.org/english/docs_e/docs_e.htm.

———— (2003) "Implementation of Paragraph 6 of the Doha Declaration on the TRIPS Agreement and Public Health, Decision of 30 August 2003" (online), WT/L/540, www.wto.org/english/docs_e/docs_e.htm.

World Trade Organization Ministerial Conference, Fourth Session (WMC) (2001) "Draft Declaration on the TRIPS Agreement and Public Health, 14 November 2001" (online), WT/MIN(01)/DEC/W/2, www.wto.org/english/docs_e/docs_e.htm.

World Trade Organization Working Group on the Relationship between Trade and Investment (WGTI) (2002a) "Communication from the European Community and its Member States – Concept Paper on Non-discrimination" (online), WT/WGTI/W/122, www.wto.org/english/docs_e/docs_e.htm.

———— (2002b) "Communication from India – Development Provisions" (online), WT/WGTI/W/148, www.wto.org/english/docs_e/docs_e.htm.

———— (2002c) "Consultation and the Settlement of Disputes between Members – Note by the Secretariat" (online), WT/WGTI/W/134, www.wto.org/english/docs_e/docs_e.htm.

———— (2002d) "Report On the Meeting Held on 16–18 September 2002: Note by the Secretariat" (online), WT/WGTI/M/19, www.wto.org/english/docs_e/docs_e.htm.

———— (2003) "Communication from the European Community and its Member States – Concept Paper on Policy Space for Development" (online), WT/WGTI/W/154, www.wto.org/english/docs_e/docs_e.htm.

World Trade Organization Working Group on Trade and Transfer of Technology (WGTTT) (2002) "Provisions Relating to Transfer of Technology in WTO Agreements; Communication from Cuba, Egypt, Honduras, India, Indonesia, Jamaica, Kenya, Mauritius, Pakistan and Zimbabwe, Revision, 21 October 2002" (online), WT/WGTTT/3/Rev.1, www.wto.org/english/docs_e/docs_e.htm.

———— (2003) "Report of the Working Group on Trade and Transfer of Technology to the General Council, 14 July 2003" (online), WT/WGTTT/5, www.wto. org/english/docs_e/docs_e.htm.

World Trade Organization Working Party on GATS Rules (WPGR) (2003) "Communication from the European Communities: Government Procurement of Services" (online), S/WPGR/W/42, www.wto.org/english/docs_e/docs_e.htm.

Xu, B. (2000) "Multinational enterprises, technology diffusion, and host country productivity growth," *Journal of Development Economics* 62, 477–93.

Xue, L. (1997) "Promoting industrial R&D and high-tech development through science parks: the Taiwan experience and its implications for developing countries," Special Issue of R&D Management, *International Journal of Technology Management*, 13:7/8, 744–61.

You, J.I., and H.J. Chang (1993) "The myth of free labour market in Korea," *Contributions to Political Economy* 12.

Young, A.A. (1928) "Increasing returns and economic progress," *Economic Journal* 38, 527–42.

Yu, E.S.H., and C.-C. Chao (1998) "On investment measures and trade," in P. Lloyd and C. Milner (eds), *The World Economy* 21:4, 549–61.

Zarrilli, S. (2002) "International trade in energy services and the developing countries," in *Energy and Environmental Services: Negotiating Objectives and Development Priorities*, 23–69. New York and Geneva: UNCTAD.

Zedillo Commission (2001) "Report of the high-level panel on financing for development" (online), Report for the Monterrey Conference, www.un.org/reports/financing/full_report.pdf.

About the Contributors

Alice H. Amsden obtained her Ph.D. from the London School of Economics. She is currently Barton L. Weller Professor of Political Economy at MIT's Department of Urban Studies and Planning. Her research interests include economic and industrial development. She was recently awarded the Leontief Prize for Advancing the Frontiers of Economic Thought by Tufts University's Global Development and Environment Institute. Her recent publications include *Beyond Late Development: Taiwan's Upgrading Policies* (co-author Wan-wen Chu; MIT Press, 2003). She also wrote *The Rise of "the Rest": Challenges to the West from Late-Industrializing Countries* (Oxford University Press, 2001). She has served as a consultant with the World Bank, OECD, and various United Nations organizations. She has written extensively on problems of industrial transformation in East Africa, East Asia, and Eastern Europe. Currently, among other courses, she teaches Economic Development and Technical Capabilities.

Amit Bhaduri is Professor Emeritus at Jawaharlal Nehru University, Delhi. He has been appointed Professor of Political Economy at the University of Pavia. Previously he was a Reader at the Delhi School of Economics and Professor at the Indian Institute of Management, Calcutta. He has been a Visiting Professor at various academic institutions (Colegio de Mexico, the Universities of Stanford, Vienna, Linz, Bologna, Bremen and Trondheim). He has also been a Research Officer at the United Nations Industrial Development Organization (Vienna), and a Visiting Fellow at the Centre for Development Studies, Trivandrum, India; a Fellow at the Wissenschaftskolleg zu Berlin; and at the Swedish Collegium for Advanced Study in the Social Sciences. He obtained a Ph.D. at the University of Cambridge and taught at

Pembroke College, Cambridge. He has published many papers in academic journals and a number of scholarly volumes, including *The Economic Structure of Backward Agriculture* (Academic Press, 1983); *Macroeconomics: The Dynamics of Commodity Production* (Macmillan, 1986); *Unconventional Economic Essays* (Oxford University Press, 1993); *The Intelligent Person's Guide to Liberalization* (co-author; Penguin Books, 1996); and *On the Border of Economic Theory and History* (Oxford University Press, 1999).

Ha-Joon Chang is Assistant Director of Development Studies at the University of Cambridge. He has worked as a consultant for numerous international organizations, including various UN agencies (UNCTAD, WIDER, UNDP and UNIDO), the World Bank, and the Asian Development Bank. Among his publications is *The Political Economy of Industrial Policy* (Macmillan, 1994). He has also edited a number of volumes, including a collection of speeches by Joseph Stiglitz, *Joseph Stiglitz and the World Bank: The Rebel Within* (Anthem Press, 2001), and has published numerous articles on issues ranging from theories of the state, market and institutions, to the transition economies. His most recent book is *Kicking Away the Ladder: Development Strategy in Historical Perspective* (Anthem Press, 2002).

Albert H. Cho is a consultant at the World Resources Institute in Washington, DC. He has worked on trade and sustainable development issues at WRI, the Smithsonian Institution, the International Centre for Trade and Sustainable Development, and Harvard's Center for International Development. His prior work has focused on investment, trade in services, and the political economy of ethnic diversity. He holds an M.B.A. and an M.Sc. in development economics from the University of Oxford, where he was a Rhodes Scholar, and an A.B. in Social Studies, summa cum laude, from Harvard University.

Carlos M. Correa, following studies in economics and law at the University of Buenos Aires, from which he also obtained his doctorate, has pursued a career in academia, with activities for a time in government. From 1984 to 1989, he was Undersecretary of State for Informatics and Development in the Argentine national government. During this period he was coordinator of the Inter-ministerial Group on Intellectual Property. From 1988 to 1991 he was a government delegate in international negotiations on intellectual property. Since 1991 he has been the Director of the Masters Programme on Science and Technology Policy and Management, and of the Post-graduate Courses on Intellectual Property of the University of Buenos Aires. He was also appointed Director of the Center for Interdisciplinary Studies of Industrial Property Law and Economics of the same University. He is currently in charge of the "Innovation, Development and Intellectual Property Policy" project at the South Centre, and he chairs the Genetics Resources Policy Committee of the CGIAR.

Navroz K. Dubash is a Senior Fellow and IDFC Professor of Governance and Public Policy at the National Institute of Public Finance and Policy, New Delhi. His current work focuses on the development of institutions and the design of governance mechanisms with particular relevance to electricity and water infrastructure. Prior to joining NIPFP, he worked as a Senior Associate at the World Resources Institute (WRI) in Washington, DC. At WRI, he co-directed WRI's International Financial Flows and the Environment (IFFE) project, which explored the impact of financial globalization on problems of environment and development. His areas of publication and expertise include the political economy of electricity restructuring, international financial institutions and development assistance, the implications of a global invest-ment agreement for domestic policy in developing countries, climate change policy, mechanisms for democratic global governance, and local institutions for groundwater management. Dr Dubash holds Ph.D. and M.A. degrees in Energy and Resources from the University of California, Berkeley, and an A.B. in Public and International Affairs from Princeton University.

Peter Evans is Professor of Sociology at the University of California, Ber-keley. His research and writing deal with the comparative political economy of developing countries, with a focus on industrialization and the role of the state. His most recent books include *Embedded Autonomy: States and Industrial Transformation* (Princeton University Press, 1995); *Double-Edged Diplomacy: International Bargaining and Domestic Politics* (co-edited with H. Jacobson and R. Putnam; University of California Press, 1993); and *High Technology and Third World Industrialization: Brazilian Computer Policy in Comparative Perspective* (coedited with C. Frischtak and P. Tigre; International and Area Studies Publications, 1982). Current work includes *The Challenges of the 'Institutional Turn': New Interdisciplinary Opportunities in Development Theory* and *The FTAA's Impact on Democratic Governance.*

Kevin P. Gallagher is an assistant professor in the Department of Inter-national Relations at Boston University and a Research Associate at the Global Development and Environment Institute (GDAE) at Tufts University. He directs GDAE's Globalization and Sustainable Development Program, which works to develop a more empirical-based understanding of the globalization process in order to draw out lessons for future trade agreements by examining the relationship between economic integration and economic development in late industrializing societies. His most recent books are *Free Trade and the Environment: Mexico, NAFTA, and Beyond* (Stanford University Press, 2004); *International Trade and Sustainable Development* (Earthscan, 2002); and various volumes in the *Frontier Issues in Economic Thought* book series (Island Press). He has served as a consultant to a number of developing-country governments and to international organizations such as the North American Commission for Environmental Cooperation, the Economic Commission for Latin America and the Caribbean, and the OECD.

Nagesh Kumar is Director-General of RIS (Research and Information System for Developing Countries), a New Delhi-based policy research institution devoted to international economic issues. Dr Kumar obtained his Ph.D. in Economics from the Delhi School of Economics and joined the faculty of RIS in 1985. During 1993–98, Dr Kumar served on the faculty of the United Nations University – Institute for New Technologies (UNU/INTECH), Maastricht, the Netherlands, and directed its research programme on Globalization, FDI, and technology transfers in developing countries. He has also served as a consultant to the World Bank, ADB, UNDP, UNCTAD, UNIDO, UN–ESCAP, ILO, the Commonwealth Secretariat, the Commission on Intellectual Property Rights, among other organizations. He is recipient of the Exim Bank of India's first International Trade Research Award in 1989 and a GDN Medal for best research awarded by the World Bank and the Japanese government in 2000. He is author of *Globalization and the Quality of Foreign Direct Investment* (Oxford University Press, 2002); *Protecting Foreign Investment: Implications of a WTO Regime and Policy Options* (Zed Books, 2003) (with Carlos Correa); and editor of *Towards an Asian Economic Community: Vision of a New Asia* (ISEAS, 2004).

Sanjaya Lall is a professor of development economics at the University of Oxford. In 1982, he became a fellow of Green College, Oxford. His research interests include technology and technical change in developing countries; direct foreign investment and multinational corporations; industrialization (especially in India and Southeast Asia); and export performance of developing countries. From 1985 to 1987 he was on leave from Oxford as a senior economist at the World Bank in Washington, DC. He was an Honorary Director of Studies at the Indian Council for Research on International Economic Relations (ICRIER), New Delhi, in 1981–82. He has written over 30 books and monographs, 75 articles in refereed journals, 72 articles in books, and 67 reports for international agencies and governments. In 2002 alone, he was an adviser to the Ministry of Industry, Syria, on industrial upgrading and competitiveness; lead consultant to UNCTAD for its *Investment Policy Review* of Lesotho; Consultant to the International Labor Office on the employment implications of globalization; consultant to the World Bank, assessing the progress and impact of its Industrial Technology Development project in Turkey; consultant to FIAS, ADB and DFID on a workshop on FDI promotion in South Asia, held in Dhaka; and consultant to the World Bank and UNCTAD on FDI for an Integrated Framework analysis of Lesotho.

Ajit Singh is an Indian economist who graduated from Punjab University, obtained his Ph.D. at the University of California, Berkeley, and has been teaching economics at Cambridge University since 1965. He is currently Professor of Economics at the university and Senior Fellow at Queens' College Cambridge. He has been a senior economic adviser to the governments of Mexico and Tanzania and a consultant to various UN developmental organizations, including the World Bank, the ILO, UNCTAD, and UNIDO. He is the author of *Takeovers: Their Relevance to the Stockmarket and the Theory of the Firm*, and coauthor of *Growth, Profitability and Valuation* (both Cambridge University Press). He has also published extensively in academic economics journals. His most recent books are the edited volume (with A. Dutt and K. Kim), *The State, Markets and Development* (Edward Elgar, 1994); and the monographs, *Corporate Financial Patterns in Industrialising Countries* (Technical Paper No. 2, World Bank/IFC, Washington, DC, 1995); and *The Effects of Hyper-Inflation on Accounting Ratios: Financing Corporate Growth in Industrialising Economies* (with G. Whittington and V. Saporta, Technical Paper No. 3, World Bank/IFC, 1997). In 2000, the University of Michigan Press published his co-edited volume (with C. Howes) *Competitiveness Matters: Industry and Economic Performance in the U.S.*

Joseph E. Stiglitz was born in Gary, Indiana, in 1943. A graduate of Amherst College, he received his Ph.D. from MIT in 1967, became a full professor at Yale in 1970, and in 1979 was awarded the John Bates Clark Award, given biennially by the American Economic Association to the economist under 40 who has made the most significant contribution to the field. He has taught at Princeton, Stanford and MIT, and was the Drummond Professor and a Fellow of All Souls College, Oxford. He is now University Professor at Columbia University in New York. In 2001, he was awarded the Nobel Prize in economics. He was a member of the Council of Economic Advisors from 1993 to 1995, during the Clinton administration, and served as CEA chairman 1995–1997. He then became Chief Economist and Senior Vice-President of the World Bank from 1997 to 2000. Recognized around the world as a leading economic educator, he has written textbooks that have been translated into more than a dozen languages. He founded one of the leading economics journals, the *Journal of Economic Perspectives*. He has recently published a new book, *The Roaring Nineties* (W.W. Norton). His book *Globalization and Its Discontents* (W.W. Norton, 2001) has been translated into twenty languages and is an international bestseller.

Robert Hunter Wade is Professor of Political Economy at the London School of Economics. He writes about globalization, inequality, economic growth, capital markets, financial crises, industrial and technology policy, Asian development, international environmental politics, international NGOs, the World Bank and other multilateral economic organizations, and world governance. His book *Governing the Market: Economic Theory and the Role of Government in East Asian Industrialization* has just been reissued by Princeton University Press. He has conducted field research in Pitcairn Island, Italy, India, South Korea, Taiwan, and the World Bank. He worked earlier as an economist in the World Bank and in the Office of Technology Assessment (US Congress). He has taught at Victoria University (Wellington), UCSD, Sussex, Princeton, MIT, and Brown. He has been a Fellow of the Institute for Advanced Study, Princeton; the Institute for Advanced Study, Berlin; and the Russell Sage Foundation, New York City.

Index